India and the European Union

Perceptions of the Indian Print Media and Elites

India and the European Union

Perceptions of the Indian Print Media and Elites

Dr. Shreya Pandey

KNOWLEDGE WORLD

KW Publishers Pvt Ltd
New Delhi

ISBN 978-93-86288-96-7 Hardback
ISBN 978-93-86288-97-4 ebook

Published in India by Kalpana Shukla

KNOWLEDGE WORLD

KW Publishers Pvt Ltd
4676/21, First Floor, Ansari Road
Daryaganj, New Delhi 110002
Phone: +91 11 23263498/43528107
Marketing: kw@kwpub.com
Editorial: jose@kwpub.com
Website: www.kwpub.com

Printed and Bound in India.

Contents

Preface

European Union-India relations are one of the most salient partnerships that India has sought to cultivate. It is widely believed that it is a healthy, positive and non-controversial relationship that needs to be worked upon and strengthened further for reaping of optimal benefits by both sides. The purpose of writing this book has been to conduct an in-depth analysis of the dynamics of EU-India relations through the prism of the perceptions about the relationship in the Indian print media and amongst the elites of India.

This book makes an attempt to define the true nature of EU-India relations in the drastically changed world scenario as a result of the growing importance of complex interdependence and the advent of multipolarity. An attempt to clearly understand the nodal points of the strengths and weaknesses of these ties has been made. The study concentrates on locating the gap between formulation and implementation of EU-India policies. It has tried to delve deep into the nuances of this relationship and come up with a holistic perspective on EU-India relations. The general perceptions, the available literature on the relationship, the coverage in the newspapers and the insights of the elite has helped this study to arrive at concrete conclusions and recommendations for furtherance of the relationship.

A perception can either be a fleeting opinion or long-lasting in nature which makes a mark on the individual's thinking. Such long-lasting perceptions become a sound basis for knowledge. The increase in diversification of contact and cooperation between two countries in areas such as extending mutual political support, scientific and technological exchange, collaborations in educational and cultural activities and the movement of people from one place to another leads to the growth of knowledge about the other country, which ultimately leads to the shaping up of perceptions. The Indian press thus becomes the disseminator of perceptions and makes them popular, while the elite employ these perceptions for the purpose of policy-making and justifying their viewpoints. Public opinion in India is greatly influenced by the perceptions of the Indian elite and the media, as a majority of the people in the country choose to rely on these two sources for information and analyses rather than work towards finding things out for themselves.

The research undertaken is relevant for examining the changing dynamics of the EU-India relationship triggered by the elevation of their respective roles in the international scenario. The shift to multipolarity is bound to increase the venues of engagement between the two partners as a result of new issues such as terrorism and climate change occupying centre-stage. The standpoint of the European Union and India commands respect in the international community. It therefore becomes imperative to revisit the nuts and bolts of the relationship which has evolved tremendously in the last few years. The study makes a sincere effort to bring to the fore the overall perception about the relationship between the EU and India. It makes an attempt to highlight the vacuoles and gaps between initiatives resolved to be undertaken by both parties and the actual results on the ground.

The study seeks to examine India-EU relations by means of presenting an adequately informed assessment of initiatives in the social, economic, political environmental and developmental areas. An attempt has been made to contribute towards the building up of subject matter and information on perceptions about EU-India relations. The study has made an attempt to provide further insight regarding the visibility, influence and acceptance of the EU in India.

One of the limitations of the study is that it is not an exhaustive study of print media publications. Moreover, the study does not include a comparative analysis of the perceptions about the EU in India with that of another player in the arena such as the United States.

The research is based on primary sources as a result of data collected through the day to day scanning of three national dailies— namely, *The Times of India* (an English newspaper), *The Economic Times* (a business newspaper) and the *Dainik Jagran* (a vernacular newspaper) for an entire year— from 1st of July 2009 to 30th June 2010. The book includes interviews of about 38 elites of India affiliated to areas of politics, media, civil society and business in the period from 2 February to 10 May 2010, who were asked to comment on how they perceive the European Union.

An attempt has been made to examine the strengths and weaknesses of the relationship and the ways and means of strengthening the EU-India partnership further, especially in the light of the inputs based on the investigations about the perceptions of the print media and the Indian elite.

1
Introduction

This chapter traces the trajectory of relations between the European Union and India right from ancient times to the year 1963 when diplomatic relations were established between the two —and further on up to the present scenario. It shall make an attempt to contextualise and identify the very obvious crests and troughs of the relationship. An attempt shall be made to suggest immediate steps and measures that should be taken for further consolidation of the EU-India partnership.

Historical Background

The relations between Europeans and Indians is said to have existed even before the Christian era. The Greeks, who came to ancient India were referred to as Yavanas. The name "India" first appears in Greek literature in the 5th century B.C. in the works of Heaktaios and Heradotos. The word is derived from the Indus River and it originally meant only the Indus region, which then belonged to the Persian Empire. Heradotos, however, had already used the term in a wider sense to denote the whole country— and classical Greek usage followed his example.

Among the colonial powers, it was the Portuguese who were the first to arrive in India in 1498. Portuguese explorerVasco Da Gama discovered India when he arrived in Calicut by sea. The Portuguese made Goa their seat of administration. England's East India Company began trading with India in the beginning of the 15th century. The French were the next to come to India and by the 18th century, they captured a sizeable portion of southern India, which included Pondicherry, Karaikal, Yanam, Mahe and Chandernagore near Kolkata in West Bengal. But the French suffered defeats in many of the Anglo-French wars and lost their possessions. Like the Portuguese and the French, the Dutch also had a brief stay in India. They controlled the east coast of Malabar and established trading stations in Travancore, Pipely, Chinsurah and Murshidabad in West Bengal and at Balasore in Orissa. The Danes were the last Europeans to come to India. They established trading posts in Tranquebar in Tamil Nadu, Serampore in West Bengal and the Nicobar Islands. They lost their remaining outposts to the British in India by 1845 (Indianetzone 2009).

It was the British who ruled over India for the longest period, about 200 years, starting from the 15th century. The British rule in India began with the rule of the East India Company, which initially destroyed the Dutch monopoly over the spice trade and went on to rapidly increase and consolidate its position in India and eventually started running the administration of the country. The East India Company faced stiff opposition from the Indian rulers and the local people and consequently the control of the administration in India was transferred from the Company to the British Queen. The British annexed many princely states and formed laws and policies of their own and very soon the entire Indian sub-continent was subjected to British rule. Railways, telegraph and postal services were introduced in India with the intention of ensuring the permanent presence and control of the British in the country.

The people of India were highly resentful of the acts, policies and intentions of the British in India, which led to a revolt against British rule, fuelled by a group of Indian's headed by Mahatma Gandhi, Jawaharlal Nehru, Lala Lajpat Rai and Subhash Chandra Bose. These leaders of India's freedom movement openly declared that they had been inspired by a long list of European thinkers including Voltaire, Garibaldi, Mazzini, Max Mueller, Hunter, Monier Williams, Hobbes, Locke and Rousseau. India finally succeeded in becoming an independent and sovereign country on 15 August 1947. The new constitution of India, which came into being, following this historic change, borrowed a number of provisions from the Government of India Act 1935 and other constitutions of Europe.

Thus as history shows that Europeans made attempts towards advancing their economic interests by political and military means similar to the strategy adopted by other invaders arriving in India in the past. But it was British rule with its "much deeper penetration, that moulded India's colonial experience from near-total economic dependency to the traumatic experience of partition". India's world view and its international identity in the post-independence period were largely shaped by the nature of British colonial rule and the resistance launched against it. The British left behind the legacy of a politico-administrative system which had its own merits and the new Indian government of independent India readily embraced these features which included "Westminster-style parliamentary democracy, military deference to civilian leadership, an independent judiciary and vibrant free press". But it is also true that the Indian experience with British colonial rule has led to a consistent discourse of "mistrust towards the West" in the media and in Indian textbooks. Nevertheless, Europe played a positive role in India as was evident from the "established trade patterns to India's military procurement as a result of the flaring up of the conflict with Pakistan" (Muenchow- Pohl 2012).

India, in time, approached the United States, England and other European countries for steel, armaments, defence and infrastructural technologies. However, the clear message that came from these quarters was that "we will not give all this to you unless you practically join up on our side". The philosophy of non-alignment during the Cold War was not accepted, appreciated and understood in the manner in which India desired. India's request for help and cooperation went unheeded between 1947 and 1953, after which it moved on to choose and accept , in 1955, the Soviet Union as a partner in economic and industrial cooperation. Thus, the European powers rejected all the overtures made by India, which was rather disappointing (Jain 2000:78).

Beginning of the Partnership

It was on 2nd March 1962 that India established diplomatic

relations with the European Economic Community (EEC) which was based on a common market for its six member-states that had agreed upon the abolition of custom duties and adoption of a common policy on agriculture and trade (Delegation of the European Union to India1a). It introduced general tariff preferences for 91 developing countries, which included India, under the Generalised System of Preferences (GSP) scheme in 1971, (which also happens to be the year when India was engaged in efforts to liberate East Pakistan, which led to the creation of the independent country of Bangladesh) and consequently the annual rate of India's Gross Domestic Product was 1.71 per cent (Good Governance 2009). Denmark, Ireland and the United Kingdom joined the original six members of the EEC, which was buoyed by its success in 1973 (Europa 2009). Britain happened to be India's most important trading partner at the time and British membership of the EEC led to India's loss of imperial trade preferences.

It would appear that India was now ready to break ties with Britain and assert its freedom following its recognition of the EEC. On the contrary, Britain's membership of the EEC was likely to hurt the Indian economy as it meant that the country would no longer enjoy imperial preferences as before. The change in the status quo had also made it clear that India would require striking a new relationship with Europe. The Joint Declaration of Intent (JDI) concluded between the UK and EEC stated that the problems being faced by Commonwealth countries, as a result of removal of trade preferences, would adequately be dealt with. The brevity of the JDI suggested that this particular issue concerning the erstwhile colonies figured very low in the priority list. France had, in fact, been able to secure many more benefits for its erstwhile colonies in Africa. The top-most consideration at the time was to ensure the smooth entry of the UK into the EEC. The other colonial powers who had ruled over India did not show much concern for its plight as India was largely regarded as “Britain’s baby”. They shrugged off all responsibility to provide aid and succour to India (Abhyankar 2007: 452).

India’s efforts were initially directed towards concluding an Association Agreement with the EEC on the lines of the agreement done with the countries of the Mediterranean Basin, Asia and Caribbean and Pacific (ACP) countries. However, this was denied to India and other countries of South Asia as they were called “non-associables”. India’s efforts coincided with the Lome Convention, according to which ACP countries would be extended trade preferences including subsidies on agricultural products. Another important process which was taking place at the time was the formulation of Generalised System of Preferences for developing countries and the idea had originated and was inspired from the second UNCTAD Conference held in Delhi in 1968 (Abhyankar 2007: 452-453).

When the negotiations collapsed in 1963, India was relieved for a while as the impending doom of disruption of Indo-British trade and the consequent losses to be suffered by India were swept under the carpet. But India was keen on finding a way to engage and define its links with the EEC. For an entire decade, India busied itself in trying to get better market access for its exports and reduce its huge trade deficit with the EEC which was the largest amongst its trading partners. India made attempts to inch towards this goal product-wise by means of concluding agreements on an annual basis for the purpose of partial or total suspension of custom duty levied on the products. The introduction of GSP by the EEC was not an act of charity but simply a means to maintain relations with erstwhile colonies and developing countries. The GSP did not address the specific grievances and problems being faced by India as a consequence of removal of trade preferences. India’s important “exports of jute, coir, cotton textiles and tobacco were either excluded from the scheme or else subjected to special arrangements” (Jain 2011: 224).

India's decision to come up with an entirely new device for charting out relations with the EEC was due to the tact and intelligence of K.B. Lall, the then ambassador to the EEC. The Commercial Cooperation Agreement (CCA) framed by him was used as the template for future trade agreements with other South Asian countries. The CCA retained the provisions of the GSP and included the elements of trade development and trade promotion. It was based upon sovereign equality of two entities and restructured India-EEC relations in such a manner that it would not impinge upon India's bilateral relations with EEC member-states. The first CCA set up a Joint Commission to facilitate interaction between the two partners. The CCA was expanded between 1973 and 1993 in order to include "economic cooperation and investment in keeping with the changing needs and priorities of the relationship". The Council of the EEC Chamber of Commerce was set up in 1982. At this juncture, India-EEC trade was increasing and amounted to 20 percent of India's total trade turnover (Abhyankar 2007: 453).The European Union strengthened its roots in India with the establishment of the EC Delegation in the country's capital, New Delhi in the very next year in 1983 (Delegation of the European Union to India 2001).

The 1990s and the Post-Cold War Period

The EU-India engagement deepened and widened and consequently transformed itself into an inter-twined complex relationship in the post-Cold War period. India and the EU are accorded greater significance as international players than before. EU-India cooperation has witnessed a shift from being solely limited to trade and economic transactions to cooperation in political and security-related affairs. The EC was recognised as India's largest trading partner for a long time and in the 1980s, trade with EC, which constituted 22.8 per cent share of India's total trade, shot up to 29.36 per cent in 1990. It is largely believed that it was the end of the Cold War that provided economic and political impetus to move the relations beyond trade relations. The collapse of the Soviet Union ensured that India was now "freed from the Cold War rubric" and this provided India the opportunity to strike new relationships and form new alliances. The winds of liberalisation, privatisation and globalisation blew across the country, leading to unprecedented economic growth and then caught the attention of the rest of the world. India's growth story was infused with a very high dose of enthusiasm and energy which led to its recognition as an emerging power in the international order. The nuclear test in Pokhran in 1998 was another milestone achieved by India.

The winds of change were brought about by liberalisation of the Indian economy in the 1990s, alongside reformulation of India's foreign policy in accordance with the nature of the emerging world order. Similarly, the EEC was transformed into the EU, which was accompanied by the launching of the Common Foreign and Security Policy. As a result of these changes, the new Asia Strategy of the European Union was launched in order to give adequate attention and priority to countries of the region in the light of their increasing economic and political stature. The document aimed to provide "an integrated and balanced view of the relations between the EU and its Asian partners". However, the Asia Strategy seemed to concentrate more on East Asia and South East Asia and strategic attention directed towards South Asia and India was comparatively minimal. The reason for such a stance of the EU can be attributed to the fact that India had just embarked on the exciting journey towards liberalisation of the country and still had a long way to go in becoming a strong and dependable international economic player. Thus, it took some time for India to be recognised as a formidable actor and critical partner of the EU (Bava 2013).

With the end of the Cold War, India was provided the opportunity to combine normative and realpolitik goals. However, Indian leaders were very slow in making an attempt to utilise this change of engaging with the world. It was only in the early part of the twenty first century that the Indian leaders made a marked effort to reach out to the world. The new decision-makers thought differently from "Indian Cold War leaders". They were of the view that "if India was to pull its weight internationally, it would have to become an economic and regional power". The first wave of economic liberalisation in 1990-91 had involved the removal of bureaucratic shackles on industrial growth, while the second wave emphasised upon resource and infrastructure development. The leaders of the Indian state realised that this could be made possible only through integration with the world economy. Therefore, a vigorous and vibrant diplomatic offensive was launched by India in order to strengthen relations with the major powers of the world which included the EU apart from US, Japan, Russia and China (Kumar 2009: 165-166).

India demanded, in the early 1990s, that its cooperation agreement with the EU should be revisited and political dialogue should go up another level, because EU was not only a trading area for India but also a centre for conducting diplomatic relations with Western Europe which was the more developed part of the region. A third generation agreement on partnership and development was signed between the two partners in 1993. Annual troika meetings have been taking place since 1984 and they are currently taking place under the 1994 Joint Statement on Political Dialogue to further enrich relations in the economic, political, cultural and technological fields.

EU remained the largest trading partner of India in the 1990s. India also received the largest share of development assistance from the EU during this period. Trade with the EU absorbed 26 per cent of Indian exports and one fourth of total Indian imports came from the EU. A total of 60 per cent of the total exports of India to the EU were headed for the UK, Germany and France. An asymmetric trade relationship existed between EU and India. India's share in trade with the EU was marginal when compared to EU's economic relations with other countries. While EU-

India trade reached $20 billion, the trade balance with the EU continued to be negative for India. India's trade deficit with the EU was recorded to be $2 billion in 1995. The obstacles that India faced while doing trade with EU included the use of trade protection instruments in the textile sector, as well as in the area of marine and agricultural products. The EU's misgivings were related to the automobile sector and quantitative restrictions on imports. (Jain 2001:138).

However, progress was made to resolve these issues, especially in 1997, through an agreement, according to which quantitative restrictions on imports of about 2400 items were planned to be phased out in about six years. One of the major drawbacks in the relations during this phase was the fact that the major part of "foreign direct investment, joint ventures and industrial collaborations" came from only four out of the15 member-countries of the EU which included Germany, UK, France and Italy. The other member-states were more interested in engaging with the East European economies (Jain 2001: 139).

Situating EU and India in the International Order

The drastic changes in the nature of international politics and its actors have been given due recognition by scholars. Henry Kissinger, despite being one of the main exponents of the classical tradition has stated that

> ...the traditional agenda of international affairs – the balance among major powers, the security of nations – no longer defines our perils or our possibilities....Now we are entering a new era. Old international patterns are crumbling; old slogans are uninstructive; old solutions are unavailing. The world has become interdependent in economics, in communications, in human aspirations.

Robert O. Keohane and Joseph S. Nye have espoused the theory of complex interdependence in the light of the new realities of international politics which counter the assumptions made by the realists. Interdependence refers to "situations characterised by reciprocal effects among countries or among actors in different countries." Realism perceives the world to be continuously embroiled in active or potential conflict with an extremely high degree of possibility of the use of force. The realists believe that only a well-oiled system of balance of power aided by the prompt and adequate use of force at all times shall ensure the stability of the world order. Keohane and Nye counter the realist assertions with three main characteristics of complex interdependence. The first characteristic is that there are multiple channels which include informal ties between governmental elites as well as formal foreign office arrangements and informal ties among non-governmental elites and transnational organisations that participate directly in world politics. The second characteristic is that there is the absence of hierarchy among issues and hence the overbearing and all-important presence of military concerns over all other issues is no longer acknowledged. The line of distinction between domestic and foreign policy issues has significantly been blurred. The third characteristic is that force is considered to be an ineffective instrument of policy. Military force for instance, would be an extremely irrelevant tool for resolving economic issues. Keohane and Nye however, state that complex interdependence is an ideal type and that reality mostly lies between these two extremes. They nevertheless believe that complex interdependence provides a "better portrayal of reality" (Keohane and Nye 1977).

The shift from bipolarity to multipolarity, and the resultant increase in importance of the European Union and India, have been adequately acknowledged. John Pinder, Simon Usherwood and Simon McDougall Usherwood have stated that the confrontation between the United States and the

Soviet Union has been replaced by American supremacy and the growing prospect of the emergence of a multipolar world, which is likely to include China followed by India, apart from Russia and others. The bipolar economic order is being rapidly replaced by a multipolar world economy as a result of the meteoric rise of China and India. The European Union will have to find its true place in this new scenario (Pinder et al. 2008). Feng Geng has asserted that the European Union has certain considerations in mind as it makes attempts at strengthening ties with India. The American preference for unilateralism has forced the European Union to seek partners in different regions of the world to counter such designs of the US. This reflects the contradiction in EU-US relations as both envisage a different structure of the world in the future. The EU aims to bring about an increase in its influence in the international arena by means of the establishment of a multipolar world, while the US has an alternative plan, which involves its consolidation as the hegemon of the world (Geng 2006). C. Dale Walton is of the view that with the degradation of unipolarity, a number of young actors are bound to play an increasingly significant role in international affairs. This group will certainly include the European Union which is yet to take its final shape as well as India with its parliamentary democracy which is a little older than half a century. Thus, EU, India, China, Japan, Russia along with the United States are the “most plausible potential poles in the developing multipolar international political system”. He goes on to say that since these polities continue to act as great powers, an extremely vigilant multipolar power system will emerge. However, it shall be imperative for the European Union to undertake the military responsibilities that are indispensable for achieving great power status. India on the other hand, is confounded by “regional, ethnic, religious and socio-economic” centrifugal forces which it shall have to overcome (Walton 2007).

Benefits of Forging a Strong EU-India Partnership

There is an abundance of literature available exhorting the European Union and India to close in ranks for mutual benefit. Mario Telo has emphasised upon the necessity for the European Union to look beyond "inward looking theories of integration" and draw comparisons between its federal system and that of the United States. The European Union should examine the "alternative kind of powers" such as India and its international role. He believes that external legitimacy for the European Union is crucial because 'external credibility is likely to have a decisive impact upon its internal democratic performance. He stated that it is in the interest of the EU and India to lend support for the consolidation of the existing global and regional regulating framework and contribute towards building more multilateral regimes as a background for establishing a sustainable bilateral partnership (Telo 2008).

D.K. Giri has argued that the European Union should do all within its capacity to enhance its image in India as it shall pave the way for its recognition in South Asia. The EU should not delay taking cognisance of the fact that the size, population and economic potential of India make it an important player to contend with. Therefore, innovative and constructive synergy and sustainable convergence in the areas of trade and economic and development cooperation should be encouraged (Giri 2001). Joel Sandhu has asserted that it is imperative for the EU political leadership to take bigger and decisive steps to ensure the progress of EU-India Strategic Partnership, which has proved to be a useful "institutionalised mechanism" for both sides, to confabulate on issues of mutual importance. He is of the belief that "deepened EU-India cooperation" would lead to better results for both the parties in the area of climate change, trade negotiations in the WTO and on issues pertaining to non-proliferation.

It was stated at the EICC-ASSOCHAM-EIAS-GOPIO Trade and Business Summit that the ever-growing gigantic Indian market "exerts a gravitational pull for economic interests" from all corners of the world. The economic and political changes that have come to the fore as a consequence of globalisation include the acquisition of European companies by India. The enterprises from India have established themselves as sources of international capital. Thus, the summit concluded that "India's geopolitical virtues and strength, its democratic record and values and political stability" make it imperative that the EU should make every possible effort towards consolidation of relations with India (EICC-ASSOCHAM-EIAS-GOPIO Trade and Business Summit 2007).

Strategic Partnership

The 1994 cooperation agreement signed between EU and India helped widen the ambit of relations and the focus was no longer merely on trade and economic ties. The Joint Political Statement signed in 1993 provided for the holding of annual ministerial meetings and starting a broad and comprehensive political dialogue after which the first EU-India summit was held in Lisbon in 2000 and it was hailed as a big step forward in the evolution of the relationship.

The first EU-India summit proved to be one the most significant milestones which helped to break the ice between the two partners ever since the European Commission took upon itself the task to persuade the Council and the European Parliament for forging a "substantially enhanced partnership with India". The EU-India Summit acknowledged the importance of India as a significant economic and political player who "had been left in the cold after its key ally, the Soviet Union crumbled at the end of the Cold War". India thought of this as an opportunity to gain prominence as a global player in the international arena. Thus, "a broad consensus" was seen to emerge "among the Member States to positively engage India through dialogue" on issues of common concern and mutual benefit that could be jointly advocated in the "multilateral fora". The EU exhibited the prescience to realise that India is likely to be one of the most powerful partners in the New Economy especially in the fields of information technology and bio-technology. The EU lauded the huge waves of economic reforms that had swept India and revived it financial health. The EU understood that there was immense economic potential in the partnership with India which at that time was largely an under-valued market. The bilateral trade and investment was also way below expectations and the two sides were keen to expand business by means of adopting sound trade and investment policies (Delegation of the European Union to India 2000). Building upon these sentiments, it was decided at the summit that EU and India should "build a new strategic partnership in the 21st century founded on shared values and aspirations characterised by enhanced and multi-faceted cooperation". It was stated that this was an apt moment for launching "a new phase of constructive and mutually beneficial partnership" in the wake of the "enhanced and sustained growth" of India and integration and enlargement of the EU (Delegation of the European Union to India : 2000a). The document entitled "Agenda for Action" talked about the specific areas and action sought to be taken by both the partners, including enhancement of bilateral dialogue, promotion and protection of human rights and fundamental freedoms, dialogue on preventing and promoting terrorism, cooperation to combat international drug trafficking and drug abuse, furthering common interests in international organisations, eradication of chemical, biological and nuclear weapons. Cooperation in the fields of information technology and communications, science and technology, elementary education, environment and trade was also emphasised upon for further action (Delegation of the European Union to India: 2000b).

The first security strategy document was adopted by the EU in 2003 and it was entitled "A Secure Europe in a Better World European Security Strategy" in which terrorism, proliferation of weapons of mass destruction, regional conflicts, state failure and organised crime were identified as the key threats to peace and stability in the world. It was stated that since these problems were common to all, international cooperation would be necessary to deal with such problems. The EU stated that this could be made possible through "multilateral cooperation in international organisations and through partnerships with key actors". The EU was of the opinion that it should look to develop strategic partnerships with Japan, China, Canada, India as well as with all those who share their "goals and values" (Delegation of the European Union to India : 2003).

The Communication from the Commission to the European Council, the European Parliament and the European Economic and Social Committee which was titled "An EU-India Strategic Partnership" was presented in 2003. It stated that EU-India relations have been bolstered since the first EU-India Summit in Lisbon in 2000 through "meetings at all levels- including business and civil society- and extensive dialogue and cooperation on political, geo-political and multilateral issues, economic and trade questions". The Commission believed that EU and India "already enjoy a close relationship, based on shared values and mutual respect" and they should therefore adopt "a new strategy" to take the relationship further and they came up with detailed "analyses and proposals" for strengthening the "strategic partnership". Both partners were exhorted to increase international cooperation through multilateralism, conflict prevention and post-conflict reconstruction, non-proliferation of weapons of mass destruction, combating terrorism and organised crime, tackling the issue of migration, promotion of democracy and human rights and promotion of peace, prosperity and stability in South Asia. A slew of measures were proposed for strengthening the economic partnership. It was stated that a strategic policy dialogue should be initiated between EU and India for the sake of regulatory and industrial policy and on the issue of environment. It called for strategic sectoral dialogues in the areas of information society, transport, energy, biotechnology, global satellite navigation system and space partnership. It also called for boosting investment at the bilateral and multilateral level. The proposal encouraged business-to-business contacts, cooperation in finance and monetary affairs and synergies in science and technology. The EU and India were asked to engage in extensive development cooperation which would include the goal of achieving the Millennium Development Goals by India. Mutual understanding was sought to be increased through parliamentary exchanges and academic contacts and exchanges apart from cultural cooperation notably in the fields of film and music. It was opined that both partners should take necessary measures for increasing reciprocal visibility. It was stated that attempts should be made to strengthen the institutional architecture of EU-India relationship by holding summits and ministerial meetings, biennial meetings, brainstorming sessions and EU-India Roundtables. It was suggested that there should be regular interaction between leaders and representatives of missions from both sides. The Commission stated that it hoped that this would be "the starting point of collective reflection on upgrading EU-India relations to a truly strategic partnership". It was expected that further deliberations between the two sides would lead to deepening of EU-India relations "in the form of an Action Plan and a new Joint EU-India Political Declaration" which could be endorsed at the sixth EU-India summit (Europa Summaries of EU Legislation: 2004).

The European Commission's request elicited a response from India in the form of a Strategy Paper. It is believed to be the first document of its kind to be released by India. The Indian response recommended "a relationship of sovereign equality based on comparative advantage and a mutuality of interests and benefits" which would in turn be "immune from the vicissitudes of either side's relationship with a third party". India proposed "prior consultations on the eve of major multilateral conferences, institutionalised dialogue between EU and India on UN matters, exchange of views on the unfolding events and developments in

South Asia, Middle East, Afghanistan and Iraq. India advocated for the creation of a Joint Working Group on Security Cooperation and intensification of dialogue on energy and environment (Ministry of External Affairs: 2004).

The five EU-India summits held since then assured that progress was made in all possible areas of interaction. The fifth EU-India summit is largely considered to be a "landmark" summit as the proposal for upgrading the EU-India relationship to the level of a Strategic Partnership was endorsed. The Partnership is regarded by both sides to be much more than the sum of its parts. It is looked upon as a "qualitative transformation" as India and the European Union are known to "engage as equal partners and work together in partnership with the world at large". The European Union has included India into the elite club of countries such as the United States, China, Canada and Russia with which it has a strategic partnership which is recognition of India's growing power and "potential to be one of the world's most important international actors"(Delegation of the European Union to India 2005).

The EU and India have adopted a "comprehensive and forward looking" Joint Action Plan in acknowledgement of the Strategic Partnership at the sixth EU-India summit in order to deal with the current diverse and complex global challenges which would invariably involve strengthening of the multifaceted EU-India partnership (Delegation of the European Union to India 2005a). The two sides decided to strengthen dialogue and consultation mechanisms. They decided to carry on dialogue consistently at the Summit and Ministerial level on all issues of mutual interest. It was decided that progress in the implementation of the Joint Action Plan would be assessed before each annual summit and an overall assessment would be made at the eighth EU-India summit. Political dialogue and cooperation sought to be enhanced by emphasising upon pluralism and diversity, effective multilateralism, peace-keeping, peace-building and post-conflict assistance. It was stated that regular parleys would be held on issues such as regional cooperation in the EU and SAARC, disarmament and non-proliferation of weapons of mass destruction, combating terrorism and organised crime.

The EU and India decided to make an effort to bring together the people and cultures of both sides by organising parliamentary, educational and civil society exchanges and by means of increasing mutual visibility. They decided to facilitate the movement of people on both sides by addressing migration and consular issues. The two sides aimed at accelerating economic policy dialogue and cooperation in the areas of industrial policy, science and technology, finance and monetary affairs, environment, energy, clean development and climate change, information and communication technology, transport, space technology, pharmaceuticals and biotechnology, agriculture, customs, employment, social policy, development and business cooperation. The European Union and India expressed their keenness to increase trade and investment with the help of the High Level Trade Group and by utilising the opportunities and concessions provided by the Doha Development Agenda. The two sides sought to encourage Public Private Partnership (PPP) and remove irritants in the areas of Intellectual Property Rights (IPR), sanitary and phytosanitary issues, services and public procurement (Delegation of the European Union to India 2005b).

The seventh EU-India Summit was held in Helsinki on 13 October 2006. The leaders of both sides "reiterated their commitment to the Strategic Partnership launched at the fifth EU-India Summit in the Hague" after which a comprehensive and forward looking Joint Action Plan was launched at the sixth EU-India Summit in New Delhi. The two sides expressed their satisfaction with regard to the implementation of the Joint Action Plan and expressed their resolve to take it forward. The leaders observed the significant strides taken by both sides towards "intensification of dialogue between the strategic partners". The two sides laid special emphasis upon stronger financial and business links which would be "mutually advantageous and would buttress the Strategic Partnership" (Delegation of the European Union to India 2006).

The European Union and India reviewed the progress achieved in the implementation of the Joint Action Plan at the eighth EU-India summit and were satisfied with the results. They stated that further progress would be welcome. The two sides intended to make an overall assessment of the Joint Action Plan in 2008 and suggested ways and means of further "upgrading the overall framework of EU-India relations". Thus, the framework of the Joint Action Plan is credited with making an extremely significant contribution towards strengthening Strategic Partnership in the areas of dialogue and consultation mechanisms, political dialogue and cooperation, bringing together people and cultures, economic policy dialogue and cooperation and developing trade and investment (Delegation of the European Union to India 2007).

India and the European Union signed the Memorandum of Understanding on the Country Strategy Paper for India 2007-2010 which would support the Indian endeavour to achieve the Millennium Development Goals and help in the implementation of the India-EU Joint Action Plan. The European Union welcomed India's participation in the Asia-Europe Meeting and "reiterated its endorsement of the incorporation of India into the fold of the ASEM process dialogue and cooperation which links Europe with Asia. India also welcomed the willingness expressed by EU to engage in the East Asia Summit process and its intention to join the Treaty of Amity and Cooperation (TAC) (Delegation of the European Union to India 2007).

The review of Joint Action Plan at the ninth EU-India summit revealed that new formats of dialogue were created through the conduits of Indian membership of the ASEM and the EU observer status at SAARC. Indo-EU trade more than doubled and bilateral investment increased ten-fold. A dialogue process was initiated on macro-economic policy and financial services which highlight the salience of financial and monetary stability and that of inclusive growth particularly in the context of price rise associated with food, basic metals and energy. An EU-India Energy Panel was established and the International Thermonuclear Experimental Reactor (ITER) Agreement came into force. A spurt in activities in the area of science and technology was witnessed and "exchanges have elevated to ministerial level, with increased co-operation across the board, shared partnerships with co-investment in research and technology development, and renewal of the EU-India Science and Technology Agreement."

Cooperation in the field of information and communication technologies continues to be strengthened as a result of cooperation between the European high speed research network— GEANT2 and its Indian counterpart— ERNET, enabling European and Indian researchers to develop joint projects. Considerable progress has been made towards validating Ayurveda products as para-medicines or food supplements. There have been numerous activities organised under the "Sector Policy Dialogue and Associated Work Programme" in the field of employment and social affairs. Specific funding has been made available to bring about an increase in the participation of Indian students in European graduate programmes (Delegation of the European Union to India 2008).

The leaders of both sides expressed their determination "to reinforce their strategic partnership" at the 11th EU-India summit "for their mutual benefit in all areas and to better contribute to the resolution of the challenges of the twenty-first century". The two sides took up bilateral, regional and global issues of common interest and concern for discussion. The leaders took note of the development priorities of the EU as well as the changes brought about in the functioning of the EU as a result of coming into force of the Lisbon Treaty (Delegation of the European Union to India 2010).The President of the European Council Herman Van Rompuy emphasised upon the necessity to bring the EU-India strategic partnership launched in 2004 to a higher level. He stated that there is a need to make it wider (in the areas to be unfolded) and deeper (in those already launched). He also stated that the new institutional EU setting would facilitate the achievement of these objectives (Delegation of the European Union to India 2010a). Jose Manuel Borroso, President of the European Commission, stated that the 11th summit held in the "Lisbon setting" has contributed towards strengthening the Strategic Partnership between India and the European Union. He highlighted considerable progress made in the areas of reaching towards a broad- based EU-India Trade and Investment Agreement, cooperation in the field of energy, exploiting green and clean technologies, climate change and developing a common stand on global affairs. He stated that the results of the EU-India summit clearly reflect that the EU-India "Strategic Partnership is not a theoretical concept but a very concrete relationship that delivers" (Delegation of the European Union to India 2010b).

The factsheet of the twelfth EU-India summit referred only to the historicity of the EU-India strategic partnership and stated that

> EU-India relations date back to the early 1960s when diplomatic relations were established. It was however the 1994 Cooperation Agreement (which is still the current legal framework for cooperation) that opened the door to the broad political dialogue that has since evolved, notably through annual summits since 2000, and through regular ministerial and expert-level meetings. In recognition of both sides' political and economic importance the EU-India strategic partnership was created in 2004 to enable the partners to better address complex international issues in the context of globalisation. To underpin the strategic partnership, leaders at the 2005 summit adopted the EU-India Joint Action Plan (JAP) which defined common objectives and proposed a wide range of supporting activities in the areas of political, economic and development cooperation. The Joint Action Plan was reviewed at the 2008 summit and has since

focused on promoting four priorities: peace and comprehensive security, sustainable development, research and technology and people-to-people and cultural exchanges. Besides ministerial and expert level meetings, the EU and the Republic of India hold regular annual summits. The previous EU-India Summit was held in Brussels on 10 December 2010.

Political cooperation, trade relations, climate change, energy and science and technology were identified as the main areas of EU-India cooperation. Science and technology has been identified "as a central element in the EU-India strategic partnership". A new initiative called the Strategic Forum for International Cooperation (SFIC) "aims at making Europe's international research policy towards non-EU countries more effective and coherent through enhanced dialogue and cooperation between EU and other major partner countries outside Europe". The SFIC has selected India "as the strategic partner country for implementing its first pilot initiative" (Delegation of the European Union to India 2012).

The broad-based trade and investment agreement for which negotiations began in 2007 have not been concluded till now. The statement issued at the 12th EU-India summit mentioned trade negotiations to be "close to completion". It is widely believed that "serious cooperation" in many fields in which dialogues have been initiated is conspicuous by its absence. Indian policy makers are largely known to be unconvinced about Europe's role as a strategic player in Asia. The EU is generally not regarded as a factor to reckon with "in India's foreign policy debates" (Sachdeva 2014: 428-429). However, we also see a simultaneous strengthening of India's bilateral ties with UK, France and Germany. The absence of political will in the EU to engage more constructively with India is owing to the choice of the larger and more powerful member-states of the EU to engage with India on a bilateral level rather than as a united whole under the EU umbrella. Therefore, it would not be unfair to state that despite the upgradation of relations to the level of strategic partnership, EU-India relations suffer from "a certain degree of mutual neglect and lack of attention" (Baroowa 2006: 747-748).

The Economic Dimension of EU-India Relations

EU-India trade increased from $1640 million in 1973 to $5700 million in 1980. EU-India trade grew about five times in the period 1981-1990. As a result of economic reforms being ushered into India in 1991, EU-India trade increased around 20 per cent in four years in the period 1990-94 and registered further growth of around $19,500 million in 1996-97 (Jain 2011: 228-229).

EU-India trade in goods more than doubled in value. Exports increased from €13.7 billion to €31.6 billion while imports registered an increase from €12.8 billion to €29.5 billion in the years between 2000 and 2008. The EU had a surplus in trade with India which grew from €0.8 billion in 2000 to €2.1 billion in 2008. India accounted for 2.4 per cent of exports and 1.9 per cent of imports in 2008. India was EU's tenth most important trading partner. In the first half of 2008 EU exports to India fell from €15.7 billion to €12.7 billion in the first half of 2009, while imports fell from €14.9 billion to €12.9 billion. Consequently, EU trade balance with India changed from a surplus of €0.8 billion in the first half of 2008 to a deficit of €0.2 billion in 2009 (Eurostat news release 2009).

The same trend continued for the rest of the year as exports decreased from €31.6 billion in 2008 to €27.6 billion in 2009 and imports declined from €29.5 billion to €25.3 billion in the same period respectively. The decline in EU-India trade during this period was in line with the general trend of decline in the EU's total external trade over the period. The EU trade surplus with India increased from €0.8 billion in 2000 to €2.3 billion in 2009. The EU's trade surplus remained stable at €0.7 billion in the first nine months of 2010. India's share in the EU exports of goods and services increased to 2.6 per cent of the total exports and 2.2 per cent of the imports in the first nine months of 2010. India has consequently become the EU's ninth most important trading partner (Eurostat news release 2010).

The EU's trade in goods with India soared to a new high in 2010 after the decrease recorded in 2009 owing to the global economic slowdown (see Table 1.1). Thus, the EU's exports to India declined from €31.3 billion in 2008 to €27.4 billion in 2009 and then rose to €34.8 billion in 2010. Imports decreased from €29.5 billion in 2008 to €25.4 billion in 2009 and then increased to €33.2 billion in 2010. As a result of these fluctuations, the EU's trade surplus with India declined from €2 billion in 2009 to €1.6 billion in 2010. The EU's trade in services with India occupies a special place and continuously increased its share in EU-India bilateral trade (see Table 1.2). Continuous growth was witnessed in EU-India trade in the first months of 2011. Both imports and exports registered a growth of 20 per cent each between the first ten months of 2010 and the same period of 2011 with exports amounting to €33.4 billion and imports amounting to €33.3 billion each. The EU's trade with India recorded a relatively moderate surplus of €0.1 billion in the first ten months of 2011. India is the EU's most important trading partner (Eurostat news release 2012).

Table 1.1:EU27 Trade in Goods with India

Million euro 2000	2001	2002	2003	2004	2005	2006	2007	2008	2009	2010	
India											
Exports	13 678	12 950	14 330	14 572	17 154	21 322	24 392	29 177	31 263	27 427	34 797
Imports	12 846	13 463	13 682	14 064	16 369	19 086	22 614	26 587	29 530	25 443	33 228
Balance	832	-513	648	507	784	2 236	1 778	2 591	1 732	1 984	1 569
Total Extra-EU27											
Exports	849 739	884 707	891 899	869 237	952 954	1 052 719	1 160 100	1 240 984	1 309 218	1 097 990	1 349 610

Imports	992 698	979 145	936 972	935 241	1 027 522	1 179 569	1 352 787	1 435 083	1 566 379	1 207 810	1 509 092
Balance	-142 959	-94 438	-45 073	-66 004	-74 567	-126 850	-192 686	-194 099	-257 161	-109 820	-159 481
India / Total											
Exports	1.6%	1.5%	1.6%	1.7%	1.8%	2.0%	2.1%	2.4%	2.4%	2.5%	2.6%
Imports	1.3%	1.4%	1.5%	1.5%	1.6%	1.6%	1.7%	1.9%	1.9%	2.1%	2.2%

Source: Eurostat newsrelease (2012). "EU-India Summit EU 27 trade in goods with India increased by 20% in the first ten months of 2011", URL: http://ec.europa.eu/eurostat/documents/2995521/5152694/6-09022012-AP-EN.PDF/97fd2c7e-6c3e-4337-9926-3d721a6d10f7?version=1.0.

Table 1.2 -EU27 Trade in Services with India

Million Euro Exports						**Imports**		**Balance**	
2008	**2009**	**2010**	**2008**	**2009**	**2010**	**2008**	**2009**	**2010**	
Total	**8 938**	**9 137**	**10 862**	**8 129**	**7 390**	**8 692**	**809**	**1 747**	**2 170**
of which:									
Transportation	2 850	2 391	3 577	1 821	1 488	1 835	1 029	903	1 742
Travel	1 018	874	1 230	2 017	1 470	1 660	-999	-597	-430
Other services	5 069	5 868	6 052	4 282	4 426	5 182	788	1 442	870
of which:									
Communications services	278	261	230	267	207	187	10	55	43
Construction services	322	487	481	132	224	204	190	263	277
Insurance services	73	70	81	54	55	89	18	15	-8
Financial services	350	322	310	80	133	187	270	189	123
Computer and information services	1 356	1 732	1 811	1 125	1 288	1 530	230	444	281
Royalties and license fees	212	247	268	50	29	49	162	218	219
Other business services	2 243	2 548	2 693	2 472	2 333	2 835	-229	215	-141

<table>
<tr><td>Personal cultural and recreational services</td><td>28</td><td>21</td><td>32</td><td>30</td><td>69</td><td>33</td><td>-2</td><td>-48</td><td>-0.2</td></tr>
<tr><td>Government services other</td><td>208</td><td>181</td><td>146</td><td>71</td><td>89</td><td>69</td><td>137</td><td>91</td><td>77</td></tr>
<tr><td>Total extra-EU27</td><td>525 304</td><td>483 493</td><td>539 028</td><td>454 045</td><td>416 271</td><td>453 604</td><td>71 259</td><td>67 222</td><td>85 424</td></tr>
<tr><td colspan="2">India / total extra-EU27</td><td>1.7%</td><td colspan="2">1.9%</td><td>2.0%</td><td colspan="2">1.8%</td><td>1.8%</td><td>1.9%</td></tr>
</table>

Source: Eurostat newsrelease (2012). "EU-India Summit EU 27 trade in goods with India increased by 20% in the first ten months of 2011", URL: http://ec.europa.eu/eurostat/documents/2995521/5152694/6-09022012-AP-EN.PDF/97fd2c7e-6c3e-4337-9926-3d721a6d10f7?version=1.0.

The EU is recognised as India's largest trading power. The relationship has undergone a massive transformation as India has evolved from being an aid-recipient to being an aid donor and an equal partner. This in turn has led to a partnership which has been mutually beneficial. The EU and India are recognised as the world's largest democracies and global actors in a multi-polar world who have entered into a Strategic Partnership, of which, the commercial angle is considered to be most important. There has been an exponential growth in the frequency and intensity of EU-India trade relations (see Table 1.3). The EU-India trade in goods has witnessed growth of more than five times between 2000 and 2014 (Government of India 2014: 133-134).

Table 1.3: Trade with European Union (US $ million)

Year	Exports	Growth rate (%)	Imports	Growth rate (%)	Total Trade	Balance of Trade
2009-10	36,028	-8.5	38,433	-10.06	74,461	-2,405
2010-11	46,078	27.89	44,540	15.89	90,618	1,538
2011-12	52,603	14.16	56,530	26.92	109,133	-3,927
2012-13	50,469	-4.06	52,275	-7.53	102,744	-1,806
2013-14	51,595	2.23	49,504	-5.30	101,099	2,091

Source: Government of India, Ministry of Commerce and Industry, Department of Commerce Annual Report 2013-2014 (2014). "Commercial Relations, Trade Agreements and International Trade Organisations", URL: http://commerce.nic.in/publications/pdf/anualreport_chapter6-2012-13.pdf.

The two-way flow of goods, services and investment has undoubtedly strengthened EU-India relations and has led to the establishment of "a real economic partnership". The EU is the largest economy and internal market in the world as it has successfully managed to represent a single goods and services market of over 500 million people and a GDP of €13 trillion. The EU has been recognised as India's most important trade and investment partner with a total two-way trade close to €100 billion in goods and services in 2012. India is the EU's ninth largest trading partner and is roughly at par with Brazil and South Korea. Two-way trade in goods has grown three times since 2000 from €27 billion in 2000 to €76 billion in 2012 (see Figure 1.1). India's exports of services to the EU have more than tripled since 2000 and EU export of services to India has increased more than four times since 1999 (see Figure 1.2). Trade between EU and India has exhibited a positive growth trajectory of 43 per cent in goods and 40 per cent in services since the global crisis started in 2008. Despite a marginal reduction in bilateral trade in 2012, because of insignificant increase in GDP last year, it has not affected the subsequent increase in EU-India trade. About 20 per cent of Indian goods and around 10 per cent of its services are exported to the EU. Indian export of goods to the EU is greater than its exports to China, Japan, Brazil and Russia together. A similar trend is being witnessed in services. Consumers in the EU, as well as in India, enjoy the advantage of access to high-end, greater range and lower price of products. India has been one of the largest beneficiaries of the Generalised System of Preferences offered by the EU to third countries on account of the fact that India's most competitive exports of goods are covered by the scheme. Hence, not less than €17 billion worth of goods are exported to the EU on preferential terms. India is also recognised as the most important source of imports under the GSP scheme. The EU had to forgo about

€900 million as a result of according tariff preferences to India under the scheme (Delegation of the European Union to India 2013: 7). The EU exported goods worth €35.9 billion to India, while India exported €36.8 billion worth of goods to the EU, which marks a new trend as the balance of EU-India trade in goods was in India's favour. The EU export of services to India amounted to €12.5 billion, while India exported services worth €11.2 billion to the EU. The balance of trade was in favour of the EU and was recorded at €1.3 billion (European Commission 2014).

Figure 1.1: EU-India "Trade in Goods" Statistics

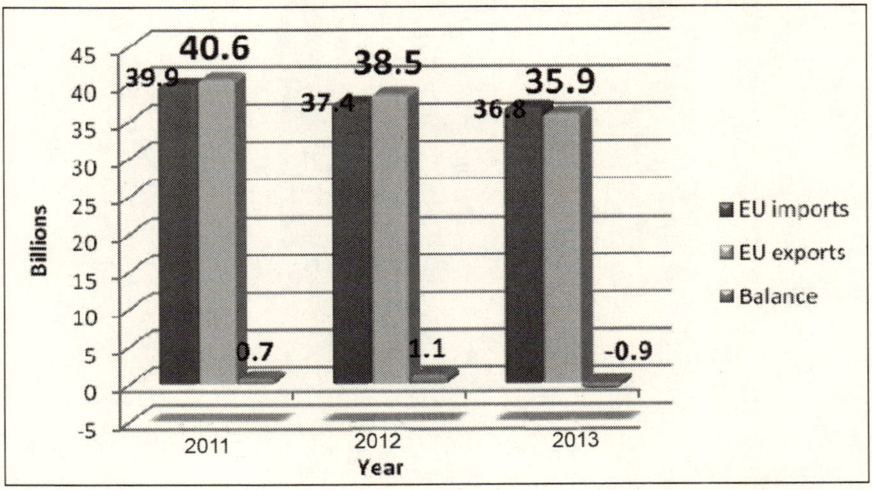

Source: European Commission (2014), "Trade Countries and Regions India", URL:http://ec.europa.eu/trade/policy/countries-and-regions/countries/india/.

Investment by the EU in India increased three times over from €759 million in 2003 to €3 billion in 2010. The EU investment in India further shot up to €12 billion in 2011, while Indian investment in the EU reached €1.9 billion (see Figure 1.3). Cumulative EU investment in India since the year 2000 reached €35.6 billion in 2011 compared to €10 billion of

Indian investment in the EU. Despite the fact that the EU is the world's number one location for FDI, it continues to adopt a pro-active attitude towards overseas investment (Delegation of the European Union to India 2013: 7-8). EU investment in India shot up to €41.8 billion in 2012, while Indian investment to the EU amounted to €8.8 billion (see Figure 1.4). This marked a decline of €1.2 billion compared to the previous year (European Commission 2014).

Figure 1.2: EU-India "Trade in Services" Statistics

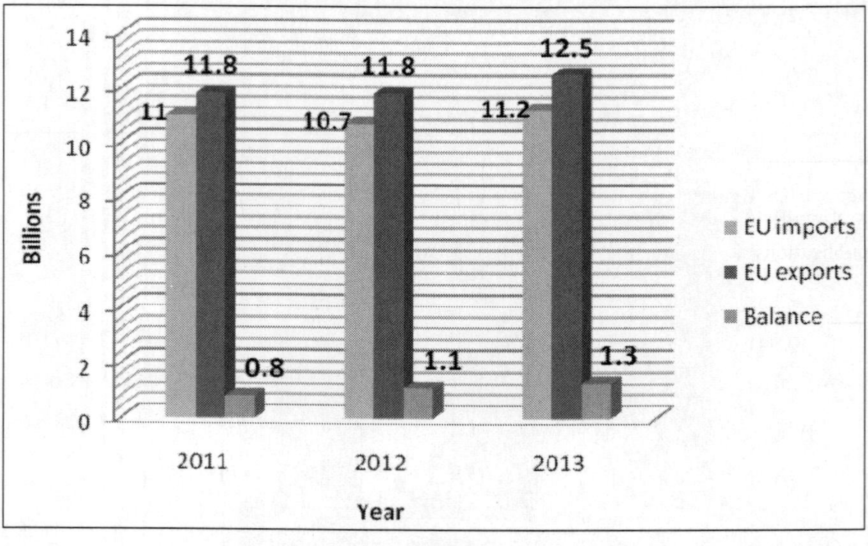

Source: European Commission (2014), "Trade Countries and Regions India", URL:http://ec.europa.eu/trade/policy/countries-and-regions/countries/india/.

Figure 1.3: FDI Flows between EU and India

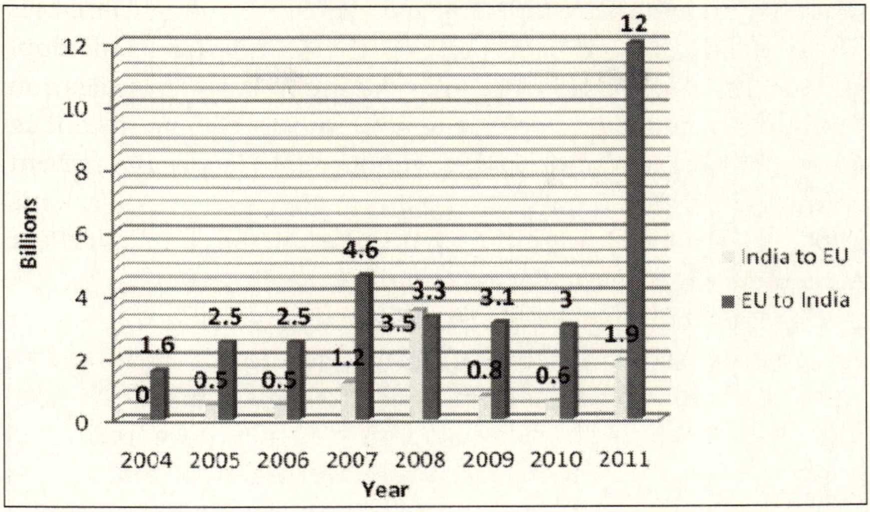

Source: Delegation of the European Union to India (2013). "The European Union and India Fifty Years of Partnership", URL: http://eeas.europa.eu/delegations/india/documents/publications/the_eu_and_india_fifty_years_of_partnership.pdf.

Figure 1.4: Foreign Direct Investment in 2012

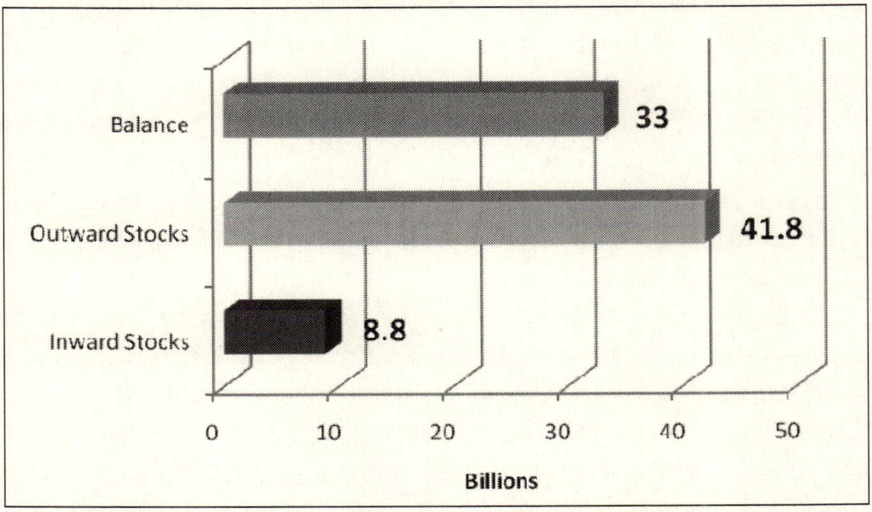

Source: European Commission (2014), "Trade Countries and Regions India", URL:http://ec.europa.eu/trade/policy/countries-and-regions/countries/india/.

India and the EU have enjoyed robust economic relations. These relations have been built on the foundations of several agreements such as Cooperation Agreement between European Community and India on Partnership and Development, 1993, Agreement on Scientific and Technological Cooperation, 2001 (renewed in 2007), Agreement on Customs Cooperation, 2004, EU-India Horizontal Civil Aviation Agreement, 2008, Agreement on Nuclear Fusion Energy Research, 2009 and Joint Declaration on Culture, 2010. India has bilateral framework agreements with a number of individual the EU countries in areas of trade, investment and avoidance of double taxation. India has concluded agreements for investment promotion and protection with EU member-states (Government of India 2014: 134).

EU-India bilateral relations are periodically reviewed at the official level by the India-EU Joint Commission. Three Sub-Commissions on Trade, Economic Cooperation and Development Cooperation and seven Joint Working Groups on agriculture and marine products, textiles, steel, food processing industries, pharmaceuticals and bio-technology, customs cooperation and technical barriers to trade (TBT)/ sanitary and phytosanitary (SPS) issues are active. In 2014, the meetings of Sub Commission on Trade, Sub Commission on Economic Cooperation and Sub Commission on Development were held in the month of June.

India's trade with the EU is hampered by "non-tariff barriers such as sanitary and phytosanitary standards, technical barriers, complex system of quota/ tariff and anti-dumping/ anti-subsidy measures against Indian products". These issues are of salience as far as market access for India's exports to the EU is concerned. They are therefore regularly taken up for discussion in the Joint Working Groups and Sub-commission on Trade. The EU market has stringent quality norms and standards. Nevertheless, India requires meeting these norms in order to increase the market share of Indian products in the EU. This continuous process of dialogue and exchange of views helps in creating an environment conducive for facilitating and increasing bilateral trade and investment flows (Government of India 2014: 134).

A massive change is taking place in India as an increasing number of people in the lower-middle class slab are shifting to the upper middle class category. There has been an accelerated increase in the strength of the upper middle class. Even more noticeable has been the rise in numbers of the very rich class, which consists of a total of 100,000 households with net worth of upto $1 million. It has been predicted that the country will have the "largest middle class population and consumption" in the world, even if a modest growth of GDP of about 6-7 per cent is estimated by 2030. The MNCs are at loggerheads with each other to tap one of the biggest markets of the world and satiate the appetite of a bouregoning Indian middle class.

India is the most preferred destination for many European corporations. There are some well-known European brands which also happen to be household names in the country—amongst them Unilever (Anglo-Dutch), Mercedes- Benz (German), Danone (France), and Ferrero (Italian). The rate of success of these companies inevitably increases as a result of "earlier entry, greater control of entry mode and local leadership".

Most MNCs recognise India to be a valuable source of "offshoring knowledge work" and market that is likely to "boom" in the near future owing to India's population of 1.2 billion people which is the country's asset. Graduates who are added to the workforce each year amount to a total of 3.1 million and India also happens to be the largest English- speaking market owing to its colonial past. About 65 per cent of the global offshoring work comes to India annually. Outsourcing to India assures access to abundance of talent and large-scale benefits of cost arbitrage. A number of Indian IT services companies underwent phenomenal growth by the turn of the century, owing to their focus on low-cost IT services delivered outside the country. This led several European IT vendors such as Capgemini (France), Atos (France), Steria (French), SQS (German) and others to follow suit and provide employment to staffers in India with numbers ranging from 4000 to 45,000. Most of these European companies have also gone ahead and established off-shore R & D centres in India (see Table 1.4).

A firm can internationalise by either making a Greenfield or Brownfield investment. A Greenfield investment is one in which "a company sets up its de-novo subsidiaries, affiliates, factories or delivery centres in the target market". When a company makes an entry into the market "through an acquisition, joint venture or majority participation in the local firm", it is called a Brownfield investment. (Charlie 2014: 19-20).

Table 1.4: Investment made and acquisition of companies in India by the EU member-states

UK Investments in India (2004-2013)	UK- headquartered Companies in India
Number of greenfield investment projects (Companies) -683 (431), value -$37.3 billion Number of acquisitions / joint ventures – 489, value- $33 billion Total Investment projects- 1172,value- $70.3 billion	Aviva (Insurance Group) Barclays (Banking and Financial Services) BP (Energy and Petrochemicals) Cable & Wireless (Telecommunications) Cadbury (Confectionary) Cairn (Energy Oil and Gas Exploration) GSK (Pharmaceuticals and Drugs) JCB (Construction and Farming equipment) Standard Chartered Bank (Banking and Financial Services) Rolls Royce Holdings (Power systems company) Tesco (Grocery and General Merchandise retailer) Virgin Atlantic (Aviation)

German Investments in India (2004-2013)	German-headquartered Companies in India
Number of greenfield investment projects (Companies) -564 (327), value-$22 billion Number of acquisitions / joint ventures -193, value- $12.47 Total Investment projects- 757, value-$34.4 billion	Siemens (Engineering and Electronics) Adidas (Sports Clothing and Accessories) Bayerische Motoren Werke (BMW) (Automobile and Engine manufacturer) Audi (Automobile manufacturer) Volkswagen (Automobile manufacturer) SAP Enterprise (Software) Deutsche Telecom (Banking and Financial Services) Bosch (Engineering and Electronics) Bayer (Chemicals and Pharmaceuticals) Lufthansa (Air Travel) Carl Zeiss (Opto-electronics)
French Investments in India (2004-2013) Number of greenfield investment projects (Companies)- 303 (164), value- $17.95 billion Number of acquisitions / joint ventures -171, value- $3.69 billion Total Investment projects – 474, value-$21.64 billion	**French-headquartered Companies in India** Alstom (Power Generation, Transmission and Transportation) BNP Paribas (Banking and Financial Services) Capgemini (IT Services) Schneider Electric (Electrical Equipment) Alcatel Lucent (Telecommunication Equipment) Faurecia (Automotive Parts Manufacturer) Saint-Gobain (Building Materials) L'Oreal (Personal Care) Accor (Hospitality and Tourism) Carrefour (Retailing) Renault (Automotive) Atos Origin(IT Services)
Italian Investments in India (2004-2013) Number of greenfield investment projects (Companies) -144, value- (102) $5 billion Number of acquisitions -82,value- $1.54 billion Total Investment projects-226, value-$6.54 billion	**Italy –headquartered Companies in India** Fiat (including New Holland and Magneti) Marelli) (Automotives) Pirelli (Auto Components) Ferrero (Food and Confectionary) Armani (Fashion and Leisure) Piaggio (Automotive and Engines Lavazza (Retail Coffee) Eni (Oil and Gas) Danieli (Metal and Manufacturing) Assicurazioni Generali (Financial Services) Luxottica (Eyewear) Bisazza Glass (Mosaics)

Spanish Investments in India (2004-2013)	**Spain-headquartered Companies in India**
Number of greenfield investment projects (Companies) 123 (100), value- $3.76 billion Number of acquisitions / joint ventures – 61, value- $2.09 billion Total Investment projects-184, value- $5.85 billion	Befesa Infrastructure (Water Treatment) Banco Sadabell (Financial Services) Borges (Olive Oils) Gamesa (Renewable Energy) Gestamp (Engineering and Renewable Energy) Navantia (Navy Construction) Inditex Group (Zara) (Clothing and Accessories) Isolux Corsán (Infrastructure and Construction) Acciona (Engineering, Construction and Infrastructure) Coinma (Office Furniture) Grupo Cobra (Engineering)
Swedish Investments in India (2004-2013)	**Sweden-headquartered Companies in India**
Number of greenfield investment projects (Companies) -98(56), value- $4.96 billion Number of acquisitions / joint ventures-25, value- $1.55 billion Total Investment projects-123,value- $5.31 billion	Nepa (Brand tracking services) Seco Tools (Cutting tools and Equipment) Handelsbanken (Financial Services) Ericsson (Telecom Equipment) Saab (Defence and Aerospace) Eletta (Measurements and Under-water Cleaning) Atlas Copco (Industrial Tooling and Equipment) Ikea (Furniture and Home Accessories) Volvo (Automotives and Construction Equipment) Tetra Pak (Food Packaging and Processing) Gunnebo (Security Solutions) KappAhl (Clothing Chain)

Source: European Business and Technology Centre Enhancing EU-India Collaboration in Clean Technologies (2014). "European Companies in India: Reigniting Economic Growth Foreign Direct Investment", Charlie, A. URL: http://ebtc.eu/images/ebtc-website-assets/publications/sector-publications/cross-sector/market-reports/140505_REP_ebtc-eicc-report_european-companies-in-india.pdf.

EU-India FTA

The EU-India Strategic Partnership was followed up by the EU-India Joint Action Plan where the partners agreed that the economic aspect of the relationship was under-utilised. Negotiations on EU-India FTA expanded the strategic partnership. The conclusion of the EU-India FTA would cater to a huge market of 1.5 billion consumers. A High Level Trade Group which included government officials and business leaders was set up in 2006, this recommended a slew of measures beckoning towards greater liberalisation as the basic foundation for inking EU-India FTA. At the end of the year, the European Commission "requested negotiating mandates from EU member-states for bilateral trade agreements with India, Korea and ASEAN" who were selected on the basis of certain criteria, which included the size of their market, economic growth and the existing level of protection against EU exports. The initiative was understood as an attempt to bring in a new generation of FTAs which would be implemented after the disappointment at the multilateral Doha Round Talks in WTO. Moreover, the mandates were part of the "Global Europe-Competing in the World" (Global Europe Strategy) trade policy framework that was initiated a year earlier. Competitiveness was chosen as the main motivation behind FTAs. The Global Europe Strategy brought about a shift in emphasis from development objectives to competition and corporate-driven growth. Thus, the EU was seen to be engaged in facilitating "economic cooperation and trade" rather than bringing about "human development and poverty reduction". FTA negotiations were considered to be necessary as attempts on the part of WTO to reach a consensus on issues such as services and investment, liberalisation and intellectual property rights protection because of the clash of interests between the developed and developing countries. The civil society raised its concern on the adverse effects that uncontrolled liberalisation in these sectors could bring about (Wouters et. al 2013).

The Indian economy has undergone tremendous transformation since independence through economic reform and integration with the global economy. Despite the fact that EU-India trade links are considered to be strong, its trade and regulatory framework is considered to be restrictive on account of imposition of tariff and non-tariff barriers that hinder trade with the EU. The non-tariff barriers are imposed in the garb of "quantitative restrictions, import licensing, mandatory testing and certification for a large number of products" along with complex and long-drawn customs procedures. Hence, the promising economic growth and mutually beneficial trade and protectionist policies were factors that propelled the EU to seek a free trade agreement with India (European Commission 2014).

The European Parliament Panel on International Trade sent seven members to India to discuss the EU-India Free Trade Agreement and they met members of the Standing Committee on Commerce and Civil Societies. The leader of the delegation, Pawel Zalewski, remarked that the FTA would be a "game changer for both sides" as it would help in increasing trade volumes as well as the presence of Indian businessmen in the EU market as non-trade barriers would be effectively dealt with. He also divulged that based on the estimation of three impact studies that were conducted, it can safely be said that EU-India FTA shall prove to be highly beneficial for India. It would create more than 2 million jobs in India and India's trade to the EU would increase in all probability by 5 to 10 per cent (Zeebiz 2013).

The FTA negotiations between EU and India were launched way back in 2007 and they reached a "critical phase" five years later in 2012 when issues such as improved market access for goods and services, a chapter on government procurement and retrospective taxation were taken up for discussion. The EU had "disengaged itself" from EU-India FTA talks before this and for a little over six months when the erstwhile UPA government in power at the Centre was unable to accept and accommodate the EU demands. The talks during this phase hovered around "eliminating or drastically reducing duties on European-made vehicles, vehicle components and wines and spirits". The Indian side has been demanding data secure nation status from the EU as it would facilitate the consolidation of business of IT companies from India in the EU. Besides, India has persistently been asking for non-restrictive visas for its professionals and greater market access in the services and pharmaceutical sectors. Apart from asking for huge duty cuts in automobiles, the EU has been insisting on tax reduction on wines and spirits and dairy products and a strong intellectual property regime (F.Business 2014).

India is seeking greater market access in the EU in the services sector. It is interested in facilitating and enhancing Information Technology Enabled Services (ITES), Business Process Outsourcing (BPO) and Knowledge Process Outsourcing (KPO) ,covered under Mode 1 of the BTIA, while Mode 4 deals with movement of skilled professionals like software engineers. Greater market access in Mode 4 will enable skilled professionals such as software engineers to reside and work on a temporary basis in EU countries. The obstacles in facilitating Mode 4 include work permits, wage-parity conditions, visa formalities and non-recognition of professional qualifications. India is also urging the EU to grant data secure status because the high costs involved in adhering to the extant EU's data protection laws and procedures makes the Indian small and medium enterprises highly uncompetitive.

The EU has persistently demanded for greater opening up of the Indian economy for FDI in multi-brand retail and insurance and greater liberalisation of the currently impervious sectors of accountancy and legal services. The European banks have expressed their keenness to fill the vacuum in the Indian banking space. However, some banks such as Goldman Sachs, Morgan Stanley and UBS have surrendered banking licenses as they were unable to withstand the pressure of priority sector lending and financial inclusion.

India has taken a firm stand on the intellectual property regime (IPR). It is very clear that it does not want to make any commitment over and above the WTO's Trade Related Aspects of Intellectual Property Rights (TRIPS) as it will militate against India's capacity to produce generic drugs. India is apprehensive that data exclusivity protection measures that permit pharmaceutical companies to exclusively hold onto the rights to their test results for a particular period will delay the supply of Indian generic medicines. European pharmaceutical companies on the other hand, find Indian patent laws to be extremely unpalatable as they do not allow greening which permits companies to renew patents on old drugs by making minor changes (Singh and Priya 2014).

India has brought down duties on auto parts and components but has continued with the policy of imposition of high import duties on assembled vehicles. The EU alleges that this high level of protectionism should be done away with. The Indian argument is that "the auto manufacturing focus cannot be sacrificed". An FTA with tariff reductions is largely unacceptable to the Indian automobile sector. Imports from the EU coming in at lower tariffs will kill the manufacturing sector. Besides, India's other partners such as Japan and Korea are likely to be unhappy at the undue preference that will be given to the EU in the automobile sector in the proposed FTA (CNBC TV18).

On 20 November 2006, the WTO heard the issue concerning "importation of wines and spirits" from the EU to India. The European Communities had "requested consultations with India regarding duties applied by India and restrictions on retail sale applied by the Indian state" (World Trade Organisation 2010). India offered to break the deadlock by going for significant cuts in duties on wines and spirits to 40 per cent from the current 150 per cent in 2013. In addition to this, the Indian government proposed to cut the entry price per bottle of wine to \$3.7 and whisky to \$5.5. The EU has not been satisfied with this offer and has demanded further reduction in duties for wines and spirits by 30 per cent and in the price of a bottle of wine and whisky to \$3.5. India's wine industry is opposed to the overtures made by the Indian government to the EU. The industry is of the view that significant reduction of duties would lead to flooding of cheap imports into the Indian market which would in turn lead to the pulverisation of the wine industry and the farming community would be ruined (Basu 2013). It was suggested in some circles that the EU should be pushed so that the export of grapes into the EU could be increased while India could allow import of wines at lower duties from the EU, because wines comprise a much smaller sector in comparison to whisky and other spirits (Indian Wine Academy 2011).

The turn of events in the EU with regard to agriculture are alarming for India as the EU has set aside a whopping €363 billion package for agriculture in its seven-year budget for the period 2014-2020 which adds up to almost 38 per cent of the EU spending on agriculture. Consequently, Indian farmers will face tough times and a threat to their livelihood once the EU-India FTA is sealed. This has been confirmed by a study done by Misereor and Heinrich Boll Stiftung of Germany and four other international institutions and they believe that Indian farmers are bound to lose heavily once the EU-India FTA comes into force. India will have to do away with more than 90 per cent of all applied tariffs towards the EU within a period of seven years. This will only make matters worse as EU tariffs are much lower and will not offer India additional market access. Export of Indian products to the EU, which are not subsidised —such as the famous Malabar pepper, Basmati rice, Darjeeling tea and Benaras silk,will face heavy losses.

The dairy sector is expected to bear the heaviest brunt if the FTA decisions regarding the sector go in favour of the EU. Dairy cooperatives such as the Gujarat Co-operative Milk Marketing Federation, which is the producer of the famous Amul brand, has generated demand and employment opportunities for not less than 15 million dairy farmers in rural India who reside in 140,000 villages. The EU-India FTA will have a direct bearing on the lives of 3.2 million dairy farmers. The WTO had provided India a safety mechanism by means of which it could increase the tariff to up to 113 per cent on a number of food items, in case an increase in imports was damaging the domestic sector.The EU-India FTA will have a corrosive effect on such measures. An overview of agricultural trade makes it obvious that India will have minimum gains as a result of trade asymmetries (Nair 2013).

The European Chambers of Commerce, which represents 20 million enterprises and 45 member associations, was of the view that the EU is keen on the signing of the EU-India FTA as they are unable to experience "smooth penetration by foreign companies in the Indian market". They are of the opinion that an amenable business environment is conspicuous by its absence in India. They are known to persistently urge for a "stronger IPR chapter" and for "opening of the public procurement market to EU companies." In case, the negotiations are not concluded anytime soon, a new impact assessment exercise should be carried out jointly by the European Commission and the Indian government in order to raise awareness about the Free Trade Agreement, as it would help both sides to better appreciate the concessions that would be needed to be made in key sectors of the economy, so that EU-India FTA can see the light of the day (Euractiv.com 2014).

There is indeed a certain amount of speculation and hope that the finalisation of the EU-India Free Trade Agreement will be expedited by the new foreign trade policy put in place by the new government at the Centre headed by Narendra Modi. EU Ambassador Joao Cravinho expressed similar sentiments and stated that he expected the FTA to be "finalised in the next year or so" as the two sides "are actually not very far from the agreement but [we] are not there yet" (The Economic Times Foreign Trade 2014).

Strengths of the Relationship

Robust Trade Links

Trade relations between the EU and India are considered to be the well-spring of the positive vibes that abound in the context of EU-India relations. No convincing is required on either side that the economic angle is the umbilical cord of the relations of India with the European Union. India is the ninth largest trading partner of the EU. The bilateral trade is slated to exceed €160.6 billion by 2015 (European Commission 2010). The FDI flows from the European Union to India have shown a sharp rise from €3.2 billion in 2009 to €41.8 billion in 2012. The European Union is very keen on increasing its share of FDI into India as expressed by the Head of the Delegation of the EU to India (Indian Express. com 2010). India's total foreign exchange reserves were recorded at $319,710 million in December 2014 out of which $299,395.9 were kept in the form of Foreign Currency Assets (FCAs) (Reserve Bank of India 2014). Foreign currency assets refer to the appreciation or depreciation of non-US currencies in US dollar terms, which include the euro, pound and yen (Indian Express. com 2011). A portion of the foreign exchange reserves of India are stashed away in euros, which reflects the confidence India has on the viability and success of the euro as an international currency, even in the wake of the sovereign debt crisis that plagued the eurozone recently. When we look at the big picture, it is evident that the EU gains more in the economic partnership with India. However, it must be borne in mind that India has higher stakes in fostering economic ties with the EU and consequently values the EU more as a trade partner compared to the degree of importance accorded by the EU to India. Therefore, the economic engagement can be considered to be of a veritable quality and is expected to grow by leaps and bounds in the coming years.

Deepening Defence Cooperation

Mighty powers such as the United States are vying for a share of the huge Indian defence pie. The feeling of being vanquished for not being able to win the bid and strike a military deal with India was made apparent by the resignation of US ambassador to India Timothy Roemer who described the rejection of US defence majors Boeing and Lockheed as "deeply disappointing" (Malik and Roche 2011: 4) . They in fact failed to clinch the deal despite Barack Obama lobbying for them during his high-profile visit to India in 2010. The deal has been slated as one of the most valuable and sought-after military contracts in recent years involving the purchase of 126 fighters and has witnessed tough competition among Boeing and Lockheed Martin, Sweden's Saab AB and the Russian makers of the MiG 35 (The Economic Times 2011). A report released by the Swedish Think Tank, the Stockholm International Peace Research Institute (SIPRI) states that India has overtaken China as the world's largest arms importer, receiving 9 per cent of the volume of global arms transfers in 2006-2010. India selected France's Rafale for the $20 billion deal, which is hailed as the mother of all defence deals. In another major deal, India finalised a $2.4 billion deal with Dassault Aviation and Thales to upgrade 51 Mirage 2000 aircraft. This development is largely being seen as an attempt by India to deepen its strategic ties with the EU (Reuters 2011). This is a big positive for EU-India relations and reflects upon the growing mutual trust and confidence that the European Union and India have for each other.

France will enter the Indian submarine market as and when the first boat under the Scorpene project is handed over by the Mazagaon Dock Limited to the Indian navy in 2015. Other projects, which India has inked with France, include the development of the Kaveri engine for LCA and the Shakti engine for ALH variants apart from the Maitri Missile Project which is estimated to cost up to $6 billion.

India ordered 66 Hawk AJTs from Britain worth $1.7 billion which was further augmented by 57 additional Hawks worth $1.1

billion during the British Prime Minister David Cameron's visit to India in 2010 to be built by HAL. Britain is seeking tie-ups with India's DRDO. Britain has also sought Indian participation in the Global Combat Ship (GCS), a flexible role frigate programme. Germany's A330 MRTT has been selected owing to its lower-life cycle costs and is now awaiting clearance from the newly elected Indian government at the Centre before the contract worth $1 billion is signed. Italy is involved in the Indian navy's indigenous aircraft carrier programme and the Italian firm Selex Sistomi, which is a subsidiary of Finmenccanica, provides its radar systems. Italy's Alenia Aermacchi is also slated to participate in India's intermediate jet trainer programme.

India has purchased major weapon systems such as aircraft, missiles and helicopters for its army, navy and airforce. In addition to this, it has also acquired sub-systems and components for its indigenously developed weapon systems from the different member-states of the EU. It has been predicted that India shall spend $150-200 billion for purchasing arms in the next decade, a substantial portion of which shall go to the member-states of the EU who shall finalise weapon deals with India (Bhatia 2014).

Cooperation in Science and Technology

The European Union and India have had numerous fruitful collaborations in the vital field of science and technology. The first EU-India Science and Technology Agreement was signed in 2001 and it was extended in 2009. The "New Delhi Communique", which was released during the India-EU Ministerial Conference on Science in New Delhi in February 2007, states that cooperation in the field of Science and Technology (S&T) should be based on the principles of "symmetry, reciprocity, mutual benefit and, where appropriate, the co-investment of resources in joint actions". It was stated that there is immense scope for increasing the "breadth and depth" of cooperation in the field especially through the modicum of the EU's Seventh Framework Programme (FP7) for

Research and Technological Development 2007-2013 and India's Eleventh Five Year Plan. India has become the European Union's fourth largest international partner under the FP7 (Europa 2010). Both the European Union and India have undertaken to spend €5 million every year on research areas of mutual interest. About 130 Indian research organisations have been declared eligible for funding under the FP7 programme in over 90 projects, the total cost of which will amount to €317 million. The EU and India are known to have made forays into numerous areas of S&T such as materials research, transport research, computation, material science, energy, biotechnology, food, agriculture, ICT, health, climate change and the environment.

Besides, India is also a partner of the EU in numerous prestigious endeavours such as International Thermonuclear Experimental Reactor (ITER) project, GALILEO, the European Satellite Navigation system and the interlinking of India's Education Research Network, ERNET to its pan-European equivalent GEANT2 (Delegation of the European Union to India 2011).

The promotion of research and innovation is regarded as a salient policy objective, as is evident by the "Innovation Union" flagship initiative of the EU and the "Decade of Innovation" which is India's initiative. The participation of Indian universities, research centres and companies in the EU Framework Programme has gradually been increasing. In the EU's Seventh Framework Programme, India ranked fourth in terms of participation and third in terms of the total amount of financial contribution received by the EU (Delegation of the European Union to India 2014).

New Mode of Cooperation for Development

There has been a complete role-reversal for India as far as the development sector is concerned. It has graduated from being an aid-seeker and donned the new avatar of an aid-giver and a donor country. The European Union had helped India whole-heartedly by providing concessions through provisions such as GSP (Generalised

System of Preferences) in 1971 which happened to be the year when India was engaged in efforts to liberate East Pakistan, which led to the creation of the independent country of Bangladesh, and consequently the annual rate of India's Gross Domestic Product was an abysmal 1.71 per cent due to the country's war efforts (Good Governance 2011). The EU has provided massive funds and assistance to all the three phases of the Operation Flood Programme (1970 -1996) which aimed at an increase in milk production, augmenting rural incomes and providing reasonable prices for consumers (National Dairy Development Board). The main objective of EU-India Development Cooperation is to significantly contribute towards achieving the Millennium Development Goals (MDGs) and support the implementation of EU-India Joint Action Plan (JAP) of 2005 which was revised at Marseilles in 2009, in order to set the agenda for the future keeping in mind the shared values and the progress already made and the new challenges that have come to confront the two sides and the world at large in the "areas of security, sustainable development, research and technology and people to people and cultural exchanges" (Delegation of the European Union to India 2008). The first Multi-annual Indicative Programme (MIP) under the 2007-2013 planning period allocated a total of €260 million for 2007-2010 and €210 million was allocated for the second MIP.

Primary and elementary education has been recognised as a priority sector by both partners. A total of €270 million has been committed by the EU to this cause from 2000 to 2013 in order to achieve the goals of Sarva Shiksha Abhiyan (SSA). The EU further allocated a sum of €80 million in 2011 to support elementary and secondary education. The EU has earmarked €32 million for its State Partnership Programme to further the cause of spreading education in Chattisgarh and is a partner in many NGO-led initiatives. The EU has entered into two State Partnership Programmes with Chhattisgarh and Rajasthan respectively and it will spend a total of €160 million on both these states. In addition to this, the two sides have finalised a Financing Agreement for the Sector Policy Support Programme known as National Rural Health Mission- Reproductive Child Health II which avails a sum of €110 million in order to achieve two specific objectives outlined in the MDGs. The two goals focused upon are concerned with reducing child mortality and improving maternal health in India "through better health service delivery" and by supporting the "institutional capacity" of the country's health systems (Delegation of the European Union to India 2014a). Thus, the legacy of EU-India participation in developmental activities continues.

Commonality of Values

The European Union and India are known to share and espouse the values of democracy, rule of law, civil liberties and respect for human rights, which explains why they find it easy to arrive at a consensus on wide-ranging issues (Delegation of the European Union to India 2010). They can be considered to be each other's alter-ego as far their political outlook on issues pertaining to India's neighbourhood is concerned. India is known to appreciate the attributes attached to soft power in international relations and is therefore highly appreciative of the manner in which the EU conducts itself in the international arena.

The Indian sub-continent has been inflicted with chronic ailments for a considerable period of time. Human rights abuses, military coups, dictatorships, insurgencies, proliferation of terrorist camps and frequent change of governments have become the order of the day. In the midst of this volatility, India stands out as it zealously safeguards its democracy and parliamentary system of government. This steadfast role of India, towards upholding the freedom of its citizens and the rule of law and towards preserving its territorial integrity and sovereignty naturally, draws the EU towards India.

Consensus on Issues

The 12th EU-India Summit was held in New Delhi on 10 February 2012. The Indian delegation was led by Prime Minister Manmohan Singh, while the EU was represented by Mr Herman Van Rompuy, President of the European Council and Mr. Jose Manuel Durão Barroso, President of the European Commission. EU and India expressed their satisfaction at the "deepening comprehensive bilateral ties and mutually acknowledged each other as "long-standing strategic partners".

The two sides expressed their optimism regarding the Bilateral Trade and Investment Agreement as significant progress was made in the negotiations. The leaders appreciated the holding of the business summit aimed at improving the business climate and exploring opportunities for further collaboration in EU and India. The two sides noted the signing of the Memorandum of Understanding on Statistics. EU and India welcomed the holding of the India-EU Security Dialogue in 2011 which reaffirmed their commitment to "maintain and expand cooperation in the field of security". The two sides welcomed the holding of the meeting of the India-EU Joint Working Group on Counter Terrorism in 2012 in response to the Joint Declaration on International Terrorism which was adopted at the eleventh summit in 2010. Both sides acknowledged the relevance of the activities of the UN Counter-Terrorism Committee and pledged to conclude the negotiations on the Comprehensive Convention on International Terrorism at the earliest. The two sides acknowledged the necessity of regular dialogue and exchange of information with regard to anti-piracy efforts, cyber-crime and cyber-security. EU and India pledged to enhance bilateral cooperation in the areas of energy, ICT, aviation, EU Emissions Trading System, science and technology, space, nuclear energy, migration and vocational training.

Both sides emphasised upon the fact that democracy should be fully restored in Pakistan and that the perpetrators of the Mumbai terrorist attack of November 2008 should be brought to book. The two sides stated that regional cooperation is extremely crucial and it ought to be enhanced between them via SAARC and other regional platforms. EU and India reiterated their pledge to assist Afghanistan and encouraged the reform process taking place in Myanmar. Both partners expressed their solidarity with the struggle for democracy waged by the people of the Arab world.

The two sides expressed their concern regarding the international economic situation and reaffirmed their adherence to the Doha Development Agenda. They reiterated their commitment to Sustainable Development based on the Rio Principles, adherence to the principles of UN Framework Convention on Climate Change and reaffirmed the importance of the implementation of the Strategic Plan for Biodiversity 2011-2020. The leaders of both sides also pledged that eradication of poverty would remain the main task of the global development agenda and they resolved to pursue maximum achievement of MDGs by 2015. The EU and India expressed their concern about the Iranian nuclear issue and called upon Iran to settle the issue amicably by holding a constructive dialogue with the IAEA and the UN Security Council. The two sides stated that they were committed to a nuclear non-proliferation regime and urged for an early agreement on Fissile Material Cut-off Treaty in the Conference on Disarmament (Delegation of the European Union to India 2012).

The two sides thus make it a point to follow up on the developments in the bilateral relationship every year at the EU-India summit. There is a marked doggedness with which the two sides pursue mutually-acceptable goals in the bilateral, regional and global sphere.

The EU-India political partnership has been marked by consistency, owing to the utilisation of a sturdy institutional infrastructure, which facilitates regular ministerial meetings, summits and expert-level discussions. The two parties consistently keep in touch and hold political dialogues on issues pertaining to trade and investment, development cooperation, economic relations, scientific and technological exchanges, humanitarian aid and culture. This regularity of interaction and resultant progress in various fields bears testimony to the fact that the European Union and India have a serious intent to engage with each other.

Scope for Betterment of Relations

Disputes Galore

There are numerous disputes pertaining to the pharmaceutical, automobile and textile industries which should be resolved at the earliest. The irresolution of these disputes is creating a dent in the performance of these sectors and is adversely affecting the overall EU-India trade figures. All sides which including buyers, suppliers and consumers apart from the governments, should be given a patient hearing so that the interest of all sides is taken into account.

The temporary ban imposed by the European Commission on the import of mangoes, eggplants, taro plants and bitter gourds and snake gourds from India is a case in point (The Hindu 2014).

India is also not happy when the European Union imposes non-tariff barriers or blocks Indian exports on the grounds of non-conformity to EU standards and alleged employment of child labour and unsuitable working conditions.

India is also irked with the attitude of the EU towards alleged human rights violations in Kashmir. India and the EU find each other on the opposite side of the fence in the WTO and climate negotiations.

Spanner in the Works of EU-India FTA

The EU-India FTA negotiations which began way back in 2007 have not been smooth, being mired by a host of problems. Although an increase in market access of goods and services is expected on both sides, a number of apprehensions have been expressed. It is largely believed that the FTA will considerably reduce India's bargaining power at the WTO. The elimination of 90 per cent of duties on both sides will lead to an import surge which is likely to lead to job losses and the closure of manufacturing units in India. The Most Favoured Nation Clause in the FTA will compel India to extend to the EU the better treatment that it has been providing to other countries, which will undermine India's strategic position in future trade negotiations, especially with other developing countries (Centre for Education and Communication 2011). The EU is perceived to be championing the cause of multinational pharmaceutical companies who are advocating the adoption of data exclusivity, which will ensure nothing but the preservation and protection of monopolies (Public Service Europe 2011). Both the sides seem to be dragging their feet on the FTA which is hampering economic growth on both sides.

The Ever-growing Importance of Trade in EU-India Relations

The overemphasis on India-EU trade has led many in India to view the European Union as a trade bloc and less as an emerging pole in a multipolar world. However, such a perception ought to be altered. The European Union and India must look beyond the well established trade and economic agenda and must consolidate and focus their energies upon working together on issues of terrorism, promotion of democracy and human rights, global environment threats, sustainable development, scientific research and telecommunications.

Absence of a Common Approach towards Security

There is no common India-EU approach towards security. However, the Indo-US partnership is manifested through joint military exercises, whereas no such joint endeavours are ever visible in the case of the European Union and India. This naturally leads to greater prospects of forging of stronger bonds with the United States rather than the European Union. India and the European

Union should work towards building a strong partnership not only in the sphere of economics only but also in the areas of politics and security (Institute for Security Studies 2011).

Selective Support to the Strategic Partnership

The strategic partnership between the European Union and India does not mean that the two are co-equal partners (Sisodia and Bhaskar 2005: 188). It is largely believed that the focus of the EU-India strategic partnership largely does not exceed beyond ensuring economic deliverables while the other aspects of the relationship are limited to 'a dialogue level' (Sachdeva 2008). The strategic interest between the two partners is also considered to be limited as there is no geographical or territorial contiguity between the two partners. It is also stated that the word 'strategic partnership' has been overstretched and has become part of rhetoric and does not suggest anything new or vital anymore.

The thrust to the India-EU strategic partnership is mainly applied by those member-states who have a substantial stake in furthering economic relations with India, which in turn leads to the dissipation of political will in Brussels and gives rise to the preferred option of dealing bilaterally with India. The institutions of the European Union and the conservative member-states are more often than not found to be at loggerheads regarding the steering of EU-India relations (Jain 2005).

Excessive Bureaucratisation

The institutional framework of the European Union is characterised by a super saturation of bureaucratisation which renders "de-linking a bilateral relationship from the European Union" officialdom an extremely formidable task. The Strategic Partnership happens to have lost the tenacity and direction for cooperation and development due to the countless consultative mechanisms set up for its functioning (Sachdeva 2009). The bureaucracy in India and European Union should explore all possibilities of streamlining the method of consultation and decision-making to enable concrete action for achieving timely results.

EU Visibility Negligible vis-à-vis the United States in the Indian Sub-continent

The European Union ought to play a more proactive role as the United States emerges as the decisive actor in international issues while the EU is invariably relegated to the background. This appears to have lessened EU's relevance to the rest of the world and the US has come to be regarded as the undisputable hegemon of international politics. The EU bloc disintegrated and fell like a pack of cards and failed to arrive at a unanimous decision on Iraq. The evident discord among the European powers over the intervention in Libya and lack of unanimity regarding ways and means to control the resultant deluge of immigrants coming into Europe does not portray a very convincing picture of an EU which is capable and ready to lead the world (Thornet 2011). The United States almost invariably succeeds in hogging the limelight in India's neighbourhood, whether in executing relief and peace-keeping operations in Afghanistan or maintaining calm and bringing Osama Bin Laden to justice in Pakistan. The European Union hardly figures in news coverage on these issues in the Indian media. Thus the European Union has extremely low visibility in the Indian subcontinent and this prevents the charging up of the atmosphere for dynamic and fruitful relations. The EU needs to be more proactive, assertive and should come out of its shell in order to occupy a position of relevance.

The Emergence of Pakistan as a Liability

India sees Pakistan, rather than China, as the source of current major threats.It is extremely concerned about the developments in the border region between Afghanistan and Pakistan, which is currently not under the control of either state. The fact that India is the regional power to reckon with cannot be discounted owing to its employment of soft power in the region for the fulfilment of its national security objectives. Pakistan has become a strategic liability of the United States, its immediate neighbours and the world at large. Some scholars believe that the restoration of security and stability in Afghanistan should be the top-most strategic objective of the European Union and not the retrieval of Pakistan from state failure (Subhash 2009). The Taliban has secured their position in the Swat Valley which is at a distance of 100 miles from the Pakistani federal capital of Islamabad. They have also infiltrated and taken control of the Buner district which puts them just around 60 miles away from the capital which will quite possibly have extremely dangerous implications as they continue to move closer to the centre of power (Cnn.Com/Asia 2011). The Pakistani Taliban carried out the deadliest attack to date and killed 132 children and nine staff members at a Pakistani school in Peshawar. A total of seven Taliban attackers wearing bomb jackets cut through a wire fence and stealthily entered the school before launching an attack in the month of December 2014 (BBC New Asia 2014). The EU should be more vocal in condemning state support to terrorism and the mushrooming of terrorist camps in the area and support India in its struggle against terrorism.

Agreement on Afghanistan and the Concern over China

The European view of India's strategic interests in Afghanistan can best be fathomed by the views expressed by Richard Gowen. He states that the best possible manner of forging a relationship with Indiawill be to initiate a joint effort to deal with the crisis in Afghanistan, as this in turn shall infuse a new sense of urgency in the European Union's strategic dialogue with India which will create an extremely strong foundation for closer cooperation and lasting relationship in the future (Pragmatic Euphony 2009).

India continues to remain anxious about China's increasing presence in the Indian Ocean, the repression in Tibet, which India considers to be an autonomous region, and China's increasing military capabilities. China's attempt to establish its hegemony through its String of Pearls Strategy in the Indian Ocean is a cause of concern for both sides. The dumping of Chinese goods, undervaluing of its currency and other unfair trade practices continue to irk both India and China. India and the EU should join hands to check and contain China for mutual benefit.

Permanent Seat in UNSC for India

India represents almost a fifth of humanity and occupies the third position in terms of global purchasing power parity. It has also established its credentials as a responsible nuclear power. India's case for a permanent seat on the UNSC is considered to be largely undisputable.UK and France occupy two permanent seats of the UNSC which means that Europe occupies 40 per cent of the total permanent seats available although it represents only 7 per cent of the world population. In the light of these circumstances India had expected that the EU would come out in support of its bid for a permanent seat in the United Nations Security Council (Mahbubani 2014). But the EU seems to be dilly- dallying on the issue. The European Union chose to go only half-way with India by agreeing on the requirement to reform the United Nations and adopt it to the new realities of the 21st century, which are different from the scenario that existed in 1945, and very cleverly refrained from specifically supporting India's candidature for a permanent seat in the UNSC (The Financial Express 2005).

The Lack of Mutual Understanding

India and the European Union need to reach out to each other for bridging the information deficit that exists despite the large number of high level visits that take place on either side. A lot is not known about the European Union in general and the new Accession Countries in particular in India (Jain 2004). There exists a dire need for the improvisation of mutual perspectives about each other by ensuring the availability of information and better communication between the people of the European Union and India in order to enhance the process of getting to know and understand each other better.

The Need to Acknowledge the Importance of SAARC

The importance of SAARC also needs to be realised for strengthening of relations with the European Union. It should not be utilised merely as an organisation ensuring economic cooperation, but rather, as a forum bringing about durable political cooperation amongst its members which shall ultimately contribute to more dynamic relations of it members with that of the European Union (Jain 2007). SAARC and the European Union are huge entities that cater to diverse populations. India and the EU would undoubtedly benefit from a rigorous exchange of views and perspectives about the developments in regional cooperation in Europe and South Asia.

More Interaction in the Field of Education and Among People of Both the Regions

The visibility of the European Union in India continues to be at very low levels in spite of the increase in presence of the European Union despite numerous increments in the awareness and availability of information about the European Union. It is necessary to give credence to well-thought out multilateral initiatives, over bilateral efforts, in order to develop more effective synergies. This realisation has led the European Union to take active interest in the development of EU studies in India and other parts of Asia so that the methodology of teaching and research can be modified in the desired manner by making efforts to improve the skills of the faculty and by providing the facilities required for the progress of European studies in India. The establishment of chairs of study in the academic institutions of both sides should be taken up seriously (Jain 2008). The recently held European Higher Education Fair is a step in the right direction as it brought together nearly 100 globally renowned European higher education institutions from

21 European countries in order to spread awareness about "educational, scholarship and career opportunities available in Europe" (Delegation of the European Union to India 2014b). A lot more needs to be done in the area of understanding each other's cultures. The reach of the civil-society dialogue has undoubtedly increased but it is largely steered and propelled by the Government. This hampers its uninterrupted spread and growth and the inclusion of larger sections of society in such exchanges. The movement of persons based on a well-thought out approach on migration issues also needs to be facilitated (European Commission 2011).

Need to do the Right Thing at the Right Time

The United States was confronted with the choice of either continuing to believe that the Indian nuclear genie could be put back in its place or whether its power and potential should be harnessed by the hegemon for its own strategic and vested interests, before the power becomes unwieldy or is made use of by others like Europe or China (Varadarajan 2005).The United States was not even a tad hesitant in realising the potential of India and went ahead, against all odds to sign, the civilian nuclear agreement with India. The European Union ought not to miss such opportunities, for they will undoubtedly be grabbed by others who are wooing India. India has always called for the formulation and implementation of stronger foreign and defence policies by the European Union because post-modern EU is of no real relevance and concern to India which is subjected to traditional security threats (Grant 2006). President Barack Obama did not miss a single photo opportunity to project himself as a true and dependent ally of India during his recently concluded visit to India in the first month of January. We have witnessed no such effort on the part of any leader from the EU in the recent past. It can be ominously said that this is what makes all the difference. Thus, it is high time that the European Union wakes up from it blissful slumber and caters to and engages with India in the manner that befits respectable and potentially beneficial partners.

Conclusions

Europe and India have known each other even before the Christian era. The Europeans initially came as traders and then transformed themselves into colonisers. India was ruled by the British for more than two centuries. Independent India established cordial relations with the EEC which chose to provide India development assistance and trade concessions. The 1990s saw the signing of the Commercial Cooperation Agreement which forms the legal basis of the relations till this day. The first EU-India summit took place in 2000.The Strategic Partnership Agreement was signed in 2004 which upgraded the status of EU-India relationship. The EU is the largest trading partner of India while India is EU's ninth largest trading partner. Bilateral trade has always increased despite a few hurdles posed by domestic and international events such as the global economic recession of 2008 which slowed down growth of economies, including the GDP of India, and contributed to the eurozone crisis. The balance of trade is always in favour of EU but India gains considerably from trade with the EU and therefore it is a mutually beneficial partnership.

The trajectory and nature of EU-India relations validate the point that liberalism and complex interdependence portray reality in a much better way than realism and pursuit of self-interest. Efforts are being made in order to make the Strategic Partnership more meaningful through goal-based and time-bound action in various spheres of cooperation. It is a fact that the economic aspect is the most vital part of the relationship. Therefore, the primary goal of both sides has clearly been the conclusion of the EU-India FTA for quite some time. However, overemphasis on the commercial aspect of relations leads to ignorance of other aspects of the relationship.

Preference accorded to bilateral relations between India and EU member-states also hurts EU-India relationship. Defence cooperation between the two sides is gradually increasing. But this cooperation is basically being nurtured in the bilateral context between the EU-member states and India. It is therefore extremely essential that both sides develop a common approach towards security. The EU and India continue to engage each other in research and innovation in the field of science and technology. Development cooperation between the two sides has undergone a sea-change as India is no longer an aid-seeker. It has become a donor country. However, the EU is currently providing India development assistance especially in the field of health and education to help India achieve its MDGs. A campaign against excessive bureaucratisation as launched by the incumbent government at the Centre in India should be emulated by the EU in order to check corruption and prevent unnecessary delays in paper-work. The EU and India have a very similar value-system which leads to commonality of standpoint on various international issues. India has quite a few expectations from the EU. India wants the EU to unequivocally condemn state-sponsored terrorism in Pakistan, work together in Afghanistan and contain China. India seeks EU support for its bid for a permanent seat at the UNSC.

Greater cooperation is also sought through the platform of SAARC and greater exchanges in the field of culture and education are called for in order to enhance mutual trust and friendly relations. The EU is required to assume a more proactive role in the sub-continent so that it is recognised as a power to reckon with just like the United States. This will further strengthen EU-India relations.

If we dissect the relations between the European Union and India, we witness an interesting scenario. It is a fact that progress on every issue is taking place at its own pace and each issue has charted it own course. We therefore see a melee of activity on the EU-India front. There is a strong sentiment of optimism that blankets the relations. It is important that EU and India build up on this sentiment by bolstering mutual confidence in each other more by deeds than words. It is not an insurmountable task to dissolve the irritants and settle disputes that exist between the

European Union and India owing to the fact that both sides have a lot in common and are always willing to negotiate.

Thus, European Union-India equation can undoubtedly be termed as a sanguine relationship. The realisation ought to translate into concrete and decisive measures that should be acted upon by both sides for enhancement of their status bilaterally and in the world at large. The European Union and India should make every effort to accord importance and priority to each other at every global forum so that they optimally benefit from this partnership and are identified as natural and inseparable allies by the rest of the world.

2

An Overview of General Perceptions on EU-INDIA Relations

The chapter deals with the conceptual discussion of perceptions. It shall aim to identify and locate the possible levels and areas of analyses of perceptions regarding EU-India relations. It shall seek to examine the importance of perceptions for policy making especially with respect to EU-India relations. It shall make an attempt to identify and highlight the major trends and lines of thought pertaining to the perceptions about the relationship.

Conceptual Understanding of Perceptions

Perception is understood as "a belief or opinion, often held by many people and based on how things seem" (Cambridge Dictionaries Online 2015). It refers to "cognisance by the senses or intellect; apprehension by the bodily organs or by the mind of what is presented to them". Perception involves the process of "discernment, apprehension and cognition". It can be defined as "man's constitution by which he has knowledge through the medium or instrumentality of the bodily organs". It is an "idea or a notion" distinguished from "conception". It refers to the "quality, state or capability of being affected by something external" (Webster's Online Dictionary 2015).

Perception can be defined as the process of "cognitively selecting, organising and evaluating the wide variety of stimuli" that we are exposed to in our daily lives. The first stage in the formation of a perception involves the decision regarding the focus of our attention, which is followed by organising the selected stimuli for evaluation. For instance, the information in the media outlets needs to be given a structure before they can be interpreted. The final stage involves evaluating and attaching meaning to the stimuli which gives rise to a perception. Perceptions represent our beliefs, values, attitude systems as well as our world-view (Samovar et al. 2009).

Scholars of international relations seemed to have paid much less attention to the study of perceptions compared to psychologists. Although the work of the psychologists on the subject of perceptions has helped to bring to the fore the relevance of perceptions, their approach suffers from a few drawbacks. More attention seems to be paid to emotional rather than cognitive factors. All data used for validating the theories are acquired through laboratory experiments which leaves one wondering whether the "settings and manipulations that are employed reveal processes that are at work in the real world". The analysis generally suffers from a policy bias as the aspect of conflict of interest is discounted in international relations—especially upon analysis of the period of Cold War. The structure of the international system is not given adequate attention and the disadvantages and benefits that accrue from it are either "overlooked or misunderstood". Thus, there are too many psychological variables for explaining behavior which could be better understood by means of policy analysis. Hence,

> ...images and reasoning drawn from the hardline approach to foreign policy are examined to show the operation of emotional influences and cognitive processes that inhibits intelligent decision-making, but arguments and belief systems that support conciliation are never analysed in these terms ...we can also go on to compare different actors' perceptions of the same object, situation or other actor. If we can find appropriate comparisons, we can try to locate systematic differences in perceptions traceable to differences in ways of processing incoming information, differences in pre-existing images of others or general views of the world, or differences in specific views of the world (Jervis 1976).

The central theme of the cognitive paradigm is that cognitive predispositions, or mindsets of an individual, have a highly disproportionate contribution in shaping his or her perceptions. This leads to "selective attention to information, to premature cognitive closure, for people to see what they expect to see based on prior beliefs and world views, and consequently to the perseverance of beliefs and world views", which means that perception is more theory-driven than data driven (Jervis 1976).

Jervis came up with his views when the cognitive revolution in social psychology was capturing the maximum attention. He emphasised upon the "role of emotion or motivation in perception", which was in contrast to the cognitive view. This led to "motivational biases or motivational reasoning" that are assumed to be dictated by "people's emotional needs, by their need to maintain self-esteem, and by their interests-diplomatic, political, organisational or personal". It leads to "wishful thinking" and people tend to see "what they want to see" rather than "what they expect to see". Hence, motivated reasoning is expected to rationalise and justify "policies that are perceived to support one's interests and emotional needs". It is extremely difficult to empirically distinguish between cognitive and motivated biases and both can in fact lead to the very "same pathologies of judgment and decision". Nevertheless, since the belief that the cognitive model is more parsimonious and more easily testable has been in currency, scholars of international relations continue to prefer cognitive to motivational explanations.

A shift in priority was witnessed by the end of the 1990s as greater emphasis was laid upon emotions in social psychology and in the study of American politics. This change took place on account of the shift from the "view that emotions are a source of deviation from rationality to a view in which emotions were necessary for rationality". This argument won further support from the breakthrough in neuroscience by means of which the ability was acquired to differentiate centres of cognition and emotion in the human brain. In the discipline of international relations, Mercer rejected the "common view that psychology can only explain deviations from rationality and argued that psychology should be used to explain accurate judgments." He also argued that beliefs such as trust and credibility are based as much on emotion as on cognition. A lot of work has been done in the field in the last decade (Levy 2013).

In international politics, "friendliness/hostility and strength/ weakness constitute the building blocks of the image of the other". Boulding used the term image and defined it as "the total cognitive, affective and evaluative structure of the behavior unit, or its internal view of itself and its universe" to analyse international systems. By adding onto the psychological concept of schema, it has been proposed that "images of the other are not a collection of unrelated traits, but rather a constellation of features that cluster together in meaningful ways". They seem to be dictated by the interaction of three factors which include "the perceived relative capability of the actor, the perceived threat and /or opportunity represented by that actor and the perceived culture of that actor". The particular image which is activated shall decide the manner in which people react to an action carried out by a foreign country. Hence, image determines interpretation of the action. This perspective helps us understand "how actors in international relations are perceived by looking at how the perceiver apprehends the content of these actor's images" (Levy 2013: 450).

Sonia Lucarelli and Lorenzo Fioramonti came up with a model consisting of two levels that took into account a "long term variables/ framework" and "interactional/contingent factors". Drawing from the Social Identity Theory, they considered

> (i) political identity, (ii) historical memories and (iii) socially shaped conceptions of the world order to be fundamental components of the prevalent cognitive maps within a society, the same maps that we assume influence the society.

Based on international relations and analysis of the nuances of foreign policy, they identified a few more variables that influence and shape the perceptions of an external other that included

> (iv) positional variables (that is, those preferences, interests, perspectives, that the interviewee assumes as a player in a particular social role (that is, leader of a non-governmental organisation or a political party), (v) power related variables that account for asymmetries with respect to the EU (vi) interaction variables (eg, the specific political interaction experience with the EU in an issue area within a bi/multilateral context (Lucarelli and Fioramonti 2009).

The EU is considered to be a unique beast in the international political system because neither does it qualify as a state of the Westphalian model nor can it be understood as a "classic international organisation". And just as blind men come up with different interpretations of the size and shape of the elephant, scholars have grappled with the issue of making sense of the EU, especially in the external world. The EU is considered to be in the process of evolution and there is no finality that can be attached to its identity. Attempts have been made to categorise the power and functions of the EU and it has been assigned different nomenclatures and called a civilian power, normative power, ethical power and a model power. Attempts to derive the external identity on the basis of internal processes and ideas leads to ignorance about "what outsiders think about the EU and what it does"(Torney 2013: 7).

The behavior of countries, their policy priorities and their approaches to foreign policy are embossed on the perceptions which shape their foreign policy outlook (Pattanaik 2004). The EU has had to constantly strive to maintain its relevance in the global arena. The unique characteristics of "consensus, soft power, rule of law and regionalism" are looked upon by the outsiders in a different fashion. They often find it difficult to analyse, assess and appreciate the EU for what it stands and for what it does. Consequently, the dominant impression of the EU in the eyes of others makes it stand out for "its complexity, ineffectiveness and delay". With the onset of the 21st century, the EU embarked upon the task of finding out the manner in which it is looked upon and understood by the outside world. The 2009 Lisbon Treaty which led to the establishment of the European External Action Service and the creation of the post of the High Representative for Foreign Affairs and Security Policy were a testimony to the fact that the EU had become extremely conscious of its international image in world affairs (Chaban and Holland 2013: 2).

The constantly changing "EU external images and perceptions are fascinating cognitive puzzles". But more importantly, they need to be looked upon with utmost concern as it happens to be a vital factor contributing to EU foreign policy. A number of reasons have been outlined for undertaking a study of external perceptions. External perceptions are a source of information to fine tune EU foreign policy in the present and future. They throw light on the external identity of the EU. Studying external perceptions brings to light the performance of the EU as a global actor and helps it decide upon the goals and objectives that it should have with regard to international issues. Although, deciding upon the future line of action in the area of foreign affairs is solely the discretion of the EU, identity-formation in the context of the external world takes into account not only the feedback from within, but also the ideas and opinions beyond its borders. External perceptions also help in gauging the reach of the EU. It is also serves like a report card on the performance of the EU and gives a verdict on its effectiveness, legitimacy, visibility, coherence and consistency in external affairs (Chaban et al. 2006: 247-248).

The perception of the Indian elite about the EU is predominantly influenced by the Anglo-Saxon media which militates against a comprehensive and holistic understanding of EU's institutional framework, processes, functions, role and ideas. The EU seems to be more of an intricate puzzle to Indians owing to its unique characteristics and because of the sheer size and complexity of its working.

India feels at ease in dealing bilaterally with EU member-states. There is adequate clarity regarding policies of EU member-states. But generally India is at a loss and is quite clueless when it comes to policy matters pertaining to the EU on the very same issues. It is also felt that the democratic form of government in India and commonality of values with the EU does not hold out any advantage for India as China seems to be the constant priority of the EU, if not the apple of its eye. India gets the occasional pat on the back and the assurance that the relationship will come of age and be as important as EU-China relations. Jain places people in the EU in three categories and comments on their attitude towards India in particular and South Asia in general. He also talks about three "circles" of people who seem to be taking the relationship forward. He explains that

> there still continue to be three kinds of people in the EU: those who are otherwise very well informed and knowledgeable, but who do not try to understand South Asia because others have tried it before and failed to do so; those who neither understand anything, nor wish to understand anything; and then a small minority of those who have the courage and perseverance to make an effort to understand the more complex problems of India and wish to do something about it. Relations with India are still driven in India by very 'small circles' in Brussels. In the first circle are those that have substantial economic stakes – primarily the 'Big Three' (France, Germany and the United Kingdom). When push comes to shove, they are the ones that bring the requisite energy to move things forward in an increasingly heterogeneous Union. In the second circle are those member states that have interests in certain sectors,

> but that do not quite have the big picture. In the third circle are the remaining member-states, which broadly feel that if some things are good for others, it is fine with them (Jain 2011: 225-226).

Promotion of EU Visibility in India

The communication from the Commission to the Council entitled "Towards a New Asia Strategy" talked about "raising the profile of Europe in Asia". It was suggested that the business community could help in this task and the Union's image could act as "an important selling point" internationally. Programmes and activities based on the theme of cooperation especially economic cooperation were also expected to be utilised. It was expected that the EU would be held in higher regard if people were better informed about the EU and its activities. It was urged that further efforts should be made towards dissemination of information on European financed activities in Asia, especially economic cooperation and also development projects. This goal was to be achieved through the implementation of policies. An attempt has been made to formulate a more effective "information policy of which a baseline all-media study of the European image in Asia is an essential part". An enhanced visitor's programme which would invite distinguished Asian politicians, journalists, academics and other leaders to Europe was proposed. Efforts shall be made towards strengthening higher education and training links with Asia including university cooperation schemes. "Town twinning and cultural exchanges" were encouraged in order to bring about decentralised cooperation between institutions as they are considered to be an intrinsic part of the pluralistic civil society. It was also decided to build upon European expertise on Asia by supporting a network of European centres specialising in Asia (Commission of the European Communities 1994: 19).

The EU-India Economic Cross Cultural Programme was approved in 1995 and it busied itself in developing links between organisations based in the EU and India that were structured in networks at the university, media and enterprise level. It was entrusted with the task of increasing the visibility of the EU in India and that of India in Europe apart from enhancing cultural and economic presence and mutual understanding in the two continents (Community Research and Development Information Service 1997).

A couple of years later, there was another communication from the Commission entitled EU-India Enhanced Partnership and it emphasised upon increasing cultural understanding, not only through working groups but also by extending the EU-India dialogue by involving the civil society, media and the academic community. The earlier communication of 1994 had mainly emphasised upon economic cooperation. However, the communication from the Commission in 1996 realised that the conduct of economic and political relations would be hampered by lack of dialogue and a broad understanding of each other. It was stated in the communication that in order to make its economic might and presence felt in India, it was necessary for increasing the European profile in Asia. It was realised that in order to achieve this, special efforts needed to be made towards improving the visibility of European activities in India. It was also noted that the great size and immense diversity of the country called for a special effort for strengthening its image in India. It was also emphasised that awareness about India and the sub-continent needs to be increased in Europe on the same lines. Therefore, the Commission proposed to

> ...facilitate cross cultural cooperation initiatives, encourage the establishment of a network of organisations interested in Europe-India relations; promote an increased flow of press and media information on Europe in India and vice-versa.

It was also mentioned that this phase of activity would find strength and support from activities launched in the European

Parliament, Economic and Social Committee and the Committee of the Regions if these institutions find it appropriate (Commission of the European Communities 1996:13-14).

The communication from the Commission in 2001 entitled "Europe and Asia : A Strategic Framework for Enhanced Partnership" stated that for expressing better EU's economic and political might in the region, benefitting from the adoption of the euro and pursuing a more effective common foreign and security policy, it was imperative to increase awareness of the EU in Asia. The need for strengthening and broadening the network of Delegations across the region was felt, apart from enhancing coordination at all levels and intensifying information and communication efforts. It was also thought that one needed to strengthen educational, scientific and cultural exchanges with Asia. The need to reverse the trend of most Asian students opting for North America and Australasia was pointed out as a first priority. It was also pointed out that the number of European academics with links to Asia was very small and European Studies continues to remain an undeveloped area of study in most Asian countries.

The need for increasing and strengthening contacts with intellectuals and networking was also emphasised upon (Commission of the European Communities 2001: 23-24). It was pointed out that it was high time that stereotypes of all kinds were dispensed with so that Europe was no longer considered to be introspective and old-fashioned while Asia is looked upon "as a distant and exotic continent" (Commission of the European Communities 2001: 14).

The Communication, from the European Commission to the Council, The European Parliament and the European Economic and Social Committee, on the EU-India Strategic Partnership, thought it relevant to mention that a lot remains to be done in order to accelerate "reciprocal visibility". The communication recognised that the "Indian public opinion needs to receive information about the EU's many facets beyond trade issues. It was stated that sufficient resources should be deployed for this task and "close cooperation and coordination between all Member-States and Institutions" should be ensured. The diplomatic and cultural representatives of the Member-States in Delhi were instructed to report on the visibility of the EU and make meaningful contributions towards "a future awareness raising and communication strategy". Information was provided about the research project to be launched by the European Commission which would identify target audiences, key messages, main instruments and how best to deploy them. The Commission called upon the EU member-states and the European Parliament to meaningfully contribute towards this project. The Communication highlighted the fact that information should be exchanged on high level visits and "all high level EU visitors should promote EU in India". The Government of India was to be encouraged to make frequent visits to EU institutions and India was urged to work out its own communications strategy (European Commission 2004: 10).

The EU-India Strategic Joint Action Plan stated that India and the EU would enhance their "multifaceted relationship and build upon these foundations through deepening political dialogue and consultation mechanisms, bringing together people and cultures, enhancing economic policy dialogue and cooperation and developing trade and investment. One of the means of bringing together people and cultures was through increasing mutual visibility. It was stated that both sides should make efforts to "inform each other's public opinion". Since the societies are undergoing rapid change, there is a need to "update the media image on both sides". Efforts to "enhance mutual visibility" should involve upgrading and making more effective the available means and exploring new instruments for reaching out to the populace on both sides. In order to further this purpose, both sides proposed to

> promote more intensive media coverage of India in the EU and vice-versa; enhance journalistic exchanges between the two sides, organise short term information courses and thematic conferences for journalists on a reciprocal basis, promote tourism in both directions and especially enhance interaction between youth groups including cooperation in the field of sport; develop periodically EU-India thematic cultural years (eg cinema, music, dance, literature) (Delegation of the European Union to India 2005b).

Baroness Catherine Ashton, the EU High Representative for Foreign Affairs and Security Policy, had stated that the European External Action Service, which is one of the most important innovations of the Lisbon Treaty that came into force on 1 December 2009 would enable the EU to have a more ambitious, effective, coherent and visible foreign policy. She stated that the EEAS would be "the principle interface with international partners, i.e. Europe's eyes, ears and face" (Delegation of the European Union to India 2010).

The European Business and Technology Centre aims at spreading information and awareness for increasing research and innovation collaboration between the EU and India. It organises a number of activities and aims at transforming itself from "visibility to incubation by promoting Europe in India and India in Europe, providing information and intelligence, supporting the market entry process from the scratch, providing full service, incubation, support for businesses and R&D". It aims at bringing about collaborative research and product development, business development for EU entities, assisting Indian companies with the EU solutions for its projects, helping Indian entities to work jointly and leverage cost advantage, bringing value to the EU and Indian entities and lowering the cost of technology transfer. It aims at facilitating linkages from the EU to India through developing technologies suitable for Indian conditions, knowledge and technology collaboration and brain circulation in the field of academia. It seeks to bridge research needs through technology forecasting and research competency mapping. It tries to bring about better coordination through research cooperation between different institutions from the EU and India, organisation of events and facilitating the formation of smaller and medium sized projects and partner consortia (Delegation of the European Union to India 2012).

Gauri Khandekar, a researcher at the Brussels office of the Madrid-based FRIDE think tank and head of its Agora Asia-Europe programme, gave an overview of the twelfth EU-India summit and suggested that “reciprocal visits from Indian politicians are called for to increase EU’s visibility in India”. She stated that this would also lend clarity towards comprehending each other’s role in the developing global architecture. She opined that “getting the bilateral compact right” was a key precondition for better relations as the two sides enter a new phase of partnership (Euractiv.com 2012).

The Second European Standardisation Expert in India (SESEI) project is geared towards promoting the EU-India cooperation on standards and related policies and regulation. It seeks to open channels of communication and increase cooperation between the EU/ European Free Trade Association (EFTA) and Indian decision-makers, opinion setters and stakeholders in the standardisation and regulatory system. It also seeks to increase the visibility of European standardisation and promote the EU/EFTA-India cooperation on standards related issues (ETSI World Class 2014).

The main aim of Erasmus Mundus Students and Alumni Association India chapter (EMAInd) is promotion of the EU as a centre of excellence in the field of higher education among Indians. EMAInd functions in consonance with the Erasmus Mundus Association (EMA) to “enhance visibility and attractiveness of European higher education in India”. The

EMAInd is engaged in spreading awareness about the Erasmus Mundus Master Courses and Joint Doctorates in India. It also aims at establishing and intensifying a network of professional universities throughout India. Erasmus Mundus increases its visibility by organising information events at various Indian universities. It also organises seminars on inclusive education and workshops on higher education in the EU. It is known to hold charity and community service events for specially abled people. The EMAInd encourages participation at the events of the European Commission and the EU Delegation in India which aims at discussion of EU-India cooperation in the context of EU-India policy on education and student mobility (Erasmus Mundus Students and Alumni Association 2014).

Perceptions about EU-India Relations

Political Dimension

Europe has been conspicuous by its absence in the list of countries which Prime Minister Narendra Modi has chosen for making foreign policy overtures. His primary focus was on immediate neighbours such as Bhutan and Nepal after which East Asia caught his attention and he was seen confabulating and signing deals at break-neck speed with the leaders of Japan and China in full media glare. The BRICS summit attended by mainly non-European powers and Russia made it obvious that India was emphasising upon Eurasian credentials and its foreign policy priorities were manifesting a marked shift from courting the EU. Modi's visit to the US was recognition of the fact that the United States mattered in Indian foreign policy calculations just as India's neighbours East Asia, Russia and Australia did. Although, foreign ministers of UK and France have called on Modi, the EU has not been made out to be a significant partner of India in the briefings of the newly elected government. Clearly, the priorities of the Modi government have diverged from the EU, or so it seems, owing to lack of visibility of the EU.

The fact that the EU is India's biggest trade partner is often discounted when the United States and China are acknowledged as India's important trade partners. Trade with the EU showed an upward trend and reached $72.7 billion. Our trade is known to be largely balanced with the EU, unlike China, which is allegedly destroying parts of our manufacturing sector by means of underpriced exports. Europe, and not China, is a source of high technology for India. EU-India economic ties have been strengthened due to the highest FDI being brought to India by the EU. Both partners are eagerly awaiting the conclusion of EU-India FTA negotiations which began in 2007 to further boost EU-India ties. The EU has enabled India to keep its supply sources of defence equipment diversified as it has emerged as a key defence partner of India next only to Russia. The relationship is nurtured through cultural interaction and people to people contacts through projection of soft power by both the partners. The EU seems to matter in the UNSC as France and UK are permanent members while Germany is rooting for membership along with India. China and the US are known to have glibly dealt with the matter with no firm commitment of taking action on the issue. However, France and UK have emerged on the forefront as strong supporters of India, which in turn has increased levels of trust and affinity between the EU and India.

The EU and India have posed a united front on terrorism and religious extremism, although EU appears to be restrained about condemning state-sponsored activities of terrorism in Pakistan while the EU has had problems in grappling with extremism in West Asia (Sibal 2014).

India and the EU are made of up similar constituents as both entities are an economic and political union of little less than 30 states exhibiting linguistic, cultural and ethnic diversity. However, the cultural affinities and other similarities in their make-up have not led to the forging of very strong political and strategic bonds.

Although India happened to be one of the first countries to establish diplomatic relations with the European Economic Community in 1962 and then conclude a Strategic Partnership and a Joint Action Plan in 2005 and 2008 respectively, that offer a framework for furthering cooperation on security-related matters, it shall take more time for a common strategic culture to take shape between the two sides. This is on account of the fact that such measures lead to "dialogue, commitments to further dialogue, and exploratory committees and working groups, rather than to significant policy measures or economic breakthroughs".

There has been a constant flow of appreciation from Indian leaders for the EU as a model that can be emulated in South Asia. The EU has been acknowledged to have an equitable structural framework which makes it extremely suitable for South Asia "ethically and strategically" despite economic and political disparities that exist between the EU and India (Jain 2007: 186-187). EU-SAARC cooperation has not been substantial largely due to internal divisions within SAARC. The lack of political consensus and unity among the SAARC members themselves, especially the hostile relationship between India and Pakistan has prevented the organisation from carrying on a meaningful political dialogue with EU (Jain 2007: 181).

Another aspect of the relationship that needs to be factored in is the Indian preference to deal with EU member-states through bilateral arrangements rather than negotiating with the EU as a whole. This becomes a necessary evil in the light of the absence of solidarity in European institutions on strategic questions. Although, the EU has claimed ever since the Maastricht Treaty that has a common foreign policy, the reality suggests otherwise. It is contended that if the EU had a single voice, there would be no need for two EU member-states to be permanent members of the UNSC along with another member-state known to be lobbying really hard for a third permanent seat. Besides, it is individual member states of the EU rather than the EU who are known to take a firm stand on issues against key global actors such as the United States, Russia and China. The current euro zone crisis has also caused loss of credibility in the EU's image as a global actor in world politics. India is able to connect with London, Berlin or Paris but not with Brussels. This increases the chances that "New Delhi will write Europe off as a charming but irrelevant continent, ideal for a summer holiday but not for serious business". The "old Continent and the rising new sub-continent" should consolidate upon their ties based on commonalities and mutual trust so that they emerge as a strong and worthy contender to the "blandishments of the United States and China" (Tharoor 2012).

Others choose to point out the differences between the EU and India. They are of the view that the partners could not be more dissimilar with respect to culture, history and demography. The absence of geographical contiguity or even proximity renders the task of locating common strategic interests extremely difficult. However, both have been anxious about their role and position in global affairs in the light of China's rise which in turn has compelled them to reassess their relationships with global players such as the United States, Russia and Japan. Politics in India has been described as "big and messy" with voters in millions belonging to divergent backgrounds who have a different take on every issue. Local and state-level politics often takes precedence over national politics and national politics appears to be an "amalgam of assorted local rivalries". The very same description can be transposed to EU politics where all member-states vie with each other in order to get their "competing national interests onto Brussel's agenda of priorities".

Both sides face similar challenges in their neighbourhood. The EU is expected to deal with the threat from Russia and adequately respond to the rapid and complex changes taking place in Middle East politics. Similarly, states in the Asia-Pacific look towards India to counter Chinese hegemony in the region. The relationship that exists between both sides is largely perceived to be "overly cautious in its ambitions and lacking in concrete elements", which also limits their "political clout". The lack of "internal coherence" within the EU and India is considered to be a constraining factor. Although each entity has its own sets of problems, most of them are not insuperable (Bomassi 2013).

The attempts made by the EU towards being recognised as a crucial political partner of India would "mystify" Indians even before the coming of the dark clouds of the euro zone crisis on the horizon since 2010. The EU's efforts go in vain in trying to convince India that it is a relevant dialogue partner and "induces yawns in Delhi". It is clearly evident in India that European member-states are engaged in stiff competition with each other in trying to get contracts and expand business in India along with the fact that these countries accord little or no priority to the EU and its institutions when they further their relations with India on a bilateral level. This could change if the EU chooses to wake up from its slumber and act as "a convincing, cohesive and coherent personality" in India. Therefore, if the EU becomes a more active and assertive actor in the context of EU member-states, promising trends of EU-India trade and forward-looking minds can help a meaningful political dialogue to take shape in the years to come (Malone 2011). Both are plagued by a very high level of bureaucratisation that renders the process of decision-making painstakingly slow.

It comes as a surprise for many that although India was one of the first countries to establish diplomatic relations with the EEC in March 1962, the Commission opened a delegation in India only in 1983 and India does not have a separate mission to the EU in Brussels. India's relations with the EU have gone well beyond the economic aspect of the relations with the emergence of the EU as a solid "pillar in the multipolar world". It is on account of this reason that "traditional diplomacy towards the EU" should be promoted. The EU-India summit is one such measure that has led to positive results. (Austermann 2014: 171).

A large number of opinion makers expressed the sentiment that they would prefer that the EU plays a greater role in global affairs. They do not consider the EU to be occupying the first place in geopolitical importance. Consequently, the EU trails behind the United States, China, Japan and Russia in the list of India's most salient international partners. The reason attributed for this low priority accorded to the EU is not an Indian assessment and analysis of the "likely evolution of the EU's internal political integration" but rather "a clear and possibly growing distinction and divergence of both strategy and sentiment between Europe and US" (Lisbonne-de-Vergeron 2014: 49).

The European Commission's communications of 2003 and 2004 respectively to the member-states at the European Council and European Parliament highlighted the arguments in favour of forging a strategic partnership with China and India. The EU expected that both the powers would contribute towards stability, regionally and globally, especially through the multilateral frameworks and the United Nations. The EU hoped that a considerable increment in global responsibilities would lead to natural convergence of interests.

India was disgruntled with European responses to the Arab Spring in general and its opinion about the events in Syria in particular. However, India's standpoint has undergone a shift lately as seen in the latest voting on the issue at the UN. India's relatively less emphatic insistence on non-interference and opposition to the right to protect were motivated by the necessity to "carefully balance its relations with Syria against its growing economic ties with the Gulf states" because India is heavily dependent upon the region for it energy imports. India faced a similar dilemma in the case of Iran and voted along with the EU to censure Iran for its non-compliance with the nuclear non-proliferation regime. However, China refused to support stricter UN sanctions against Iran (Muenchow- Pohl 2012).

The other unifying factor in the bilateral relationship could be the China factor. India is perceived as a counterweight to China. India has since long established its credentials of being a benign power with a responsible and democratic form of government and no designs of mounting aggression against its neighbours. India is as cautious and "wary" of China as the United States and EU. It is an established fact that China supplied a large portion of Pakistan's nuclear-weapons technology and beat India in the 1962 war, as a result of which there are numerous unresolved border disputes between the two countries. But it is also very clear from the conduct of EU and India that they would not prefer their partnership to be a part of anti-China axis. India has tried its best "in ending the chill that set in after 1998" when it declared that her nuclear weapons would mainly target China. Nonetheless, it is widely anticipated that the friendship of India, the EU and the United States could easily be transformed into an alliance, should China become hostile (Tannock 2006).

It becomes clear from the wording of the 2004 communication that the EU had very high expectations from India with regard to effective multilateralism on account of "shared values with India and its active role in UN peacekeeping, conflict prevention and post-conflict reconstruction, which was highlighted and taken note of as a specific area for closer EU-India cooperation. However, these expectations failed to materialise and therefore the strategic partners did not move past the level of political dialogue. The gap between vision and action can be traced to the "different perceptions of the global order". EU's endeavours towards "effective multilateralism" depend almost entirely upon the "dominance of the West" and it "seeks to establish its norms as the ground rules for global governance". However, this is not palatable to India, which, along with China, continues to repeatedly challenge

American and European hegemony in the UNSC, World Bank, IMF and WTO. The demand for a redesign of the multipolar order, keeping in mind the demands of the emerging powers and the developing world rings loud and clear. The economic side of the relationship will remain the anchor of EU-India relations. The EU should utilise and lean on this strong aspect of the relationship in order to further the political partnership between the two entities (Muenchow- Pohl 2012).

Security Dimension

The EU has been accredited with a new identity of a civilian power that aims to civilise international relations and promote effective multilateralism and contribute towards global governance. These happen to be the positive arguments that emanate from the EU. The Indian perception is not as enthusiastic about the identity discourse. Its primary concern lies in assessing the effectiveness of the EU's foreign policy and its ability to achieve tangible results. It has been alleged that the European debate revolving around its new identity of being a civilian power or normative power is often utilised as a smokescreen for shortcomings in its military capabilities and for its lack of a security and defence policy. India's strategic community has expressed lack of clarity regarding relations between the EU and the North Atlantic Treaty Organisation (NATO) which is considered to be a vital component of the EU's military power. Besides, India's attention is focused on security threats and challenges that emanate from Asia, the Gulf Region and the Asia-Pacific where the EU does not play a vital role which "explains the low opinion of the EU as a security actor". The EU's engagement as a military power in Asia is limited to its presence and contribution to the NATO-led International Security Assistance Force Mission in Afghanistan and an anti-piracy mission off the coast of Somalia. Therefore, the EU presence cannot be accounted for as a formidable military power in Asia, and this often leads to the portrayal of the EU as "an irrational and inconsistent actor" as its member-states compete with each other for more influence in the bloc and do not shy away from the occasional use of force for furthering their national interest. The EU, which only enjoys enhanced observer status in the UN General Assembly and in its committees, has no voting rights. Many EU member-states have shown solidarity with the Indian position of reforming the UNSC. However, no common EU policy for supporting India's candidature for a permanent seat in the UNSC has evolved. Moreover, Brussels is largely perceived as incapable of doing much as far as supporting India is concerened to gain acceptance in the Multilateral Export Control Regimes, the Australia Group, Wassenaar Arrangement, NSG and the Missile Technology Control Regime, because it is EU member-states, and not the EU, who are members of these exclusive groups and call the shots. It is therefore recommended that

> its time to address the partnership in a more practical fashion and stop dwelling on the same topics. European and Indian decision-makers often complain about the same issues, but from different angles. While New Delhi perceives Brussels as unable to communicate its message of security, the European side complains that no one in New Delhi is interested in listening. Instead of trying to work on the whole range of security issues at the same time and getting nowhere, both partners should come together to identify overlapping priorities. Topics like terrorism, maritime and cyber security could be promising (Brisch 2014).

The EU provides "very little value added" support for dealing with India's main security threats. The EU can be written off as almost irrelevant to the most important areas to India, in strategic terms, such as India' neighbourhood, the Gulf region, the United States and China. The EU has no role to play in furthering India's security interests in Central and Southeast Asia. The EU-India collaboration in the areas of global security, such as "nuclear proliferation, civil conflict and terrorism", do not appear to be worthy enough to take note of. India's efforts at attaining energy sufficiency are not buttressed by the EU. In fact, it is not the EU itself, but the member-states of the EU such as UK and France who are part of the UNSC that bring "more value to the table for India". India would do well to gain European cooperation in dealing with counter-terrorism and in sharing European remote surveillance technology. However, it is more than evident that it is bilateral relationships with European member-states that shall prove more instrumental in this exercise than the EU itself (Tharoor 2012).

However, the EU cannot be completely written off as it is more liberal in terms of technology transfers compared to the United States. Therefore, it makes sense to extend a hand of friendship towards the EU who could be our major "suppliers of co-development and co-production of military hardware" which would enable us to achieve the goal of developing "an indigenous defence manufacturing base. Besides, the US has indicated its preference for dealing with the Indian private sector, while the EU has shown no reservations whatsoever in dealing with the public sector for the purpose of defence manufacturing. While it is imperative to appreciate the need for the involvement of the private sector for expediting the process of building up our indigenous capacities, the mandatory requirement of exercise of state control in such a vital sphere cannot be ignored. This makes the EU a more suitable partner than the US in the defence manufacturing sector as the Indian government's bargaining power would be much greater than that of the private sector. However, the cancellation of tenders especially after completion of negotiations due to lack of coordination has raised doubts in the EU defence industry circles about India as an appropriate partner for defence deals. Two EU member-states are nuclear weapon states and they therefore have a say in the "non-proliferation-related technology-denial export control regime" whose membership is sought by India. France has signed a uranium supply agreement with India and is all set to overtake the United States in setting up nuclear power plants in India. France has been India's leading partner from the EU in space as Arianespace has launched India's INSAT series satellites and India shall be launching French SPOT satellites which shall translate into increase in business and visibility of India as a space power (Sibal 2014).

The bulk of the problem areas in the world happen to be located between India and the EU. For instance, the death toll in Europe was much more due to drugs that made their way into the EU from Afghanistan, than the total number of lives lost in two decades of fighting in the area. India's geographical proximity and security concerns in Afghanistan open up the scope for cooperation with the EU in the context of the region in question. India's rising persona in the geopolitics of the Indian Ocean and in security issues of the Gulf which is an important source of energy for the EU, is another possible area for cooperation (Tharoor 2012).

The relationship between the EU and the US has always been a very special relationship as they have been partners in recent history and share commonality of values. This led the Americans to emboss a permanent security footprint in Europe. Hence, when the United States started extending better security guarantees to the Pacific Rim, in its individual capacity rather than as part of the transatlantic partnership, panic waves passed through the EU. The United States has increasingly become vocal about the fact that it expects the EU to play a much bigger role in providing European security and beyond. This is however less likely to materialise until the EU completely recovers from the financial throes inflicting the euro zone. A parallel between the US-EU and US-India relationship can be seen in this context, because just as EU is being asked by US to play a greater role in security matters, India is also being coaxed by the United States to assume a bigger role in security affairs in order to diminish Chinese hegemony in the region in the wake of Chinese antagonism towards its neighbours in South China Sea. India would face the dilemma of making a choice between its non-interventionist policies, for which it is known, and its aim to emerge as a credible player in global affairs. Both EU and India seem to be passing through a difficult phase where they

> ...have come to be perceived as the sick men of their regions. Once full of spirit and vitality, not stagnating and spluttering-struggling to overcome internal divisions... and find a suitable space for themselves in the global order. Yet if they can find the political will to match ambition with strategy, there are opportunities for both Europe and India to make a difference and begin the ascent towards a more secure place on the world stage. And the challenge both are facing can perhaps be overcome by shared solutions.

India and the EU could play a meaningful role in Asia in cooperation with each other to simultaneously counter-balance the Chinese economic and political presence and check the military shift of the United States towards the Asia-Pacific. The EU could provide important inputs to India on its Atlanta mission, off the Horn of Africa, which would be vital in protecting sea-lanes across the Hormuz and Malacca Straits in cooperation with India. This would contribute substantially to their status in Asia-Pacific. India has abundance of renewable energy sources such as solar, wind and biofuels while EU is the regarded as the leading proponent of renewable energies on account of the bountiful experience of European companies with these technologies. It therefore seems that EU-India relations hold "much untapped potential" and the way forward is to "temper expectations, remain realistic about what can be achieved and find the niches where both can act as partners to achieve mutual goals" (Bomassi 2012).

India' nuclear cooperation with EU has become an extremely controversial issue as EU doubts the "quality of the commitment made by India" in order to secure the US-India nuclear deal, which allowed the export of nuclear fuels and technology to India despite its unchanged status of being a de facto nuclear weapons state outside the ambit of the Non-Proliferation Treaty. The EU is mighty uncomfortable regarding the consequences of handing out concessions to India in the context of the non-proliferation regime as a whole.

Some member-states however, chose to make the most of the situation and even before the signing of the US-India 123-Agreement for peaceful nuclear cooperation, President Sarkozy signed a bilateral agreement on civil nuclear cooperation with the Indian Prime Minister Manmohan Singh on the margins of the EU-India summit in Marseilles in 2008, which opened the Indian market for French nuclear technology. The United Kingdom followed the French line of action and also inked a deal with India. However, doubts about feasibility of nuclear energy have risen in response to the Fukushima nuclear accident and has slowed down EU-India cooperation in this area. The EU-India summit of 2012 took note of the slow rate of progress and called for "progress and finalisation of a research and development agreement" between India and the European Atomic Energy Arm, EURATOM. However, doubts that have crept in regarding the dangers associated with nuclear energy became evident in the EU's official fact sheet circulated among journalists just before the summit which chose "to narrow the prospects for nuclear energy cooperation with India to the aspect of nuclear safety" (Muenchow- Pohl 2012).

It is strongly argued in various quarters that "maritime security cooperation between India and EU should be the next port of call". The Indian navy is focusing its energies on strengthening its maritime security, as maritime security challenges in the near and distant neighbourhood are on the rise. However, EU member-states have been reducing their naval assets lately for budgetary reasons despite a spike in global maritime security challenges. India and EU member-states are known to meet on a regular basis through EU and NATO missions. The primary concern has been to safeguard global trade against Somali pirates in the Gulf of Aden and the broader Indian Ocean. The potential to intensify cooperation in counter-piracy operations was highlighted at the last EU-India summit held in 2012 as one the three areas which also included terrorism and cyber security. However, not much has been done on the ground to achieve this goal. Individual EU member states, with large interests in maritime affairs, have played a constructive role in coming up with new propositions for cooperation and collaboration. For instance, Netherlands looks upon India as a promising country to engage with in the maritime industry sector. Therefore, the multi-annual maritime project entitled "Focus on India" has sought to increase the chances for Dutch companies to do business with India while India would be hoping of climbing up a few notches to become a strong global maritime security actor (Kamerling 2014).

The Indian perception about the EU is that it suffers from an "agency deficit especially in security matters" as for most of the time it is majorly recognised as a "trade bloc". However limitations on part of the EU reveal only part of the whole story. It is imperative to examine the Indian side of the tale. Not everyone is convinced that India truly wishes to engage with the EU more intensively and extensively. India has donned the new avatar of an emerging power which is ready to shoulder global responsibilities in its immediate neighbourhood and afar. However, this has not led the EU to figure prominently in India's foreign policy considerations. This calls for a review, as giving the EU a key position in the Indian radar of security objectives and priorities would prove to be mutually advantageous.

There is widespread agreement on the issue that the EU is a key economic and commercial player in the Asian region. But many scholars point to the strategic weakness displayed by the EU in tackling security challenges in the region. EU member-states are known to have a noticeable military presence in the region by means of "military dialogues, joint exercises, arms sales, technology transfers, Asian participation in the Galileo global navigation satellite system, French military deployments in the Indian Ocean and British participation in the Five Power Defence Arrangement". Despite this, acceptance of a greater EU role as a security actor in Asia does not come by easily owing to the "complexity of security challenges in Asia and EU's lack of research capacity which would enable it to grasp Asian perceptions of security challenges". For example, India was not happy with meddling of EU-member states during the Indo-Pak standoff in 2001 in trying to persuade India not to go to war. India was predictably irked by such interference as it has made it amply clear that it "believes in bilateralism and would be reluctant to accept any kind of EU intervention or mediation" (NFG Asian Perceptions of the EU 2013).

Normative and Cultural Dimension

The Indian perception is that EU remains in isolation "in a Westphalian world with pre-modern and modern mindsets. A growing "normative disconnect" is reported between EU and the emerging powers including India which are increasingly losing fondness for Europe as a supplier of norms to the rest of the world for they seem to be engaged in a sort of "regulatory imperialism" that indulges in the imposition of "norms and standards" irrespective of the country's stage of development. Emerging powers constantly challenge American and European hegemony and demand for a redesigning of the global order by playing a larger role in the formulation of rules in the international political and economic order. Most people in India are not happy with the EU belief that they have a "civilising mission" in the developing world and that their "transcendence of power holds lessons for others". The EU is accused of having a condescending and "patronising attitude" of teaching everyone else "how to do things". The narrative of the EU portrays it as a global entity that is making efforts for the welfare of the people around the world and in the midst of this EU mission, the emerging countries are looked down upon as they are "unwilling to cooperate and adopt its high global standards". Thus, the EU and India tend to have divergent views about the same issue. For instance, there is a tendency to consider the issue of climate change in India in "developmental rather than environmental terms". A clear distinction is recognised between the "survival emissions of a developing country" and the "lifestyle emissions of the West". India looks upon the aggressive attempts made by the developed world including the EU to get the developing world sign on the dotted line as an attempt to "restrict the development potential of developing countries and impair their competitiveness". The environmental agenda of the EU is more often than not brought under the scanner by India which considers it as a means for the EU to safeguard and further its commercial interests under the garb of trying to save mankind and the planet (Jain 2014: 35-36).

A similar sentiment was expressed by Indian negotiators at the Rio+ 20 summit that due to less than satisfactory performance of the world economy, there is "no stomach for genuine action on the environment as this always carries a price tag". Moreover, the EU has adopted "a confrontationist attitude and has led a campaign arguing that "emerging economies like India and China are too wealthy to be allowed to have a differentiated approach". The EU has in fact won over some African states with this argument. India believes that the EU shall make use of climate change negotiations for the purpose of "blunting the competitive edge of the developing economies and improve its competitiveness" at a time when it finds itself in the throes of an economic crisis (Chaudhari 2012).

Indians are known to suffer from "an allergy to being lectured to" and consequently, one of the great irritants of the EU-India relationship has been the tendency of EU to "preach to India on matters" that India is convinced it can handle on its own. India looks upon human rights as a vital domestic issue. It has been claimed that there is no issue related to human rights exposed by Amnesty International, Human Rights Watch and EU institutions which have not been brought to the fore first by Indian citizens, journalists and NGOs and handled within the "democratic Indian political space". Hence, the attempt of the EU to slide in human rights into a free trade agreement invites displeasure from the Indian bastion. The Indian argument is that trade issues should not be decided based upon the moorings of internal European politics revolving around human rights declarations and agreements. India has clarified that the "substance of human rights is far more important than the language or the form". In fact, it is also held that India and the EU happen to be on the same side as far as "the substance" is concerned. Therefore, once a rapprochement takes place on the issue, the negotiations on EU-India FTA would be concluded, which would transform trade relations for the better. The presence of numerous structural impediments in EU-India relations has been acknowledged. It is no hidden fact that EU has long favoured China over India as an investment destination despite its abysmal human rights record. For every euro invested in India, the EU invests €20 in China. It was pointed out that both sides have their eyes trained on the most powerful actors in the international system but they tend to ignore each other and do not build upon the foundations of a strong partnership (Tharoor 2012).

The promotion of democracy and human rights, which constitute the EU's normative agenda, were the principal set of objectives that it employed for defining its relations with India. India being the world's largest democracy is looked upon by the EU as an important partner for promoting the shared objectives in the Indian subcontinent and beyond. The EU promptly established a regular bilateral human rights dialogue focusing on developments taking place in the EU and India. But the real value of this understanding "was expected to materialise in multilateral cooperation and joint initiatives in third countries". The annual human rights dialogue between the EU and India has managed to dispel mutual doubts and tensions on sensitive issues like the Kashmir and the Gujarat riots in 2002. It has become a platform for constructive and open exchange of views and information. It is believed by some scholars that the EU expectations that India shall become "an active promoter of democracy and human rights did not materialise". Although India is a contributor to the UN Democracy Fund and has provided all kinds of assistance in local democratisation projects in Afghanistan and other countries, it insists on the consent of the host government as a pre-condition for any financial or technical support which is considered by the EU as a redundant measure. India is known to have abstained in the event of any country-specific resolution that has come up for voting at the UN Human Rights Council in Geneva on account of adherence to the principles of non-alignment and non-intervention in the internal affairs of other countries which is criticised by the EU. The only exception to this rule came in the form of Indian solidarity in condemning the Sri Lankan government for reneging on its promises of safeguarding the rights of the Tamil minority. However, an argument was made against India that its condemnation of Sri Lanka was driven by domestic politics. The EU expected that India would be instrumental in spreading shared values abroad and it would lend political support to people and civil society movements against unpopular and dictatorial regimes during the Arab Spring. However, the EU was disappointed by the Chinese and Indians who did not agree with the western interpretation of the right-to-protect clause and categorically stated that regime change was out of bounds of its foreign policy (Muenchow-Pohl 2012).

Indian cultural actors belonging to the private and public sector consider international cultural relations to be an end in itself. The terms that are mostly used to denote EU-India interaction in the cultural sphere include "international cultural relations, cultural exchange and to a limited extent, public diplomacy and cultural diplomacy". The Public Diplomacy Division at Ministry of External Affairs and some prominent Indians are seen abundantly using the "instrumental language of soft power".

Cultural ignorance is known to exist on both sides. Europe and its diversity are virtually unknown in India. Indians mostly have a stereotyped knowledge about Europe and. apart from UK, they tend to know about Western and Northern Europe while "Central and Eastern Europe are very little known". As far as EU-sponsored academic cooperation is concerned, it is largely known to be "very cumbersome and lacking in transparency". Not much salience is attributed to research in humanities and the social sciences in the DG Research Framework and Erasmus Mundus programmes while the EU's Visitor Programme involves journalists and not academicians. Thus it becomes clear that

> ...the attitudes of many governments and cultural players in the EU are perceived as being paternalistic and out of date in a globalised world, ignorant of Indian realities. Indian artists and NGO activists argue for the value of collaborative ventures- of which several have already occurred- in which mutual learning occurs symmetrically across continents, in a mode of co-curation and mutual learning. Some see future EU-level cooperation as both a challenge and opportunity, recognising Europe as a terrain in which multilayered cultural cooperation can transcend both propaganda and the pitfalls of nation branding. Thus any European strategy would have to be very broad-based and bottom up in order to have any impact on the pan-India scale, or for the slogan of building "people to people"

> exchanges to have any substance for that matter. Furthermore, unless the EU were able to reach out effectively in the digital environment, its strategies would have little or no impact on the country's young people, and would remain confined to older generations of people in the major cities working principally in the traditional high arts, heritage and crafts sectors. The EU also needs to work through India's large number of universities, many of which had already become centres of cultural production and presentation, in order to envisage cultural relations as a process of mutual cultural education (Isar 2015).

European social and cultural stolidity constitutes of "anti-discrimination, laws and institutions that aim to combat discrimination and exclusion on the grounds of religion, gender or ethnicity, viable democratic institutions, efficient governance, an uncompromising commitment to the rule of law, and a relentless striving for collective self-introspection and self-correction". India would do well to learn from the European experience about how to "limit the influence of kin and nepotism in politics". A major strength of Europe, unlike India, is that the EU has "stable political institutions, including norms of coalition governance which are more driven by issues and stability" (Jain 2014:36).The EU is looked upon as the new melting pot of the world as it is increasingly becoming "multicultural, multiethnic and multilingual" and consequently it is facing "a major challenge of diversity management and accommodation". A sizeable number of educated Indians are of the view that EU tends to be "socially and culturally protectionist". There is a widespread feeling that the EU is not doing a good job in dealing with diversity of cultures and multiculturalism has malfunctioned in Europe. Besides, European societies have not extended a warm welcome and have not been able to meaningfully integrate non-Western ethnic minorities, especially Muslims.

India on the contrary, shows us a different picture as it has ably assimilated diversity in "a constitutional framework within a discourse that is not about dominance, but coexistence" (Jain 2014: 37). Indians fails to recognise a single European culture as a result of the "ambiguity of the discourse about EU cultural identity within the EU itself, which has been seeking to foster a European identity and common European values" (Jain 2014: 37-38).

Europeans need to bear in mind that with gradual shift of balance of power towards the East, the phenomenon of Europeans wielding influence in the rest of the world does not exist anymore (Jain 2014:40). Europe ought to appreciate that it should "listen more and lecture less" for very often they are perceived by Indians to be "intrusive and preachy". The new European narrative is required to be "more open, inclusive and accommodating". An ongoing meaningful dialogue and a decisive step towards learning about each other shall considerably enhance the quality of the bilateral relationship (Jain 2014:42).

India and the EU share "striking similarities" which includes being an economic and political union of almost 30 member states that are culturally and linguistically disparate from each other. Both have "strong democratic traditions, historical ties and priorities for governance in a multilateral framework" and therefore they can be regarded to have "great potential to be close, natural partners". However, there seems to be a lack of common understanding about the role of strategic partnership between the two sides. The perception of the EU as a security actor is also engrained in historical experiences. Europe's history explains their preference for soft power and non-military instruments of foreign policy. Traditional security which refers to protection from external attack is the resultant effect of the European integration process. The Indian experience is diametrically opposite as the "EU shares sovereignty as a post-modern actor" while India subscribes to the "more traditional view of state sovereignty" in order "to protect its strategic autonomy". Although non-interference and non-intervention are largely considered to be the hallmark of India's general foreign policy imperatives, the security environment in South Asia has prompted India to focus much more than the EU on "military dimensions and hard power capabilities". India and EU may share common values and goals "such as multilateralism, democracy, human rights and global governance" but they tend to differ as far as "approaches and strategies" are concerned (Britsch 2014).

India and the EU share a common perception of international security to a considerable extent as both have expressed the desire for a stable Middle East and a stable Afghanistan but their ways and methods have different normative underpinnings which seems to emerge in the form of a "normative Europe and a realist India" (NFG Asian Perceptions of the EU 2013: 10).

In the current scenario, normative conditionality cannot be expected to have much scope and it cannot be very productive. This should not lead the EU to entirely "give up its ambition to become an international norm-setter". The achievements, policies and standards of the EU could be emulated at a very fast pace by the developing world once the latter attains economic self-sufficiency and political unity. In the meanwhile,

> EU should concentrate on its liberal standards for internal use and ensure that it meets the preconditions of its post-modern policies: enhanced economic integration, political democracy and equal opportunities for its people. Even retired super powers can have a long life, if they keep in good form. This requires for example more ambitious economic innovation, support for private creative initiatives, increasing the effectiveness of governance and assuring that welfare for its citizens can be further developed. Only if Europe modernises itself and succeeds in legitimising its policies internally, might it have a chance to constructively engage the new giants. If it manages to uphold its

> economic competitiveness and raises its political effectiveness, Europe would inevitably obtain a strong bargaining position in the new power politics of this century. Not strong enough to impose its conditions, but sufficient to ensure that its core interests are not harmed and that it maintains confidence in itself (Holslag 2015: 17).

The Dimension of Development and Climate Change

India considers the EU to be an "increasingly important development partner" as it has immense scope as far as "market, high technology and foreign direct investment" are concerned. India has expressed willingness "to adapt many European best practices in various socio-economic fields" (Jain 2014 40). When compared with the emerging powers such as Brazil, China and South Africa, India seems to have the least possibility of establishing "meaningful cooperation with the EU on development". This is on account of the fact that India is more than willing to shrug off its association and identity of belonging to the "traditional donor community" as it currently chooses to "selectively engage in those multilateral frameworks that appear to be more genuinely open to Southern representation and leadership." However, India does not have an extremely rigid stance on the issue and makes an exception or two, as in the case of Afghanistan, where there seems to be a possibility of forging development links between the EU and India. The EU authorities and decision-makers should take note of the fact that quite a few of "their normative assumptions about international development" are found to be problematic and seldom agreed upon by Indian policy-makers. This does not amount to complete negation of "progressive EU principles" but it is indeed a pointer that the theme of development has emerged as a problematic area in which assertion of values by the EU will pose difficulties more often than not. In fact, some small steps in the right direction seem to have been taken by some of the EU member-states such as UK, Germany and Netherlands in order to move towards greater South-South cooperation approaches. This entails focus in the area of "economic growth as opposed to poverty reduction alone, on infrastructure and productivity, a growing role for the private sector, the relative decline of official development assistance (ODA) and rise of various forms of blended finance". This is regarded as a much more practical approach towards bringing about international development which shall create new opportunities for EU-India cooperation in this field especially in the areas of "infrastructure and agriculture". However, it is also feared that this process could lead to "deepening competition and a race to the bottom in terms of environmental and labour standards". It is necessary that irrespective of "the difficult context", both partners should continue to work in unison in this area by drawing "on the relative strengths of both actors in achieving "economic growth, social welfare, human rights and peace-building". The EU-India strategic partnership is "unlikely" to offer "a strong basis for such dialogue and collaboration" (Mawdsley 2014). India's participation in the multi-billion dollar Galileo satellite project launched by the EU would have proved to be one of the milestones in development cooperation. However, India withdrew from the project as it realised that it was not being treated "as a co-decision maker" even after committing €300 million for the project. India was of the view that they must have a say in the control of the satellite so that they are not denied access during war. As the costs increased, the EU was unimpressed by India's modest offer of investment and ultimately EU took upon itself the full managerial and financial burdens of the development of the satellite (Winand et al. 2015: 279-280).

Despite a few drawbacks, there still remain a number of areas for boosting development cooperation between EU and India. The information communication technology (ICT) sector in India has been bursting at the seams with vitality and growth since the 1990s and it has attracted the attention of the United States as well as the EU. The resultant loss of jobs due to a very high rate of outsourcing has been a cause of worry and displeasure in the developed countries. Indians belonging to the ICT industry have the opportunity to make use of their skills to work in the USA and the EU countries. Another reason for the emergence of the EU as an avenue for jobs for Indians is the increasing rate of greying population which has led to a decline in the working population of EU member states. India is in the process of "capitalising on this demographic dividend". India's quest to develop "all-round infrastructure of roads, air links, ports, airports and power sector" gives ample opportunity for fostering of EU-India development cooperation. The World Trade Organisation and other international agencies have helped both sides resolve issues such as "problems related to goods, general agreement in trade and services, agriculture and textiles, new trade-related areas in intellectual property rights and trade-related investment measures" which impact development cooperation. The practice of offering very high subsidies to farmers in the EU and other developed nations has led to a strong protest by India and other developing countries. Besides, India can afford liberalisation and lowering of barriers to a certain extent only till it attains development up to a certain level. India shall have to "activate South Asian cooperation" in order to have the gumption to meet such conditionalities (Harshe 2007: 1421).

The European Commission had taken a decision to phase out development cooperation with India after 2013. However, development aid would continue to remain an aspect of the relations "as regional and thematic programmes" would be in operation even after 2013. The EU is continuously engaged in the process of improving effectiveness of its aid. A decisive shift has taken place as we have watched previous aid recipients like India become well known aid donors in the international community. The global recession of 2008 brought to the fore the weakness of the economies of the world including that of the EU which compelled them to implement internal austerity measures, which in turn affected their "foreign aid expenditure". The EU preferred investing in social sectors such as health and education while India has a marked preference for investing in infrastructure projects. India provides aids through programmes which are unconditional. However, the aim of these projects is that it should bring in benefits both for the aid recipient country as well as India. The EU is best suited for the role of tendering advice to India "on best practices in external aid implementation" because it has a "comprehensive history as an aid donor and its constant efforts toward improving aid delivery" are worth emulating (Winand et al. 2015: 333).

The rapid growth of the Indian economy and population of the country makes India a salient partner of the EU in many sectors including energy and climate change. The EU-India Initiative on Clean Development and Climate Change, EU-India Energy Panel and EU-India Science and Technology Steering Committee are part of the bilateral framework put in place since 2004 for enhancing cooperation between the two partners on the issue of climate change. However, work under most of these heads has been slow-paced at its best. Meetings have not been held frequently, which has impeded the strengthening of ties in this sphere despite the setting up of "working groups on clean coal, energy efficiency and renewables". The European Commission and EU member-states such as UK, France, Germany and Spain have provided funding for some small-scale projects in India. But these flagship programmes have not been able to fire up cooperation between the two sides. It is widely felt that the partnership between EU and India requires

> further development, not least because of India's growing significance in respect of realising global climate security objectives. Bilateral problems on technology transfer (where respect for intellectual property rights is again an issue) need to be resolved, and, overall, India needs continued assistance to decouple population and economic growth and poverty alleviation from emissions growth. The country is home to

> over a billion people, and according to government estimates, energy consumption (based mainly on black coal) is projected to increase 50 per cent by 2015.

There is widespread "energy poverty" in India as thousands of villages remain unconnected to the electricity grid or have intermittent connections. Therefore, assistance provided by the EU "in order to improve livelihoods in rural communities" would considerably increase their strength and capability to adapt to the effects of climate change. India offers a fertile ground for "technological leapfrogging" which could provide ample opportunity to companies of the EU to invest and do business in area of conventional and renewable energy. Hence the European Council remarked that although relations have been expanding, there is substantial scope for much closer cooperation with India (Afionis and Bailey 2012: 67-68).

India and the EU have generally found themselves in opposing camps on the issue of climate change. The EU has been asking India to extend its support for a legally binding agreement and do much more in order to deal with the challenge of global warming. India on the other hand, points out that the EU, along with the other developed countries of the world which had undergone the process of industrialisation much earlier, are largely responsible for carbon emissions and degradation of the environment of the planet. Hence, it is the developed world that should take on the responsibility and burden of correcting the wrongs that have been committed by them and led to the problems of global warming and climate change. India has been a consistent campaigner for "adequate and predictable finances" to be provided by the developed world to the developing countries so that they can do their bit in tackling this global menace. The EU and India have made efforts in the recent past to set aside their differences on the issue of climate change. The EU authorities have stated in their defence that they intend to have "an open-minded engagement with India" and they believe that "everyone needs to bend towards each other". The EU has made efforts to assuage fears of India that it would be compelled to reduce carbon emissions when it would be imperative for its economy to grow. India is far from attaining energy security, sufficiency and stability and therefore the EU is not asking for a reduction of emissions in absolute terms in India. EU authorities however, very cleverly point out that just as India should not be compared with EU, India should also not be compared with China as the latter is the biggest greenhouse gas emitter and India's close ally in the climate negotiations (Goswami 2014).

Economic Dimension

The economic component undoubtedly dominates EU-India relations despite the lofty political ideals and ambitions outlined in every summit statement. The lack of "domestic consistency" in India as well as the EU poses a problem for development of a vibrant, continuous and growing economic relationship and there are occasional bumps which both sides have to contend with. It is imperative that both sides should make attempts to iron out the differences that are preventing them from finalising the EU-India FTA, negotiations for which have been going on for two years short of a decade.

The perks of having a liberalised and open market in India do not automatically translate into an economic relationship that is "low maintenance or free of conflict". The EU has to contend with regulatory problems, high levels of bureaucratisation and red tapism. Moreover, the Indian government has placed limits on foreign ownership in key areas of the economy, especially the service sector and "props up public enterprises through a complex system of cross subsidies". The EU has expressed a strong distaste for the intellectual property rights regime in India, especially in the context of the pharmaceutical industry. Trade with India also tends to "get hampered by frequent and opaque changes in the overall tariff structure or imposition of import or export restrictions" with a view to regulate and control flow of goods and services as well as prices of commodities. Both sides are not ready to budge from their stand and renege on their core interests such as "lower duties on automotive imports from Europe or unrestricted market access for Indian IT services providers". As many of these issues have been picked up by political circles and have been highlighted in the media, especially in India, the assurance at various summit meetings that the FTA is headed towards an early conclusion seems no longer credible. While the EU-India trade has been registering growth at a steady pace, the EU-India FTA would undoubtedly take the economic partnership to an entirely different level. It shall be extremely beneficial for European investment in India which has been registering a decline lately for want of further liberalisation in India. The conclusion of the EU-India FTA is largely anticipated to be the most tangible deliverable in EU-India relations (Muenchow-Pohl 2012).

Despite the settling in of pessimism with regard to the conclusion of the EU-India FTA, a new ray of hope has come on the horizon with the formation of the new government at the centre in India. It has given the assurance that the EU-India FTA shall see the light of the day once the Narendra Modi government finalises its foreign trade policy. The EU authorities have expressed similar views that the EU-India FTA would be finalised in the "next year or so". Once the Free Trade Agreement comes into force, it shall last for as long as 15-20 years. Therefore, both sides have decided to show perseverance. EU has stated that it understands India's growth imperative and therefore is willing to accept "an asymmetrical agreement'. The EU called for proportionate, if not equal, taxation to be imposed on either side especially in the case of the automobile sector. Taxes of up to a 100 per cent are imposed on cars imported from the EU to India, while only 7-8 per cent taxes are imposed on cars exported to the EU. India exports around 200,000 cars to Europe while EU exports only 40,000 cars to India. The EU has stated that the ban on import of alphonso mangoes from India on the grounds of allegedly being “contaminated by pests such as fruit flies and other quarantine pests” shall be lifted soon.(The Hindu, 28 April 2014).

It has also been stated that the EU is optimistic about economic growth in India which “currently is a level well below its potential as an investment destination than many of its competitors”. The investment climate seems to have changed in psychological rather than substantial terms. The Indian government is all set to push for increasing investment flows into India which in turn will give a boost to the country’s manufacturing capacity. The Modi government’s Make in India initiative is expected to help India enter the global value chain (The Economic Times, 14 December 2014). The Indian government has urged the EU to “energise it constituents across the EU because India has opportunities” and it will make the experience of doing business as comfortable as possible. India’s trade volume with the EU has declined in the recent past in whole terms although India’s exports to the EU have increased, but overall EU imports to India have declined in the past few years. EU-India trade exchanges amounting to a yearly €70 billion is no match for EU-US trade which was recorded at around €1500 annually. There is a growing realisation that no stone should be left unturned for “fostering bilateral trade, investment and economic relations between EU and India”. Efforts should also be made towards building bridges of communication between large, small and medium-sized enterprises in EU and India for the purpose of “integrating resources and technical knowhow” (The Economic Times, 21 November 2014).

The Indian economy was able to recover from the shock of the global financial recession in 2008 and the initial shock of the Eurozone crisis did not cause a divergence in its path. However, in case the sovereign debt crisis worsens, India will eventually come under severe economic stress. The “five principal channels” through which the Eurozone crisis can make its way to the Indian economy include trade, currency, investment, banking and commodity price. Although the fiscal health of India is much better than that of the EU member-states, the Indian government has preferred to take adequate measures for safeguarding its economic interests by means of embarking upon a policy of fiscal consolidation. The other measures suggested for economic reform include cutting public expenditure, increasing efficiency in tax collection and minimising subsidies. The deregulation of retail fuel prices has been hailed as a step taken in the right direction by the government at the centre (Mahambare 2010: 21).

Deliberations on the ways and means of dealing with the financial woes of the Eurozone have dominated the agenda of most meetings of European leaders held since the last two years. This has led to the free fall of foreign policy issues to the bottom of the priority list of the EU. This has exerted an impact upon the manner in which "EU is viewed by its partners". The Indian perception has been "critical about the ability of an aging Europe to retain a competitive edge vis-as-vis the emerging economies and even more so about its willingness to set aside national special interests and member states prerogatives for a coherent EU foreign policy". The longer the EU remains in the throes of a financial crisis and the more India feels the negative impact of the crisis on its economy, it shall be more likely that India shall not regard the EU as a global player in the same class as the United States (Muenchow- Pohl 2012).

Coverage of EU News in the Indian Press

Newspapers are the most effective conduit through which the reach and engagement of the European Union with India can be assessed. Indian journalists and media pundits have been active participants in the debate on India's foreign policy agenda. A comprehensive and widespread coverage of international news has become a priority for the print media owing to the "massive readership of Indian newspapers" despite the fact that the main focus of the media continues to be local and national issues. The lack of full-time foreign correspondents, albeit the few based in major cities such as Washington D.C. and London, proves to be a great impediment in international reporting. Despite these limitations, Indian newspapers continue to play a primary role in foreign policy debates and most news items on foreign policy are "hashed out in impressive, sometimes excruciating detail bolstered by commentary from a stable of well known former government officials". For instance, in the Ministry of External Affairs, the mandatory daily dose of reading includes news and op-ed pages from three or more newspapers (Markey 2009).

The European Union is found to be "a little known actor and an unclear entity" in the Indian press. It is recognised as an economic and political power in the media but it occupies a distant second position after the United States. There is frequent mention in the press about the human rights policy, aid policy and soft security of the European Union. Most discussions about the European Union take place within the broader context of the India's relations with individual European countries. There seems to be very little general awareness about what exactly the EU is and much less about its policies, motives and goals (Fioramonti and Lucarelli 2007).

Some analysts have put forth the question as to why India seldom makes it to the front pages of newspapers in the EU and why the EU is inadequately reported in the pages of Indian newspapers. He goes on to say that the European Union is undoubtedly of great consequence to China and Japan, which is a fact corroborated by the sheer number of Chinese and Japanese journalists based in Brussels (Subhan 2005). Some scholars share the belief that there seems to exist an overall sentiment that the flow of information between the EU and India is insufficient and therefore the existing networks within EU and India need to be pooled together and streamlined (Cameron et al.). The lack of information inevitably leads to the emergence of stereotypes and misconceptions owing to the power imbued with the journalists in the information age to influence and mould opinion based on what they choose to write. The mutual sharing of knowledge by journalists on the Indian and EU sides will facilitate a better understanding of mutual perspectives (Schumacher 2005).

Misperceptions and Lack of Communication

There seems to be a widespread feeling in Brussels that the Indian policy-makers largely refuse to consider the EU as a power to reckon with. The European Commission President Romani Prodi expressed the view that the United States is accorded the highest degree of importance in the course of formulation and implementation of Indian economic and foreign policy which amounts to ignoring the European Union and not giving recognition to its might as a strong actor in the economic and political affairs of the world (Jain 2009).

It has been argued that "images and the representations" that the European Union and India have of each other do not represent the real picture and causes friction between the two. India would like to be seen as the "new emerging political and economic power" rather than as a "very fast growing developing country". The EU, on the other hand, would like to be acknowledged as "an important political and normative actor" even if it is not widely recognised as such. This happens on account of "stereotyping and prejudices" that tend to adversely impact the relations between the two actors (Wulbers 2008).

Since Indian perceptions are largely recognised to be shaped by the Euro-skeptic English media, the differences are not between a "security and realpolitik obsessed India and a (perceived) de-securitised Europe" but rather between a "values based discourse and a needs-based discourse (NFG Asian Perceptions of the EU 2013:9).

The reasons for the building up of misperceptions about India and EU can thus be attributed not only to information deficits alone but also to historical experiences and contexts. It is alleged that "Asian minds are still set on massive domestic development needs and historical injustice that reflect on a perceived power asymmetry at the international level, generating different perceptions of security" (NFG Asian Perceptions of the EU 2013:10).

It is imperative to "invest heavily in research and knowledge about South Asia" as Europeans have largely been "blinded by a passion for the colourful India with all its traditions, languages and religions." A need for the EU to "become much more active diplomatically and increase its visibility, establish networks, promote student exchanges and create advocacy groups" has been felt in order to strengthen relations with South Asia in general and India in particular (Britsch 2014 :3). Therefore both sides need to strive to

> make a conscious effort to overcome perceptional differences since misperceptions constrain greater mutual cooperation and dialogue. It is essential to explore innovative ways so the EU can better target and synergise its media and communication strategies with key strategic partners like India in order to enhance its visibility and overcome stereotypes and misperceptions. More importantly, it is about overcoming the enormous information deficit that still persists about the EU in India and about India in the EU, largely because of mutual indifference and neglect. Clearly, both have a visibility issue to address and an imperative need to devise more coherent and effective public strategies (Jain 2014: 40-41).

Definition, Rationale and Scope of the Study

This study aims to add "a non-European perspective to what has largely been an inward-looking scholarly debate on the role of the EU in the world" (Torney 2014: 1358). Studies began to be conducted on Indian perceptions about the EU only from the year 2001 onwards. Only a few studies have been conducted on how the Indian print media portrayed individual EU Member States ((for example Anne Vaugier-Chatterjee 2002,2006). These studies comprised of historical overviews (Subrahmanyam 2005), reminiscences of former diplomats (Dixit 2001) or assessments based on conversations and elite interviews (Lisbonne-de Vergeron 2006, 2011). Some describe Europe as 'the hub of the West' or express great admiration for the creation of a peace community and collective prosperity of the Community (Vivekanandan 2001). Others seek to explore how public opinion, the political elite and civil society organisations have perceived the EU (Fioramonti 2007; Fioramonti and Poletti 2008; Mitra 2006), but without conducting a primary public opinion survey or face-to-face elite interviews (Jain and Pandey 2012: 333).

This study is a first of its kind as it will examine perceptions about EU-India relations through the prism of the print media and the Indian elite. It is absolutely essential to know the exact nature of the picture of the EU being portrayed in India. Besides, Indian elite opinion is widely circulated, acknowledged and respected in the media as well as in the decision-making and policy-making circles. Hence, this study aims to address the research gap that exists as a result of no attempt at a detailed analysis of the source of perceptions and misperceptions about the EU which are ultimately circulated in India. The studies conducted so far deal with perceptions at a superficial level without trying to locate the outlet of such perceptions and examining the reason why such perceptions are being ultimately accepted as established fact. This study shall help in ensuring dissemination of accurate and adequate information about the EU in the media and through the elites by pointing out the current faults and deficiencies of the process which shall go a long way in refurbishing the image of the EU and contribute to strengthening and further consolidation of EU-India relations.

The study undertaken makes an attempt to define the true nature of the EU-India relations in the drastically changed scenario as a result of the growing importance of complex interdependence and the advent of multipolarity. An attempt to clearly understand the nodal points of the strengths and weaknesses of these ties has been made. The study concentrates on locating the gap between formulation and implementation of EU-India policies. It has tried to delve deep into the nuances of this relationship and come up with a holistic perspective on EU-India relations. The general perceptions, the available literature on the relationship, the coverage in the newspapers and the insights of the elite should help in arriving at concrete conclusions and recommendations for furtherance of the relationship through this study.

A perception can either be a fleeting opinion or long-lasting in nature which makes a mark on the individual's thinking. Such long-lasting perceptions become a sound basis for knowledge. The increase in diversification of contact and cooperation between two countries in areas such as extending mutual political support, scientific and technological exchange, collaborations in educational and cultural activities and the movement of people from one place to another leads to the growth of knowledge about the other country which ultimately contributes to the shaping up of perceptions. The Indian press thus becomes the disseminator of perceptions and makes them popular while the elite make use of these perceptions for the purpose of policy-making and justifying their viewpoints. The Indian public opinion is greatly influenced by the perceptions of the Indian elite and the media as a majority of the people in India choose to rely on these two sources for information and analyses rather than work towards finding things out for themselves.

This study is required for examining the changing dynamics of the EU-India relationship triggered by the elevation of their respective roles in the international scenario. The shift to multipolarity is bound to increase the venues of engagement between the two partners as a result of new issues such as terrorism and climate change occupying centre-stage. The standpoints of the European Union and India command respect in the international community. It therefore becomes imperative to revisit the nuts and bolts of the relationship which has tremendously evolved in the last few years. The study has tried to make a sincere effort to bring to the fore the overall perception about the relationship between EU and India. It shall therefore in the process highlight the vacuoles and gaps between initiatives resolved to be undertaken by both parties and the actual results on the ground.

The study examines EU-India relations by means of presenting an adequately informed assessment of initiatives in the social, economic, political environmental and developmental areas. It has aimed at contributing towards the building up of subject matter and information on perceptions about EU-India relations. An attempt has been made to provide further insight regarding the visibility, influence and acceptance of the EU in India.

One of the limitations of the study is that it is not an exhaustive study of print media publications. Moreover, the study does not include a comparative study of the perceptions about the EU in India with that of another actor such as the United States.

Hypotheses

The following hypotheses have been tested in the study:

ó Complex interdependence and the consolidation of multi-polarity are leading to greater engagement between the European Union and India.

ó The economic and political dialogue has contributed towards visibility of the European Union in the Indian print media.

ó On specific issues, the coverage of the EU-India relationship creates prejudices and stereotypes.

Research Methods

Reference to all the relevant material pertaining to relations between the European Union and India has been made. The matter is organised under the main themes that are aimed to be discussed and comprehended in the study. The study is based on facts and is supported by the theoretical premise of complex interdependence and the phenomenon of multipolarity. The study shall be descriptive and analytical in nature.

The study is based on primary sources as a result of data collected by day-to-day scanning of three national dailies namely *The Times of India* (English newspaper), *The Economic Times* (business newspaper) and the *Dainik Jagran* (vernacular newspaper) for an entire year from the 1 July 2009 to 30 June 2010. According to round two of the Indian Readership Survey (IRS) 2009 released in the month of November 2009, all the three newspapers chosen for undertaking this study retained the number one slot. *The Economic Times* continues to be the leading business newspaper of India with a readership of about 757,000. *The Times of India* retained its number one position among the English dailies with a readership figure of 13,347,000 and it added 185,000 readers to its fold. *The Dainik Jagran* emerged as the most popular newspaper of India and recorded a readership of 54,791,000 and gained 208,000 readers. The last twelve rounds of the survey have also declared *Dainik Jagran* to be the largest read daily of India.

The news items mentioning the EU or European Union have been included in the data-set for content analysis. The quantitative tools of analysis include the number of news items on the European Union, the monthly distribution of the items, the coverage of such news in each newspaper, the sources of information and the placement and length of the articles. The qualitative tools include the categorisation of the EU as an economic, political, social, developmental or environmental actor based on its area of involvement in the news item. The articles have been subjected to evaluation of being positive, negative or neutral contingent upon the immediate response that it triggers. The focus of centrality has been determined by means of assessing the importance and visibility of the European Union as a major or secondary or minor actor in the news article. The dataset thus created shall be utilised for both qualitative and quantitative analysis.

The study involved interviewing a total of 38 elites in India affiliated to areas of politics, media, civil society and business. The political elites include former and present members of parliament. The media elites consist of editors, Chief Executive Officers and leading reporters of different media outlets. The civil society elites comprise of Indians leading NGOs, INGOs and think-tanks. The business elite include members of chambers of commerce, CEOs and top officials of companies, members of official business networks and persons associated with the formulation of Indo-EU trade and economic policies. The elites were asked a total of 18 questions revolving around EU-India relations. They were asked to comment on issues such as professional association with the EU, on the matter of the EU's great power status, the importance of EU to India in relation to other prominent regions, the Commission Delegation and factors that should be kept in mind while formulating governmental policy with the European Union. The data collection technique involved face-to-face interviews and the content was recorded and transcribed.The data thus collected would be utilised for the purpose of analysis, comparison and for the identification of new trends in EU-India relations if any.

The research undertaken involved the use of data collected both from primary and secondary sources. Primary sources include documents and reports released by governments and various organs of the European Union. The newspapers are a secondary source of information but the data collected is considered to be primary as it has been analysed for the first time. Secondary sources include research work done by experts and organisations available in books and academic journals, commentaries and news items from newspapers and internet sources.

Conclusions

Perceptions are an important element which has to be kept in mind for effective foreign policy formulation and implementation. Perception is an idea, notion or belief of how things external to us appear to be. It can be regarded as an effect, which is external, on man. Both psychologists and scholars of international relations have engaged themselves in the study of perceptions with the former emphasising more on emotions while the latter stressed upon cognitive aspects. It has been realised in the past that both elements are vital for perception-formation. Another concept closely related to perception is that of the image which is considered to be a collection of features that come together in a logical manner. The image helps in the interpretation of action of the subject which can be an individual or state or a supra-national identity like the EU.

The EU is a unique beast which is constantly evolving and thus it becomes difficult to ascribe a definiteness to it which further complicates the image of the EU in the eyes of the beholder who lives beyond its boundaries. Therefore, external image portrayal in an accurate fashion becomes imperative for the EU in order to ward off undeserved negative feedback so that it gets due acknowledgement for its effective and constructive foreign policy. This will inevitably help the EU to cultivate a healthy relationship with other countries of the world. Therefore, the element of external perceptions needs to be taken into account so that the right approach can be adopted in dealing with international actors and issues. The EU took a concrete step to double its efforts in order to disseminate the correct information about itself by means of the creation of the European External Action Service and the post of the High Representative for Foreign Affairs and Security

Policy. A study of external images not only yields interesting results about the nature of impressions that the external world has about the EU but it also gives an opportunity to the EU to introspect and learn from its mistakes in order to conduct it relations more smoothly and in a better fashion in future.

The Indian perceptions about the EU are influenced to a very large extent by the Anglo-Saxon media which results in the formation of a distorted image about the EU. Indians look upon EU as a strange entity which is too complex to understand and too distant to engage with. The Indian media under the influence of the Anglo-Saxon imagery makes no effort to bridge the gap between the EU and India through their writings. No attempt is made to highlight the relevance of the EU to India and everything is reported in a very impersonal and matter-of- fact manner.

It is not only the Indian on the streets but also the Indian government that finds it easier to deal with EU member-states than the EU both of which work more often than not at cross-purposes. The EU-member-states are more concerned about furthering their interests rather than trying to take every one along and negotiate as a collectivity with India.

Indians have been curious about Europe since a very long time and we find interesting and often contradictory descriptions of the Europeans who happened to come to India. They were described as strange people who fought bravely and who did not like to use water much. They were looked upon as very curious people who followed rules in matters of punishment, but had no regard for the rules of pollution and purity.

A flurry of activity was witnessed after signing of the Maastricht Treaty for the purpose of increasing the visibility and popularity of the EU. The initial decision taken was to place the economic potential of the relationship into the spotlight. However, it was subsequently decided to make amends by working equally on every aspect of the relationship as growth in every sector was interdependent on the enhancement of the relationship in other sectors. Thus, an attempt to intensify a EU-India dialogue by involving all possible stakeholders was made.

The newly-elected government at the Centre does not seem to have been charmed by the grace of the Old Continent as the EU hardly figures in the list of foreign destinations which the globe-trotting Indian Prime Minister has chosen to make a spectacle of. He did occasionally brush shoulders with the European leaders but did not feel the urgency to project India in the EU like he did in Australia or at Madison Square in the United States.

A common EU-India strategic culture is yet to take final shape although the EU is continues being an important partner of India in the defence sector. Cooperation between the two sides along with the involvement in SAARC has proved to be a non-starter. The EU member-states and the EU are seen taking firm and often conflicting stands on international issues which dents the image of the EU as a unified entity. Hence, the EU should make it a point to emerge from the clouds as a distinct actor with a strong voice which will compel India to prefer it over the EU member-states for entering into negotiations and inking deals. Both the EU and India are accused of being hesitant and slow-paced actors who seem to have lost the enthusiasm of being the go-getters in international politics. It is necessary that both the EU and India are imbued with the spirit of becoming more active in global affairs and the means to go about this task would be to build up a joint front. There is a strong sentiment in India that the EU should become a prominent player in international relations just like the US. The EU in turn expects India to extend help and support in this mission and take the its side on every issue. However, India has given utmost importance to its national interests and has taken stands in the UN and on other international platforms accordingly. However, it is believed that the two would come together to contain China, cooperate in reconstruction and rehabilitation efforts in Afghanistan, participate in joint counter-piracy missions, ensure energy security and continue collaborating in the nuclear sector and defence manufacturing.

India is not happy with the EU's exercise of normative power in India's internal affairs. India considers itself to be a responsible democracy and is most conscious of ensuring fundamental rights to all its citizens. Besides, human rights violation is often over-hyped in India's case while the EU turns a blind eye towards state-sponsored widespread blatant violations of human dignity in China.

It is largely felt that cultural exchanges will be promoted at all levels and among all sections of society as a very high degree of mutual cultural ignorance is believed to exist in both EU and India. Most Indians feel that multiculturalism has failed to become the essence of the European style of living while on the other hand, India extends a warm welcome to all. This is not entirely true and it is necessary that such myths are dissipated through greater cultural interaction between the two partners. Such interactions are likely to lead to better understanding about strategic issues as EU and India tend to have a different comprehension about the same concept which makes arriving at a consensus a very difficult task.

The economic aspect is undoubtedly the most mature and vital aspect of the EU-India relationship. However, it would not be very wise to assume that it is a smooth-sailing relationship. Numerous disputes arise in this sphere only to be resolved amicably over a period of time. The tenacity and perseverance shown by both sides to conclude the EU-India FTA agreement is a case in point.

India has donned a new avatar in the area of development cooperation. It has become a donor country and continues of encourage South –South cooperation approaches. The EU member-states have begun supporting such ventures. Meanwhile, EU-India cooperation continues as the EU is assisting India in drawing closer to the MDGs.

Not much headway has been made in climate and energy cooperation. The EU and India are found to be at loggerheads as far as the issue of climate change is concerned because the EU sides with the developed world, while India is part of the developing world brigade. However, the EU keeps assuring India that it will not be compelled to go for an absolute reduction of emissions in the light of its compulsions to reach development targets, especially in the villages. Besides, the EU is expected to invest in businesses in India for helping it in the task of technology-leapfrogging and attaining energy self-sufficiency by bypassing stages of development that are not cost-effective and are harmful for the environment.

It is amply clear that misperceptions about each other are thriving mainly on account of an information deficit and communication gap in EU-India relations. It is vital that such wrong notions are dispelled by frequent interaction and through exposure to each other's ethics and mode of working. The Indian media should share the responsibility of covering EU news adequately and draw the attention of the Indian public towards various dimensions of the relationship, so that they are able to connect and associate themselves with the activities of the EU. It is also imperative to highlight the notions, opinions and ideas that the Indian elite have about the EU-India relationship, for they have a far reaching influence in ascertaining the conduct of Indian foreign policy. This alone will help in giving the EU its rightful place in India's foreign policy priorities and also increasing the stature of the EU, which is currently highly underestimated in the eyes of the Indian populace. Hence, this study about how the EU is perceived by the Indian print media and its elite can be regarded as appropriate and suitable for ascertaining Indian foreign policy priorities in the context of EU-India relations.

3

The Visibility of EU in the Indian Print Media

This chapter shall examine in detail the degree of salience accorded to the European Union in the Indian print media. It shall involve an elaborate quantitative and qualitative analysis of the news items mentioning the European Union which in turn shall enable the identification of major areas of engagement, issues of concern, the visibility of the EU in the Indian press as well as an assessment of the dimensions and aspects of the relationship.

The Relevance of Newspapers

Newspapers are considered to be one of the most important tools for feeling the pulse of a nation. It is also a conduit through which decision makers convey their standpoint on domestic and foreign policy.

The people of America became aware of important events taking place in other countries and foreign policy issues through discussions held on television or radio and also through newspapers and magazines. In the early years during the time of Thomas Jefferson, it was the newspapers that dominated the process with almost 200 newspapers in circulation. The ability of newspapers to spread information in a rapid and comprehensive manner has received a boost through the operation of specialised wire services such as the Associated Press (Ray 2013: 164).

Similarly, the study of contemporary Chinese foreign policy continues to rely on traditional research materials including printed sources which include newspapers, journals and books apart from interviews and opinion polls. The digital revolution has enabled editions of newspapers backed by powerful search engines become easily accessible. In addition to this, Chinese bulletin boards sponsored by newspapers are established sources for understanding with clarity about public attitudes towards Chinese foreign policy and attitudes towards other countries (Johnston 2006: 403-404).

There is a wide range of Russian perspectives on foreign policy that are reflected on various occasions in the "policy choices and direction of the Kremlin". The various hues of foreign policy interests appear in Russian newspapers and journals and get reflected in speeches made by policy-makers (Oliker, *et al.* 2009: 84). It has been reported that Russian foreign policy elites were more likely to read domestic newspapers in order to gain information about relevant domestic and international events (Zimmerman 2002: 25).

The standpoint and perceptions of political parties, pressure groups and the academic community in India is adequately reflected in the print and electronic media. The Indian dailies with mass circulation conduct opinion polls frequently and publish results along with the analysis. Despite the fact that these newspaper polls are largely confined to internet users, they provide a substantial statistical sample of public opinion on disparate issues of foreign policy (Bandyopadhyaya 2003: 129).

An independent judiciary and a thriving media buttress democratic institutions in India (Gaur 2005: 273). The history of the Indian print media is interspersed with India's struggle for freedom. It is popularly known as the fourth pillar of democracy. The liberty of the press has been duly safeguarded by the Indian Constitution. Newspapers are largely seen as perishable commodities with a shelf life of a day which necessitates that "news served is fresh, crisp and accessible everywhere". This line of thinking has taken over the old methods when most newspapers were family enterprises (Ranganathan and Rodrigues 2010: 53-54).The performance of the Indian print media draws a lot of attention from the developed world. This is due to the fact that the percentage of paid-for newspapers grew by 11.22 per cent in India in the year 2007 while at the same time it declined by 0.56 per cent in North America and by 2.37 per cent in Europe respectively. The World Association of News reported that Indian newspaper sales had increased by 35.51 per cent in five years from 2003 to 2007 (Ranganathan and Rodrigues 2010: 52).

Although, "the death of print, the rise of online, the rise of social media, smart phone and tablet penetration" cannot be denied as very visible trends, the print media is all set to grow in countries such as China, Brazil and India, unlike the markets in US and Europe. A total of 19 out of the top 100 dailies of the world are Indian which is less only to the Chinese dailies which are 25 in number. The newspapers in India have "operating margins upwards of 25 per cent" while the American newspapers make a profit hovering around 10 per cent. This establishes beyond doubt that the newspaper industry in India is bound to see happier days and shall make rapid strides towards greater demand and profits (Khandekar 2013: 1).

India is a land inhabited by more than 1.2 billion people who speak 18 major languages and 1600 regional dialects. This explains why India has the largest number of newspapers in the world. A total of 69,323 newspapers (English language-10,000, Hindi language- 27,527) were registered till 31 March 2008 with a circulation of 207,108,115(Government of India 2010). The aim of the current study has been to examine the perceptions of India about the EU through the lens of the newspapers. For all practicable reasons, three dailies were chosen for content analysis of articles mentioning the EU in the newspapers. These dailies came out at the top in each of the three categories chosen for the study. The three categories adopted for choice of newspapers for the study were English newspaper, Hindi newspaper and Business newspaper with the largest circulation respectively. The choice of newspapers with the largest circulation in each category ensured that the dataset would be the most representative and that reference was being made to newspapers which were considered to be authentic sources of information by the largest chunk of the population. The business newspaper category was included because economic cooperation forms the backbone of the relationship between international partners. The EU-India relationship is essentially understood as an economic relationship which rendered the inclusion of a business newspaper in the study to be indispensable. The Hindi and English newspaper categories were essentially included in the study as they happen to be the official languages of India. The knowledge of either or both languages is widely prevalent which would lead to a substantial database.

The business newspaper chosen for research was *The Economic Times* which is widely read with a readership of 757,000 (Livemint 2009). It provides a comprehensive view of economic and financial trends at home and abroad. In fact, the President of India Pranav Mukherjee who was also the Union Finance Minster in the previous UPA government is known to be an ardent fan of the newspaper which he has been reading every morning for many decades. *The Times of India* qualified under the English newspaper category and was recorded to have a total readership of 13,347,000 which has catapulted the daily to number one position in the category (Livemint 2009). *The Times of India* has a wide range of subscribers as it is a newspaper that has something for everyone and for people belonging to all ages. It has extensive coverage of news from across the world on all possible aspects. Therefore, it comes as no surprise that it is the most popular newspaper among the English speaking urban populace. The *Dainik Jagran* has been chosen under the Hindi newspaper category as it recorded readership amounting to a whopping 54,791,000 (Livement 2009). It is an immensely popular newspaper not only in rural areas but also in urban areas because this newspaper is not only read by those knowing Hindi but also by those who are bilingual. *Dainik Jagran* essentially concentrates on local and national news and politics which directly impact upon the lives of the readers which explains the most immediate and pertinent reason for the continuous subscription of this newspaper by the teeming multitudes in India.

Volume and Distribution of News Output

The three newspapers selected for the study contributed 944 news items altogether on the European Union in the time period of one year (1 July 2009 to 30 June 2010). The entire spread of EU news items shows that *The Economic Times* which is the business newspaper contributed 61 per cent of EU news items which indicates the relevance attached to the economic aspect of EU-India relations. The majority of news items totaling 577 in number were related to trade, business, finance, banking, competition laws and the Eurozone crisis which shows a marked preference for tracking EU-India relations in the economic sphere. *The Times of India*, the English newspaper, registered a 36 per cent contribution to the total dataset with 343 news items. Although the news focus was led by economic issues, the daily does provide an insight into other activities and involvement of the EU at home and abroad. It provides a holistic picture with focus on EU's participation in economic, political, social and environmental affairs. *The Times of India* tries to spice it up and believes in reporting on relevant and disparate issues in order to live up to its reputation of being the most popular English newspaper of India. The *Dainik Jagran* published a total of 24 new items which constitutes only 2.5 per cent of the total news items on the EU which clearly shows the obliteration of the EU from the radar of the Hindi newspaper. *Dainik Jagran* has a pointed focus upon tracking news as it happens in the Indian federal system. Thus, the newspaper enjoys the credibility of supplying authentic and detailed news pertaining to domestic and national level politics. It is out and out an inward looking newspaper. This becomes evident from the manner in which the reporting is done of the few news items totaling 24 in number that mention the EU. The local angle is never ignored when other regions of the world are examined. Almost every article tries to draw out a parallel or emphasise upon the connection between developments in the EU and its fallout on India or the strategy that should be pursued by India for safeguarding its interests in international politics (Figure 3.1).

Figure 3.1: Distribution of EU news among the three news outlets

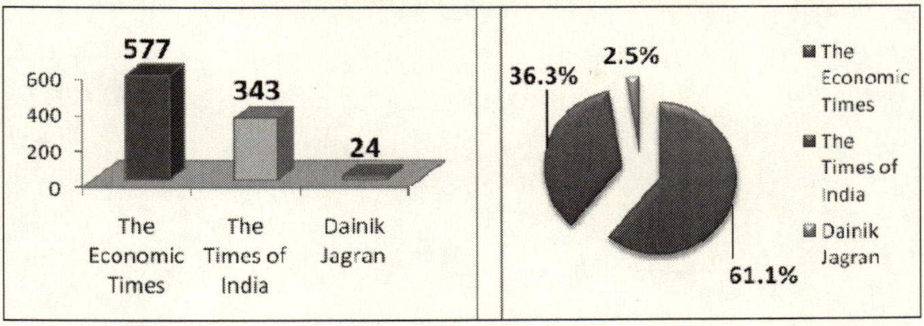

News Coverage on a Monthly Basis

The trajectory of monthly distribution of EU news over a period of one year reveals some patterns (Figure 2). We see news output in modest numbers in the first five months of the study from July to November (July-26, August-36, September-44, October-33, November-35). We suddenly see a spike in EU news items at the end of 2009 in December with 61 news items being reported owing to the global climate negotiations taking place at the Copenhagen Summit. There was a slump in January with only 47 EU news items finding a place in the coverage. In fact, this can alternatively be seen as reverting to the normal volume of EU news generated in the previous months. However, the months of February (90) March (80) and April (106) registered a dramatic increase in news items hovering around the century mark on account of concerns over the impending Eurozone crisis, increasing intensity of negotiations and controversies regarding EU-India FTA and trade and industry-related issues. The month of May (219) reported the highest volume of EU news items by far followed by the month of June (167) owing largely to the thickening of the eurozone crisis cloud. The unprecedented increase in volume of news in the last five months can largely be attributed to heightened concerns over the eurozone crisis and the contagion along with its likely fallout impacting India and the world at large.

Figure 3.2: Monthly Distribution of EU News among the Media Outlets

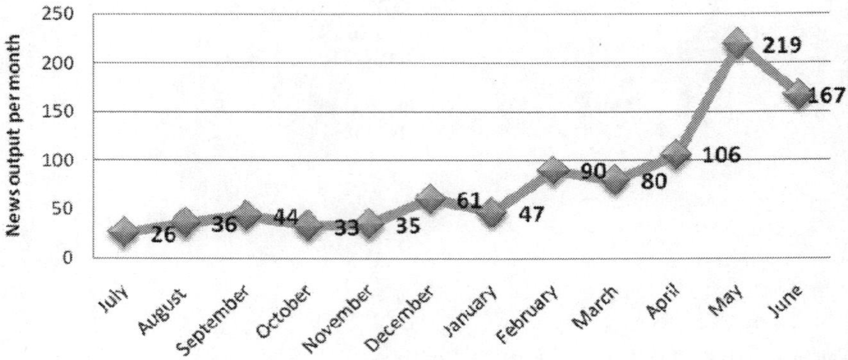

Out of the 26 EU news items reported in July, *The Economic Times* published 20 articles, 15 of which could be classified as news related to the economy. News related to various industries was reported. The likelihood of an increase in demand in the textile sector in India from the EU and the US was predicted (Koley and Ghosh 2 July 2009: 22). However, the non-availability of any major concessions in the budget for reviving the tottering textile industry of India was also pointed out (Mehta 7 July 2009). The conspiracy by the developed world to attack the sturdy domestic generic drug companies of the developing world as the former are no longer able to withstand competition also found space (Narendranath 28 July 2009: 13). The EU was also seen to be taking an aggressive stance as it threatened to take legal action against India at the WTO for imposing higher local taxes on imports than on domestic liquor (The Economic Times 18 July 2009:7). The Free Trade Agreement and comprehensive partnership with India along with the measures that India should adopt for increasing exports and the health of its economy were also discussed (Sen 2009: 11). *The Times of India* published 5 articles out of which 2 articles could be classified as environment related news while 3 of the articles were related to agriculture. The news items included the decision of the European Union to do away with the ban on the sale of twisted vegetables (The Times of India 1 July 2009: 23). The commitment of the US to GM crops as opposed to the cautious stand take by the EU was also taken up as an issue of debate (Bannerjee 20 July 2009: 9). Light was also thrown upon the issue of ensuring that temperature does not arise beyond 2 degree Celsius in order to check global warming (Bagchi 17 July 2009:11). The *Dainik Jagran* featured a solitary news item which highlighted the different opinions of countries of G-8 regarding the economic slowdown and measures to deal with it (Brajesh 11 July 2009: 10).

The month of August recorded a total news output of 36 news articles, 24 of which were reported in *The Economic Times* and they were predominantly related to the WTO ministerial meeting held in Delhi ahead of the Doha negotiations. Attempts were made towards forming a robust coalition at WTO (The Economic Times 19 August 2009: 9). Concentration on the technical aspects for successful conclusion of the Doha negotiations was duly recommended (The Economic Times 23 August 2009: 6). The European Commissioner for Trade was advocating for an increase in global trade by working towards the successful conclusion of the Doha round (The Economic Times 31 August 2009: 15). *The Times of India* published 11 news items on a mélange of issues. It included news items on political matters related to United States and China, Russia and Georgia, Sri Lanka and Afghanistan's presidential elections. It featured environmental news that touched upon climate change and energy-saving light bulbs. It also carried an article on an unconventional topic about conflicting claims that have been made over the country of origin of the chicken tikka masala in Scotland and the EU (The Times of India 6 August 2009: 17). *Dainik Jagran* published only one article on the European Union and talked about how the EU, Russia, Japan and India can help the United States in perpetuating its hegemony all over the world (Dainik Jagran 9 August 2009: 10).

The month of September reported a total of 44 news items out of which *The Economic Times* published 28 news items which amounted to slightly more than half of the total volume of coverage. There were 24 news items that carried information related to the economy. About 8 news items dealt with trade and a majority of them were based on the World Trade Organisation. Attempts were made at the mini-ministerial held in Delhi for ending the bitterness in Doha negotiations (The Economic Times 2 September 2009: 9). It was reported that although the ministerial took forward the Doha agenda, a lot more requires to be done (Pant 11 September 2009: 12). The role of the developing countries and their willingness for favourable results was also emphasised upon (The Economic Times 21 September 2009: 7). There were 8 news pieces that dealt with business and finance in general and competition laws in particular. There were 7 news items published under the category of environmental affairs. They generally dealt with climate change and global warming. There was a debate regarding limiting the increase in global temperature to 2 degrees Celsius, as promised by the European Union and the G-8 as it would cost a phenomenal 12.9 per cent of GDP by the end of the century (Lomborg 3 September 2009:14).

The Times of India published 13 news items on the EU. A total of 4 news items related to political affairs were published. They dealt with presidential elections in Afghanistan, Syria and the occupation of Golan Heights and concerns over the making of the atom bomb in Iran. Ending all forms of discrimination (Mitta 28 September 2009: 11) and drafting of a new technical standard to limit the volume of mobile music players were the social issues that were dealt with in the three news items on the EU (The Times of India 29 September 2009: 14). Only 3 news items talked about economic affairs and they mainly dealt with the proceedings at the WTO. Environmental news appeared in 4 news items that put forth the standpoints taken by different countries on climate change. It was reported that the US had to take back its threat of blocking UN negotiations on climate change in the wake of the pressure exerted by the G-77 countries

(Sethi 30 September 2009:17).The EU had clarified that it would be unwilling to provide funds for mitigating the effects of climate change to India and other emerging economies (Sethi 12 September 2009: 10). Indian plans to introduce legislation for guarding against green house gas emissions also found spotlight (Sethi 12 September 2009: 10).

The month of October reported a total of 33 news items. *The Economic Times* dealt with 17 news items out of which the lion's share of 14 news items dealt with economic affairs. A total of 9 news pieces dealt with issues of business and finance related to competition laws. The EU raids of the French unit of India's largest pharmaceutical company were reported in this regard (The Economic Times 8 October 2009: 7). In other news in the same category, it was made clear that the EU reserves the right to place limits on the prices charged by mobile phone companies for protecting the internal mobile market (The Economic Times 2 October 2009: 8). The efforts of the EU at making the "filing of private damages actions for compensation in law courts easier" also found space (The Economic Times 3 October 2009:14). A mêlée of events were reported in the 15 news items that appeared in *The Times of India*. The news on the economic front appeared in 5 news items and mainly dealt with competition laws and taxes on foreign investment. A total of 4 news items on political affairs were reported. They dealt with the Iranian nuclear issue, Lisbon Reform Treaty and the question of accession of Ukraine into the European Union. The issues discussed under the category of social affairs in three news pieces included immigration of Indian workers to Europe apart from piracy and trafficking of drugs. A total of 3 news items on Copenhagen climate change negotiations were reported. A possible dilution of India's stand on the UN Framework Convention on Climate Change was also highlighted as an area of discussion and debate (Sethi 19 October 2009:10). The *Dainik Jagran* also chose to flag environmental concerns in the single news item mentioning the EU which appeared this month. It called for not giving in to the wishes of the developed world at the Copenhagen summit (Gupta 31 October 2009: 10).

The volume of news output in November was 35 articles in all. A total of 19 articles were published in *The Economic Times*. The news mainly emanated from the textile, pharmaceutical and liquor industry. There was also reporting on the possibility of further delay in the EU-India Free Trade Agreement on account of the consideration of extraneous issues by the EU (The Economic Times 6 November 2009: 9).The issue of a possible economic recovery in the Euro]one was mulled over and the continuance of stimulus measures in the economy was advocated (The Economic Times 16 November 2009: 1). As far as environmental affairs are concerned, a couple of articles were published that saw less scope for an agreement between the developed and developing countries at the last round of negotiations in Barcelona ahead of the Copenhagen summit in December (The Economic Times 2 November 2009: 3).Only one, but very relevant, EU news item relating to political affairs appeared this month. It was stated that the filling up of the post of the new foreign policy chief of the EU is proving to be problematic (Castle 16 November 2009: 1). A solitary news item about social affairs talked about Indian companies joining the wellness brigade in line with health initiatives being taken all over the world (Sen 8 November 2009: 8). *The Times of India* published 16 news items in all. There were 5 economy related news items that talked about economic recovery, competition laws and the settlement of anti-trust and patent disputes (The Times of India 13 November 2009: 22). The news in the political domain largely emanated from Europe. The Lisbon Reform Treaty, twenty years of the fall of Berlin Wall, and election of the European President were discussed in the 4 news items related to politics. A couple of news items related to the environment talked about the proposition of imposition of a carbon tax to ensure adherence to the rules of carbon emission reduction (Parashar 30 November 2009: 11). The issue of piracy featured in 2 news items under the category of social affairs (The Times of India 18 November 2009: 25).

The month of December saw EU news coverage rise to a total of 61 news items. *The Economic Times* published a total of 34 news items. The economic news was dealt with in 19 new items and covered a wide range of topics such as unemployment, banking, WTO, anti-monopoly cases, rise in steel prices and duty on wine and liquor. The environment news figured in 14 news items. The biggest climate talks in history taking place in Copenhagen were subjected to extensive coverage as there was widespread hope that a deal to combat climate change was very much possible (Cowan and Fogarty 8 December 2009). There was a single news item on politics dealing with the US and EU ban on arms exports to China following the Tiananmen Square incident in 1989 (Kondapalli 20 December 2009: 11).*The Times of India* covered a total of 22 news items. The political news, 8 in number largely emanated from Israel, Balochistan, Myanmar and discussed EU's outreach programme with India and EU as a model for South Asian Unity. The economic news figured in 4 articles. It mainly dealt with banking and finance news such as the decision of the ECB to offer an unlimited one-year loan to Eurozone banks in order to check speculative borrowing (The Times of India 16 December 2009: 26). A total of 7 news items covered environment-related news. These articles basically focused upon the Copenhagen summit, UN climate talks, climate change and European Emissions Trading Scheme and Carbon-free Congress in the Czech Republic. Only 2 news items dealt with social affairs. One of them talked about the attempt at funding violent attacks against the Swedish PM and Parliament (The Times of India 3 December 2009: 19) while the other talked about a possible withdrawal of money by Muslims from Swiss banks over a referendum vote that banned the construction of minarets in the country (The Times of India 26 December 2009: 18). *Dainik Jagran* reported 5 news items in all out of which 4 focused upon Copenhagen summit talks.

The month of January saw the reporting of 47 news items in all. A total of 28 news items on the EU were covered in *The Economic Times* out of which 22 articles referred to economic matters. The first month of the year reiterated the importance attached to the economic element of EU-India relations. At least 10 news items referred to various industries such as pharmaceuticals, wheat exports, agro-chemical and seafood industry. Commenting on the state of the economy, it was reported that the West would in all likelihood witness a recovery in 2010 (Sruthijith 25 January 2010:1). The news items covering environmental affairs were inclusive of the issues of climate change, global warming, carbon emission reduction commitments, Copenhagen and its aftermath. *The Times of India* reported 19 news items on EU in all out of which 7 were related to political affairs. The role of the EU in global politics was showcased in articles based on themes such as the global balance of power, projecting the EU in the external world, visit of EU Delegation to the site of ethno-communal clashes and the Istanbul meeting on Afghanistan. There was less emphasis on the economic role of the EU this month with only 4 news items being reported on a couple of topics that included the Eurozone crisis (Krugman 12 January 2010: 18) and the EU-ASEAN Trade respectively (The Times of India 15 January 2010: 19). The news items on social affairs although six in number, included within its umbrella a number of issues of current concern such as health care, education, gender parity, crime and privacy of the individual. There was a single news item dealing with the environment that talked about the EU project called Safe Road Trains for the Environment (The Times of India 5 January 2010: 19).

The month of February registered an output of 90 news items which was almost the double of news items reported in January. *The Economic Times* published a total of 62 news items out of which 25 articles focused on the state of economy that reflected concern over the performance of the Eurozone economies. The industry-related news was discussed in eight news items and it dealt with palm oil, shipping, sugar, steel, floriculture, textiles and the information and technology sectors. Trade-related news amounting to 13 in number mainly focused upon EU-India FTA apart from dealing with EU's trade relations with Turkey and a major slump in exports. The theme of politics was dealt with only in three news items hovering around the Indian-subcontinent. The discussion was mainly about the Af-Pak policy, withdrawal of troops from Afghanistan and peace in Pakistan and neighbouring areas. There were four news items based on environmental affairs. They dealt with disparate themes such as carbon tax imports from advanced developing countries, green fashion and energy saving ICT devices. The news items related to social affairs totaled three in number and covered disparate themes such as privacy rights of European citizens, the mutual opening up of the educational sector in Hungary and India and Turkey as a fetching tourist destination. *The Times of India* reported a total of 25 news items out of which 15 news articles dealt with economy-related news. About eight articles dabbled with the issue of the state of economy. Industry-related news was reported in only three articles that confined themselves to discussing developments in the poultry, textile, steel and tyre sectors. About four news items that dealt with business and finance related news discussed mergers, acquisitions, competition laws and protectionist policy for labour in the US and EU. Political news was published in five news items and it mainly dealt with EU news with an inward focus such as creation of a European army, the vote of the European Parliament against transferring bank data to the US, collapse of the Dutch coalition government and parleys between EU leaders. The news volume related to social affairs amounted to a total of 4 news items. Apart from discussing themes such as crime and immigration, special emphasis was laid upon the news from the education sector. Hence, global cooperation for higher learning and quality control across universities found mention

(The Times of India 15 February 2010: 41).The only news item that touched upon environmental affairs discussed the politics surrounding the role and office of the UN panel chief (Sethi 19 February 2010: 16). *Dainik Jagran* with its India centric focus discussed issues such as the complexities involved in acquisition of weapons by states, the dubious role of Pakistan in international affairs and India's attempts to check cheap exports from China.

The month of March reported a total of 80 news items on the EU and the lion's share was reported by *The Economic Times*. It reported 52 news articles in all out of which 46 were economy-related news items. The state of economy was discussed in 19 articles. The news items mainly voiced concern about the eurozone crisis and the value of the euro (The Economic Times 26 March 2010: 21). A total of 14 news items related to various industries such as pharmaceuticals, civil aviation, insurance, handicrafts, textiles, software, telecom and automobile were reported. Trade-related news was reported in eight news items out of which seven dealt with EU-India FTA. The differences between EU and India over the inclusion of new and contentious issues in the negotiations were reported (The Economic Times 5 March 2010: 17). A total of five news items related to business and finance were reported and concerned themselves with measures to improve and expand EU trade through harmonisation of non-tariff rules, trading in currency futures and the creation of a European Monetary Fund. Only two news items dealt with political affairs. The first article dealt with the EU decision of denying tariff-free entry to Sri Lankan textile goods into the EU (Mehta 5 March 2010: 16) while the second article talked about EU role's in ensuring better representation of emerging and developing countries in the G-20 (Sapir 22 March 2010: 13). There were two news items related to gender parity and immigration reported under the category of social affairs. The volume of environment-related news was very less this month. Only a couple of news related to the impact of GM foods (Aggarwal 8 March 2010: 14) and the race for the UN's top climate change job were reported (The Economic Times 16 March 2010:2). *The Times of India* chose to examine the political angle of economic issues such as the reform of Bretton Woods institutions, the global extension of balance of power and the existence of multipolarity which reflects the desire on the part of the EU to retain its sway and position in international affairs. About four articles also discussed the presence and role of the EU in Nepal, Sri Lanka, Israel and Spain. The news items related to social affairs dealt with a plethora of issues such as gender parity, immigration, multiculturalism, art, culture, sports, education, human rights and crime. A total of eight news items related to the economy were published. Half of the news items catered to trade-related affairs while the other half dealt with news items based on the state of economy with one item catering to the expansion of trade in the EU.

The month of April registered the volume of news output to be at 106. *The Economic Times* published 54 news items out of which 42 news items catered to the economy. Half of the economic news items dealt with the issue of the state of the economy. A total of eight news items dealt with the medicine, pharmaceutical, civil aviation, poultry, textile and steel industries. The news items focused on EU-India FTA while others focused on countervailing duties (Sen 26 April 2010: 13), anti-subsidy duties (The Economic Times, 15 April 2010:11) and trade barriers (Sen 14 April 2010: 11) that have an adverse impact upon EU-India trade. There were four news items emanating from the area of business and finance. The coverage included issues such as investment in mobile industry, competition laws, IT outsourcing and International Financial Reporting Standards. There were three news items on political affairs that were reported which included coverage of the Nuclear Security Summit (The Economic Times 5 April 2010: 2), the shift in global economic power (Chaudhuri 13 April 2010: 12) and the spat between Gujarat Chief Minister Narendra Modi and delegation of German parliamentarians (Ganapathy 17 April

2010:2). The environment news was reported in seven news items and they solely focused on negotiations and bargaining taking place on climate change among various actors in the post-Copenhagen atmosphere. A couple of news items about social affairs were reported. They were essentially about immigration into Europe. *The Times of India* reported a total of 49 news items in all out of which 22 news items were economy-related. News related to the Eurozone crisis featured in a total of 10 news items. A total of nine news items were industry-related and featured the aviation, pharmaceutical, steel and gambling sectors. A couple of news items on trade talked about WTO and Russian export taxes on wood (The Times of India 16 April 2010: 24) and a single news items related to business dealing with laws governing service providers was featured (Lohia 12 April 2010: 14). A total of 14 politics-based news items were reported. Political news about the external world featured news about aspersions on Modi, the EU's role in world affairs, Polish-Russian relations, Somali pirates, enhancing nuclear security and Pakistani Prime Minister's visit to Europe. Internal news within the EU included the role of Kaczynski brothers in Polish politics, the death of the Polish President in a jet crash in Russia, roadmap for dealing with volcanic ash, British elections and rift between Sarkozy and his female ministers. A total of four news items on the environment were reported. A couple of news items talked about new safety standards related to electromagnetic radiation and discussed the conflict over Kyoto Protocol. There was talk about the Meat-free Monday campaign in EU which would encourage one meat-free day per week to reduce carbon emissions (Sharma 22 April 2010: 38). It was reported that a global shortage of cricket bats is likely to happen on account of the EU directive to outlaw "before export the chemical methyl bromide" which is used for treating the wood used for making bats because it damages the ozone layer (The Times of India 17 April 2010: 30). A total of nine news items on social affairs were reported. They were about introduction of courses on EU and German laws in India, a device to check blood clotting levels, ban on veil, mass-market GPS, immigration and tighter visa norms. *Dainik Jagran* published three news items and they covered the area of diplomacy and news about the aviation and tourism industry.

The month of May recorded the largest bounty of news items, which amounted to 219 articles. *The Economic Times* published a total of 130 news items. The predominance of economic news especially pertaining to the Eurozone is evident in the news spread which shows that 122 articles reported in *The Economic Times* dealt with economic news out of which 81 news items specifically delved upon the state of the economy. The news from the business and finance section basically consisted of elements aiming at damage control in the wake of the Eurozone crisis such as regulating hedge funds in Europe, the impact of credit rating agencies, monetary policy tightening and bailout of Eurozone banks. A total of 19 news items were reported from the industry sector, eight of which dealt with pharmaceuticals, while poultry, chocolate, agri-business, seafood, plastic, tea, sugar and carpets were the other sectors covered. Trade related news items, 11 in all, mainly reported news on the India-EU FTA. A total of three news items related to political affairs were reported. They mainly stressed upon the virtues of unity and leadership for external influence and the relevance and utility of economic and political integration in international affairs. Similarly, environment-related news formed a miniscule part of the total coverage with only four news items reported on Petersburg Climate Dialogue, equitable sharing of carbon space, hazardous wastes and energy efficiency. A sole news item related to tourism was reported under the category of social affairs. *The Times of India* reported a total of 81 news items out which a major portion, totaling 57 new items, reported economic news. A total of 51 news items out of 57 were related to the state of the economy reflecting upon the Eurozone crisis. A meagre five industry-related news items dealing with pharmaceuticals, aviation, textiles and steel were reported. A total of 12 news items related to politics were reported. The news emanating from outside the EU included events such as shootout involving Russian ships, pressure upon the Nepal king to quit, selling of arms to Sri Lanka and Chinese perceptions about the EU. The political news emanating from within the EU included reforming air-traffic control system, the French-German scuffle over Greece, the need to cultivate close economic and political relations among EU member-states, British foreign policy and British elections. A total of three news items were reported under the bracket of environmental affairs and they predominantly discussed different dimensions of climate negotiations. News related to social affairs appeared in eight news items and they mainly dealt with the theme of education, research, science and technology. Thus, the issues of global positioning system, saving digital data, fibre-based packaging, EU-China joint venture for funding education centres and awards for development journalism found mention. A total of eight news items were reported in *Dainik Jagran* and all of them analysed and commented upon the Eurozone crisis.

The month of June reported a total of 167 news items out of which 109 were published by *The Economic Times*. A total of 95 news items reported were related to economic affairs and a major chunk of the articles, 69 in all, dealt with the state of the economy. Half a dozen news items discussed issues related to business and finance which included the EU transaction tax, trade unions, auditing and the expansion of the Royal Bank of Scotland. The concerns at WTO and the decline of exports were the themes discussed in six news items related to trade. There were five news items that featured environmental news of which climate change negotiations and an emission reduction pact formed the crux of the discussion. There were five news items reporting on political affairs and they covered news emanating from different regions of the world such as Sri Lanka, Gulf of

Aden, Israel, Turkey and Zimbabwe. Health, immigration and crime were the broad themes discussed as part of social affairs news in the four news articles that were reported. Industry-related news totaled 14 in number and reported news about sugar, pharmaceuticals, IT industry, automobile, horticulture, basmati rice exports, insurance, shipping and agro-based products. *The Times of India* reported a total of 58 news items out of which 38 news items dealt with the economy. There was a predominant coverage of the Eurozone economic crisis in this segment as 36 news items revolved around this topic. There were 10 news items that carried news related to politics. All news items dealt with the role of the EU in the external world and reported news about EU-Russia relations, EU-India relations, China-Pakistan nuclear cooperation, Turkey's bid to become part of EU, investment in Sri Lanka, sanctions on Iran and monitoring of peace in Gaza. News items relating to social affairs were seven in number and they covered news about migration to Europe, visa-free policy for Indians, gender equality, launching of IR courses with emphasis on EU and crisis management through visual analytics. There were only three news items pertaining to the environment and they dealt with varied issues that included banning of sex-toys by the EU, energy efficiency through green IT and saving bluefin tuna. *Dainik Jagran* did not carry any news item on the EU.

Sources of News

It is imperative to examine the sources of EU articles that appear in the three newspapers (Figure 3.3). The entire dataset reveals that not less than 301 (31.8 per cent) articles were procured from international sources. The local sources contributed 506 (53.6 per cent) articles on the EU. There were 137 (14.5 per cent) articles that found space in the newspapers sans any information about the source. It is indeed an encouraging trend that 85.4 per cent of the news items duly specified the source of reporting. This in turn leads to confirmation of credibility of the news items being published in the newspapers. The Indian print media seems to have begun the process of harnessing news from international sources in order to give the readers an authentic and holistic view of news emanating from the EU. Tapping international sources also means extra costs which they have started to bear. This hints at a positive trend attached to EU-India relations by the editors of the newspapers who pay for the news and are willing to give space to such news items. The local sources of EU news items appear much more frequently in the dataset and reflect a constantly growing interest in the affairs of the EU in India. It reflects familiarity with the EU that is being gradually cultivated among the local contributors of news as well as amongst the readership of the newspapers. This trend also suggests attempts made by the print media to take the help of the local contributors to make EU news India-relevant and explain events taking place in the EU within the overall context of EU-India relations. However, EU news items that appear without a source are a reflection of the lackadaisical attitude towards EU-India affairs wherein newspapers publish news from the EU as a necessary evil or for filling up space in the economy or international page. It also reflects a lack of perseverance and tenacity to inquire about the source of news items. In such cases, only coverage matters and not the dissemination of news from a trustworthy source. However, the silver lining is that news items without an affiliation to a source form a small percentage of the total coverage of the EU. Besides, such articles are very short and generally seem to be used as fillers compared to articles that have a credible source of information. Therefore, they do not necessarily militate against the avid interest of the reader in EU-India affairs for want of precise and authentic information.

Figure 3.3: Sources of EU News

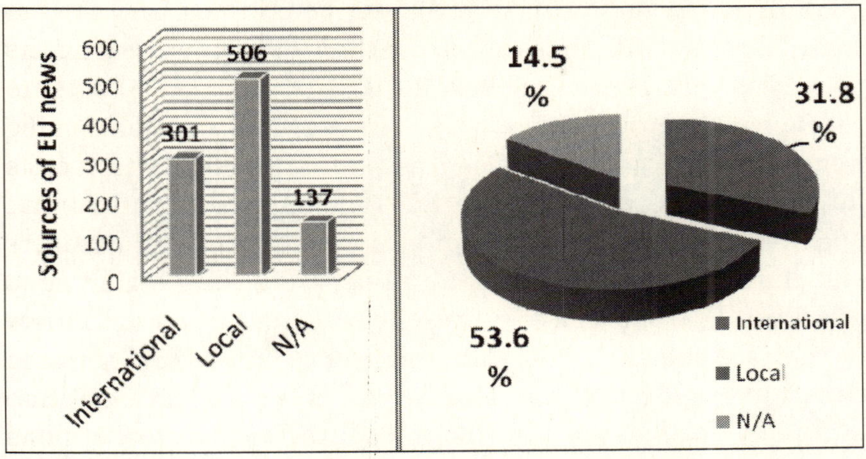

International wires are a major source of information related to the EU. Global media wires are in fact a quintessential part of the global communication network. The expansion of the global economy has led to the simultaneous expansion of international wires. The wire services had an interesting history which began with focus on news emanating from the colonial powers. Thus it comes as no surprise that the three major global news wires namely, Thomson Reuters, Associated Press and Agence France Presse were initially based and operated from London, New York and France respectively. Reuters and the Associated Press have established themselves as gigantic entities in the business of reporting news around the world. They have a large share of the business in television news reporting and have huge interest in online reporting apart from the comfortable lead that they enjoy in print-based journalism. AFP enjoys the distinction of spreading its network to almost every nook and corner of the world and it brings to the table the most extensive coverage of news especially from parts of Asia, Africa and the Middle East. The coverage of Bloomberg essentially revolves around economic news and includes within its purview financial markets, business, technology, global stock markets and trends (McPhail 2010: 274-

283). The New York Times News Service provides daily articles from The New York Times and more than 30 partner newspapers (The New York Times Company 2014).

Reuters contributed a total of 108 (44.08 per cent) news items and emerged as the leading international media service for news items related to the EU. This comes as no surprise because Reuters has consolidated its hold over Britain's erstwhile colonies because of its all-pervading and highly rated services. The overbearing presence of Reuters is testimony to the fact that it becomes increasingly difficult for India to extricate itself from the colonial construct and Anglo-Saxon attitudes. This has led to formation of skewed and stereotypical impressions about European affairs in India. The AP supplied 37 (15.1 per cent) and AFP 29 (11.83 per cent) news items respectively. Bloomberg and the New York Times News Service were responsible for reporting 26 (10.6 per cent) and 14 (5.71 per cent) stories respectively (Figure 3.4). Reliance on Bloomberg has been for the obvious, which is due to the over-emphasis upon the economic aspect of EU-India relations in the reportage. New York Times News Service has emerged as a significant contributor and it is known to be constantly gaining currency in the Indian media industry (The New York Times Company 2014). A total of 105 news items in this study on the EU were reported by international correspondents and contributors.

Figure 3.4: Distribution of International Sources of News

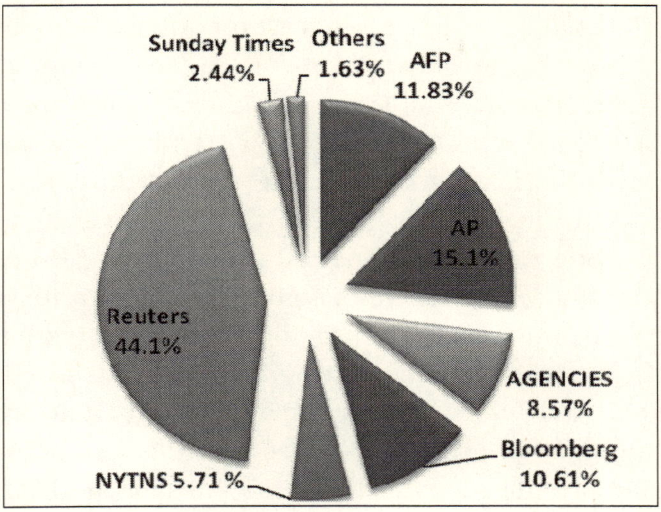

The Press Trust of India is India's premier news agency which was established after a couple of years of India's independence in 1949. PTI's reach extends to almost all districts and towns in India with 400 journalists and 500 stringers working under its roll. PTI correspondents are also based in various capitals and business and administrative centres around the world. PTI is recognised to command 90 per cent of the news agency market share in India. President K R Narayanan had remarked on the occasion of completion of 50 years of PTI that "we got independence in August 1947. But independence in news and information we got only with the establishment of PTI in 1949. That is the significance of PTI..." (Press Trust of India 2014). The Press Trust of India contributed a total of 24 (12.37 per cent) news items on the EU. It was the only significant local news wire utilised by *The Economic Times* and *The Times of India*. *The Economic Times* chose to make use of its own wire, resources and manpower and therefore a total of 52 (26.80 per cent) news items were attributed to The Economic Times Bureau, ET Now and ET Bureau. Similarly, *The Times of India* did not rely on any other local news wire and solely depended upon its own team of journalists and stringers who contribute to the news output and were alternatively known as Times News Network, Team Times of India and Times Insight Group. A total of 112 (57.73 per cent) news items were reported by the local wire of *The Times of India* (Figure 3.5). *Dainik Jagran* is also known to make use of its sources for reporting. However, our dataset shows only one news item reported by the Jagran Bureau. It is interesting to note that EU news items in *Dainik Jagran* show the Press Trust of India as the source of EU news items for almost half of the total news items reported which tends to reflect the reliance of *Danik Jagran* on a national news wire. It does not seek news from other international wires and seems to be in favour of swadeshi or indigenous instruments at its disposal. The other half of news items are reported by local correspondents and not even a single international contributor's article appears in the newspaper. A total of 364 news items on the EU were reported by local correspondents and contributors in the three newspapers.

Figure 3.5: Distribution of Local sources of EU news

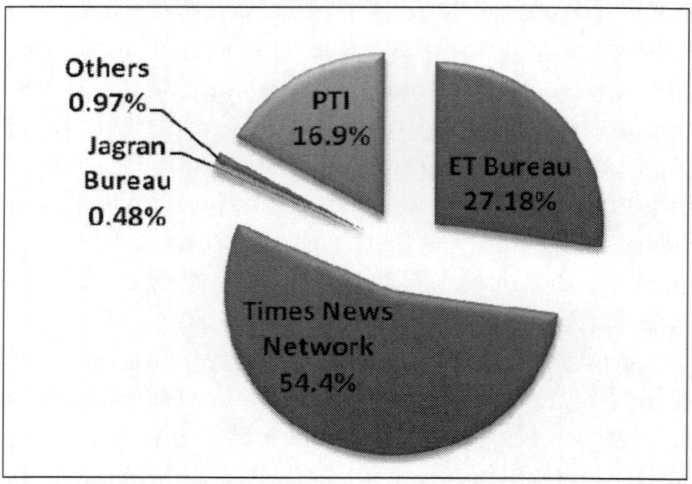

Not less than 137 (14.5 per cent) of the news items fall under the N/A category. It refers to those news items that have been reported without any mention of the correspondent or news wire responsible for contributing the news. This automatically gives way to skepticism in the mind of the reader who expects a credible source to be mentioned for a news item that she takes the pain of reading. A number of news items about the EU have been published without mentioning the source which further contributes in diminishing the interest of the Indian reader in EU affairs. This no doubt reflects the lethargy and lackadaisical view of the newspapers regarding international news. The effort seems to be wanting in tapping credible and authentic sources of international news that are easily available and accessible. Such an attitude smacks of the extreme degree of confidence and complacency in the marketability of these three newspapers. They are keenly aware of the segment of the population that they are catering to and they are tenaciously holding on to it as years of experience have demonstrated ways and means for keeping their readership intact. Unfortunately, retaining and increasing interest in the affairs of the European Union does not seem to be part of the priority list of these newspapers. These newspapers seem to cater to the curiosity generated among the people through television and they simply satiate the appetite of the readers by solely focusing upon and reporting on problems which are essentially local and national in nature. For instance, it is not surprising to find national and international news clubbed together on the same page and thus even a single whole page is not dedicated to international news. Such attitudes lead to less attention being paid to the coverage of international news in general and EU news in particular.

Local Sources

A decisive tilt towards local sources of news items on the EU across the three newspapers was observed (Figure 3.6). *The Economic Times* has 312 (54 per cent) news items in all emanating from local sources. As many as 247 news items on the EU were reported by local correspondents or contributors and 64 news articles were reported by local news wires in *The Economic Times* newspaper. Local sources registered a share of 171(49.8 per cent) news items in its coverage of EU news in *The Times of India*. The coverage included 42 news items reported by local correspondents and 65 news articles reported by local news wires. There were another 64 news items where both the local correspondent and the local news wire were mentioned. *Dainik Jagran* relied heavily on local sources and 22 (91.6 per cent) news items were reported on the EU. A total of 10 news items on the EU were reported by local correspondents and 12 news items were reported by local news wires. These local correspondents or contributors of articles and news pieces include journalists, stringers, area-experts, academicians, environmentalists, activists, editors, politicians, businessmen and columnists.

Figure 3.6: Distribution of Sources of EU News across the Three Newspapers

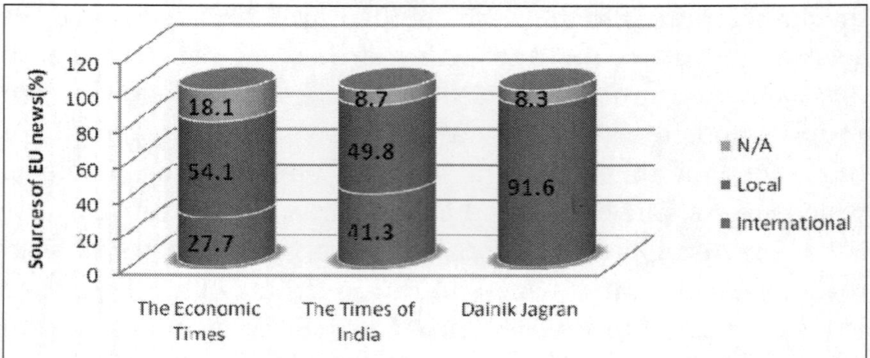

International Sources

The international sources of news items on the EU contributed 160 (27.7 per cent) news items on the EU in *The Economic Times*. International news wires contributed a total of 82 news items on the EU while the international correspondents reported a total of 45 news items. This indicates that *The Economic Times* despite being India's leading business newspaper is more interested in the perspective of India about global business rather than in a direct account of overseas affairs and business which it can readily access and make available to its audience. This reflects an inward-looking attitude of the newspaper which can be detrimental towards fathoming the real business sentiments in the rest of the world if there is overly dependence upon local wires and correspondents about news emanating from across the borders and beyond.

The Times of India reported a total of 142 (41.39 per cent) news items on EU affairs. A total of 115 news items were reported by international wires and 12 news items were reported by international correspondents respectively. A total of 15 news items mentioned both the international wire as well as the name of the international correspondent contributing the news item on the EU. *The Times of India* largely caters to the English speaking urban population that has a great degree of familiarity with all things foreign and most of them nurture ambitions to settle abroad. There is a widely felt need for keeping up with the latest trends in lifestyle and fashion apart from keeping abreast with international economic and political affairs. Therefore, in order to fulfill the need to cater to both the interested and compulsive cosmopolitan Indian who is or aspires to be a globe trotter, *The Times of India* reports a decent percentage of news coming from international sources.

The *Dainik Jagran* exhibited a decisive tilt and preference towards local sources of news and in the process chose to do away entirely with the option of using international sources of news items which consequently leaves the largest readership of India which is essentially the Hindi speaking population, completely deprived of the international perspective and news and information about the EU.

N/A (No Source Mentioned)

A total of 137 (14.51 per cent) news items reported in the newspapers fall under the N/A category. *The Economic Times* leads the tally with 105 (18.19 per cent) of the news items that have no source mentioned. *The Times of India* and *Dainik Jagran* reported 30 (8.74 per cent) and two (8.33 per cent) news items respectively under this category. This category of news items tends to leave the reader clueless as to from where the news is emanating which sows seeds of uncertainty in the mind of the reader regarding the authenticity of the news item and often a wholesome picture of the event or the issue is unable to take shape. Most of the news items under the N/A category tend to deal with the performance of markets, currency movements in the stock exchange markets and are generally fact-based with a miniscule degree of analysis.

Focus of Domesticity

It is important to investigate the focus of domesticity of the news items in order to know the area, the region or country from which the news item has originated. The study of the dataset reveals that news originating from the EU (EU focus) amount to 247 (26.1 per cent) of the total news items. News originating from India or local in nature (local focus) contributed 490 (51.9 per cent) of the news items while news reported from countries other than India and EU (third country focus) comprised of 207 (21.92 per cent) of the total news items.

The Economic Times – EU news

A total of 132 (22.8 per cent) EU news items were reported in *The Economic Times* (Figure 3.7). They were solely concerned with what was happening within the European Union. On the economic front, the decision of the EU to raise imports of palm oil from tropical rain forests was reported (The Economic Times 12 February 2010: 20). An increase in wheat exports in the European Union found mention in the newspaper. (The Economic Times 27 January 2010: 14). The ash cloud from the Icelandic volcano that spread across Europe and caused the biggest air travel chaos since the September 11 attacks was widely reported (The Economic Times 18 April

2010: 5). A number of concerns were voiced regarding the increase in unemployment rate in the EU (The Economic Times 29 April 2010:23) and the deteriorating government credit quality in the EU in the context of the Eurozone crisis (Biggadike 23 June 2010: 16). The proposed cut in stimulus measures and giving austerity a thrust to ensure the easy bailout of debt-ridden countries were one of the main issues of debate and discussion (The Economic Times 9 June 2010: 15). The hype around the sovereign debt crisis was seen to be building up during this month (Sen 29 March 2010: 13). The EU was seen to be vigilant regarding consumer rights and also for protecting its internal mobile market against cheap imports (The Economic Times 12 February 2010: 15). The imminent merger of the nationalised Deutsche Bank and ABN Amro banks enjoyed the spotlight (Jagannathan 24 February 2010: 11). The ECB was pitted to play a huge role in recovering from the Eurozone crisis. The ECB made attempts to garner more information from banks regarding the collateral that they give the ECB in return for loans (The Economic Times 25 June: 2). The EU tried to free its economy from non-transparent standards pertaining to hedge funds that enter the region and have been considered to be one of the major reasons for unfolding of the Eurozone crisis (Azhar and Ullatil 18 May 2010: 19). The internal politics of the EU was concerned with lobbying over the choice of a new EU President and Foreign Minister in anticipation of the approval of the Lisbon Treaty in the near future (The Economic Times 6 August 2009 :7). The social affairs news talked about a number of issues including public health, controlling crime and cultivation of genetically modified crops. The European Union sought to minimise hearing loss by imposing tough standards to be complied with by the music industry (The Economic Times 29 September 2009). The European Parliament categorically denied sharing information about bank transfers aimed at tracking people suspected of being terrorists (Kanter 13 February 2010: 8). It was reported that member-states of the European Union would be left free to take the decision on the question of cultivation of new GM varieties of crops (The Economic Times 5 June 2010:9). The EU news emanating from the environmental sphere mainly dealt with the Copenhagen climate negotiations and its aftermath. This segment of news included attempts made by the EU to resuscitate its influence and credibility on the international stage on environmental issues. For instance, the EU pledged an annual endowment to the world's poorer countries in order to jolt the Copenhagen climate negotiations back to life apart from trying to raise targets for cutting emissions within a decade (The Economic Times 10 December 2009:6).

Figure 3.7: Focus of Domesticity

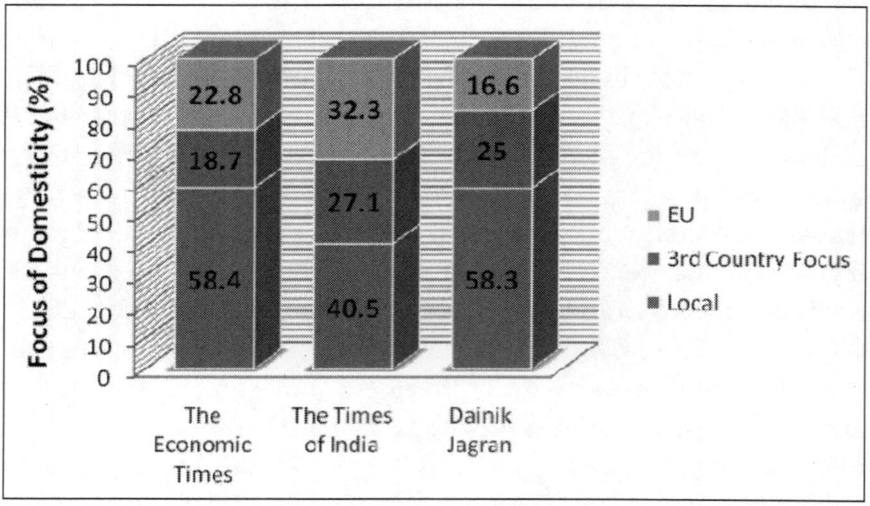

The Economic Times – Third Country News

The performance of the EU as part of the international system and in other parts of the world has been categorised as news with a third country focus and such news found coverage in a total of 108 (18.7 per cent) news items. The majority of the news items refer to the EU's role in the world rather than in a particular country. Therefore, reference to the EU appears in news items that reflect the concern of the world at large. This was seen in the case of reportage about the price of gold and oil in world markets in the wake of the Eurozone crisis. The world at large expressed its concerns regarding the value of the euro currency. The world was majorly consumed with the Copenhagen climate negotiations and talks that followed immediately in order to salvage the situation by reaching a consensus in which the EU played a vital role. The political sphere discussed the potential political role of the major powers including the EU in reforming the Bretton Woods Institutions so that it is able to meet the current challenges confronting the global economy (Sapir 22 March 2010: 13). European Union's engagement was also witnessed in other parts of the world such as United States, China, East Asia, Sri Lanka, Myanmar and SAARC. EU participated in decision-making and implementation through many international fora such as OECD, BASIC, WTO, MEFs, G8 and G20.

The Economic Times – Local News

The local news refers to news about the EU emanating locally from India. A total of 337 (58.4 per cent) local news about the EU was reported in *The Economic Times*. The major portion of news reported belonged to the economic sphere with a total of 303 news items (89.9 per cent). The Eurozone crisis and its impact upon India were reported in a total of 120 news articles. Trade-related articles, 75 news articles in all, mainly dealt with the negotiations taking place in the context of EU-India Free Trade Agreement. The news items relating to the industrial sector reported a total of 83 news articles out of which 25 news items reported about the pharmaceutical sector. The articles mainly dealt with issues of large scale seizures of drug consignments from India made by the EU (Dutta 14 August 2009: 7). Textiles, automobile, steel, software industry, liquor, sugar and poultry were the other industries that formed part of the coverage in the context of EU-India relations. The news items related to business and finance mainly dealt with banking, exports, capital outflows and trading in currency futures. The environmental news was reported in 19 news items and included topics such as India's role in Copenhagen negotiations, reducing carbon emissions and bringing about energy efficiency. News related to politics amounted to a total of 8 news items and they reported on Af-Pak policy, peace in Pakistan and neighboring areas, Nuclear Security Summit and economic and political integration. A total of 7 news items were included under the category of social affairs which included varied topics such as solar power research, global health initiatives, tourism and migration into Europe.

The Times of India – EU News

The Times of India reported a total of 111 EU news items. The economic news totaled 64 news items (57.6 per cent) out of which 54 news items reported about the state of the economy in the EU. The possibility of the collapse of the euro and the European project was not ruled out (The Times of India 24 June 2010: 26). The economic status of Greece was a cause of concern as its credit rating was reduced to non-investment grade owing to the possibility of the country defaulting on its debt (The Times of India 15 June 2010:20). The International Monetary Fund (IMF) chipped in to join the European Union in pledging support for Greece in its struggle to bring its ballooning budget deficit under control and contain the debt crisis (The Times of India 13 February 2010: 24). The banking news dealt with efforts of the EU to check speculative borrowing (The Times of India 16 December 2009: 26) and the amount given by banks as a portion of the Eurozone bailout package (The Times of India 11 May 2010:1). The competition laws reported payment of fines for infringement in dealings in the power generation industry (The Times of India 8 October 2009: 27) and for settling anti-trust and patent disputes in the software industry (The Times of India 13 November 2009: 22). Only 3 industry-related news items were reported and all the three dealt with the aviation industry. One article talked about a possible merger between the Spanish airline Iberia and British Airways (Clark 9 April 2010: 26) while the other two talked about the shutdown and disruption in travelling due to the volcanic ash from Iceland that had spread across the skies of Europe (The Times of India 20 April: 16). The political news constituted 23 news items of the total coverage of EU news and reported upon the Lisbon Reform Treaty and the election of the EU President, British elections, showcasing the EU and the creation of a European army. The news related to social affairs was reported in 17 news items on themes such as education, research, science and technology and sports. The issue of immigration was given maximum coverage. The news was reported mainly from UK and talked about the likelihood of the introduction of new and tougher restrictions on immigration as well as more vigilance regarding student visas (Ray 12 April 2010:16). A total of 7 news items related to the environment were reported on climate change, European Emission Trading Scheme, the carbon-free Congress in the Czech Republic and energy-saving light bulbs.

The Times of India – Third Country News

The role of the EU in a third country was reported in 93 news items. A total of 29 (31.1 per cent) news items threw light upon EU's role in the international system as a whole rather than in a specific country. Apart from Copenhagen climate negotiations and concerns about the global balance of power and multipolarity, the EU was reported to be active in the economic sphere. Thus, the news coverage included issues such as the Eurozone crisis, World Retail Congress, internet piracy, anti-counterfeiting trade agreement, saving digital data, law governing service providers and crisis management through visual analytics. The news from the Middle East appeared in 10 news items and revealed the EU's role on issues such as nuclear proliferation in Iran and imposition of sanctions on the country, the Israel-Palestinian issue and monitoring of peace in Gaza and call for an inquiry into the lethal seizure of a Turkish ship by Israel (The Times of India 10 June 2010:17). A total of 14 news items talked about EU's role in international bodies such as WTO, BASIC, ASEAN, G8, UN and UNHRC. China, Russia, Canada and

Somalia also featured in the news reporting. The European Union's involvement was reported in the Indian sub-continent in 11 news items in Afghanistan, Balochistan, Myanmar, Sri Lanka, Pakistan and Nepal.

The Times of India – Local News

A total of 139 new items about the EU were sourced from India out of which 75 (53.9 per cent) news items were related to the economy. A total of 47 news items dealt with the sovereign debt crisis in the EU and its adverse affects upon the Indian economy. Local news about the EU related to business and finance, dealt with expansion of EU-India trade, strengthening of EU-India economic partnership through Turkey, mergers, acquisitions and taxes on foreign investment. Industry related news items were mainly related to the pharmaceutical, steel and textile industry. Trade related news focused on EU-India FTA while a couple of articles discussed India's foreign trade policy (The Times of India 18 August 2009:28). Environment-related news was reported in 17 news items in all and dealt with climate change negotiations, reducing carbon emissions, introduction of new safety standards related to electromagnetic radiation, energy efficiency, hydromorphology and conflict over processing of bats. News emanating from the political sphere consisted of 25 news items that dealt with Iranian nuclear development, EU as a model for South Asian unity, counter-terrorism cooperation, India-EU ties, trade and investment as a foreign policy tool and enhancing nuclear security. Events happening in the Indian neighbourhood were also reported such as the Istanbul meeting on Afghanistan, China-Pakistan nuclear cooperation, supply and sale of arms to Sri Lanka and pressure upon the king of Nepal to abdicate his throne. News items related to social affairs numbered 22 in all and were based on themes such as consumer rights, social legislation, crime, culture, education, health, research, migration, travel and tourism.

Dainik Jagran – EU News

Dainik Jagran reported 4 news items originating from the EU. They reported the announcement of a $10 billion package for bailing out European countries who found themselves in a situation similar to that of the Greek economy (Dainik Jagran 11 May 2010: 10). It was also announced that violation of budgetary rules by any EU member-state would not be tolerated (Dainik Jagran 23 May 2010: 10). The EU resolved to take a tough stand against hedge funds and private equity funds (Dainik Jagran 20 May 2010: 10). Thus, we see that the EU was reported to be primarily engaged in reviving the confidence of the markets and ensuring financial stability.

Dainik Jagran – Third Country News

A total of 6 news items were reported on the activities of the EU as a global actor. The bargaining between the developed and developing countries in an attempt to reach a consensus on the issue of climate change and especially carbon emissions in Copenhagen was reported in 4 news articles. The other 2 articles reported on the economic slowdown (Brajesh 11 July 2009: 10) and the pressure being exerted upon the developing countries like India to open up their agricultural markets by the developed world which included the EU (Dainik Jagran 3 December 2009:10).

Dainik Jagran – Local News

Local news items about the EU included 14 news articles in all out of which 9 related to the state of economy in the EU and measures to be taken by the India to minimise the fallout of the Eurozone crisis on its economy. The European Union and India were mentioned in 4 news items in the course of discussing relevant political issues such as the global balance of power and (Dainik Jagran 9 August 2009: 10) the identity of the EU as a military power in world politics (Subramanyam 14 February 2010:8). There was a single news item on the environment which urged India not to bow down to the wishes of the developed world at the Copenhagen Summit (Gupta 31 October 2009: 10).

Thus, we see that the leading business newspaper concentrates on the Indian angle of news about the EU which constitutes 58.6 per cent of the total coverage. This is indeed logical and corroborates the fact that it is the economic sphere of the relationship with the EU which excites India the most. EU news and EU news reported from other countries amounted to 22.8 per cent and 18.7 per cent of the total coverage respectively which indicates a decent effort on the part of *The Economic Times* to keep its readers abreast with all major news and events concerning the European Union. *The Times of India* follows the cue of *The Economic Times* in reporting 40.52 per cent of news items with a local focus. *The Times of India* reported a total of 32.3 per cent of EU news and 27.1 per cent of EU news from destinations other than EU and India which was roughly 10 per cent more news items covered in both categories in comparison to *The Economic Times*. The increase in coverage in both these categories can be attributed to the very nature of The *Times of India* which on account of being the most popular English daily has to cater to the conditioning of the English-speaking urban populace which believes in keeping itself updated about all news happening in the West, which includes the EU and the rest of the world. The nature of coverage by *The Times of India* is in keeping with the cosmopolitan culture that it caters to and promotes. The *Dainik Jagran* with the largest readership which includes a substantial rural population largely concentrates on local EU news items which illuminate the role of India. The news from the EU along with the coverage of EU news unfolding in other parts of the world have a substantially low coverage which amounts to 16.6 per cent and 25 per cent respectively. This is owing to the fact that *Dainik Jagran* makes no pretence of being a balanced and all-encompassing daily in terms of coverage. It takes pride in the fact that it covers local news most extensively and keeps the nation informed about local and national politics and is unrepentant for not providing extensive coverage of international news unless India has a stake in the unfolding events.

Evaluation of News

The data analysis reveals that 183 (19.38 per cent) news items with a positive tone were reported while 434 (45.97 per cent) news items were characterised as negative news. A total of 327 (34.63 per cent) news items had a neutral tone. News items with a negative tone led the tally in the case of *The Economic Times* (49.5 per cent) and *The Times of India* (41.1 per cent) while in the case of *Dainik Jagran* the negative (29.1 per cent) and positive news (33.3 per cent) items were separated by a very narrow margin (Figure 3.8).

Figure 3.8: Evaluation of EU news

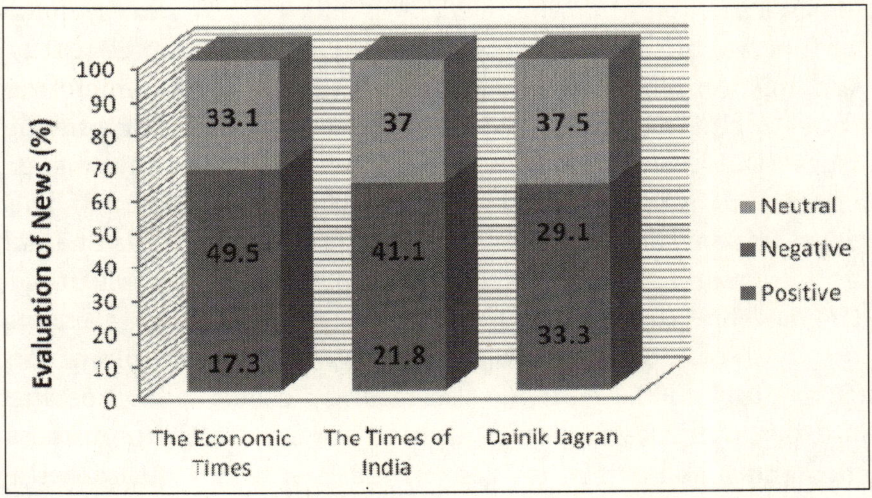

The Economic Times – Positive News

The Economic Times reported a total of 100 positive news items out of which 75 (75 per cent) dealt with the economy. The positive news related to the state of economy was reported in 24 news articles. The unveiling of the shock and awe $1 trillion rescue package went a long way in restoring confidence in the euro as well as in standby funds and loan guarantees. The commitment of the ECB to buy government bonds in the open markets along with other measures to control the contagion enabled global markets to heave a collective sigh of relief (Sen 11 May 2010:17). The

European Union's resolve to keep their currency and the union on the go was in fact applauded by markets around the world including India (The Economic Times 11 May 2010:12). Developing nations like India were able to ward off the ill-effects of the contagion on account of the inherent strength of economic fundamentals and due to massive intervention by the European Union and IMF to check losses and ensure financial stability in the eurozone (Ganesh 20 June 2010:13). Trade related news appeared in 21 news articles and was primarily about EU-India FTA. It was stated that India and EU could benefit immensely with the conclusion of the EU-India FTA not only in terms of bilateral trade but also through long-term economic partnership (Subramaniam 22 March 2010:12). Attempts were made to assuage fears regarding many contentious issues including the likely increase in the price of life-saving drugs (The Economic Times 4 May 2010:11). As a result of such agreements, it was expected that about 60-70 per cent of India's global trade would either become free from duty barriers or shall attract lesser levies (The Economic Times 10 February 2010:9). The measures that India ought to take up for increasing its exports and the health of its economy were also taken up for discussion (Sen 3 July 2009:11). India also recorded a double digit growth in exports in December 2009 from a year ago which suggested a "demand pick-up" in the Western markets which included the United States and the European Union (The Economic Times 2 February 2010:9). As far as global trade negotiations are concerned, Brazil and India were touted to be players who could help in bringing about politically-saleable deals while EU was portrayed as an actor willing to take up "a leadership role" (Chatterjee 15 March 2010: 15). Industry related news was featured in 16 news items in all. It was repeatedly reiterated that the US and EU still account for the bulk of orders to India due to their market size and purchasing power while the new markets pale in comparison (Ghosh 9 February 2010:6). An "uptick in orders from the US and EU" have led the textile companies which are India's largest employers, hire workers in hordes, leading to increase in employment (Ghosh 15 March 2010:6). Although it was declared by the Government of India that there would be no significant commercial exports of sugar in 2010-2011, exports would be limited to "quota (EU) countries" which indicates the preference accorded to EU by India (The Economic Times 13 May 2010: 15). Positive news emanating from the "mid and low value garment space", has been that markets in EU are also importing carpets from India as well as South America which was not the case earlier (Mary 9 May 2010: 1). Agriculture, drugs, palm oil, wheat exports, insurance, metal and steel industries were the other sectors which were part of the coverage of EU news with a positive tone. A total of 14 EU news items were reported, based on the theme of business and finance. The regulators in European Union were called upon to tackle distortive developments caused by the scrapping of the four-decade old system of annual price-setting which has led to huge losses to be borne by European carmakers who are the biggest users of steel (Biesheuvel 2 April 2010: 7).The European Union was also found to be vocal on accounting matters as it called upon the IASB to accelerate reforms of its fair value or market-to-market rule to ease pressure on banks that have to "price assets at depressed going rates". It also called for a principle-based approach towards setting rules (Jones 16 February 2010:10). A total of 15 news items relating to environmental matters with a positive tone were reported. The EU was appreciated for having been the driving force behind getting climate change on the top of the global agenda. It was stated that despite the debacle in Copenhagen, EU has the resolve to continue being a strong force (Goswami 10 April 2010:3). The EU was lauded for its efforts at the Bali Conference in 2007 where it made common cause with the developing countries and counterbalanced and engaged and even isolated the US which finally led to the adoption of the Bali Action Plan (Goswami 1 May 2010:3). It was suggested in one of the articles that India should make efforts towards developing a national strategy based on the model of Japan and EU who have addressed unique challenges with policies tailored to their respective political realities (Vishakantaiah 4 February 2010: 36). There were 4 news items of political nature that reported about the European Union. The European Union along with Turkey and the United Nations called for an international inquiry to investigate the lethal seizure of a Turkish ship bound for blockaded Gaza (Macdonald 4 June 2010:3). The Indian navy stated that other navies such as those of NATO forces and the EUNAVFOR (EU Naval Forces) contributed to the efficiency and effectiveness of their operations in the Gulf of Aden (The Economic Times 21 June 2010:23). It was strongly recommended that India's defence sector must take a cue from the European Union as far as investment practices for greater FDI in defence are concerned. It should adopt more stringent licensing and export control regulations to address legitimate apprehensions about majority ownership of sensitive defence companies falling in the hands of foreign players and enemy countries (Varma 7 June 2010: 12). It was stated that the Indian subcontinent can make its way towards peace in the same way as Europe did by overcoming history, war and genocide. The EU extended economic cooperation and within one generation, centuries of conflict has become a distant reality in Europe (The Economic Times 19 May 2010:8). The socially relevant news items with a positive tone that were reported totaled 6 in number. They dealt with measures taken by the EU to protect privacy rights of European citizens, minimise hearing loss through digital devices, facilitate immigration from third countries to EU and make concerted efforts to control crime.

The Economic Times – Negative News

The negative news falling under the political category totaled 6 in number. One of the articles exhorted the EU to assume special responsibility to contribute towards reforming the Bretton Woods Institutions where EU member-states are believed to be grossly over-represented in terms of voting rights (Sapir 22 March 2010: 13). The EU along with the United States was accused by India of deliberately ignoring India's soft power edge in Afghanistan in order to appease Pakistan (The Economic Times 10 February: 2). The Eurozone is said to be laboring with many problems since 2008-09 including doubts about the future of the euro, the large fiscal burden on all member nations despite high rates of taxation and the struggle to re-establish national competitiveness while living in a monetary straitjacketed framework (Chaudhuri 13 April 2010: 12). The other articles talk about the lack of unity and leadership in the EU required for external influence and the need to build up economic, political, intellectual and cultural capital.

Only 5 news items reported about social affairs related to the EU in a negative tone. An article on gender parity highlighted the inadequacy of representation of women as directors on corporate boards both across the world including EU and India (Duggal 25 March 2010:12). The World Health Organisation drew attention towards a worrisome fact that economic costs related to mental illness accounted for 3-4 per cent of GNP in EU nations (Sahay 1 June 2010: 12). The majority of the articles discussed the issue of immigration to the EU. One of the articles pointed towards the growing level of intolerance towards immigrants in the wake of economic recession (Sen 7 June 2010: 13). One of the articles reported that immigrants from third countries or non-EU people do not have access to benefits or pensions or housing despite paying council tax for local services (Sen 26 April 2010: 15). The issue of free flow of international talent from outside Europe also led to a division down the middle among policy makers (Sen 24 August 2009: 11).

A total of 13 news items related to the EU with a negative tone were reported from the environmental sphere. It was opined that with a fall in the prices of the European Union Emission Trading System, firms will have less incentive to reduce emissions and a far less inclination to invest in innovation that would reduce emissions in future (Stiglitz 18 January 2010:13). It was also alleged that EU and other developed countries had broken ranks with the G-77 in order to make the Copenhagen Accord a legally binding treaty (The Economic Times 27 January 2010:3). Mr. De Boer was alleged to be more of an EU representative rather than an unbiased player and in this context, UN Secretary General Ban Ki-Moon called for building trust between industrialised and developing countries (The Economic Times 16 March 2010:2). It was also stated that the EU benchmarking of sectors prone to carbon leakage is mainly on the basis of trade intensity rather than GHG intensity which reflects that the intent is directed towards trade protectionism rather than environment conservation (Nair 18 May 2010:12). It was speculated that EU's unilateral emission restrictions shall not be economically viable and it shall have negligible impact on global temperatures (Lomborg 14 June 2010:11).

The Economic Times reported a total of 286 news items with a negative tone out of which 262 news items were based on the economy. A total of 184 news items discussed issues related to the state of the economy and found it to be worrisome. It was reported that Greece went along with the rescue package because the economic and political costs of non-conformity with EU initiatives would have spelled a lot of trouble for the debt-ridden country (Mohan 13 May 2010: 12). It was reported that the Stability and Growth Pact which required EU member countries to maintain a minimum degree of fiscal health had proved to be an unsuccessful measure (Bhat 14 June 2010:10). The growth in the Eurozone was predicted to be weak owing to the strained balance sheets of the PIIGS countries namely, Portugal, Italy, Ireland, Greece and Spain which required EU financial support of about $1 trillion in order to sidestep the financial crisis (Suri 31 May 2010: 18). The Indian rupee was affected by the Eurozone crisis and was on a downward spiral because the deteriorating public finances of European nations including Greece and Portugal led investors to favour safer bets than emerging market assets (The Economic Times 5 February 2010:13). As a result of the crisis in Eurozone, central banks from all over the world chose to invest in US government bonds or treasuries and reverse a four-month trend that saw them pull out of the greenback (The Economic Times 5 May 2010: 16). Adverse news from the European markets and India along with apprehensions about rise in interest rates due to high inflation resulted in increased volatility of share prices (Gurav 23 June 2010: 18). It was surmised that advanced economies including those of EU and US continue to be mired in problems as a result of their overstretched public finances. However, the erosion of confidence in Europe especially in the Eurozone is considered to be more pronounced in comparison to the US. India's problems are said to be compounded due to the effects of the financial crises and the very high inflation that has hit Indian markets (Chaudhuri 18 June 2010: 14).

A total of 39 industry-related EU news items with a negative tone were reported out of which 14 were related to pharmaceuticals. India has opposed the EU proposal that shall allow it to inspect facilities of exporting countries. The Indian pharmaceutical industry considers this to be yet another attempt by the West to render India uncompetitive because the pre-inspection of manufacturing facilities shall slow down the rate of export of medicines from India to the EU (Sen and Singh 29 April 2010: 11). The EU-India scuffle on the issue of confiscation of genuine generics from India being exported to third countries at European ports was reported. India took up this issue at the WTO stating that such acts of the EU would deny access to the poor of the world to cheap medicines. The developing countries likely to be affected include Mauritius, Peru, Cuba, Bolivia, Ecuador, Egypt, South Africa, Brazil and African nations (Sen 19 June 2010: 7). Thailand and Indonesia among others supported India's position at the recent World Health Assembly which is an annual gathering of 193 members of the World Health Organisation in Geneva. They agreed that adherence to intellectual property laws that went beyond International Trips Agreement should not be allowed to become the norm (Sen 1 June 2010: 11).

Indian IT companies were reported to be giving tough competition to their peers in Philippines and China. They are soon be engaged in intense competition with these countries with companies in US and Europe framing policies in order to discourage offshoring. The recent EU proposal to levy 15 % Value Added Tax (VAT) on services delivered from outside the EU is a case in point (Pramugdha and Mishra 8 February 2010: 5). India has banned the import of poultry, poultry products and live pigs from countries reporting high pathogenic and low pathogenic influence which includes the EU. The EU has retorted by stating that India ought to provide scientific evidence justifying its strict measures to bring EU imports in conformity with international standards (Sen 10 May 2010:11) The civil aviation industry reported about millions of passengers being stranded by the closure of most of Europe's airspace due to the spread of volcanic ash across the skies of Europe. Fast air freight and trade in general were hard it (The Economic Times 20 April 2010: 15). The decline in exports was registered in many industries due to the Eurozone crisis. The other industries which were covered as part of EU news items with a negative tone included textile, sugar, plastic, seafood, basmati rice and wine.

A total of 26 trade related EU news items with a negative tone were reported. The EU-India Free Trade Agreement was discussed and opinion was expressed regarding the possibility of its successful conclusion. The EU Parliament was reported to have taken a rigid stand on the inclusion of "new issues like child labour and environment" in the discussions on EU-India FTA. However, India did not find this palatable and stated that the EU-India FTA is not the appropriate forum to discuss these issues (The Economic Times 5 March: 17). It was reported that countervailing duties, anti-dumping duties and safeguard duties are imposed every year on a number of products being exported from India to EU including drugs, chemicals and metals which are largely a means of trade protectionism being practiced by the

EU (The Economic Times 15 April 2010: 11). It was reported that decline in orders from EU had started hitting exporters in India (The Economic Times 21 June 2010: 11). The Eurozone crisis, the rupee's spectacular gains against the euro and the expected rise in interest cost due to introduction of base rate mechanism have led to further shrinking of India's already declining trade with the EU (Mulay and Pai 10 April 2010: 8).

There were 13 EU news items in all, that reported on matters related to business and finance. There was a constant worry among "emerging Asia's policy makers" that Europe's export demand would be affected drastically in case the Eurozone governments tried to contain their budget deficits and get back to the bloc's 3 per cent limit (Plumber 11 May 2010: 16).

The EU move to impose Value Added Tax (VAT) on services delivered by non-EU nations such as India was not received well as it would put a renewed squeeze on the profit margins of these global outsourcing service providers which would prompt them to look at the North American economy which seems to be recovering. Europe is a major client of Indian service providers and accounts for $60 billion revenue of the Indian outsourcing industry. The other news items under this segment show that attempts were being made to prune, refurbish and make the economy more robust through dealing with concerns such as monetary policy tightening, restoring confidence in the euro, shrinking trade barriers, regulating hedge funds and preventing naked-shortselling.

The Economic Times – Neutral News

A total number of 191 EU news items with a neutral tone were reported out of which 145 news items dealt with the economy. There were 45 news items that carried news about various industries in a neutral tone. The pharmaceutical sector reported 10 EU news items in a neutral tone. They basically reported news about greater market access of Indian generics by means of fast-tracking registration of drugs and through mergers and acquisitions such as that of Elder Biomeda (Singh 13 March 2010: 6) and the Glenmark-Sanofi deal (The Economic Times 4 May 2010: 8). The IT sector reported 8 news items about the rising importance attached to hiring of senior professionals in EU, US and India (Mukherjee and Ghosal 4 January 2010: 16), digitisation grant for the EU with must use clauses and mergers and acquisitions (Mishra 5 January 2010:1) such as the EU takeover of Sun Microsystems by Oracle Corp. (The Economic Times 13 January 2010:11). Several interesting aspects of various industrial spheres were highlighted such as the attempt by EU to define chocolate and the view from the floriculture industry that roses never go out of business. There were 38 trade-related items reported in a neutral tone. The news about negotiations regarding EU-India FTA was reported along with India's negotiations on FTA with Australia and Turkey. EU and India started negotiations to sign the Free Trade Agreement (FTA) in June 2007 and Turkey decided to start the same in June 2008 which would enable Turkey to benefit from a preferential market access to obtain industrial inputs necessary for some of their export products to the European Union and to other export markets. It was made clear that India would keep foreign players out of trade in government procurement and the issue would not be broached during discussion of the FTA with Australia as is in the case of the EU (Sen 8 May 2010: 9). The need to establish a comprehensive bilateral trade linkage through partnership between European Free Trade Association and India was recognised. Unlike the EU and US, which restrict companies to own dominant marketshare, the developing world including India was reported to be liberal on competition issues which allowed companies to own dominant market share such as L.N. Mittal owned Arcelor Mittal that owns 10 per cent of the global steel industry with many of its units located in the developing world (The Economic Times 11 May 2010: 1). Substantial coverage was given to the mini-ministerial held in Delhi in order to end the bitterness in the Doha negotiations (The Economic Times 2 September 2009: 9). Key countries including India, US, Brazil, EU, South Africa, Malaysia and Egypt were expected to participate in the Doha talks which had suffered a setback in the last eight years due to conflict of interest between developed countries including EU and US and leading developing countries such as India, China and Brazil (Sen 16 November 2009:9). The EU news with a neutral tone emanated from the banking and finance sector. The attempts by the EU to force banks which took state aid to restructure were reported (The Economic Times 27 October 2009:17). It was also observed that European banks are emerging from the credit crisis bigger than before and should thereby be considered a risk to their national economies. It was pointed out that although the EU was highly appreciated for breaking up bailed-out banks, regulators have not done the needful to rein in firms that have shunned state aid and are too big to fail (MacAskill and Menon 3 December 2009:17). The business and finance section reported news about competition laws, anti-dumping tariffs, anti-monopoly cases, creation of a European Monetary Fund, credit rating agencies, hedge funds, harmonisation of non-tariff rules, capital outflows and trading in currency futures. The news about the state of economy was entirely devoted to the reporting of Eurozone crisis in a neutral tone. The article contributors familiarised the readers with the fact that Europe is a major international actor which has been struck by the current economic crisis and the international system should consequently ensure that a collapse does not happen in Europe and that a contagion is contained (Shibata 7 June 2010:16). Most parts of the world as well as companies in Europe kept a tab on the likely impact of the sovereign debt crisis on their current business and deal flows (The Economic Times 5 June 2010: 11). The performance and stability of the Indian rupee and the US dollar was strongly pinned to the value of the euro. This indicates that the unfolding Eurozone crisis had become an essential element of economic and financial decision-making and its impact had to be factored in to realistically contemplate a positive outcome (The Economic Times 7 June 2010:16).

The environment-related EU news was reported in 26 news items in all. It essentially revolved around Copenhagen climate negotiations and steps taken after the climate conference. At the outset, the European Union stated that it will sharpen its carbon-cutting bid if the United States paid more for carbon cuts in poor nations, especially to curb deforestation (Cowan 8 December 2009). It was reported that European leaders attempted to agree to a €2 billion annual endowment to the world's poorer countries in order to jolt the Copenhagen climate negotiations out of slumber. However, many of the EU member-states were ill at ease about diverting funds from national budgets in the midst of the economic crisis (The Economic Times 10 December 2009:6). Amidst the loosening up and breaking down of cohesiveness as a result of the Danish text at the Copenhagen summit, the developing countries decided to adopt a co-ordinated approach on the lines of the EU which acted as a formal and disciplined bloc (The Economic Times 11 December 2009: 2). A meeting of the Major Economies Forum took place in order to discuss "issues for moving forward" after the Copenhagen climate conference. While the US wanted the Copenhagen Accord to become the crux of the negotiations, EU and Russia were in favour of introducing the practice of issue-based discussions that would "cut across the two tracks (Kyoto Protocol and Bali tracks)" of climate negotiations (Goswami 20 April 2010:3). The reduction of carbon dioxide emissions was reported from several quarters. One such industry was the automobile sector where Daimler was reported to be making attempts to reduce carbon-dioxide emissions of its vehicles by 19 per cent to avoid fines by European regulators. EU emissions legislation has been an important driver and has gone a long way towards ensuring tougher environmental regulations (The Economic Times 8 April 2010:5).

A total of 14 EU news items covered political developments with a neutral tone. The ratification of the Lisbon Treaty was expected to open doors for the appointment of a new EU

President and foreign minister for which intense lobbying was expected. Hong Kong's last British governor, Chris Patten signaled his availability for a top European job. Mr. Patten stated that he wishes to combine his current job of Oxford University Chancellor with that of Europe's first foreign minister (The Economic Times, 6 August 2009: 7). The issue of Myanmar and the treatment meted out to Aung Sang Su Kyi led to strong reactions of the members of the United Nations Security Council. The British Prime Minister Gordon Brown called for a global arms embargo while French President Nicholas Sarkozy stated that EU sanctions ought to target their sources of profit for Myanmar such as wood and ruby mining (The Economic Times 13 August 2009:3). Once the Lisbon Treaty was ratified on November 3, there seemed to be no takers for the office of the new and more powerful foreign policy chief. Britain, France and Germany in fact stated that they were more interested in securing lower-profile but influential economic posts inside the European Commission (Castle 16 November 2009:14). It was reported that China suffers from limitations as far as maneuvering of foreign policy is concerned on account of ban of arms exports to China following the Tiananmen Square incident of 1989 (Kondapalli 20 December 2009:11). The Pakistani establishment had expressed the hope that US and EU would leave it to Pakistan to contain terror in the region by drawing inspiration from the success of a similar strategy under General Zia (The Economic Times 19 February 2010:12). The tiff between EU and Sri Lanka also made news. Sri Lanka expressed its displeasure upon the withdrawal of Generalised System of Preferences which provided preferential tariffs for trade with EU. The EU had demanded for certain conditions to be fulfilled such as repealing sections of its emergency rules, Prevention of Terrorism Act as well as adopting a national human rights plan (The Economic Times 25 June 2010:2). The holding of the Nuclear Security Summit was also mentioned and it was stated that the outcome has been negotiated over the past six months among EU, IAEA and 44 other countries (The Economic Times 5 April 2010:2).

A total of 6 EU news items were reported on social affairs. It was reported that the European Union is supposed to radically overhaul its approval system for genetically modified crops which shall open the way to large-scale GM cultivation in Europe. Only 2 varieties of GM crops have been approved for growing in 12 years compared to more than 150 in the rest of the world because Europeans have shown no appetite for GM produce in food (The Economic Times 5 June 2010:9). A couple of news items covered issues related to voting rights of immigrants (The Economic Times 22 March 2010:12) and identity issues related to immigrants (Sen 10 April 2010:13). One news item dealt with the declaration of Turkey as the European cultural capital for the year 2010 by the European Union as it is a country embracing Asia as well as Europe (The Economic Times 8 February 2010:28). Another news item talked about the inroads made by the marketing gurus and chefs from Asian countries and European Union into the Indian tourism scene (Venkateswaran 17 May 2010: 4).

The Times of India – Positive News

A total of 25 EU news items reported economy-related news in *The Times of India* with a positive tone out of which 23 articles revolved around the issue of the eurozone crisis. European leaders were believed to be committed to the survival of the euro and they were reported to have enough money to bail out the heavily indebted member-countries (The Times of India 9 June 2010:26). Following up on this, it was reported that the European Union announced a rescue package of almost $1 trillion with support from the International Monetary Fund in order to revive the finances of the weakest economies of the Euro-region (The Times of India 15 June:20). The news soon came of a Greek bailout package worth €25 billion being put together by the finance ministers of the Eurozone countries. The financial assistance would comprise of loans and guarantees with the burden being spread amongst EU member-states (Dey and Watts 22 February 2010:22). It was reported that such measures led to less worry in the markets over the Eurozone debt crisis which led to lessening of panic in the rest of the world including India. In the light of these circumstances, India stated that it would not go for a full-fledged interest rate hike and that it would rather gradually inch towards a tighter monetary supply (The Times of India 15 June 2010:1).

A total of 25 EU news items related to social affairs were reported with a positive tone out of which 11 news articles dealt with the theme of education. A certificate course entitled EU and German laws was offered in Amity Law School in India as a result of the exponential increase in economic and academic interaction between EU and India (The Times of India 19 April 2010:38). A new course on International Relations was launched in Spain with special emphasis upon the EU as it was considered to be "a model for every process of regional integration on the planet" and one of the main factors influencing the process of globalisation (Ray 21 June 2010:62). A joint venture with funding from the European Commission and the Chinese government led to the establishment of the China Europe International Business School in 1994 and it was reported that it now had a new campus (Ray 17 May 2010: 50). It was reported that models may emerge very soon where two universities in two different countries come together and credit systems are merged in new ways as witnessed in the Asia-Pacific region and European Union (Ray 15 February 2010:42). It was reported that the EU code of conduct for data centres in the software industry shall be introduced in India (Khattar 15 March 2010:46). A couple of articles reported news about consumer protection against shocking totals on phone bills and data protection. Health-related reports with a positive tone talked about devices to check blood clotting levels, cure for diabetes and obesity and EU prescription on limits for plastic teethers that were largely found to be toxic in nature. News items related to prevention of crime were also reported. It was reported that presence of warships from the European Union had been successful in thwarting attacks on merchant and leisure ships in the Gulf of Aden (The Times of India 31 March 2010: 17). The EU legislation known as the Physical Protection of Nuclear Material and Facilities was reported to have laid down duties for verification of radioactive substances so that containers being used to transport hazardous radioactive isotopes become a remote possibility (Deshpande 11 April 2010:9). EU negotiators rejected a US backed proposal which required internet service providers to take tough steps against digital piracy because of the lack of transparency in the trade agreement and the undue influence that it would have on the working of the internet and on people all over the world (Pfanner 9 February 2010:20).

A total of 20 EU news items covering politics with a positive tone were reported. It was advocated that annual summits and informal meetings "in-between, for a few hours on one-day trips" should take place between the two partners for better EU-India relations (Anam 2 February 2010:18). It was stated that India should strive to build a relationship with the EU based on shared ideals and principles of democratic societies founded on equality and freedom of expression (Babaria 9 March 2010: 16). It was reported that the EU considered India to be a responsible member of the international community and that the former would cooperate with and assist the latter in finding a "natural place within the multilateral treaty system". It was reported that the ongoing partnership in the context of the civilian nuclear programme between EU and India is going from strength to strength (Ray 25 June 2010:20). The EU played the role of a global actor and called for an international inquiry along with Turkey and the United Nations into the lethal seizure of a Turkish ship bound for blockaded Gaza (The Times India 4 June 2010:24). Nobel Laureate Muhmmad Yunus called upon South Asian countries to come together and build an entity on the lines of the EU with a single currency and free movement (Roy 10 December 2009:15). He stated that the member-states of the EU have proved beyond doubt that countries can set aside the scars of history and can work together for peace and prosperity (Mitra 12 December 2009:22). It was reported that the EU condemned the decision of a high court in Beijing which upheld the 11 year imprisonment given by a lower court to Liu Xiabo, a Chinese writer and a dissident and demanded his release (Dasgutpa 12 February:23). The EU along with the US decided to tighten screws on Iran's nuclear programme following the imposition of fresh sanctions by the United Nations which will target insurance firms, oil firms and shipping lines supposedly linked to Iran's atomic programmes and the Islamic Revolutionary Guards Corps (The Times of India 18 June: 21). Sim Kallas, the EU Transport Commissioner provided the assurance that he would begin working towards laying out a road map for dealing with events similar to the disruption of air-traffic in Europe by the volcanic ash cloud that spread across the European skies. He stated that an attempt would be made towards measuring the density and trajectory of an ash cloud as well as the safety threshold for each kind of engine (The Times of India 26 April 2010: 17). The other themes covered which projected the EU as a positive actor included trade and investment as a foreign policy tool, integration, close economic and political relations and the tackling of piracy and intelligence in counter-terrorism operations.

A total of 5 environment-related EU news items with a positive tone were reported in *The Times of India*. A European Union project called Safe Road Trains for the Environment would involve a "carpooling roadtrain theory for use on motorways" which would save energy "in the region of 20 per cent". It would also enable road capacity to be utilised more efficiently. The aim of the project is to develop a safe and environmentally-effective road train without the need to invest in changes to road infrastructure (The Times of India 5 January 2010:19). It was reported that the European

Union has proposed to ban sex toys as the PVC used in electrical goods is harmful for the environment when it ends up at rubbish dumps, which is subsequently heaped in landfill sites often in developing countries (The Times of India 14 June 2010: 17). Governments across the European Union have enacted new safety standards related to electromagnetic radiation, which calls for minimising exposure and advising limited use for children (Deora 3 April 2010:16). It was argued that Information Technology can play a vital role in reducing greenhouse gas emissions so that the European Union can bring about "20 per cent energy efficiency improvements targeted for 2020" (Singh 21 June 2010: 57). It was reported that hydromorphology which involves the combined study of the hydrological and geomorphological elements of the river system, forms a major part of the European Union Water Framework Directive which is becoming increasingly relevant in other parts of the world (The Times of India 30 May 2010: 52).

The Times of India – Negative News

There were 141 EU news items with a negative tone that appeared in *The Times of India*. A total of 97 economy-related news were reported out of which 77 dealt with the state of the EU economy. It was reported that the IT sector gave signals of a rebound which was caught in its tracks on account of the Eurozone debt crisis which manifested itself in several EU member-states and led to sharp cuts in budgetary spending (Tejaswi and John 28 May 2010:32). In another news piece, the Greek Prime Minister, George Papandreou, described his economy as a sinking ship and requested for an international bailout which was likely to test the bonds of the European Union. The loans promised to Greece by its Eurozone partners are awaiting approval by the legislators of the respective countries. It was also reported that the proposed bailout had been politically unpopular in Germany and could face legal challenges before the country's Constitutional Court (Saltmarsh 24 April 2010:23). It was reported that the jittery markets were looking towards German Chancellor Angela Merkel, Dominique Strauss-Kahn, the head of the IMF and ECB President Jean-Claude Trichet, for sending a positive signal a day after Greek bonds were downgraded to junk status (The Times of India 29 April 2010: 20). It was reported that investors were worried about the possibility of the Eurozone falling back into recession with the introduction of austerity measures. Investors were not found to be convinced of the fact that recession would end soon. Amidst the growing uncertainty over the Eurozone crisis, investors largely expected further slump in the euro against the dollar (The Times of India 2 June 2010: 26). The European Central Bank stated in its Financial Stability Report that despite total write-downs from bad loans and securities between 2007 and the end of 2010 that are likely to be lower than previously expected, the write downs in the near future would be more if "heightened sovereign debt risk and the impact of belt tightening dragged down economic growth." It was reported in the newspapers that Nouriel Roubini believed that all the member-countries of the Eurozone will have to make many sacrifices. They shall have to drastically reduce their budget deficits by hiking taxes and cutting spending which is going to be an arduous task especially for the political leadership. Paul Krugman stated that the euro is definitely in danger and warned against any delay in responding to the Greek debt crisis as it would otherwise lead to "a chain reaction" and the downfall of the Eurozone. Joseph Stiglitz also gave a grim picture of the Eurozone and stated that it if the smaller and more vulnerable countries do not reduce their budget deficits, there is a high risk of speculative attack, which will not lead to their neighbours coming to their immediate assistance and even if they come, shall not be devoid of "painful and counterproductive procyclical budgetary restraints" (The Times of India 28 May 2010:32). News portraying the EU in a negative light was reported from the pharmaceuticals, steel, textile, poultry and aviation industry. It was reported that India is not happy with the EU stance of including social issues of child labour, human rights and climate change as part of EU-India

FTA negotiations as it considers them to be non-tariff barriers to trade (The Times of India 5 March 2010:25).

There were 20 news items relating to the political sphere which portrayed the EU in a negative light. David Cameron was attacked by the opposition for not conceding that 80 per cent of total migration into Britain is from the European Union which can only be controlled by transitional caps (Ray 1 May 2010: 20). It was argued that United States and EU provide two great power templates. While the US is known to boast about having military muscle, the EU's militarism is limited to conferences on climate change (Malik 5 April 2010:14). A case of embarrassment for Spain's EU presidency was also reported when visitors to the EU website were directed to a blog that showed a photograph of Mr. Bean instead of the country's Prime Minister whose resemblance to the comic television and movie actor has been a joke doing the rounds for some time now (The Times of India 6 January 2010:24). It was stated in one of the news items that the Labour Prime Minister had failed to overcome Britain's semi-detachment from the EU and had chosen to spend his political capital on an unpopular Iraq war (The Times of India 8 May 2010: 20). The people of Iceland voted an emphatic and resounding "No" in a referendum on a $5 billion deal to repay Anglo-Dutch loans fully aware of the fact that this would lead to delay in foreign aid, economy recovery as well as membership of the European Union (The Times of India 7 March 2010: 25). The other set of negative news emanated from the Indian sub-continent. Sri Lankan President Mahindra Rajapaksa has stated that EU's threat to suspend GSP Plus tariff concessions for Sri Lanka is a politically motivated decision. He also stated that these concessions were in fact offered just after the tsunami in order to help Sri Lanka deal with the disaster. He further said that now that the disaster was over, Sri Lanka would look for new markets (Venkataramanan 28 June 2010:6). The EU's endorsement of China's decision to go ahead with its nuclear deal with Pakistan did not go well with India as it believes that the move threatens to undo the progress made in the Indo-China relations since Copenhagen (Dasgupta 24 June 2010:16). The BJP President opined that no efforts are made to convert EU states or the Islamic states of Pakistan and Bangladesh into secular states but the existence of a Hindu kingdom like Nepal is not tolerated and it is converted into a secular state. He stated that he would be happy to see the new secular republic of Nepal become a Hindu state again (The Times of India 23 March 2010: 16).

The Times of India reported a total of 16 negative news items from the environmental sphere. The European Commission stated in a communiqué that it was not willing to fund mitigation actions in emerging economies such as India because many of the developing countries especially the ones that are more economically advanced have adequate financial resources at their disposal to generate the necessary domestic investment for climate change (Sethi 12 September 2009:10). The attitude of the UN Climate Panel Chief, De Boer in the course of the Copenhagen talks invoked a lot of criticism with the developing country delegates accusing the Secretariat of being biased in favour of the European Union. De Boer along with the European Union had come under fire from countries like China and India for "hardselling the Copenhagen Accord" despite the key developing countries like China and India not in favour of giving it preference over the formal UN process (The Times of India 4 November 2009:23). An EU directive outlawing the export of chemical methyl bromide because it damages the ozone layer has led to a "bizarre crisis" which may create chaos in the game of cricket. It is feared that a $10 million a year industry could be ruined unless a viable solution is put in place (The Times of India 17 April 2010: 30). It has been alleged that EU and US have "played all the negotiating tricks possible to take the life out of Kyoto Protocol because of their reluctance to accept binding emission reduction targets under the next phase of the protocol (Sethi 21 April 2010: 11).

The Times of India reported a total of 8 EU news items pertaining to social affairs in a negative tone. One of the news items highlighted the lack of gender parity in the EU. It stated that although women acquire more degrees and score higher grades than men in industrialised nations, they are still paid less salary and generally tend to work part time. Moreover, only 18 per cent of tenured professors in the EU are women (Bennhold 8 March 2010:25). The announcement by Britain's home office of a low ceiling of work permits to be issued to applicants outside the European Union was not taken well especially by India as it would be severely impacted by the decision (Ray 30 June 2010:11). A team of ambassadors from EU member-states met the Indian Home Minister P. Chidambaram and complained about their citizens being harassed because India's visa policies "were keeping them out of India". The anguish was expressed in strong language to the Indian Government and some contemplated to take reciprocal measures against Indians travelling overseas (The Times of India 5 April 2010: 12). The Somali cook who helped terrified hostages by buying cell phone cards and sneaking them guns to escape, had been refused shelter by European Union nations, Syria and nearby Djibouti which amounted to putting him to death for showing compassion (The Times of India 20 June 2010: 17). It was apprehended in one of the news items that there is a huge possibility of losing vast segments of cultural and scientific heritage when technology moves on because of loss of global data which continues to increase by the day. It was reported that EU alone loses digital information worth €3 billion annually in this manner (The Times of India 24 May 2010, 20).

The Times of India – Neutral News

The Times of India reported a total of 127 EU news items with a neutral tone. Economy-related news items with a neutral voice were 46 in number out of which 15 dealt with the state of economy. It was reported that investors were watching Greece to see whether its austerity plan will "stave off the risk of default". The EU and IMF had pledged to lend Greece €110 billion over a period of three years to enable it to pay billions in expiring debt after being shunned by the financial markets due to the high cost of borrowing (The Times of India 9 December 2009:9). EU officials were trying to come up with a proposal to create a new crisis fund which would head off market predators who threaten the economic health of the Eurozone. Although, bailouts are prohibited by EU treaties, the EU wants to employ the clause of "exceptional circumstances" which had previously allowed the EU to extend help to non-Euro member-countries including Hungary, Latvia and Romania (The Times of India 14 May 2010: 22). It was reported that the European Central Bank bought a total of €16.5 billion worth of bonds as part of the Eurozone's government bond purchase programme which began after the ECB gave up its rigidity on this count in order to resolve the Eurozone crisis at the earliest (The Times of India 18 May 2010: 26). Most of the news items dealt with providing information about various measures and funds directed at checking the spread of the Eurozone crisis. Trade related news talked about the incentives being given to Indian exporters by means of the Five-Year Foreign Trade Policy to widen their reach in global markets beyond the European Union, Japan and the United States owing to the economic crisis in these key destinations (The Times of India 18 August 2009: 28). It was reported that ministers from the US, European Commission, Brazil, South Africa and China are attending simultaneous negotiations on services, agriculture and non-agricultural market access in order to reach a deal at WTO (The Times of India 4 September 2009: 21). China was forced to change its tariffs on imported auto parts after losing a case filed by United States, European Union and Canada at the WTO. A total of 10 industry-related EU news items were reported. The aviation industry got maximum coverage. It was reported that the EU has proposed new guidelines for dealing more effectively with volcanic ash which had caused disruption of air-traffic. The new proposal aims at giving more flexibility to air traffic controllers and ensuring a smoother response to emergencies (The Times of India 23 May 2010: 21). The European Union Transport Ministers made attempts to ensure resumption of flights by dividing the northern skies into three areas namely, a "no-fly zone, a caution zone and an open-skies zone" (The Times of India 21 April 2010:20). The European Commission after a meeting of the Europe Transport Council was in favour of introducing the Single European Sky Concept in order to ease passenger burden (John 25 April 2010: 10). Sanjay Kohli and his partner Steven Chen won the European Inventor Award 2010 in the category of inventors from non-European countries for developing the powerful but inexpensive chips which first allowed satellite signals to be put to effective use in GPS devices and which were extensively used in cars, planes, ships and mobile phones (The Times of India 30 April 2010: 26). A European Commission study estimated the size of the gambling sector to rise from €51.5 billion to €64 billion by 2010 (The Times of India 21 April 2010: 15).

The Times of India reported a total of 40 EU news items related to politics with a neutral tone. A total of 15 news items dealt with internal politics pertaining to the European Union and the political issues that found mention included the Lisbon Reform Treaty, Ukrainian accession to the EU, 20 years of the fall of the Berlin Wall, election of the EU President, creation of a European army, the role of Kaczynski brothers in Polish politics, conditionalities for adopting the euro and the European Parliament vote against transferring bank data to the US. The external news in which the European Union assumed a neutral position included Israel-Palestine conflict and monitoring of peace in Gaza, nuclear proliferation in Iran, Afghanistan's presidential election, Pakistan's presidential election, selling of arms to Sri Lanka, Haiti earthquake, trade relations with Myanmar, Chinese perceptions about the EU, global extension of balance of power and enhancing nuclear security.

News related to social affairs with a neutral tone was substantial and totaled 28 in number out of which 7 EU news items were related to immigration and they mainly emanated from the UK. It was reported that both the Labour and Conservative party shall release their manifesto which is likely to include tough new restrictions on immigration as well as vigilance with respect to student visas (Ray 12 April 2010: 16). It was announced that more than 100 Indian doctors are likely to be offered jobs in the UK as authorities have resumed recruitment in order to do away with the shortage of medical professionals at the junior level despite the earlier news about reducing the total number of work permits to be given to people outside the European Union (Ray 3 June 2010: 9). News related to multiculturalism talked about the ban, proposed by President Nicolas Sarkozy, on wearing Islamic veils in public that covered the face because it "hurts the dignity of women and is not acceptable in French society". This proposition has sparked a debate on the rights of women and religious freedom and has been criticised and appreciated in France where the largest Muslim community in the 27-member European Union resides (The Times of India 22 April 2010: 23). In other news, the chief rabbi of Poland, Michael Schudrich stated that Poland was the most pro-Israel country in the EU. He said that the attitude towards Jews in the EU is reflected by a statement in which Pope John Paul II describes Jews to be "our elder brothers" (Bilefsky 1 March 2010: 15). In the course of discussing the game of hockey, reference was made to the EU rule which states that European players have been provided with the freedom to work wherever they wish (D'cruz 9 March 2010: 24). It was reported that Taiwan had introduced a visa-free policy for Indians if they possess a visa for the European Union, New Zealand, Canada, Japan, Australia and the United States apart from launching "the great quarterly tourist giveaway programme" (Dhawan 4 June 2010: 1). The EU project 3Plast which stands for 'Printable pyroelectrical and piezoelectrical large area sensor technology' has made it possible for a cellphone to be operated by pointing a finger without having to touch the display screen as a result of the use of "touchless control" made up of printable polymer sensors (The Times of India 24 March 2010: 21). Andrew Hamilton, vice-chancellor of Oxford, who earns more than the British Prime Minister, has stated that a major government review of funding of universities is going on and it shall be looking at the scope for a change in fee that is charged upon the student community in Britain and the European Union (The Times of India 28 March 2010: 22). Crime-related news was largely about the role played by the European Union's anti-piracy mission (EU NAVFOR) in dealing with the menace of Somali pirates (The Times of India 21 October 2009: 23).The member-states of the European Union presented a divided house over the issue of installation of full-body scanners following the failed attempt made by a Nigerian to blow up an American airliner. Some expressed the need to beef-up security measures while others looked upon these measures with skepticism (The Times of India 8 January 2010: 18).

The Times of India reported a total of 13 environment-related news items in a neutral tone. It was reported that 100-watt versions of old incandescent bulbs will be banned in Europe and shall be replaced by energy-saving bulbs with lower wattage as part of the European Union's wider climate change package (The Times of India 28 August 2009: 21). It was reported that the chances of reaching a consensus at the Copenhagen talks had plummeted owing to the standpoint of the industrialised countries. This group included the European Union which stated that environmental integrity was central to the UN treaty and the "equity of different countries' rights" was just one element (Sethi 12 October 2009:15). However, there was another bit of news doing the rounds that the European Union has taken the decision to provide aid amounting to $3 billion a year to help "poor countries" to effectively deal with the challenge of climate change (Kanter and Revkin 12 December 2009: 12). It was reported that one of the EU officials was apprehensive of the fact that China might enter into an "undertable agreement" with the United States in order to water-down the Copenhagen resolution that shall enable US companies to operate without bringing about major emission cuts (Dasgupta 19 November 2009: 13). In fact, the EU was reported to have made attempts to win over Asia, Africa and Latin America in order to thwart the influence of China and the United States in the Copenhagen climate negotiations (The Times of India 17 December 2009: 12). The leaders of the EU member-states were on a major diplomatic charm offensive on the sidelines of an EU summit in order to prevent Beijing from projecting itself as the spokesperson for the emerging countries. Thus one of the advisers of President Sarkozy remarked in this connection that "we have Mexico, Brazil and Indonesia with us. What we need is to rally the 51 African countries, all the little islands, the vulnerable countries, Bangladesh, and India if possible," The developing countries would require $147 billion a year by 2020 to adapt to climate change (The Times of India 18 December 2009: 20).

Dainik Jagran – Positive News

Dainik Jagran reported 8 news items that had a positive tone. Economy-related news was featured in a total of 6 news items. A total of 3 news items dealt with the Eurozone crisis. The European Union and IMF came forth with a $10 billion package for bailing out countries affected by the Eurozone crisis which exceeded all expectations and led to a much better performance of the global markets (Dainik Jagran 11 May: 10). It was reported that the 27 member states of the European Union have resolved to adopt a strict approach towards hedge funds and private equity firms in order to ensure financial stability of the markets (Dainik Jagran 20 May 2010: 10). Another step in this direction has been that the finance ministers have resolved to strictly adhere to the Growth and Stability Plan (GSP) in order to penalise countries that default on their debts and incur budgetary losses beyond the acceptable limit (Dainik Jagran 23 May 2010: 10). A couple of news items emanated from the aviation sector. It was reported that the Indian government has decided to extend the visa of stranded passengers from Europe for a period of 14 days under the "Special Lending Permit". The air-traffic had come to a complete standstill for the last five days due to the volcanic ash over Iceland (Dainik Jagran 21 April 2010: 14). This was followed by the news that Britain and Germany along with other European countries heaved a sigh of relief when the airplanes finally took flight from Iceland after a disruption of six days due to volcanic ash. This led to millions of passengers being stranded at the airport and affected trade worth millions of dollars. Germany and 18 other European Union countries also resumed their flight services (Dainik Jagran 22 April 2010: 12). A sole news item was reported about the steel sector. The Indian government was reported to have taken a tough stand against cheap exports from China and other countries including the EU (Dainik Jagran 23 February 2010: 23). Only a couple of articles falling under the political category carried a positive tone. It was argued that the countries affected by the acts of Pakistan sponsored terrorist organisations such as the European Union, Indonesia, America and Russia will not come under undue influence of Pakistan. The whole world knows that Pakistan is the biggest nuclear proliferator and is the hub of global jehadi terrorism (Subramanyam 28 February 2010: 8).

Dainik Jagran – Negative News

A total of 7 news items on the EU were reported in a negative tone in *Dainik Jagran*. All articles barring one were reported about economic issues. It is reported that the people of Germany were not happy about the economic package being doled out to countries that have defaulted on their debts (Dainik Jagran 11 July 2009). The euro was reported to have slumped to its 4 year low in comparison to the dollar for which demand has increased among banks and importers which has further led to the strengthening of the currency (Dainik Jagran 20 May 2010:10).The Eurozone debt crisis has led to a change in direction of the FIIs in India as investors have started withdrawing their money from the Indian market in order to compensate for the losses incurred domestically in Europe. This month alone saw the withdrawal of Rs.7000 crore (Dainik Jagran 20 May 2010: 10). Trade-related news expressed concern about the EU and the US being worst affected by financial crises and this was considered bad news for India as the two happen to have the largest share in India's trade volumes (Pradhan 12 September 2009: 10). It was reported that despite the economic recession inflicting the United States and the European Union, both were providing unjustified subsidies in the agricultural sector against which the Indian government had never appealed (Sharma 23 September 2009: 8). It was further stated that the unity among the developing countries including India is of great significance in the light of the pressure being exerted on them by America and the countries of the European Union for the opening up of their agricultural markets (Dainik Jagran 3 December 2009: 10). A sole news item with a negative tone was reported from the environmental sphere. It was reported that voluntary declarations of cuts in carbon emissions made by America and the European Union were considered to be highly insufficient by the developing countries in order to deal with the challenge of climate change and securing the future of mankind (Singh 13 December 2009: 8).

Dainik Jagran – Neutral News

Dainik Jagran reported a total of 9 news items in a neutral tone. Three news items dealt with economy-related news about the sovereign debt crisis. The European Union and International Monetary Fund announced a $10 billion package for bailing out European countries who find themselves in a situation similar to that of the Greek debt crisis (Dainik Jagran 11 May 2010: 10). In order to save the euro, increased selling of the dollar was resorted to. The rupee strengthened by 64 paise against the dollar. This was the biggest spike in a single day in the past 12 months (Dainik Jagran 11 May 2010: 10). News pertaining to the environment with a neutral tone found coverage in a total of 4 news items. It was reported that Russia releases 11.71, Japan 9.87, European Union 9.40, China 3.60 and India 1.2 tonnes of greenhouse gas per person respectively. Therefore it was decided at the G-8 summit in Italy this July to reduce greenhouse gas emissions by 50 per cent by 2050 (Gupta 31 October 2009: 10). Although, the European Union has increased the money that it is offering for the sake of success of the Copenhagen talks, it has also added a rider that India and China along with other large polluting countries should announce a cut in carbon emissions within the ambit of internationally binding norms (Upadhyaya 13 December 2009: 1). Meanwhile, it was also reported that Australia, European Union and America have laid the blame upon the developing countries and G-77 as well as China for the deadlock in the talks taking place at Copenhagen (Dainik Jagran 17 December 2009: 6). A couple of news items on the EU falling under the political category were reported. Although European Union, Russia, Japan and India may help America in perpetuating its hegemony, it is India that can prove to be the most influential and useful ally of America owing to its vibrant democracy and the use of English language (Subramanyam 9 August 2009: 10). It was stated in the context of Indo-China relations that the possibility of completely normal relations should not be ruled out as in the case of East and West Germany (Ram 26 April 2010: 6).

Most Visible EU Institutions

European Commission

A total of 90 news items mentioned the role of EU institutions out of which 66 news articles mentioned the European Commission (EC) (Figure 3.9). The largest share of articles (40 per cent) mentioned the EC in the segment of business and finance which majorly concerned itself with competition laws, mergers and acquisitions, anti-monopoly cases, search advertising, regulatory orders for world banks and markets, authenticity of credit rating agencies, creation of European Monetary Fund and proposals for investment in the mobile industry. A total of 17 EU news items referred to the European Commission with reference to the state of economy. The EC was reported to be in the process of chalking out a proposal to be made before the Council of Europe for putting in place the European Stabilisation Mechanism in order to preserve financial stability in Europe (The Times of India 9 May 2010: 23). The EC declared that it would assist Greece in formulating and implementing the fiscal consolidation programme falling within the ambit of treaty provisions of the Eeurozone countries (The Times of India 10 December 2009:29). The European Commission soon afterwards reported that Greece is favourably poised towards meeting a 4 percentage point deficit reduction target in 2010 but it would have to intensify deficit cutting efforts in 2011 and 2012 owing to an increase in deficit of 13.6 per cent of gross domestic product rather than 12.7 per cent as reported earlier (The Times of India 23 April 2010: 26). The EC appeared in 14 industry-related EU news items.

Figure 3.9: Most Visible EU Institutions

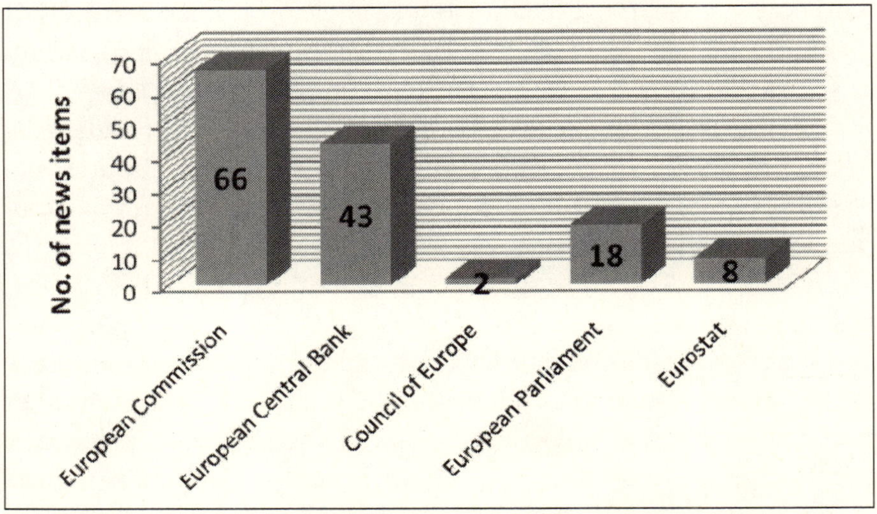

The civil aviation industry reported that Lufthansa had submitted new proposals to address EU anti-trust concerns over its plans to buy Austrian Airlines. The proposal shall be put to market-test by the EC which has been entrusted with the responsibility of ensuring fair play among the states in the EU (The Times of India 29 July 2009: 18). It was reported that EU had assured India that it would take all necessary steps to resolve the issue related to recent cases of life-saving generic or off-patent medicines sent from Indian shores and being confiscated at European ports. However, when asked whether changes would be made in the custom regulations of the European Commission, there was a non-committal reply in this regard (The Times of India 6 September 2009: 6). It was reported that the latest EU-India squabble over import duty on wines and spirits would be resolved through holding of talks and without going to the WTO as had happened in 2007. The European Commission had "dragged India to WTO" for the denial of "national treatment" to alcohol imported from Europe (The Times of India 27 October 2009:5). A positive development was reported from the Indian IT industry. Software lobby Nasscom and the European Commission had come very close towards allowing a single work visa for the EU primarily consisting of intra-corporate transferees (Ranganathan 23 June 2010: 5). A complaint was lodged before the EC by Eurofer against the biggest iron ore suppliers who were allegedly indulging in "illicit coordination of prices". Eurofer represents steelmakers of Europe and is recognised as the regulatory arm of the EC (Biesheuvel 2 April 2010: 7).

The European Commission made its presence felt in trade-related news about the EU in 6 articles. The EC was instrumental as far as representation of the EU standpoint was concerned at the WTO on matters such as subsidies on agriculture, discriminatory trade taxes on imported European liquor and import of genetically altered grain from the US. The European Commission was making an attempt to set aside all Indian concerns that the EU-

India FTA might have an adverse impact on the production of cheap life-saving drugs in the country (The Economic Times 4 May 2010:11). The Russian Deputy Prime Minister was reported to have met members of the European Commission in order to communicate the intention of his country to join the WTO by the end of the year (The Times of India 16 April 2010:24).

The EC appeared in a total of 6 news items on environmental affairs. It was entrusted with the responsibility of ensuring a smooth transition from old style 100-watt incandescent bulbs to bulbs with lower wattage in a bid to curtail carbon emissions (The Times of India 28 August 2009:21). The Commission was reported to announce through a communiqué its unwillingness to pump in funds in emerging countries such as India for the purpose of combating climate change (Sethi 12 Sepetember 2009:10). However, subsequently the European Commission stated that the EU is on track for providing €2.39 billion of fast-start finance to developing countries in order to dispel confusion about the exact quantum of money being made available to put a check on global warming so that an international deal on climate change can be reached as soon as possible (Goswami 7 June 2010: 3).

A total of 8 news items related to politics mentioned the EC. The EC was accused of "maladministration" by European ombudsmen as it failed to consider "potentially exculpatory" evidence in a case against chip maker Intel Corp. The EC responded by saying that it fully acknowledges and respects Intel's right of defence after which Intel was reported to have initiated the year-long appeal process to the European Union's Court of First Instance in which it would be allowed to mention the ombudsmen's standpoint about the case (The Economic Times 9 August 2009: 5). It was mentioned that each EU member-state would retain its seat in the European Commission as before (Castle 16 November 2009:14). The European Commission along with UK ordered the withdrawal of "GSP Plus concessions" which permit tariff-free entry of Sri Lankan textile goods into the EU which was largely regarded as a means employed to put pressure on the Rajapakse government to ensure reconciliation, accountability and respect for human rights in Sri Lanka (Castle 5 March 2010: 16).

A total of 9 news items related to social affairs mentioned the role of the EC. The British minister for Culture and Tourism stated that Britain should have notified the EC about the existence of Video Recordings Act (VRA), 1984 that aimed to regulate the industry but had supposedly failed to do so. The absence of notification to the EC implies that VRA is no longer enforceable against individuals in UK courts and people who are currently being prosecuted under the Act cannot be convicted until a new law comes into force (The Times of India 26 August 2009: 25). Another piece of news related to social legislation talked about talks held between Vayalar Ravi, Overseas Indian Affairs Minister and the EC for facilitating easier issue of work and resident permits for Indians under an “umbrella agreement” which would help in turn to “diversify the destination base for skilled and unskilled Indian workers.” (Dhawan 16 October 2009: 19). News related to research and education was reported in abundance. It was reported that the EC and Indian Department of Science and Technology have announced a joint initiative for solar power research spanning Indian and European geographies with each side committing to contribute €5 million (The Economic Times 1 August 2009: 5). Sanjay Kohli, largely known as the father of mass-market GPS technology was short-listed in the category of inventors from non-European countries for the European Inventor Award instituted by the European Commission and the European Patent Office (John 5 April 2010:20). The European Commission officially launched the Lorenzo Natali Prize for 2010 which is an international award instituted in 1992 and is given for best journalistic work on development, democracy and human rights (The Times of India 3 May 2010: 43). The EC’s involvement was reported in the area of visual analysis which refers to a multi-disciplinary activity that brings together the sciences of analytical reasoning, visual representations, interaction techniques and data manipulation in which global cooperation and cultural differences are considered to be vital factors. The EC was reported to be in the midst of developing a training platform for crisis management by employing various techniques of visual analytics (The Times of India 7 June 2010: 78). The information regarding China Europe International Business School which was established in 1994 as a joint venture with funding from the European Commission and the Chinese government also made news. It was reported that CEIBS now has a new campus in Beijing apart from the original campus in Shanghai (Ray 17 May 2010:50). The EC has stated that experts and industry shall come together to draft tougher laws to limit hearing loss and urged makers of popular digital music players to recommend users to turn the volume down in order to preserve their hearing (The Economic Times 29 September 2009). It was stated that the European Union is likely to bring about large-scale changes in the approval system for genetically-modified crops under the proposals to be adopted in the month of July. The new proposal aims at maintaining an EU-level approval system simultaneously with the freedom of EU member-states to decide whether they would like to grow GM crops or not (The Economic Times 5 June 2010: 9).

European Central Bank

The total number of EU news items that mentioned the ECB was 43 in number out of which 39 news items reported on the state of the economy. The ECB was reported to have made the decision of withdrawing the stimulus measures it had introduced in order to support liquidity in the banking sector in the wake of better performance of financial markets (Jones 4 December 2009:19). The German Finance Minister Wolfgang Schaeuble suggested that the treaty of the currency union, assumed to be irrevocable, will have to be subjected to change in order to protect and preserve the Eurozone and stability of the euro. He therefore stated that the EU should consider the option of expulsion of member-states who prove to be serious violators of debt rules. However, the ECB remarked that ejection of such a nature is "legally next to impossible" as changing the founding treaty would require unanimity among the 27 member-states of the European Union (Neuger 15 May 2010: 11). It was opined in one of the columns that the value and performance of the euro are adversely affected by the economic bailouts and the increasing complicity of the ECB in actions seen as harmful for the integrity of the euro. Under the rescue package for economically defaulting countries, it was proposed that Eurozone bonds could be used for ECB funding. Earlier on, the ECB only accepted bonds rated 'A'. or having an even better rating. However, it was reported that the ECB was willing to accept bonds as eligible collateral irrespective of rating. It was also reported that the ECB would purchase sovereign bonds in the secondary market (Das 15 June 2010: 16). The finance ministers of the Eurozone approved a giant €30 billion "emergency aid mechanism" plan for "debt plagued Greece" along with €10 billion expected from the IMF which shall make it the biggest multilateral financial rescue operation ever attempted. It was declared that all member-states of the Eurozone would pay proportionately their share in ECB's capital which would help in the emergence of Germany as the biggest lender followed by France and Italy (Strupczewski and Papadimas 12 April 2010: 9). The ECB was reported to have offered help in monitoring Greece's efforts and drawing up "necessary additional measures". The ECB would work in collaboration with the European Commission in monitoring the implementation of the recommendations by Greece (The Economic Times 13 February 2010). It was subsequently reported that Greece would ask the EU and IMF for the first tranche of debt aid worth €20 billion, for which a letter was sent to the ECB, EC and IMF formally, requesting the activation of the transfer of funds (The Times of

India 12 May 2010: 32). The ECB warned that Eurozone banks are most likely to incur a loss of up to €195 billion over the next 18 months due to the sovereign debt crisis and disclosed that it had increased the purchase of Eurozone government bonds (The Times of India 2 June 2010: 25).

Council of Europe

The Council of Europe found mention only in a couple of articles. It was stated in one of the articles that the possibility of buying of government debt of the defaulting countries could not be ruled out. However, the final decision in this regard would rest in the hands of the Council of Europe and the European Commission (The Times of India 14 May 2010: 22). It was reported that Council of Europe endorsed the French plan of having in place an economic government which largely referred to a more formalised system of coordinating economic policy (The Times of India 4 June 2010: 28).

European Parliament

The European Parliament was mentioned in a total of 18 news items on the EU. Prime Minister George Papandreou briefed the European Parliament about the austerity measures and structural reforms that his socialist government is adopting in order to ensure the stability of the euro. However, he also cited the difficulty of deficit reduction simultaneously with the very high rate of borrowing. It is expected that Athens will have to pay 6 per cent interest or more to borrow from capital markets which is by far the highest yield in the Eurozone (The Economic Times 19 March 2010: 38). The European Parliament's Economic Affairs Committee was reported to have approved its version of the draft measure which shall in turn be placed before the EU member- states for formal negotiations on a final deal pertaining to a general approach towards tighter restrictions on the activities of hedge funds and private equity groups (Jones and Desai 19 May 2010: 21).

Eurostat

Eurostat figured in a total of 8 news items, all of which dealt with the economy. Eurostat, popularly known as the statistics office of the EU, released the news that "seasonally adjusted unemployment rate for the Eurozone in May was 9.5 per cent compared to the month of April when the rate was recorded to be 9.3 per cent. The increase was expected in the light of continuous fall in output across Europe in the first quarter of 2009 with the Eurozone economy taking a dip by 2.5 per cent as global recession spread its fangs (The Economic Times 3 July 2009: 21). The Eurozone was declared to be officially out of recession along with the United States and Japan with growth of the economy by 4 per cent in the third quarter from the previous three-month period (The Economic Times 16 November 2009: 1). Eurostat stated that the unemployment rate in the Eurozone would remain the same as last month despite 134,000 individuals losing their jobs. The unemployment rate in the EU rose by 0.1 per cent to 9.3 per cent in October (The Economic Times 2 December 2009: 17). The statistics agency confirmed its earlier estimate that the economy of the Eurozone expanded 0.4 per cent quarter-on-quarter in the July-September period after registering a decline in output for five quarters. Eurostat also stated that retail sales remained the same on a monthly basis and declined by 1.9 per cent on an annual basis which was 0.2 per cent below market expectations but better than the forecast of 2.4 per cent of annual decline (The Economic Times 4 December 2009:19). Eurostat has ordered Greece to provide information on the "swaps transactions" in an investigation that may extend to other EU countries. Goldman Sachs which is Wall Street's most profitable securities firm is alleged to have aided and abetted Greece's bid to hide its deficit to comply with the euro membership criteria. Greece is facing the ire of several Eurozone countries for failing to disclose the swaps to EU regulators (Martinuzzi 18 February 2010: 16). The Eurostat went on to report that Greece which is seeking a bailout package with the European Commission, European Central

Bank and the International Monetary Fund, recorded a deficit of 13.6 per cent of gross domestic product rather than 12.7 per cent reported earlier. In addition to this, Eurostat estimated that the fiscal gap may actually turn out to be much higher (The Times of India 23 April 2010: 26). The EU member-states decided to allow access of up to €750 billion in order to rescue struggling economies. The EU also stamped its approval on the plan to grant the EU statistics agency more power for the purpose of auditing national budget reports in order to avoid understated economic figures as in the case of Greece considered largely responsible for the sovereign debt crisis. European Commissioner Ollie Rhein was of the view that Eurostat should begin with investigating the figures of Bulgaria once it these assumes powers (The Economic Times 9 June 2010: 15).

Most Visible EU Officials

Catherine Ashton

European Union High Representative for Foreign Affairs and Security Policy and Vice-president of the European Commission, Catherine Ashton featured in a total of 4 news items on the EU. Her appointment as foreign affairs chief along with that of Belgian Prime Minister Herman Van Rompuy as the union's first president was reported. Both were described as "low profile compromise candidates little known outside the EU". Consensus on the two appointments was arrived at by convincing member-states of the European Union on one hand and the European Parliament on the other, by appointing a centre-right President and a centre-left High Representative for Foreign Affairs (The Times of India 21 November 2009:23). Mauritius along with Kenya, Seychelles and Tanzania has expressed its willingness to try and jail suspected pirates, in cooperation with the EU, off the coast of Somalia— which has gained the notoriety of being known as the world's most dangerous shipping lane, and has led to Somali sea bandits earn tens of millions of dollars in ransom and raised insurance premium for ships. It was during a meeting with Baroness Catherine Ashton, European Union High Representative for Foreign Affairs and Security Policy that Prime Minister of Mauritius, Navinchandra Ramgoolam asked for financial assistance and training and the setting up of special prisons to detain pirates captured on the Indian Ocean in order to avoid them getting "mixed up with our local detainees" (The Economic Times 13 June 2010:9). The European Union High Representative for Foreign Affairs and Security Policy and Vice-president of the European Commission, Catherine Ashton on her visit to India remarked that India and EU share a commitment towards the universal values of human rights and the rule of law. She stated that the two partners must work concertedly towards checking climate change and improving the economic and financial situation. The strengthening and broadening of the bilateral economic partnership for mutual benefit is one of the major thrust areas for the partners. Therefore, India and the EU have resolved to build a solid and stable relationship (Ray 25 June 2010: 20). It was reported that Palestinian militants fired a rocket into Israel from the Gaza strip that killed a Thai worker when the foreign affairs chief was visiting Gaza (The Times of India 19 March 2010: 23). Javier Solana who was EU's top foreign policy official before Catherine Ashton, was mentioned in a sole news item and was reported to have stated that Iran has agreed to open its recently discovered uranium enrichment plant to UN inspectors. He confirmed that "Iran and six world powers" are most likely to hold a new set of talks on the issue of nuclear proliferation in Iran (The Times of India 2 October 2009: 25).

Catherine Ashton was mentioned in a total of 13 news items where her role as EU Trade Commissioner was highlighted. It was stated in this context that the EU shall make attempts to resolve the dispute with India related to the confiscation of life-saving generic or off-patent medicines at European ports. The EU Trade Commissioner, Catherine Ashton, who attended the informal ministerial in New Delhi stated that she was "aware of the problem and will try to solve it" (The Economic Times 6 September 2009: 6). Although Ashton had assured the Indian Commerce Minister Anand Sharma that she would look into the matter, she had not been candid enough to talk about bringing in changes in the European Commission's customs regulations (Sen 15 September 2009:9). Despite assurances of the EU Trade Commissioner that the problem of confiscation of Indian drugs at European ports would be addressed, it was reported that India is likely to file a case against European Union at the WTO. India will ask WTO to set up a panel which shall look into the matter and shall ask for bringing EU Customs regulations in conformity with internationally accepted norms (Sen 5 October 2009:9). It was reported that Brazil has also found itself at the receiving end of arbitrary decisions of EU Customs authorities and is therefore cooperating with India to file a case against the EU at WTO. It was reported that high-quality Indian drugs had been confiscated thrice at European ports this year, despite possession of European patents for these medicines (Sen 23 November 2009: 11). It was subsequently reported however, that India has decided to explore the possibility of solving the issue of confiscation of Indian drugs by holding consultations with the EU before pressing upon the World Trade Organisation to set up a dispute settlement panel for examining the issue. Moreover, the EU Trade Commissioner Catherine Ashton's stance also seems to have been appreciated by India as she talked about making an attempt to arrive at a satisfactory resolution of the problem through bilateral discussions (Sen 26 December 2009:7). It was later reported that following on Catherine Ashton's promise, the EU had committed that "it would make alterations in its customs regulations or its application in a manner that shipments of generics from India on the way to third countries would not get confiscated at European ports for violation of patent laws of the European countries." However, EU-India talks failed to resolve the deadlock and therefore it was reported that the Indian government is preparing to file a case against the EU's Customs regulations at the World Trade Organisation (Sen 22 March 2010: 11).

The EU Trade Commissioner wanted the issue pertaining to wines and spirits to be settled with India outside the forum of WTO. The EU is trying its best to persuade India to ensure compliance from Maharashtra, Karnataka, Andhra Pradesh and Tamil Nadu to bring levies on imported wines and spirits at par with the prices of domestic liquor. As per EU calculations, of taxes on foreign liquor amount to 200 per cent to 700 per cent of the sale price which is determined by the type of liquor, its price and also the state in which it is being sold. A positive step in this direction has been that the EU had succeeded in convincing India to bring down its custom levies to 150 per cent which is the WTO committed level, two years ago. However, India has not shown any promptness in forcing the states to bring about the required amendment in legislation (Sen 26 October 2010: 15). Thus, Catherine Ashton was the most visible EU official in the three newspapers as she was mentioned in a total of 17 news items (Figure 3.10).

Figure 3.10: Most Visible EU Officials

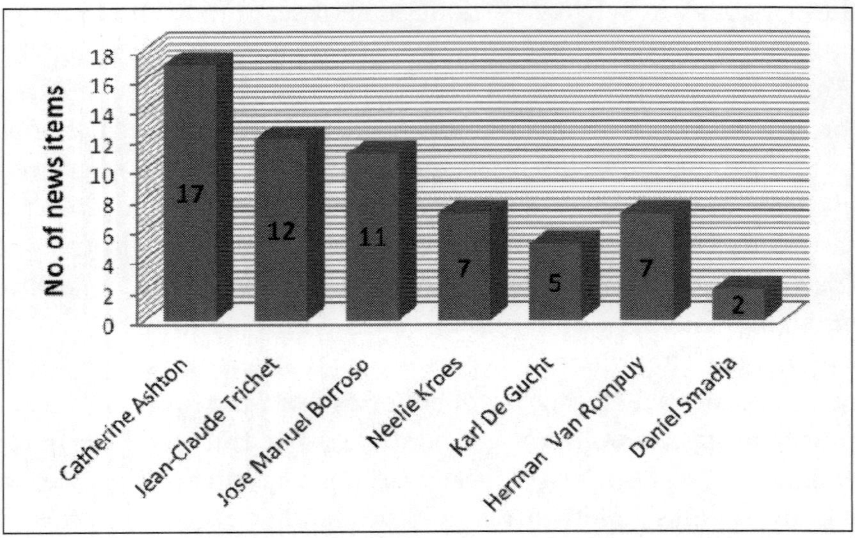

ECB President Jean-Claude Trichet

The European Central Bank President Jean-Claude Trichet was mentioned in a total of 12 news items. He was reported to have emphasised upon the fact, along with Ben Bernanke, that a lot is required to be done in order to bring the global economy to the level of self-sustaining growth (Hole 23 August 2009: 5). Trichet stated that the ECB designed its "non-standard measures" keeping in mind its "exit strategy" which would be implemented at the appropriate time. However, he pointed out that "the exit strategy should not be confused with its activation" (Kaushal 15 September 2009: 12). It was reported that Trichet would head the European Systemic Risk Board which shall watch out for financial risks. In order to get British backing for this purpose, Bank of England Governor Mervyn King could be blessed with a key role in "European Union super-watchdogs" that shall be put in place for monitoring banks and market risks (The Economic Times 23 September 2009:8). A delegation that included Trichet met the Chinese Premier Wen Jiabao and urged for "gradual and orderly appreciation of the yuan" which happens to be one of the thorniest issues between the two actors (Doran 30 November 2009: 12). Trichet announced that the ECB would undo some of the "extraordinary measures" which it had introduced lately in order to resuscitate the Eurozone economy during the global crisis. Trichet explained that in the wake of the improvement in the condition of financial markets, all measures previously introduced in order to support liquidity in the banking sector shall not be required anymore. Trichet also intimated the forecasts by European Central Bank Staff who have predicted better growth scenarios for the next year after the Eurozone comes out of the shackles of recession (Jones 4 December 2009: 19). Trichet was seen to be at loggerheads with Treasury Secretary Timothy F Geithner on ways and means to sustain growth with the former insisting on tightening budgets while the latter emphasised upon seeking stronger demand. Trichet further stated that the resultant effect of lesser budget gaps on economic growth should not be considered to be negative as it helps in bolstering market and investor confidence (Deen and Homan 7 June 2010:10). Trichet was expected to deliver a statement on the Greek financial crisis in which he was likely to talk about financial assistance to be extended to Greece which shall be subject to strict conditions as a result of "treaty prohibition on EU bail-outs" for crisis-ridden countries (The Economic Times 11 February 2010:16). Trichet was also part of the elite group that decided upon the first bailout of a Eurozone country ever since the currency was created. It was resolved that financial assistance to Greece would largely come in the form of loans (The Economic Times 12 February 2010:15). Trichet was reported to have been attending the meeting of G-20 finance chiefs in which the draft document clearly states that the EU shall seek an "effective real appreciation of the renminbi" through the forum (The Economic Times 24 April 2010:11).

Competition Commissioner Neelie Kroes

The Competition Commissioner Neelie Kroes appeared in a total of 7 EU news items. It was reported that Oracle which is one of the world's leading software makers has been taken to task by the European Union antitrust regulators who have launched an in-depth probe into its $7 billion dollar takeover of Sun Microsystems. Neelie Kroes stated that the European Commission has been entrusted with the responsibility "to ensure that customers would not face reduced choice or higher prices as a result of this takeover' (The Economic Times 4 September 2009:8). Neelie Kroes would present a proposed directive to fellow commissioners which would enable consumers to check companies that fix prices or abuse their monopoly in the market and "launch class action suits". The EU anti-trust regulators shall aim to provide compensation to victims and deter companies from violating the EU's strict rules and regulations (The Economic Times 3 October 2009: 14). The EU Competition Commissioner stated that Microsoft would allow all present users and future consumers to opt for a browser of their own choice and the company would no longer be allowed to force manufacturers to use its browser. She stated that such a step shall have a direct and immediate impact upon the market, while Microsoft was of the view that this brought them closer towards the culmination of a ten-year long episode of competition law concerns in the EU (The Economic Times 8 October 2009: 22). It was reported that the "fire-brand Commissioner Neelie Kroes" has adopted a tough posture on the issue of anti-trust enforcement rules. Consequently, a spate of inquiries in different sectors of the economy was initiated. The inquiry into the pharmaceutical sector led to investigations into the operations and dealing of 43 originator companies and 27 generic companies representing 80 per cent of the relevant turnover in the EU (Sharma 3 November 2009:15). Neelie Kroes stated that the understanding reached between Intel and AMD according to which the former would pay the latter a sum of $1.5 billion for anti-trust offences would not be impacted upon whatsoever in the wake of the two partners having settled all their litigation and exchange of money in the form of compensation (The Times of India 13 November 2009: 22).

EU Trade Commissioner Karl de Gucht

Karel De Gucht, the EU Trade Commissioner found mention in a total of 5 news items. He was reported to have stated that "it was highly regrettable" that a European-led consortium EADS, the parent company of Airbus had to pull out of the bidding of an Air Force Contract for a tanker project as the terms of the deal seemed to be tilted towards eliminating its design in favour of the American rival Boeing Co. He further warned against protectionism and stated that "open procurement markets guarantee better competition and better value for money for the taxpayer." (The Economic Times 10 March 2010: 15). Karl De Gucht is said to have remarked that India is Europe's eleventh largest trading partner constituting only 2 per cent of the total EU trade. EU-India trade therefore is less than one-fifth of EU's trade with China which he remarked "clearly falls far short of its potential (Gucht 4 March 2010: 12). Mr. De Gucht during his visit to India stated that although the new issues of child labour and the environment are not "potential deal breakers", the European Parliament would never give its blessing to a deal which eliminates these subjects from the proposed bilateral trade and investment agreement (The Economic Times 5 March 2010: 17). He pointed out that the EU includes social issues in all its trade pacts and therefore an attempt shall be made to arrive at an "appropriate language" which satisfies both partners to the agreement (The Times of India 5 March 2010: 25).

European Commission President Jose Manuel Borroso

The European Commission President Jose Manuel Borroso appeared in a total of 11 news items on the EU. The Belgian Prime Minister Guy Verhofstadt requested the European Commission President Jose Manuel Barroso to make sure that the deal involving the purchase of automaker Opel from General Motors by the Canadian-Russian consortium that included Magna and its suppliers does not give undue preference to Germany over Belgium and Britain that also have General Motors plants (The Economic Times 14 September 2009:6). The European Commission stated that the proposal for overhaul of the manner in which banks and financial markets are regulated would ensure that European taxpayers are able to avoid "a repeat of the dark days of autumn of 2008 when governments had to pour billions of euros into the banks". The proposal for reform is most likely to entrust European institutions with unprecedented amount of power over the banking industry which has been largely blamed for causing the Eurozone crisis (The Economic Times 24 September 2009:17). It was reported that Prime Minister Manmohan Singh and the European Commission President Jose Manuel Borroso would hold delegation-level talks over a whole range of issues which would include EU-India FTA, counter-terrorism measures, global economic financial institutions and climate change (The Economic Times 4 November 2009:9). Despite the fact that the US, EU and

Australia have been pushing for an "international registry", it was reported that the EU seemed to have given up on the possibility of arriving at a legally binding agreement at the climate negotiations taking place at Copenhagen. The European Commission President Jose Manuel Borroso is known to have stated that , "of course, we are not going to have a full-fledged binding treaty- Kyoto type- at Copenhagen". (The Economic Times 5 November 2009: 2). India and the EU hoped to resolve differences and sign a free trade pact within a year that shall enable the partners to reach the $200 billion mark in EU-India trade. This was asserted by leaders on both sides at a joint press conference at the tenth India-EU summit attended by Prime Minister Manmohan Singh, Swedish Prime Minister Frednik Reinfeldt and European Commission President Jose Manuel Barroso. The European Commission President went on to state that the element of trade and FTA is of vital importance for the sake of bringing about and sustaining economic recovery (The Economic Times 7 November 2009: 9).

It was reported that the EU shall bring about large-scale changes in its approval system for genetically-modified (GM) crops which is expected to open the gates for extensive GM cultivation in Europe. This proposal is based on the Austrian-Dutch plan which was endorsed by the European Commission President Jose Manuel Barroso who gave his word for implementing the proposal last year as part of his bid for reappointment (The Economic Times 5 June 2010: 9). Jose Manuel Barroso was reported to have said that "any attempt to weaken the stability of the euro will fail," as an umbrella of measures to overcome the Eurozone crisis were unveiled. These measures included a $1 trillion rescue package to guide the euro towards recovery, standby funds, loan guarantees and a pledge from the ECB to purchase government bonds in the open markets (The Economic Times 11 May 2010: 17). The German Chancellor Angela Merkel stated that Greece was in no need of financial assistance and therefore "the question of aid for the indebted country" should not be highlighted at the summit to be held in Brussels. However, the European Commission President Jose Manuel Barroso impressed upon EU member-states to agree to "a standby aid package" for Greece at the summit (The Economic Times 22 March 2010: 15). He went on to say that the decision with regard to rescuing Greece from the economic crisis needs to be taken or else the Eurozone would be rocked by economic instability and this would encourage speculation (The Economic Times 23 March 2010: 11).

EU President Herman Van Rompuy

EU President Herman Van Rompuy categorically stated that "both financial and non-financial sanctions" shall be imposed in the event of repeated violations of Eurozone's deficit cap of 3 per cent of GDP by the same member-state. Countries with deficits of more than 3 per cent face fines of as much as 0.5 per cent of GDP unless they bring their budget back in line under the provisions of the "German-inspired Stability and Growth Pact" (Neuger and Viscusi 24 May 2010:17). It was reported that the EU President Herman Van Rompuy would chair a meeting of EU finance ministers on toughening EU budget rules and improving economic governance (Holger and Rinke 20 May 2010: 26).

The euro was reported to have hit a session high versus the dollar in reaction to the speech of the EU President who stated that a deal to bail out Greece had been reached among the leaders of EU member-states (The Economic Times12 February 2010:20). The announcement by EU President Herman Van Rompuy that a landmark deal to rescue Greece and avoid a broader crisis in the Eurozone had been reached led to the steadying of oil prices above $74 per barrel. The further stabilisation of oil prices was due to upbeat forecasts for oil demand growth by the International Energy Agency and US Energy Information Administration (The Economic Times 12 February 2010:20).

The EU President stated that he is sure of the fact that Greece would receive financial assistance in time for addressing its economic problems. He went on further to say that he would like to recall the strong commitment of the euro area member states at the highest level to take necessary steps to ensure financial stability of the Eurozone as a whole (The Times of India 29 April 2010:20). The EU President Herman Van Rompuy endorsed the French proposal for a more formalised system of coordinating economic policy through creation of an "economic government" for the Eurozone. This initiative is believed to have increased pressure upon Germany which happens to be Europe's "biggest economy and chief crusader for tougher budget discipline" to accept a new political platform for discussing and negotiating on economic issues (The Economic Times 4 June 2010:28).

Daniele Smadja

Daniele Smadja, head of the EU Delegation to India, notably appeared in a couple of news items only. Daniele Smadja, mentioned as Head of the European Commission's Delegation to India interacted with reporters and stated that EU and India shall sign an agreement on civil nuclear energy dealing with India's participation in the International Thermonuclear Experimental Reactor (ITER) project during the upcoming India-EU summit. ITER is one of the largest and costliest scientific projects and it has six participants apart from the European Union. The EU-India agreement shall facilitate India's participation in the project and it shall showcase nuclear fusion as a cheap energy source (The Economic Times 5 November 2009: 2). EU Ambassador and Head of Delegation to India Daniele Smadja stated that "in the intellectual property rights (IPR) chapter (of the FTA), it will be made clear that there should be no limit on India's capacity to produce and export life-saving medicines." This clarification came in the wake of strong opposition by INGOs against the "negative consequences" of the proposed EU-India FTA which is expected to stop the supply of cheap life-saving generic Indian medicines to developing countries including Latin America and Africa (The Economic Times 4 May 2010:11).

Degree of Centrality

The degree of centrality needs to be examined in order to determine whether the EU is playing a major, minor or secondary role in international affairs. The EU is largely recognised to be playing a secondary role in 435(46.08 per cent) news items followed by minor role in 323 (34.21 per cent) news pieces and main role in 186(19.7 per cent) news items respectively. The EU is portrayed as playing the main role in the least number of news items across the three newspapers (Figure 3.11). The focus in its entirety is not upon the EU which makes it difficult for readers to register EU's exclusive role in such reportage. The finding seems to suggest that the EU has not come of its own and is therefore reported to be part of a larger picture.

As far as economic news is concerned, the EU is recognised to be largely playing a secondary role (49.17 per cent) followed by minor role (28.12 per cent) and main role (22.7 per cent) respectively in international economic matters. This finding reflects that although EU-India economic partnership is largely recognised as the mainstay of the relations, the print media reports the EU to be playing a secondary role rather than a main role in economic affairs. Hardly one-fifth of the news articles portray the EU to be playing a leading role in economic affairs.

Figure 3.11: Degree of Centrality

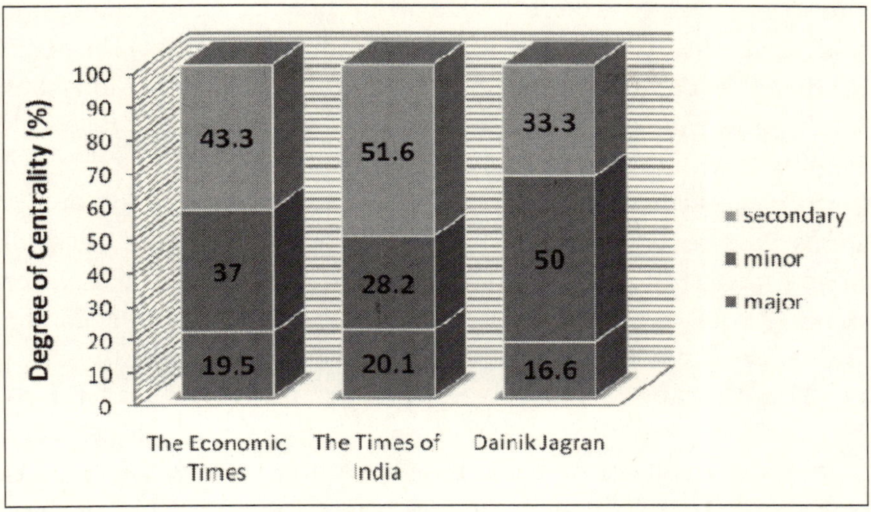

As far as political news is concerned, EU absents itself from playing the main role in European and international politics, which invariably leads to a severe dent in the role of the EU as a global actor. A meager 12.03 per cent of news items portray the EU in the main role while the EU is portrayed as a secondary and minor actor in 46.29 per cent and 41.66 per cent of news items respectively. Less coverage of the EU as a main actor relegates it to the background and leads to the erasing from elite and public memory, of its contributions in the recent past and in the present. Thus, it is clear that the Indian print media does not seem to acknowledge and recognise the European Union for its political role in the media.

The EU's visibility has undergone a further slide as far as social affairs are concerned. Only 8.97 per cent of the total news items portray the EU in a major role. The EU is seen to be largely playing a secondary and minor role in this field despite the fact that the angle of aid and development has been associated with EU-India relations since the very first phase of the relationship. This change in perception reflects the change in the stature of India from being an aid seeker to being a donor country at present. The EU is largely seen to be playing a secondary role with coverage of 48.71 per cent of the total news items on social affairs. This can be attributed to the fact that a number of issues such as immigration, crime, health, education and research dealt with the engagement between EU on one hand and third countries on the other. A total of 42.30 per cent of the total news items have reported the EU to be playing a minor role in social affairs which reflects the fact that EU is not recognised as a player making notable contribution in the field of social affairs in the Indian print media.

The EU appears prominently in a minor role as far as environmental affairs are concerned. A total of 56.98 per cent of news items portrayed the EU in a minor role while the EU was portrayed in a major and secondary role in 16.12 per cent and 26.88 per cent of news items respectively. More than half of the environment-related news items portrayed the EU in a minor role owing to the fact that EU was one among the many members who participated in international negotiations such as Kyoto Protocol and Copenhagen Climate negotiations apart from talks for reducing carbon emissions and bringing about energy efficiency. The EU was part of the big crowd taking decisions on ways and means to preserve the environment and reduce the ecological footprint.

Some Noteworthy Features

Visibility and Role of the EU in Various Spheres

The dataset reveals that EU is largely recognised as an economic actor with 70.4 per cent of the news coverage dedicated to this category. The recognition of the EU in the area of politics paled in comparison with only 11.8 per cent of new items and coverage of the EU in environment (8.26 per cent) and social affairs (9.85 per cent) respectively was not found to be so significant (Figure3.12).

Figure 3.12: Framing of EU news items

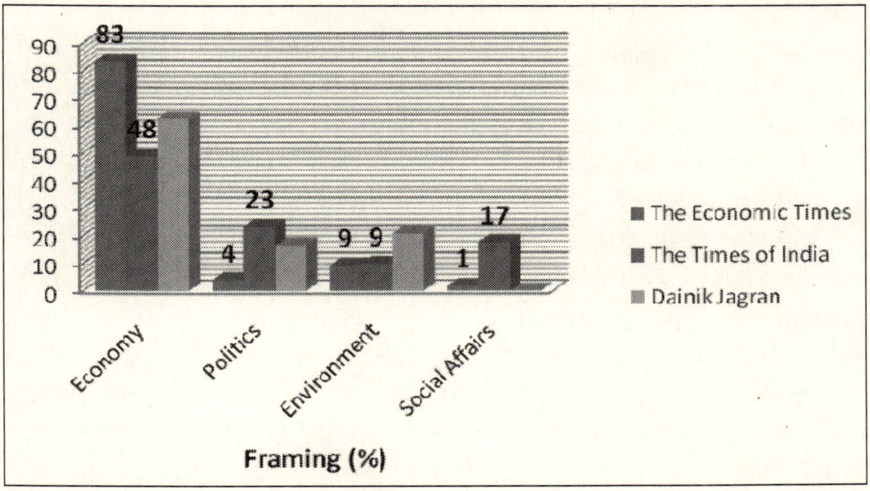

The economy-related news was bracketed under the sub-categories of state of economy, business/finance, industry and trade. The state of economy (355 new items) threw light on the economic performance of the EU as a whole and concerned itself with issues of slowdown, Eurozone crisis, recession, value of the euro, unemployment, monetary and fiscal integration, withdrawal of stimulus measures, recovery, liberalisation and growth. The business and finance segment (84 news items) covered issues such as competition laws, mergers, acquisitions, anti-dumping tariffs, EU guidelines, regulatory agencies, international finance reporting standards, banking and tariffs, hedge funds, naked short-selling and law-governing service providers. The industry segment (125 news items) included news from various economic sectors including textile, aviation, pharmaceuticals, liquor, carpets, automobile, steel, sugar, palm oil, poultry, chocolate, software industry, engineering industry, horticulture, seafood exports, insurance, shipping, tea, handicrafts, floriculture and gambling. The segment on trade (101 news items) covered issues concerning the World Trade Organisation, European Free Trade Organisation, exports, imports, EU-India FTA, anti-subsidy duties and countervailing duties.

News related to politics was further sub-divided into external and internal politics. Internal news (33 news items) covered issues such as the Lisbon Reform Treaty, European Parliament election, creation of a European army, election of the EU President and EU Foreign Affairs Chief and conditionalities for adopting the euro. Political news from the EU member-states was also part of the coverage and included issues such as British elections, collapse of the Dutch coalition government, the role of Kaczynski brothers in Polish politics and French-German scuffle over a Greek bailout. External news items (75 news items) dealt with issues such as Afghanistan's Presidential election, Af-Pak policy, Iranian nuclear issue, Israel-Palestine conflict, EU as a model for South Asian unity, reform of Bretton Woods institutions, Nuclear Security Summit, building of economic, political, intellectual and cultural capital, need for unity and leadership for external influence, EU as a model for South Asian unity and as a model for East Asian community.

News related to social affairs (78 news items) was categorised into a number of sub-categories such as consumer rights, safety and protection, aid, betterment of people, crime, culture, immigration, research and education, health and sports. News catering to consumer needs hovered around issues such as privacy rights of European citizens, robots for small and medium-scale enterprises, measures against shocking totals on phone bills, data protection and measures against internet piracy. Research-related news dealt with the solar power sector, usage of cell-phones without touching them and use and possibilities of mass-market GPS. News about education consisted of issues such as Indo-Hungarian cooperation regarding opening of universities, courses on EU and German laws in India, launch of International Relations courses with emphasis on EU in Spain, World Retail Congress, fee structure of University of Oxford, global cooperation for higher learning, quality control across universities, saving digital data and EU-China joint venture for funding education centres.

News related to gender parity concerned itself with issues such as inadequate representation of women on boards of companies in EU countries as well as dwindling numbers of females in the field of computers and engineering that are currently considered to be the most monetarily lucrative sectors. Health related news reports were concerned about global health initiatives, genetically modified crops, mental illness, device to check blood clotting levels, cure for diabetes and obesity and plastic teethers largely found to be toxic in nature. The issue of migration featured prominently as a sub-category of social affairs and mainly dealt with concerns of Indians especially belonging to the skilled sector interested in migrating to Europe. The theme of multiculturalism covered issues such as the ban on the construction of minarets in Switzerland, the ban on the veil in France, the rising acceptance and popularity of Judaism in Europe, especially Poland, and fight over the country of origin of chicken tikka masala. Most of the crime related news was about piracy, trafficking of drugs, attack on the Swedish parliament, EU legislation regarding radioactive substances and attempts to check accidents caused by drunken driving.

Environmental news was sub-divided into external and internal news. The internal news reported from within the EU dealt with European Emissions Trading Scheme, carbon-free Congress in the Czech Republic, carbon emissions, efficiency standards for electronic appliances, imposition of green taxes, carbon credits, energy-saving light bulbs, genetically modified crops, saving bluefin tuna, energy efficiency, energy-saving self-drive vehicle and new safety standards related to electromagnetic radiation. The external news dealt with climate change negotiations, Kyoto Protocol, Copenhagen climate negotiations, UN climate talks, Petersburg Climate Dialogue, Bonn II climate negotiations, EU emissions legislation, equitable sharing of carbon space, climate change, global warming and meat-free Monday campaign.

The Development Angle

The theme of aid for rescue, relief, rehabilitation and development has been a recurrent theme throughout the study. For instance, it was mentioned in the context of Sri Lanka, where it was felt that it is imperative to redress the grievances of the Liberation Tigers of Tamil Eelam (LTTE) so that the possibility of a resurgence of the violent resistance can be diminished. It was advocated that all major states of the world, including India and entities like the European Union, should act in order to salvage the situation and bring about considerable improvement in the lives of the Sri Lankans, especially the minorities. It was opined in the newspapers that India should provide aid for rehabilitation of former rebels by allowing them to study in Indian schools and universities and provide them with sufficient scholarships. The countries that were part of the Sri Lanka Donor Conference such as the EU member-states apart from Japan and Norway were urged to invest particularly in north-east Sri Lanka in order to encourage the manufacturing and services sector that could provide numerous job opportunities to the Tamil youth. The "dignified rehabilitation" of LTTE rebels who have surrendered would go a long way towards establishing peace and prosperity once and for all and will not encourage the revival of the militant organisation (Manoharan 10 June 2010: 16).

The massive earthquake in Haiti led to the death of as many as 200,000 people and left its capital, Port-au-Prince in complete ruins. The United States sent in its troops in order to provide security to the huge relief operation from chaos-creating gangs as thousands of people who survived the earthquake waited in anticipation and anxiety for promised food supplies and health-care facilities. The European Union institutions and member-states were reported to have pledged more than €400 million for emergencies and long-term development assistance to Haiti (The Times of India 19 January 2010: 19).

The EU was reported to be resorting to money and muscle power for the sake of reaching a consensus at Copenhagen for the purpose of dealing with the challenges posed by climate change. An increase in the economic dole that the EU was offering to India, China and other large polluting countries had been accompanied with the condition that the latter would be required to support a cut in carbon emissions within the ambit of international binding norms to be announced shortly. Subsequently, the EU announced it would give $10 billion dollars of economic aid in the next 3 years to the poor and developing countries to help them combat the threat of climate change. However, G-77 under the leadership of Lumumba Stanislaus Di-Aping has stated that the economic aid being extended is not adequate, which indicates the lack of seriousness among the leaders of Europe on the issue of climate change (Upadhyaya 13 December 2009: 1).

It was reported that markets were not enthused by the IMF-EU aid package for Greece which led to protests that turned violent and consequently, the list of demands has become longer. This move is looked upon as a significant change in EU policy of each member-state of the Eurozone being responsible for its own finances and marks the beginning of the era of more collective responsibility. The international financial markets welcomed the "shock and awe $1 trillion rescue package in order to restore confidence in the euro including standby funds, loan guarantees and commitment from the ECB to buy government bonds in the open market." The 27 member-states of the Eurozone agreed to the massive transfer of funds with a spirit to defend the euro at all costs ending weeks of uncertainty ever since the Greek debt crisis cast a dark shadow upon the Eurozone. There are some skeptics who point out that this will not help in solving the fundamental flaws within the economies that are not doing well. However, this move was by and large welcomed by markets from Asia to the United States in what is touted to be the biggest government rescue announcement since the G20 pumped in money in the global economy in 2008. It was reported that financial indices rose in response to these measures, as did the euro led by European bank shares (Sen 11 May 2010: 17).

Normative Power EU

The EU's role as a normative actor was also a recurrent theme in the data-set. The EU was witnessed making a pitch along with the United States, Turkey and the United Nations for an international rather than an Israeli inquiry to investigate the lethal seizure of a Turkish ship by Israel bound for blockaded Gaza (The Times of India 4 June 2010: 24).

The EU along with the United States and other western governments was reported to have mounted pressure on Nepalese Prime Minister Madhav Kumar Nepal to leave office. The western powers were reported to have adopted a candid approach towards demanding the formation of a new all-party government inclusive of Marxists (The Times of India 11 May 2010: 19).

The ETA has proclaimed itself to be the leader of the 41-year armed struggle being fought for the independence of the Basque region of northern Spain and south-west France. The European Union, along with the United States, has proclaimed ETA to be a terrorist organisation responsible for 830 deaths in the last four decades (The Times of India 1 March 2010: 15).

The EU was also reported to have raised its voice against violation of human rights in China. It vociferously condemned the upholding of the sentence of 11-years imprisonment by a high court in Beijing which was handed down to Liu Xiaobo, a Chinese writer and dissident by a lower court for "inciting subversion of state power" through his writings. In a rare move, diplomats of EU and the United States gathered outside the Beijing high court in order to register their protest where the case was put up for hearing. The EU was not supportive of the decision and called on China to release Mr. Liu (Dasgupta 12 February 2010: 23).

The EU along with the United States put further pressure on Iran's nuclear programme by means of addition of Iranian individuals and firms to a blacklist after the UN imposed a fresh set of sanctions (The Times of India 18 June 2010:21). It was reported that the European Union Delegation was scheduled to visit Kandhamal in Southern Orissa in India 16 months after violent ethno-communal clashes rocked the district (The Times of India 30 January 2010: 9).

Blockades have been a bone of contention between Israel and Gaza for a long time. After the failure of the Camp David talks in 2000, a phase of remarkable increase in violence was witnessed in the region followed by the Israeli blockade of the Gaza strip. A disengagement deal was reached by means of which the Rafah Crossing with Egypt was reopened with the monitoring done by the EU. However, with Hamas having come to power, the violent conflict between Israel and Hamas was revived, as a result of which Israel tightened the blockade which continues till this day (The Times of India 7 June 2010: 17).

It was opined in one of the articles that the entire international community is well aware of the fact that Pakistan is involved in nuclear proliferation on a massive scale and to make matters worse, it has emerged as the hub of international jehadi terrorism. Therefore, Indonesia, America and Russia, along with the European Union were expected by the international community not to entertain and encourage the nefarious activities of Pakistan (Subramanyam 28 February 2010: 8).

The EU chose not to flinch in informing Sri Lanka that it would have to comply with certain conditions in order to continue drawing benefits from the Generalised System of Preferences which hands out preferential tariffs for trade with the EU. In this connection, the EU categorically stated that Sri Lanka would be required to repeal sections of its emergency rules and Prevention of Terrorism Act apart from adopting a national human rights action plan. The EU also demanded that Sri Lanka should invite teams of the United Nations and Working Group on Enforced Disappearances and should be able to ensure that journalists are able to work in a free and secure environment unhindered by harassment (The Times of India 25 June 2010: 2).

The Theme of Integration

Billionaire investor George Soros has opined that there were trends suggesting the imminent destabilisation of the European continent with the stimulus provided by dangerous policy decisions in Germany. Soros stated that Germany is "endangering the European Union" as a result of undue emphasis upon "pro-cyclical policies" of cutting its budget deficit and holding up the rise in wages in order to make up for the fall in the purchasing power of the euro. This makes it difficult for the other countries to regain competitiveness. Soros commented that the euro was an "incomplete currency" from the start as the Maastricht Treaty of the EU established a monetary union sans a political union. He further suggested that Europe should get rid of its troubles by making efforts towards strengthening the euro by revising its structure (The Times of India 24 June 2010:26).

It was foregone conclusion that EU member-states would never be mute spectators and see Greece bite the dust. EU member-states showed no hesitation in braving the storm and this proved to be the key to the reinstating of confidence in the international financial markets about resurgence of the euro (The Times of India 12 May 2010:26). Therefore, it comes as no surprise that Angela Merkel was highly appreciative of EU's capability to manage crisis situations, stand up for the euro in solidarity and help out a member-state which finds itself riddled with debt (The Times of India 27 March 2010: 26). The political leadership was in fact reported to have shown absolute determination to stand behind the euro (The Times of India 8 February 2010: 21).

The inclusion of Russia as a member-state of the European Union was advocated by some analysts who stated that the EU ought to pursue a proactive policy of engaging with Russia. The relationship between Russia and the EU was predicted to be mutually beneficial. It was reported that a number of member-countries of the European Union were in favour of building up a European army which would lead to the recognition of the bloc as a force to reckon with (The Times of India 7 February 2010: 20).

The growing popularity of the Turkish language which is spoken in more than 24 countries of the world by more than 63 million people was discussed in the light of a possible integration of Turkey into the European Union. In the light of this possibility, business and tourism prospects are attracting language learners by the dozen (The Times of India 26 April 2010: 45).

One of the analysts threw light upon the Maastricht Discipline which the European countries had to comply with in order to become members of the Eurozone and adopt the euro as their common currency. The eligibility criteria laid down the condition that the aspiring countries should not have a fiscal deficit which exceeds 3 per cent and their economies should be largely stable (The Times of India 21 March 2010: 24).

Narayan Murthy, co-founder of Infosys Technologies Limited, cited the example of the European Union and stated that the present day European countries have “inextricably interlinked economies”. If Europe can overcome the difficulties of “history, war and genocide” in order to achieve “development and economic prosperity”, he exhorted that India and Pakistan can do the same in order to solve development issues by building economic linkages. He also pointed that the big and powerful economies had strongest trade relations with their neighbours as in the case of the United States, China and the EU. Integration of this nature could actually go a long way in ensuring free flow of goods and people between India and Pakistan (The Times of India 19 May 2010: 2). The economic integration of the EU has been a source of inspiration for many trading blocs across the world including the South-east Asian trading bloc, ASEAN, which was reported to have signed a free trade agreement to create a European-style single market which was expected to increase trade in the region by $10 billion (Patnaik 14 May 2010: 13).

Although, the British government has expressed its intention of working towards the betterment of relations with the countries in

South Asia, North Africa and Latin America where all "the economic action is focused", it has not shirked away from "highlighting the huge importance of the special relationship" with the EU and the United States. Although Britain is not part of the Eurozone and does not have smooth-sailing relations with EU-members states, it is inextricably linked to the EU which is repeatedly emphasised upon by its leaders (Ray 13 May 2010: 22). The UK's semi-detachment from the EU was very much visible when the Labour Prime Minister Tony Blair chose to expend his political capital on an unpopular Iraq war (The Times of India 8 May 2010: 20). A lot is said about Britain's skepticism about being closely knit to the EU, and the academia is known to have recently commented in the wake of the elections that the Liberal Democrats are going to have a tough time being Europhiles (The Times of India 22 April 2010:23). This scenario is highly reflective of the constant tug-of-war that is witnessed in the British political theatre on the issue of the worthiness of further integration of Britain with the EU.

Conclusions

Newspapers are a reflection of the times we are living in. They are one of the cheapest sources of information about international events and happenings. Specialised wire services have played a tremendous role in the dissemination of information across the world. Newspapers have been the lifeline of most nations and the mouthpiece of the state apart from providing space for the outlook of important stake-holders and opinion of the masses. The Indian media is credited to be the fourth pillar of democracy and press freedoms including the freedom of speech and expression have been duly assured by the Indian constitution. The liberties that the Indian press enjoys and the teeming millions in democratic India have ensured that India has the largest number of newspapers in the world. The Indian newspaper market is alive and kicking despite being constantly challenged by online access to news through sophisticated and easy to use gadgets.

The current study has aimed to study Indian perceptions about the EU through the lens of three newspapers with the highest circulation in the chosen categories. The three categories of newspapers were Business newspaper, English newspaper and Hindi newspaper under which *The Economic Times*, *The Times of India* and *Dainik Jagran* were chosen respectively.

A total of 944 news items on the EU were reported in the three newspapers in the time-period of one year (1 July 2009 to 30 June 2010). *The Economic Times* which was chosen as the business newspaper for the study reported a total of 61.1 per cent of the total EU news items. The fact that the maximum numbers of articles belong to the business newspaper comes as no surprise because the economic aspect of the relationship is widely acknowledged to be the most recognised and strongest dimension of the relationship. *The Times of India* which caters to the English speaking urban populace and is known for the most extensive coverage of news reported a total of 36.3 per cent of the total EU news items. *Dainik Jagran* which enjoys the highest circulation in the world reported only 2.5 per cent of the total EU news items in the span of one year which is worrisome as this has led to denial of exposure to EU news to a large Hindi-speaking Indian readership in rural as well as urban areas.

The monthly distribution of EU news over a period of one year shows that the first five months recorded news output in modest numbers (July-26, August-36, September -44, October-33, November-35) followed by an increase in the month of December (61) due to the Copenhagen climate negotiations after which January (47) saw the volume decrease corresponding to the modest output in the first five months. However, the subsequent months registered a noticeable increase in output in the month of February (90), March (80) and April (106) owing to the coverage of the Eurozone crisis, EU-India FTA and trade and industry related issues. The month of May (219) recorded the highest output on account of the intensification of the Eurozone crisis followed by 167 news items reported in the month of June.

A total of 14.5 per cent of the total news items in the dataset gave no information of the source of the article while 53.6 per cent and 31.8 per cent of the total news items were procured from local and international sources respectively. Thus, we see that a total of 85.4% of the total news items mentioned credible sources of news which reflects upon the fact that Indian newspapers take the task of reporting seriously. International sources are still not ultilised up to the optimum level which reveals the lack of interest, willingness and urgency on the part of the Indian print media to know the international perspective of news events. An overwhelming reliance on local sources shows that Indian newspapers are largely-inward looking and have been conditioned to be on the lookout for news with a local angle which they assume, increases the marketability of the newspaper. Reuters emerged as the most popular international news wire which explains the Anglo-Saxon orientation of the articles dished out to the readers. PTI emerged as the most popular local news wire and it was preferred by *Dainik Jagran* over other international wires even for obtaining international news.

A look at the focus of domesticity reveals that a total of 26.1 per cent of the total news items reported news originating from the EU while 51.9 per cent of EU news had a local focus and 21.92 per cent of news items mentioned the role of the EU in a third country respectively. The total share of EU news is very less and this suggests that the Indian press does not make any significant effort to educate its readership about various facets of the EU and consequently the EU continues to be considered a strange and distant entity to deal with. Most of the EU news items had a local focus which is a welcome sign as EU news originating in India gives an insight into the nature of the bilateral engagement between the partners. However, it seems the Indian press is far more concerned about news with a local focus than EU news which smacks of an India-centric approach without adequately factoring in the EU side and the international dimension of the partnership. About one-fifth of EU news articles had a third country-focus in which the EU was mentioned only in passing and therefore did not significantly contribute to enrich our understanding about the EU and EU-India partnership.

The evaluation of EU news items reveals that 19.38 per cent of EU news items were reported in a positive tone, 34.63 per cent in a neutral tone and 45.97 per cent in a negative tone respectively. The Indian press has not been keen to portray the EU in a positive light, despite there being no sensational controversies, aggressive attitudes and acrimony being on display. Therefore, hardly one fifth of EU news being reported with a positive tone does not conform to reality and it would not be an exaggeration to say that it does a disservice to the EU-India partnership. A sizeable number of EU news items were reported in a neutral tone and therefore these articles can be said to be a part of mundane reporting. Such articles are extremely factual and neither paint a positive nor a negative picture and thus make for very dull reading. The impact of such articles on the reader is decidedly low as it has no fireworks and very less appeal. The majority of the articles were reported in a negative light owing to the unfolding and intensification of the Eurozone crisis. The negative portrayal of the EU in the largest chunk of the articles will not in turn lead to a positive impression in the minds of the readership. Besides, the positive aspect of the relationship fails to get its due which makes matters worse and to top it all, there are a notable percentage of articles with a neutral tone. This finding calls for urgent attention and immediate and necessary action in order to ensure portrayal of the EU in the Indian press which is proportionate to reality.

EU institutions were mentioned only in 14.5 per cent of the total number of news articles with the EC being mentioned only in 7 per cent of the total number of articles followed by the ECB which appeared in 4.5 per cent of the total news items. Many of the EU institutions such as the Council of the European Union, the Court of Justice of the European Union and the Court of Auditors were not mentioned at all. This means that the Indian press does not consider it to be worthwhile to include EU institutions in its reportage while discussing EU-India relations. This deprives the Indian readers from knowing anything and everything about EU institutions which have an indispensable part to play in the conduct of relationship between the two sides. The near-about complete obliteration of EU institutions from the Indian press only goes onto add to the ignorance of the readers about the dynamics of the partnership.

The picture gets gloomier when we cast a glance towards the visibility of EU officials, the most popular of who appears to be Catherine Ashton who was mentioned in 1.8 per cent of the total number of articles in the data set followed by Jean Claude Trichet (1.27 per cent) and Jose Manuel Borroso (1.16 per cent). Thus, the EU appears to be largely a leaderless, faceless and voiceless gigantic machine which goes about its work and contributes mechanically to the relationship. Thus, no warmth of a human being seems to nurture the EU which must surely confound Indian leaders even more. They find it even more difficult to understand and relate to the EU and they therefore, train their gaze on engaging and understanding EU member-states as their leaders enjoy a high degree of visibility in the Indian newspapers for reasons ranging from sound policies to news about their personal lives.

The degree of centrality reveals that EU is portrayed as a secondary actor in 46.08 per cent of news items while it plays the role of a minor actor and the main actor in 34.21 per cent and 19.7 per cent of EU news items respectively. Thus, the EU appears to be playing a secondary role in majority of the articles. This means that the EU does not appear as a solo actor in most of the articles as it involves another equally important actor which is not necessarily India. Therefore, the personality of the EU is not unraveled in totality in such articles. In addition to this, the EU is portrayed as a minor actor in a notable number of news articles which provides even less information and insight about the EU because it is mentioned only in passing as one in the midst of the crowd. These articles however hint at the various fronts and areas where EU is involved. But since brevity is maintained while mentioning the EU, the Indian readers are unable to learn much about the EU from such articles. The EU appears in a main role only in one-fifth of the total number of news items which means that even when an article mentions the EU, there is an almost 80 per cent chance that it shall assume a secondary or minor role in the news story. This takes the debate of visibility to another level as we realise from this finding that visibility alone cannot be considered to be the determining factor for ensuring familiarity with the EU as visibility in which role and in what capacity becomes an equally or much more important consideration.

The EU finds most frequent mention as an economic actor in the current study in a total of 70.4 per cent of news items while it is mentioned as a political actor in 11.8 per cent of the news articles. EU is portrayed as an environmental actor in 8.26 per cent of total new items while 9.85 per cent of news items mention it as an actor in social affairs. The EU is mentioned as an economic actor in a majority of the EU news items which confirms the fact that the economic aspect of the relationship is the strongest and most visible. However, the Indian press refuses to recognise the EU as a relevant actor in political affairs which explains the reason for the Indian reader's comprehension about the EU's global political role bordering on ignorance and ambiguity. The EU has not had a significant portrayal as far as environmental affairs are concerned for it played an increasingly subdued role in the recent global climate change negotiations. The visibility of the EU as a social actor was also not significant owing to the fact that most of the articles had a third country focus and also because of reduced EU engagement due to a change in the avatar of India from being an aid seeker to becoming a donor country.

The other important themes that were discussed in the study included the themes of development initiatives, normative power and integration of the EU. The EU was reported to be involved in bringing about development in Sri Lanka and Haiti, providing an aid package to debt-ridden Greece and offering economic assistance to developing countries to help them combat climate change in their countries. The assertion of normative power by the EU was seen in a number of EU news articles. The EU protested the lethal seizure of a Turkish ship by Israel, demanded the ouster of the Nepalese Prime Minister, protested against the sentence of 11 year imprisonment of a Chinese writer and dissident, visited Kandhamal in the Indian state of Odisha sixteen months after violent communal clashes had taken place, pressurised Iran to give up its nuclear proliferation programme and warned Sri Lanka that GSP would be withdrawn lest it repeals some sections of it emergency rules and adopts a human rights action plan. The theme of integration revolved around news stories about standing up for the euro in solidarity by the EU member-states, creation of a European army, inclusion of Russia and Turkey into the EU, inter-linked economies of the EU leading to development and prosperity and the EU being a source of inspiration for regional trading blocs around the world.

On the basis of the study conducted, we can safely say that the choice of the print media as an instrument to study the perceptions of the EU in India and the relationship between the two partners stands validated. This study has yielded a fair amount of articles which have provided plenty of information and analysis of the dynamics of the relationship. The various aspects of the relationship in economic, political, environmental and social spheres have been thoroughly discussed in the articles which have enabled in-depth study of the nuances of the relationship. The study has also brought to light the most popular aspects of the relationship along with the most visible themes, institutions and leaders covered by the three different newspapers catering to a very different readership although they are published in the same country. Needless to say, the print media has proved to be an extremely useful instrument for the purpose of analysing and understanding perceptions about the EU-India relationship. The study has given a fair amount of insight into the manner in which the EU is perceived in India.

4

The Perception of the Indian Elite about EU

This chapter is based on the analysis of interviews of the political, media, civil society and business elites held during the period (2 February to 10 May 2010). It mentions their thoughts, perceptions and contribution towards the EU-India dialogue. The designations of the persons mentioned are those held by them during the period of holding of the interviews. The chapter investigates the potential areas for policy-making and for consolidating the EU-India partnership. An attempt has been made to understand the sentiment and estimate the degree of priority given to EU-India relations by the elites. An effort has been made to comprehend the exact degree of engagement of the Indian elites with the European Union.

Understanding the Concept of Elite

The term elite originally meant and can still be considered to mean the "highest, the best, or the excellent. It refers to a minority in whose hands power, wealth or privilege is concentrated, justifiably or otherwise". Elitism refers to "belief in, or practice of, rule by an elite or minority" (Heywood 2008: 80-81). The concept of elite is classificatory and descriptive and it serves the purpose of designating those who enjoy a higher position in society. Just as we witness a wide range of values in society, there are also different kinds of elites in society. The elites of power, wealth, respect and knowledge are some of the types of elites to name a few. Since a term is required to refer to "elites in relation to various values", we tend to speak of "the elite" of the society. The elite in a democratic country springs from a broad base while elites in non-democratic countries are known to be drawn from a few ruling families and thus have a narrow base (Laswell et al. 2010:14).

Modern elitism, propounded by thinkers such as C.Wright Mills, has highlighted elite rule in the hope of both "explaining it and challenging it". Mills argued that contemporary America was dominated by a "power elite" that unified industry, politics and the military which were considered to be the key spheres of contemporary society. His concern was to expose the elite and the adverse impact that it had on democracy rather than to "celebrate its inevitability" (Edgar and Sedgwick 2007:108). C. Wright Mills who coined the term power elite described them as:

> ...composed of men whose positions enable them to transcend the ordinary environments of ordinary men and women; they are in positions to make decisions having major consequences. Whether they do or do not make such decisions is less important than the fact that they do occupy such pivotal positions: their failure to act, their failure to make decisions is itself an act that is often of greater consequence than the decisions they do make. For they are in command of the major hierarchies and organisations of modern society. They rule the big corporations. They run the machinery of the state and claim its prerogatives. They direct the military establishment. They occupy the strategic command posts of the social structure, in which are now centred the effective means of the power and the wealth and the celebrity which they enjoy (Mills 2000: 3-4).

Classical elitism developed by Pareto, Mosca and Mischels considered elite rule to be inevitable and an unchangeable fact of social existence. Pareto had argued that the phenomena of circulation of elites and oligarchy have been observed throughout history. He had stated that "every human enterprise has its own elite". Pareto made use of two categories of elites provided by Machiavelli of that of Foxes and Lions in order to explain the "nature of governing elite structures". The attributes of the Fox and the Lion are completely different and isolated from each other. Pareto makes an attempt to explain that "history is a process of circulation between these two types of elites". Pareto's idea of ideal system of governance would reflect a balance of forces which shall have the qualities of both the Fox and the Lion. He explained the characteristics of the two categories of elites by stating that:

> Foxes govern by attempting to gain consent and are not prepared to use force; they are intelligent and cunning, enterprising, artistic and innovative. However, in times of crisis their misplaced humanitarianism leads them towards compromise and pacifism. Hence, when final attempts to reach a political solution have failed, the regime is fatally weakened. Lions represent the opposite pole. They are men of strength, stability and integrity. Cold and imaginative, they are self-serving and are prepared to use force to achieve or maintain their position. Lions are defenders of the status quo in both the state and civil society.They are likely to be committed to public order, religion and political orthodoxy (Evans and Coen 2003: 2).

Scholars who have dealt in detail with the question of elites can be divided into two broad categories. The first category includes Pareto and Mosca —who tend to talk of a single elite, generally called the political elite who is considered to be socially decisive, while the second category includes scholars such as Saint-Simon, Karl Mannheim and Raymond Aron— who believe that different types of elites exist who share "power, responsibilities and rewards" (Keller 1991:6). The moral and the functional perspectives are the two main views that have dominated the earlier phase of the study of elites. The former justifies the existence of the elites on the basis of notion of moral superiority of individuals, while the latter attributes their relevance to the social function of a class or group. Both the approaches seem to lose direction and sense of purpose as the moral approach gives way to "mysticism" while the functional approach encourages "tautology". Despite, such limitations, the study of elites has been found to be extremely relevant in understanding the features of a modern industrial society. The social significance of the elites has been found to be growing along with the difference between the elites and the ruling classes. A striking feature of the modern societies has been the "proliferation, greater variety and more extensive powers" of elites. As a result of the increase in "occupational and economical differentiation", elite have increased in salience "as guardians and creators of collective values and as managers of collective aims and ambitions" (Keller 1991: 5-6).

The liberal-democratic perspective encourages public participation in the formulation of foreign policy. The realists do not support involvement of the common man in foreign policy making. The critical approach agrees with the assertion of the realists that elites exercise their control over the process of foreign policy making and the public is insulated from the exercise. However, the critical theorists do not subscribe to the "normative assumption" of the realists that the status quo is acceptable. In fact, advocates of the critical perspective have built up a critique of elite domination of foreign policy. It is useful to get an insight into the role of the elites in determining foreign policy by applying the elite model to the system prevalent in the United States. While the pluralist model talks about dispersion and distribution of power across all segments of the political system, the elite model states that power is wielded by a small number of influential groups. The people who are part of these groups include "foreign policy officials, think tanks and representatives of large business interests" while the public is systematically excluded from this assembly. The confabulations and decision-making about foreign affairs consequently leads to the process of "media debate and public opinion formation" which are in sync with "elite interests and agendas" that tend to dominate "media and public debate". The generally public not only grasp and internalise "what they see and hear in the news" but they are also trained to analyse issues "in a manner congenial to elite interests" (Robinson 2012: 168).

Nevertheless, it is also true that it is the self-interest of the elites that helps in binding the social, economic and political system together. The factor that keeps a check on the reckless and selfish pursuits of interests by the elites is the realisation that the system might disintegrate and collapse if such activities are not put on the leash. The contribution of elites towards changing policies is of an "incremental" rather than a "revolutionary" nature. It is driven by the motive to protect their interests. Hence, existing policies are reformed but they are never replaced as the latter would be detrimental to the dominance of elites (Wittkopf et. al. 2003: 291).

The linkage of the Indian elite with the formulation and implementation of Indian foreign policy has been highlighted by many scholars and commentators. It is widely believed that the ruling elite that mainly consisted of leaders of the Congress party had a key role in giving final shape to the principles of Indian foreign policy. Although the Indian civil service and the military played a major role in the process, their contribution was "overshadowed by the Congress and the political elite" (Gupta and Shukla 2009: 328). This three-tiered elite had divergent views regarding the aims and aspirations of India. The Congress party was more "Indian in outlook and had definite opinions on foreign policy". The clarity and articulation of the Congress was reflected in various resolutions passed by the party in the various sessions of the party held during India's struggle for independence as well as in the post-independence period. The Indian elite belonging to the civil service and the armed forces however, were a group that was recruited, trained and nurtured by the British authorities. They had no particular ideological commitment and their loyalties to British imperialism and western forms of political and economic system were strong. This group of elites was entrusted with the task of taking care of internal administration, defence and diplomacy after independence. However, Jawaharlal Nehru, India's first Prime Minister made sure that these two groups comprising of the army and the military, served India, subject to the guidance and direction of the political elite (Bandyopadhyaya 1970: 54).

The Indian elites continue to play a major role in the formulation of opinions on international issues especially foreign policy. Amitabh Mattoo has defined policy-making elites as key decision-makers in the political, military, business and scientific fields, as well as those who are likely to occupy key decision-making positions in the next five years. He has stated that India's policy-making elite has been mulling over in an extremely systematic manner, on the issue of India's international relations and its place in the world. A consensus over the main foreign policy issues exists at the core of the strategic elite. This core is said to exist mainly in Delhi and is said to consist of about a hundred members that include prominent journalists, retired civil servants, formal admirals, generals and air marshals, academics and scientists and a few politicians and businessmen. The new members are socialised through regular workshops and seminars. This group is the main conduit of advice on issues pertaining to foreign policy to even major political parties like the Congress and the Bharatiya Janata Party (BJP) ((Mattoo 2005: 83-94).

It was stated that Indian elites have a strong realisation of the economic growth of their country. However, the Indian state has been unable to reap optimum benefits as a result of the emergence of the country as a global economic power (Malone 2011). It has been stated that countries like India who do not possess the "material capabilities" to make a change in international politics are not very appreciative of the "concept of power in foreign policy making". Consequently, the word power became associated with a pejorative connotation and the Indian political and strategic elite became sceptical about power politics. This has led to progressive loss in India's ability to assert itself in international affairs (Pant 2011: 19).

Christopher Jaffrelot has observed that a major section of the Indian elite are extremely upbeat on account of the newly acquired power and do not hesitate in showing their disapproval of a Europe which has economically stagnated and which seems to have accepted this with the "content bourgeois comfort of elderly retirees." He says that this section of the Indian elite considers the EU region to be a "has-been" which has been completely drained out morally and intellectually and has an extremely wobbly welfare state which might disintegrate very soon. For instance, there was extensive coverage by the Indian press of the suburban violence which took place in France in 2005 and it was depicted as the "degradation and degeneration" that the European society was undergoing (Jaffrelot 2006).

Kirsty Hughes has remarked that the Indian elites have an extremely ambiguous concept of the European Union. It is mostly understood in terms of its engagement at the level of trade and the World Trade Organisation but everything else seems to be extremely unclear like the Schengen which is obscure to them as the UK does not happen to be a part of it. Nevertheless, a positive trend has also been noticed as more and more Indians have become aware of the European Commission and the European Parliament and a shift in the focus of engagement although extremely gradual, is taking place from individual European countries towards the EU (Hughes 2005).

A total of 38 stakeholders working in the areas of politics, media, civil society and business were interviewed during the period (2 February—10 May 2010). The political elites included former and present members of parliament. Most of the political elites who were interviewed were still in office or had the experience of serving as a minister in the Union government. The media elites included editors, Chief Executive Officers and leading reporters of different media outlets including electronic media. The civil society elites comprised of Indians leading NGOs, INGOs and think-tanks. The business elite included members of chambers of commerce, CEOs and top officials of companies, members of official business networks and persons associated with the formulation of Indo-EU trade and economic policies. Thus, a number of well-known personalities (ten from business, eight from politics, ten from civil society and ten from media) were interviewed as part of this study.

The elites were asked a total of eighteen questions revolving around EU-India relations. The data collection technique involved face-to-face in-depth and semi-structured interviews of 45 minutes duration each and the content was recorded and transcribed for ready reference. All interviews were conducted in Delhi, the country's capital. The data thus collected can be utilised for the purpose of analysis, comparison and for the identification of new trends in EU-India relations if any.

Professional Involvement with the EU

The interviews conducted reveal that the business elites have interactions at various levels with companies, firms and people belonging to different countries of the EU. They also contend that they keep a tab on the developments taking place in the European markets. However, they do not display any urgency to do business under the aegis of the EU.

The majority of the political elites were forthright in their answers about their professional involvement with the EU. They did not make tall claims of having important linkages with the EU. Many of the elites recognised the importance of the EU as a group and expressed the hope of greater involvement in the activities of the EU.

Civil society elites seemed to be more familiar with the EU and its institutions, compared to the business and political elites. They were therefore, very clear about the nature of their exact association with the EU. Most of them succeeded in making a clear distinction between EU and its member-states when talking about their nature of work in the EU.

Business Elites

The business elites showed a fair amount of familiarity with the EU and its institutions. However, they emphasised upon their association with various member-states of the EU rather than with the EU as an entity. Akhil Alha, Associate Analyst, Dunnhumby, Gurgaon, stated that his company has offices in different member-states of the EU such as Italy, Hungary, Ireland and Britain (Alha 2010). Shashidhar

GV, National Sales Manager, Wipro Limited, Infotech Division stated that he gets a "fair amount of information" about markets, the global economy, the growing global business and the manner in which customers are reacting to various situations with respect to India and other parts of the world including the EU. He also said that the organisation's operations extend to Germany, France and Spain (Shashidhar 2010). S. Harikumar, Senior Manager, Forex, Oriental Bank of Commerce, remarked that since he works at the international bank division of a bank, his organisation has "banking relations across Europe" and therefore it becomes imperative for them to closely monitor the developments that take place in Europe (Harikumar 2010). Nadeem Iqbal, Senior Merchandiser, Radhnik Exports, belonging to the textile sector, stated that he has to take care of merchandising and therefore he tries to get as many orders as possible, and negotiates on the costs in order to "get shipments plus exports of garments to European countries" (Iqbal 2010). Santosh Desai, MD & CEO, Future Brands Limited, revealed that he occasionally goes to different places in Europe where he talks about business and has "a fair amount of business contacts with the EU both in retail space as well as in terms of a whole lot of brands" (Desai 2010). Saponti Baroowa, Manager at Global Information Centre, Travel Security Services, which is a consultancy firm that monitors risks across the world, stated that their clients are Fortune 500 and Fortune 1000 companies, many of which are from Europe. However, they do not deal with any EU body (Baroowa 2010). Ms. Shravani Dang, Group Head, Corporate Communications, Avantha Group, stated that they have "acquisition companies in outer Europe" which has led to great affinity with Europe. One of the companies deals with power systems while the other is concerned with the food processing business. Both these companies are located in Belgium (Dang 2010). Mr. Sukh Nandan Singh, Manager – API Marketing, Ranbaxy Laboratories Limited dealt with marketing in a pharmaceutical company that exports medicines to EU especially Eastern Europe. He also stated that their company has "multiple links of trade" as they export medicines from India to Europe and they also have their own offices throughout Europe. He also stated that although there is no professional involvement with the EU, he does get an occasional opportunity to interact with EU officials at various seminars and meetings (Singh 2010a).

Political Elites

Agatha Sangma, Union Minister of State for Rural Development, stated that she doesn't "really deal with EU issues at all" (Sangma 2010). Anil Madhav Dave, belonging to Rajya Sabha, the upper house of Parliament and a member of the Parliamentary Forum on Global Warming and Climate Change, stated that he does not have any professional or personal involvement with the EU. However, he claimed that he is a keen observer of the "activities of the EU" and wishes that India, Sri Lanka, Bangladesh and Pakistan can combine into a bloc on the lines of the EU although this will take time as the region is riddled with problems of poverty, terrorism, religious and ethnic strife (Dave 2010). Prakash Javadekar, Member of Parliament, Rajya Sabha and national spokesperson of BJP during the time of the study and who is currently a Union Minister, stated that as a policy-maker and law-maker he does deal with the EU. He also stated that he is involved in the Globe Movement, which stands for Global Legislators Organisation for Balanced Emissions, which also has a European chapter which he has constant interaction with (Javedekar 2010). Manishankar Aiyer, former Union Minister for Petroleum and Natural Gas and Panchayati Raj, stated that as First Secretary to the Indian Mission to the European Economic Community, he was part of the team that was negotiating with the European Economic Community along with Pakistan and Sri Lanka regarding the ways and means by which the General System of Preferences could be utilised in order to protect India and South Asian manufacturing exports to the United Kingdom which was about to become part of the European Common Market. He further stated that he tried to impress upon the Europeans that they should welcome a "gathering of democracies" and not spend their energies on China. He went on to comment that "EU-India relationship has got strengthened considerably" and there is much more interaction on the economic and political front than in the above-mentioned period of the early 1970s (Aiyer 2010). Mr. Rajiv Pratap Rudy, Member of Parliament , Rajya Sabha, National Spokesperson, Bharatiya Janata Party, stated that as commerce minister for state, he had the opportunity to be briefed about "EU activities". He stated that the ministry he was in charge of dealt with the EU. He acknowledged that the EU has emerged as an "important economic group" and that India has "reasonably good trade with the European Union" (Rudy 2010). Thokchom Meinya , Member of Parliament, Lok Sabha and member of the Indian National Congress, denied any current professional involvement with the EU (Meinya 2010). Mr. Mukut Mithi, Member of Parliament, Rajya Sabha, former Chief Minister of the Indian state of Arunachal Pradesh and former lieutenant governor of Pondicherry, stated that he looks forward to an association with the EU in future (Mithi 2010).

Civil Society Elites

Alok R. Mukhopadhyay, former Associate Fellow at Institute for Defence and Study Analyses, which is a think tank working on security and foreign policy issues, stated and he personally focuses on the Indian "neighbourhood and also observes dynamics as well as complexities of the European Union". He calls the EU a "successful model of integration" which has made him opt for "EU affairs" as an area of research (Mukhopadhyay 2010). Mr. Henri Tiphagne, Executive Director of People's Watch and Member of National Core Group on NGOs under the National Human Rights Commission of India, stated that he has had a "variety of engagements with the EU". He worked closely with the European Parliament in addressing the issue of caste-based discrimination in India. He also worked closely with the EU on a project which was based on the "EU's initiative for democracy and human rights" (Tiphagne 2010). Ms. Karuna Raina, Climate

Campaigner at Greenpeace India, stated that her organisation is an INGO which has offices in 40 countries. The origins of Greenpeace can be traced to Europe. She stated that her professional involvement with EU stems from the fact that policy measures in India "are far inferior to those in practice in the EU" especially rules and laws pertaining to GM food and the need for a regulatory board for a nuclear plant. So the learning process between the two partners necessitates her association with EU affairs (Raina 2010).

Ms. Mallika Joseph, Deputy Director of another think-tank, the Institute of Peace and Conflict Studies stated that they have initiated several high level dialogues in order to understand the centres of power in the world including the EU. Their organisation has facilitated "track-two dialogue between the Indian strategic community and member-states of the EU". The Konrad Adeneur Foundation has been their partner in this initiative. She stated that interactions have facilitated understanding about the EU perspective on global issues, the various fronts where India can prove to be a partner and has further helped in grasping the complexities and challenges of decision-making in the EU (Joseph 2010).

Mr. Jesim Pais, Assistant Professor at Institute for Studies in Industrial Development, stated that he works on economic issues related to industry and his primary focus is India. He stated that as he tends to look at issues of labour and employment in India and "then looks outside, European Union comes pretty quickly". He remarked that the EU is a large economy and is comparable with India, US and China and therefore EU figures very frequently in his analysis. He also mentioned that he did a recent study on labour regulations in India which was followed by a comparative study with three EU countries which included UK, France and Sweden (Pais 2010).

Pratap Bhanu Mehta, President, Centre for Policy Research, stated that he has been associated with EU affairs in the capacity of a political theorist and a constitutional lawyer. He stated that he is extremely interested in EU issues ranging from language policy to the principle of subsidiarity. He said that that he had "a lot of interaction with the wide range of EU institutions". He also stated that as part of "international relations policy work," they have been dealing with "European counterparts to a significant degree" (Mehta 2010).

Ruchira Gupta, the Founder President of an NGO, Apne Aap Women Worldwide, which is an initiative to end sex-trafficking, stated that she has no formal collaboration with any country in Europe but she has an established relationship and cooperation with the European Women's Lobby which is a non-governmental organisation based in Brussels and lobbies for the rights of women. She said that they have joined hands with this NGO in the past for urgent action campaigns for the sake of the protection and empowerment of women. She also has linkages with a group called World March for Women based in Norway and other women's groups in Sweden and Iceland. She also stated that women's groups in Europe are fighting to change laws on trafficking by arguing that selling of sex should not be criminalised but the purchase of sex should be criminalised. She said that she is particularly looking at the Swedish laws which provide a "fantastic model" to reduce trafficking, in order to lobby in the Indian Parliament to change laws on trafficking (Gupta 2010).

Ms. Ranjana Kumari who is a women's rights activist and Director of Centre for Social Research, stated that her organisation has received technical support from the EU for setting up of a Gender Training Institute and has cordial relations and engages in active cooperation with European Women's Lobby. A number of EU member-states have also contributed resources towards capacity building of her organisation and have in turn enriched their learning experience (Kumari 2010).

Sujit Dutta, Mahatma Gandhi Chair at the Nelson Mandela Centre for Peace and Conflict Resolution, Jamia Millia Islamia, stated that he is currently working on a "very important project funded by the EU on the theme of peace building" which shall be based on the sharing of the European and South Asian experience. The EU side consists of Dublin University, Ireland and Catholic University based in Brussels as partners while the South Asian side includes the Nelson Mandela Centre for Peace and Conflict Resolution from India and a partner from Lahore, Pakistan. The four partners meet regularly and work towards "course building and course structuring" which shall be taught in different universities of the world (Dutta 2010). Mr. Wilson John, who is a Senior Fellow at Observer Research Foundation, stated that he does invite EU diplomats to some of the functions organised by his think tank. He adds to this by stating that "there is always an interaction with EU diplomats largely to do with his research project" on Asia, Pakistan and terrorism (John 2010).

Perceptions about the EU as a Great Power

A majority of the business elites recognised the EU as a great power as it was proving to be a leader in the realm of global markets, international diplomacy, military equipment, social diplomacy, agenda and norm setting. However, there were a few who considered the EU to be largely a passive power. It was also alleged that the EU member-states had different agenda and different set of interests which led to frequent squabbles among them denting the credibility of the EU of being a consolidated economic power in global politics.

All the political elites unanimously refrained from calling the EU a great power. They cited different reasons for the failure of the EU to emerge as a great power. Some stated that the EU needs to set an example by being the first to practice what it preaches. Others stated that the EU still does not speak in a single voice. Others said that the loss of colonies has undermined the economic growth of the EU. Many believed the EU to be a very strong economic power. Most of them were hesitant to call it a political and military power to reckon with in international politics. However, they did express the hope that it is most likely to become a great power in future.

The civil society elites showed a very distinct hesitation towards accepting the EU as a great power. Some of them acknowledged the EU to be an economic power in the international arena. But some of them were reluctant to accept this view. It was highlighted that the EU is in the throes of an economic crisis. The EU was acknowledged to be leading in international trade but it was stated that it does not seem to be an economic superpower. The rift among the member-states also leads to lessening of the power and influence of the EU in the external world. It was stated that the world continues to emphasise upon bilateral partnerships rather than collaborating with the EU as a single entity. The EU was applauded for its work in social affairs and was hailed as a cultural power. However, barring a single elite, no elite was ready to vouch for the EU as a great power.

The predominant view that emanates from media elites is that all of them consider the EU to be an economic power. None of them are ready to acknowledge EU as a leader in the normative, social or military spheres. Most of them mention the lack of coherence in the external policies of the EU. Many of the media elites pointed out the absence of a united and credible EU front which would help the rest of the world to appreciate better, the perspective and role of the EU in world affairs.

Business Elites

Akhil Alha stated that he does see the EU as a great power, as countries in the EU are one of the largest spenders on military equipment. Besides, the EU is vigorously pursuing the agenda of developing "EU military force in Europe". He goes onto say they are a "great economic power" as "they stand at the top in the world in terms of their GDP and purchasing power parity". They are the key contributors in the field of agriculture, industry and services. He says that the popular view that EU economy is very advanced is corroborated by the fact that services contribute 67 per cent of their overall GDP (Alha 2010).

S. Harikumar was of the view that EU is recognised as the emerging power in the world. And it is hoped that as it consolidates its economic power, it will emerge as the leading power of the world. He further adds that the EU will have a "critical role to play in the global economic environment and thus the EU should be regarded as a key player in the global market (Harikumar 2010).

Malvika Singh, Publisher of *Seminar* Magazine, did not give a direct answer. She chose to say that the EU can be regarded "as an interesting experiment of countries coming together to work" on the basis of consensus to formulate policies that shall be applicable to the European region as a whole. She believes this leads to easier decision-making in the field of trade and foreign affairs as EU member-states have come together as a collective "in a world that is increasingly shrinking and globalising" (Singh 2010).

Nadeem Iqbal was of the view that EU is "indeed a great power" and it tends to dominate many countries including India in the economic sphere. He cited the example of the Indian textile sector. They have very stringent rules with respect to the environment and use of chemicals. For instance, if they find the use of chemicals in garments beyond the permissible limit, they burn the entire consignment and do not pay the exporter. He reconciles to such rules and treatment meted out to the exporters and says that since it is a very lucrative market and there is stiff competition among the Indian exporters, they choose to work hard and take care that no rules are violated in exporting the garments (Iqbal 2010).

Santosh Desai stated that although he is a little wary of a phrase like "great power", he considers the EU to be a powerful economic and military force from the point of view of geo-politics (Desai 2010). Dr. Saponti Baroowa does not consider the EU to be a great power. He is of the view that the EU is almost a single entity when it comes to economic issues but it is not so in the case of foreign and security policy. He points out that the rift among the member-states surfaces when "hard security issues are discussed". He however admits that the "EU has a major role to play in international diplomacy, global governance, agenda-setting, development of norms and climate change" (Baroowa 2010).

Shashidhar G.V. elaborated upon the difficulties faced by EU in becoming a great power to reckon with. He stated that it is commendable that member-states of the EU are attempting to come together. But there also seem to be differences galore. For instance, the UK does not want to be a part of the EU anymore. He highlighted the fact that the euro has still not received universal acceptance by the EU member-states. Besides, doubts persist regarding the performance of the countries of Western Europe in terms of "economy, finance, business and prosperity in the coming decade". He also cited the example of France and other Scandinavian countries where a significant reduction in the number of people, who are part of the workforce, has been observed on the one hand, whereas the number of people living on pension and doles provided by the government is increasing on the other. He stated that in the light of the above circumstances, it is very difficult to imagine EU becoming the "second superpower" in the international system (Shashidhar 2010). Mr. Surjit S. Bhalla, Chairman, Oxus Investments Private Limited, is of the opinion that EU stands out as an economic, political and social power. However, since it "is composed of different countries with different interests", it is difficult for the EU to always act as a single bloc as in the case of the United States. Thus, the EU is not as effective and influential as the United States in various international organisations of the world (Bhalla 2010). Mr. Sukh Nandan Singh adds on to this view and states that the EU is in fact a passive power. Active involvement on the part of the EU is witnessed only in the case of those "things in which the US has not shown much interest or has not done a good job" (Singh 2010a).

Political Elites

Agatha Sangma stated that although EU could be categorised as an economic power, it cannot be considered to be a prominent military or political power (Sangma 2010). Mr. Anil Madhav Dave stated that the life-span of a nation or society is thousands of years and therefore it is too early to comment on the EU, which is a fairly recent experiment. He stated that EU could be called a "development power" as development was on the mind of the member-states when they came together to form the EU. He further explained that when states come together for strategic or military purpose, the alliance is short-lived as seen in the case of the First World War and Second World War. He further stated that the harping of the EU on the issue of human rights and global warming shall not help unless it gets its house in order first, rather than pointing fingers at others especially the developing countries. He believed that only then would the EU emerge as a great power (Dave 2010).

Mr. Prakash Javadekar stated that EU has the "psychological advantage of being emotionally integrated". This facilitates "composite bargaining" on economic matters and their alliance with NATO has also proved to be immensely useful for them. However, a decline in the fortunes of Europe has been witnessed in the recent past. This is on account of the fact that that Europe created colonies and they used to partake the fortunes of these colonies. He goes on to say that now that these colonies have disappeared, the EU is deprived of a major source of economic support. The rise of emerging powers such as BRICs grabs much more attention than the EU. He also stated that everyone witnessed the sidelining of the EU during the Copenhagen climate negotiations. He contends that EU therefore has a very marginal role to play in the light of the current circumstances (Javadekar 2010).

Mr. Manishankar Aiyer stated that EU is not a great power although it has the potential to be one, on account of the fact that it is a gathering of twenty-seven different nations and the geographical area is almost equal to that of India. They are known globally for their economic strength. However, the EU is still not known to talk in a single voice as far as their external relations are concerned. He opined that unless EU becomes militarily independent of the United States, it shall remain a minor power. Gradually, it might be relegated to become a non-existent power as there is "no European policy as such" and the "European Commissioner for External Relations" hardly represents the "totality of European opinion". He was of the belief that EU is "an extremely powerful force in the world of economics" and might eventually attain the same stature in the "world of politics and diplomacy" (Aiyer 2010).

Mr. Thokchom Meinya stated that he was "not sure" about calling the EU a great power in international politics (Meinya 2010). Mr. Mukut Mithi stated that the French and the Portuguese were world powers once upon a time but the EU could not be called a great power in the present scenario. He however, referred to the member-states and stated that some of them are powerful economically and in other aspects (Mithi 2010). Mr. Rajiv Pratap Rudy described the EU as "an economic group which has been formulated" and their strength in military and diplomatic fields is for everyone to see. However, he stops short of calling the EU a great power and says that "power has many connotations" and it "would not be the appropriate word" (Rudy 2010).Vincent H. Pala emphasised upon the aspect of integration in the EU. He stated that once they are united, they will be a great power. He stated that it is the economic and diplomatic power which has made them a strong force in the international system (Pala 2010).

Civil Society Elites

Alok Mukhopadhyay was of the view that EU is majorly an economic power. It has not emerged as a strong military power of the world. The EU is in the making as far as diplomatic power is concerned because the European External Action Service has a long way to go after the Lisbon Treaty came into force. He believes that the EU does have a unique character but it has been its normative power that has constantly been challenged on various issues at the WTO and in the course of climate change negotiations. He summed up by saying that EU therefore is "still an economic power" and not a great power (Mukhopadhyay 2010).

Henri Tiphagne emphatically argued in favour of the EU and stated that "the market determines the power of institutions". He further explained that since the EU "is a very strong market power, it has to be acknowledged" as a great power (Tiphagne 2010). Karuna Raina stated that she does not consider the EU to be a great power because the EU frequently fails to translate its intentions into reality. She cited the example of the Copenhagen climate negotiations and stated that the EU role in the discussions held were far from satisfactory. She stated that although the EU is a normative power, it cannot be called a great power if it cannot convince other countries to accept and adopt its viewpoint (Raina 2010). Mallika Joseph stated that bilateral relations between EU members-states and the rest of the world are given much more prominence than relationship between EU and the external world. Therefore, "India-UK relations, India- German relations and India- France relations are much stronger compared to India-EU relations" despite the signing of very relevant documents between the two partners such as EU-India Strategic Partnership in 2005. This is because people in India do not consider the EU as a great power, rather as a group made up of distinct member-states who have strong bilateral relationships with India (Joseph 2010). Jesim Pais stated that there were high hopes that EU would emerge as a great power comparable with US and China. However, that hope seems to be dissipating as the EU seems to be in the throes of a financial crisis, with Greece being one of the first countries to be inflicted with the crisis. He goes on to say that in addition to the current financial crisis, the "EU has not been showing signs of emerging as a great power since "the last years" (Pais 2010). Pratap Bhanu Mehta stated that he does not consider the EU to be a great power "for a whole range of reasons". The EU does not have a "unitary will in foreign policy" and "its ability to project power beyond its borders is very weak". He goes on to point out that one of the most vital sources of power in the world, which the EU seems to fail to realise, is migration. Consequently, "the interpenetration of elites in the United States with interpenetration of elites in India" is much more than it is with the elites of EU. This diminishes the power of the EU in international politics and it is looked upon as a "closed society" (Mehta 2010). Ranjana Kumari was of the view that EU is not "a current great power" but has the potential to be one. She further said that the social engineering systems in place in the EU are commendable as they take care of every human being who is a member of the EU and inequalities in European societies have been managed very efficiently. This is a great strength of the EU. She also said that EU has also established its credentials for providing good governance and bringing about the system of democratisation (Kumari 2010).

Ruchira Gupta stated that she would rather call the EU a cultural power as it has shown the way towards preserving cultural identities and facilitating continuous interaction between distinctive cultural norms in the borderless member-states of the EU (Gupta 2010). Wilson John stated that EU as a group is very incoherent. They do not possess consistent policies and it shall take time before they emerge and act as a strong, cohesive and assertive group (John 2010). Sujit Dutta opines that EU should be currently seen as a process rather than as a finished product and therefore it cannot be looked upon as a great power. The member-states of EU are in fact the "real functionaries of Europe" although the EU "is gradually evolving its own identity". This renders "whatever emanate from Brussels" extremely important (Dutta 2010).

Media Elites

Ajay Setia, Input Head of Etv stated that the EU is a "great economic power" but not a global military and diplomatic power (Setia 2010).

Amiti Sen, who works as part of The Economic Times Bureau, stated that the EU is a great power and its stature has increased tremendously as "the euro is growing so strong" and it is being adopted by the majority of the member-states of EU (Sen 2010). Mr.Anil Patni, DGM, Energy Security, Communication and External Affairs, Former Press Advisor to the European Commission, former Assistant Editor at British High Commission and former Sub-editor at the Times of India, stated that he has no doubt that EU is a great power. He pointed out that EU has "formulated a single currency, a common commercial policy and a common agricultural policy" and by coming together, these small countries have "formed a formidable bloc". He further contended that the EU is the "biggest trading bloc in the world". The EU was negotiating at WTO "with the strength of 550 million consumers" and with the combined purchasing power which is higher than that of the United States (Patni 2010). Ms. Lalita Panicker, Senior Associate Editor at the Hindustan Times Media Limited, stated that she largely looks at EU as a great economic power and not a military power. She was of the view that India could emulate many of the democratic practices of the EU. For instance, India could learn from the manner in which the member-states of the EU overcame their differences and yet retained their distinct identities and at the same time, formed a viable economic union which undoubtedly is a fantastic experiment (Panicker 2010). Mr. Manoj Joshi, Deputy Editor, Mail Today, was of the opinion that EU "is a great economic power but not a great political power". He laid down certain conditions for the EU in order to become a great power. He stated that the EU shall have to "work out its system of political unity and become coherent". He stated that if Britain and France can transfer their permanent seats in the United Nations to the EU, it would "be seen" by the rest of the world as a great power (Joshi 2010). Kumar Rakesh, Group Vice-President and Senior Editor, NE TV Group, stated that the EU is not a great power, although he acknowledged that it is an economic power. He also stated that the unity among the member-states is a vital asset and they ought to preserve it. He stated that the EU should strive for complete integration of Britain into the EU. He also praised the democratic ethos practiced in EU (Rakesh 2010). Mr. Ranjit Kumar, Special Correspondent, *Nav Bharat Times* News Bureau, stated that EU has the potential to be great a power. He stated that the EU has a common president and a common foreign minister, and if they speak in one voice on every international issue, EU shall become a great power (Kumar 2010). T.K.Arun, Economic Editor of *The Economic Times,* had similar views and stated that the EU is largely an economic power and it is "a very weak political power" (Arun 2010). Mr. Shantanu Guha Ray, Business Editor of *Tehelka*, a weekly news magazine, stated that EU shall remain "after the United States a fairly important power" despite job losses and recession sweeping through Europe. He referred to EU as "a pure business zone because bulk of the EU news stories revolve around business" and get printed on business pages. The majority of the news items are carried by the business newspapers rather than the "routine normal papers" which occasionally publish political stories emanating from EU (Guha Ray 2010). Soma Das, Principal Correspondent of *The Financial Express,* stated that she considers the EU to be a great power only in terms of the economic and diplomatic mould (Das 2010).

Perceptions about the EU as a Leader in International Politics

A majority of the business elites stressed upon the point that since the EU is an established economic power in the international system, it can easily use this leverage for assuming a leading role in international politics. Many of the elites acknowledged that the EU has immense potential to become a leader in international politics. The EU's political role in Afghanistan, its mending of relations with Iran and Iraq, its role in WTO, the acknowledgement of the EU as a worthy partner by the rest of the world and its efforts to bring about democratisation were appreciated. However, most of the business elites were reluctant to acknowledge the EU as an established leader in international politics. Some stated that although the EU is an important actor in international politics, it does not possess the ability of a game-changer. Some stated that the incoherent and varied voices that are heard coming from the EU dent its credibility as a leader in international politics.

All political elites categorically denied the existence of the EU as a leader in international politics. Most of them pointed out that having an economic partnership with the EU is desirable but the EU does not have the might to become a leader in international politics. Most of them stated that the United States is the dominant power of the international system and the EU, by far, is not cut out for the job in the present circumstances. The political elites had a much stronger reaction to the notion of the EU as a leader in international affairs as compared to the business elites.

One section of the civil society elites acknowledged that the EU occupies a prominent place in international politics. They urged the EU to engage more with developing countries such as Asia and Africa and play an active role pertaining to key global issues such as terrorism, international trade and agriculture. The emphasis laid upon greater involvement of the EU in Asia was done with the motive of attracting more and more largesse from the EU for development work to be carried out by the NGOs. However, another section of elites refrained from calling the EU a leader in global politics. It was alleged that it toed the line of the United States. The EU was unable to speak with a common voice on key global issues such as the Iraq war. The EU's China policy which is highly contradictory also came up for strong criticism.

All the media elites invariably mentioned that the EU is a global economic power. However, they were quick to point out that it has not emerged as a leader in international politics. This is owing to the fact that the EU has not shown the will and ability to tackle security and military issues on its own. The failure of the EU to put up a united front on various foreign policy issues such as in the case of Iraq and Copenhagen was also pointed out. It was suggested that the individual member-countries should make use of their clout in leading international organisations in order to sway the agenda and decisions in their favour and portray themselves to be a part of the EU.

Business Elites

Akhil Alha stated that EU is emerging as a global leader in the international forum. Most of the "political tie ups and political relations are based on strategy and economic alliances" and since EU is a formidable economic power, EU has an influential political role to play as in the case of "global climate change politics" (Alha 2010). S. Harikumar subscribed to a similar view by stating that since the EU is an economic leader, it shall have to play a vital role in international politics. He talked about EU's role in Afghanistan and its participation in troop deployment. He also stated that EU has shown considerable political acumen in trying to boost relations with Iran and Iraq in order to source energy from these countries because oil and gas play a critical role in European Union energy security issues. He also commended the role played by EU in internal politics of bringing about democratisation of Central and Eastern Europe (Harikumar 2010). Malvika Singh stated that since the EU is "economically more superior", it could play a key political role and partner Asia, India, South Asia and the Middle East. She called the EU "an emerging economic powerhouse" which can effectively deal with the "erstwhile unipolar power" which is the United States (Singh 2010). Nadeem Iqbal maintained that he always keeps a distance from politics and would not like to voice his comments on this question (Iqbal 2010). Santosh Desai was of the view that EU is one of the big boys of politics in the world and EU certainly has a place on the table. The EU's role in international politics is significant. However, it is neither a defining leader like the United States nor it is among the emerging powers of the world. Thus, the EU cannot be considered to be a leader in international politics at present or in the future as things stand (Desai 2010). Saponti Baroowa stated that the EU is emerging as a leader of international politics as it has exhibited the prowess to lead the world in the areas of global governance, climate change and agenda-setting. It has taken huge strides by establishing its credentials in successfully conducting "global soft power diplomacy" (Baroowa 2010). Shashidhar G.V. stated that although EU member-states are prosperous and doing well for themselves, EU does not have the capacity to swing world politics one way or the other. China, US, India and Russia have a much greater role in international politics compared to the EU (Shashidhar 2010). Shravani Dang was of the view that performance in the global markets and economy is related to the political stature of a great power. Since the financial crisis has struck the EU, she suggests that we should wait and watch and then assess whether the EU is a leader in international politics or not (Dang 2010). Sukh Nandan Singh stated that EU is currently busy with setting its own house in order. The Eurozone crisis is sapping most of EU's energy and therefore it is not playing a pro-active role in global politics. However, the EU has not shied away from providing leadership in areas where others have chosen not to venture and intervene. For instance, it led from the front at the United Nations Forum for Forests and the Convention on International Trade in Endangered Species. It has also played a key role in global politics revolving round the WTO. He chooses to call the EU a persuasive player in international politics (Singh 2010a). Surjit Bhalla reiterates the point that the inability of the EU to speak in one voice militates against its emergence as a leader in international politics (Bhalla 2010).

Political Elites

Agatha Sangma stated that the countries of Europe have dominated the world for a long time and therefore the EU has a fairly strong presence in international politics (Sangma 2010). Anil Madhav Dave insisted that the EU should not nurse any ambitions of becoming the leader in international politics. He stated that just as United States and Soviet Union failed to establish their dominance in the world, EU would also fail in such an endeavour. He stated that working for the welfare of the European society and extending help to developing countries by the EU would be appreciated and its clout in certain spheres would certainly be acknowledged. However, an attempt to emerge as a political leader and dominate the rest of the world would have disastrous consequences (Dave 2010). Prakash Javadekar stated that the EU currently is not at the top of her game in the political, economic and military spheres. Hence, a bloc that is grappling with its own problems cannot be expected to give the right direction to the rest of the world in the sphere of international politics. He went on further to say that the UK has not even been able to stitch up an alliance three days after elections in Britain (Javadekar 2010). Manishankar Aiyer stated that the EU should "develop an independent profile "and should stop being "as hopelessly dependent on the United States as they are now". It is required that they use their own discretion "much more often". He added that the United States speaks on behalf of the EU and the latter "meekly follows" the former (Aiyer 2010). Thokchom Meinya categorically stated that he does not see the EU as a leader in international politics by exclaiming "no, no, no, never" (Meinya 2010). Mukut Mithi stated that economic partnership with other countries in the world including the EU is welcome. However, the international system is dominated by the United States and not the EU as a leader in global political affairs (Mithi 2010). Rajiv Pratap Rudy stated that EU pales in comparison with the United States and China, although its presence is acknowledged among the major powers of the world. He stated that "EU does not stand anywhere" as far as political leadership of the international system is concerned although "it is a good formulation which has come into existence" (Rudy 2010).Vincent Pala stated that he does not see the EU as a leader in international politics. He stated that although the role and presence of EU cannot be neglected, it is also true that the United States is "quite ahead of the EU" in the race for global leadership of political affairs (Pala 2010).

Civil Society Elites

Alok Mukhopadhyay observed that the EU follows the United States in all crucial global military and security issues and therefore cannot be regarded as a leader in international politics (Mukhopadhyay 2010). Wilson John had similar views about the EU and stated that the "EU at the moment "can be regarded as somebody who is not a leader but a follower" of the United States (John 2010). Henri Tiphagne suggested that the EU should make efforts to increase its role in international affairs by aligning itself with countries and regions of the world where the poorest of the poor live because it is not Europe but Asia, Africa and Latin America who shall determine the agenda on the global scene (Tiphagne 2010). Sujit Dutta talked on similar lines and stated that although the EU cannot be considered to be a "major state", it has been active in India and its neighbourhood. He cited the example of EU intervention in "Afghanistan, EU-Asia dialogue and the EU-India dialogue" which the EU carries on persistently. He went on to suggest that EU needs to play a special role in helping out the countries in Asia and Africa because the "legacy of the problems of these states" such as "poverty, disease, underdevelopment and ethnic strife owes significantly to European colonialism". Therefore, the EU should come forward and should provide backing in terms of "state-building, security, technological and manpower support". He recommended that the EU should do its bit for changing the norms of world trade as far as agriculture is concerned so that a level-playing field is provided to farmers on both sides of the globe. He stated that the EU should play a leading role in dealing with important questions such as those of global financial reforms and terrorism. He stated that efforts should be made by the 27-member bloc in the direction of bringing the "democracies of India, the EU and the United States on the same page" in order to ensure international peace and stability (Dutta2010). Ranjana Kumari stated that the EU plays a "very positive role" in international politics. She stated that EU can go a long way in bridging the gap between developed and developing countries. She urged the EU to bring about global economic development by coming to the rescue of countries "where millions of people are dying of hunger, abject poverty, deprivation, internal and international conflict". She argued that the EU could thus play a very critical role in terms of balancing and creating "a peaceful, developed and happy world" in the future (Kumari 2010). Ruchira Gupta was of the view that the EU could check and balance other emerging great powers like China. She also stated that the EU must work towards defeating the "very strong corporate and hegemonic agenda" of other "imperial powers" and make efforts to ensure social justice (Gupta 2010). Karuna Raina stated that she looks upon the EU as "more of a soft power" which has considerable influence on cultural issues. However, she pointed out that whenever it comes to hardcore politics and making changes, she fails to recognise the "EU as an entity" and calling the bloc as "a leader" in international politics would in fact "be a very bold statement to make" (Raina 2010). Mallika Joseph shared similar views as she stated that although the EU has a parliament of its own, they do not project a coherent foreign policy. She went on to say that till this happens, it shall be very difficult for the international community to look at the EU as a single political bloc. Therefore, it is too early to talk about the EU assuming the role of a leader in international politics (Joseph 2010). Pratap Bhanu Mehta stated that he does not look upon the EU as a leader in international politics as it lacks the ability to set the international agenda and suffers from an internal identity crisis. He said that it is not clear what it stands for. It was expected that the EU would emerge as a kind of alternative bulwark to the United States. However, this does not seem to have happened. He termed the "EU decision-making process to be too abrupt "as seen in the case of its very contradictory China policy" (Mehta 2010).

Jesim Pais voiced similar views and stated that the EU cannot be looked upon as a leader in international politics because they fail in emanating “the feeling of being a joint strong power”. He cited the example of the Iraq war when the EU was unable to take a stand. He talked more on the same theme by stating that it was widely expected that France, Germany and Britain would share a feeling of solidarity on the issue which would make the EU a formidable bloc. But sadly for the EU, this has not happened and new rifts and fissures constantly emerge among the member-states of the EU which further debilitates EU aspirations of becoming a leader in international politics (Pais 2010).

Media Elites

Anil Patni stated that the EU is “a leader more in economic issues and less in the area of hard foreign policy issues such as war and peace”. The general perception is that the EU is “not seen as a very strong power”. For instance, at the time of the Iraq war, France and Germany happened to be on one side while UK and Italy happened to be on the other. He cited the example of another debacle that was witnessed at Copenhagen. The EU as “the good boy” announced that it shall go for “a 20 per cent reduction in carbon emissions by two zero two zero as per the twenty-twenty formula”. However, the EU happened to be sidelined during the Copenhagen process. When the Copenhagen final accord surfaced it was clear for everyone to see that the BRICS and USA had won the round of negotiations and they represented and signified the “emerging new world order”. The “good boy” had entirely disappeared from the scene. He suggested that EU “needs to play this game in a much smarter way than they have done so far” (Patni 2010). Lalita Panicker stated that there is no single leader that we can accept as the EU leader because there are different entities with different strengths. If Germany is recognised as an economic power, France is considered to be a cultural power. There seems to be no EU collective that can effectively bargain on behalf of the entire 27 member-bloc (Panicker 2010). Manoj Joshi stated that he recognises the EU as a leader in the field of international law. Nevertheless, he points out that one thing that the "EU lacks" is that it refuses to act and assume the responsibilities of a military power. He further explains that given its size, "EU's military clout" is extremely limited. He stated that the EU should not expect to be called a leader in international politics if it is not willing to exercise its military power (Joshi 2010). Kumar Rakesh stated that it would "take time" for the EU to emerge as a leader in international politics. He stated that the powerful European countries enjoy the individual membership of many IOs and IGOs such as the UN and G8 which in turn can help them in the game of polarisation of politics and turn the tide in favour of the EU (Rakesh 2010). Ranjit Kumar expressed similar sentiments and stated that the EU is presently a dominant power in the economic area but in future it is likely to become leader in political affairs contingent upon how united the EU shall become in the coming years (Kumar 2010). Soma Das opined that politics is governed by economics and therefore the EU has a fair chance of emerging as a leader in international politics. However, it is largely considered to be an economic partner rather than a political and diplomatic power by the rest of the world (Das 2010). T.K. Arun was also not convinced that the EU can be looked upon as a leader in international politics on account of the absence of a coherent foreign policy as a result of which the EU is unable to speak with conviction for the independent individual member-countries (Arun 2010).

Perceptions about the Relationship between India and EU

The business elites looked upon the EU-India relationship as a growing relationship and a relationship with a lot of potential. None of them stated that the partnership is on a negative curve. They cited various examples to illustrate the growing importance of India to the EU and the mutual realisation of the relevant role played by the two partners in their respective markets and in the world at large. All of them urged for greater engagement of the two partners in various sectors of finance, business and industry by facilitating trade and investment, cultural exchanges, museum exhibitions, promotion of tourism, movement of people and labour migration. All the business elites were optimistic about the relationship and expected greater participation and engagement by the two powers in joint collaborations and projects.

The political elites largely subscribed to the view that EU-India relationship is a positive and stable relationship. Most of the elites hoped that the relations shall accelerate and reach a higher level of engagement. Some stated that the acceleration in the relationship shall mainly be in the economic sphere. Some of the elites were of the view that India and the EU should confabulate on issues of trade, terrorism, climate change and grass roots democracy. It was also stated that a new enthusiasm and dedication needs to be infused among the staff at the Indian embassy that take care of EU affairs. It was acknowledged that their currency is doing very well which in turn shall lead to greater economic engagement between the EU and India.

The civil society elites were of the view that there are no deep-seated strategic conflicts and ideological differences between EU and India which makes the relationship a cordial relationship. Besides, economic partnership necessitates a certain degree of engagement with the other partner which has led to further intensification of the EU-India partnership. Both partners also find themselves on the same footing as far as global aspirations such as checking China and the United States are concerned.The EU and India espouse the same values and believe in democracy, rule of law, good governance and try to ensure international peace and stability in the world which invariably makes them allies. However, some stated that differences crop up when India deals with the EU as a bloc and not with individual member-states of the EU. It was stated that the EU presidency plays a key role in determining the crests and troughs of the relationship. Some of the elites also stated that the EU needs to play a more visible and definite role in international affairs which shall bring the EU and India closer.

Business Elites

Akhil Alha stated that "EU-India relations can gradually be improved". The EU has made huge strides in the construction, pharmaceutical, cement and fashion industries. India has carved a niche for itself by providing skilled labour at reasonable prices to all industries and the demand has increased further in European societies on account of their greying population. In the light of these circumstances, he argues that strict barriers relating to immigration from India to European countries does not make sense. He argues that labour migration should become smooth. He further stated that India and the EU should work on this relationship as it would prove to be mutually advantageous (Alha 2010). S. Harikumar stated that India has realised the importance of this relationship and is constantly working towards making it better (Harikumar 2010). Malvika Singh stated that both India and the EU need to accelerate initiatives and "do soft diplomacy", which should include expansion of trade, cultural exchanges, museum exhibits and promotion of tourism. There is also a tendency among Indian students to prefer America over Europe as an education destination as they face "language problems" in the latter. Such issues need to be addressed adequately so that we could arrive at a worthwhile relationship (Singh 2010). Nadeem Iqbal stated that Indians are looked upon as more trustworthy than the Chinese in Europe. They are widely believed to be law-abiding and honest with respect to usage of chemicals in fabrics, unlike the Chinese. They are also willing to do the bidding of the European businessmen and pay money in advance which has enhanced the credibility of Indian businessmen in the EU. This hints at betterment of EU-India relationship (Iqbal 2010). Santosh Desai stated that as India and the EU start considering things from the strategic point of view, both the partners shall start acknowledging the relevance of each other and exploring new ways and means of strengthening the relationship. However, he admits that it is early days yet. The EU in fact, has been slow in waking up to the India story. The Europeans have had a longer and greater presence in India than India's other partners, but somehow they have not been able to cash in on this. He further states that nothing like the EU exists in the popular consciousness of India. It is understood as an "abstract kind of a body" and therefore it is essential that the EU has a significant presence and must stand apart. It should manifest itself as more than the sum of its total parts. It is necessary in fact to remind in "a sense and refresh those contacts" and those relationships that have existed and also "to locate them in this idea of the EU" (Desai 2010). Saponti Baroowa stated that EU-India relations "lacks the momentum it ought to have" although it is definitely not stagnant (Baroowa 2010). Shashidhar GV was of the view that "EU has not been a great help to India in whichever way" while India seems to be helping them out. India is buying jets and submarines from EU member-states. Indians are their vital customers. Nokia's second biggest market happens to be India. Companies like Ericsson and Alcatel are alive today because of the Indian market. He stated that EU as a bloc is coming to terms with the new reality after their success which they enjoyed for almost 150 years after the Second World War. Indians have achieved independence in their own right and so the partnership is steering towards "a more equal relationship and an even equation" (Shashidhar 2010). Shravani Dang was of the view that EU-India relations are largely stable and they are improving "bit by bit" (Dang 2010). Sukh Nandan Singh stated that the image of India in EU is improving. He said it is very common to see nowadays European brands of cosmetics such as L'Oreal, and watches like Tissot and Rado being endorsed by Bollywood actors. This gives India very good visibility in these markets. Thus, we see the two partners come closer and statistics show that India's exports to the EU are also "growing constantly" (Singh 2010a). Surjit Bhalla was of the view that if US and China were to ignore India in future, then India will gravitate towards the EU which will strengthen EU-India relationship (Bhalla 2010).

Political Elites

Agatha Sangma stated that EU-India relationship is a very amicable relationship, although it should not primarily be economy-focused and emphasis should also be laid upon political and diplomatic ties (Sangma 2010). Anil Madhav Dave stated that the relations would develop in the field of commerce and taking strategic decisions in world affairs in the future. He stated that India and EU should jointly work to address the issue of global warming and terrorism that have emerged as the two biggest threats to mankind (Dave 2010). Prakash Javadekar stated that India has "a good relationship with individual nations of Europe and with EU" and India would like to take the relations to another level (Javadekar 2010). Thokchom Meinya had similar views and stated that EU-India relations can further be strengthened and consolidated (Meinya 2010). Vincent Pala stated that the relationship "is stable as of now" (Meinya 2010). Mukut Mithi stated that EU-India relations are friendly and economic engagement with each other has increased by leaps and bounds as their common currency has become much more powerful in the world (Mithi 2010). Rajiv Pratap Rudy was of the view that the two partners have "a positive trade relationship and very positive ongoing dialogue". He stated that when he was the Chairman of Climate Change Forum in Parliament, a "very strong European Parliament team" had paid them a visit. He also stated that numerous delegations of the EU keep visiting India to interact on varied issues (Rudy 2010). Manishankar Aiyer remarked that EU-India relationship is a very stable one. He stated that he would love to infuse dynamism into the relationship. He stated that the relationship seems to have settled into comfortable grooves and EU summits and work of the Indian Mission in Brussels have become extremely monotonous and "routine". He then recalled his experience at the Indian mission in Brussels which he described as "very new, energetic and dynamic". He said that India then had a "remarkable ambassador in K.B. Lall", who helped each one to deliver to the best of his ability. He stated that nothing much is going to change unless a K.B. Lall kind of temperament enters into the Indo-EU relationship". He however, stated that he would have preferred that EU would take more interest than it does now in bringing about greater people to people contact by supporting the Indian experiment of bringing about grassroots democracy through the establishment of Panchayati Raj institutions. He however accepted nonchalantly, that "Indo-European stability which amounts to Indo-European stagnation" would rule the roost for a long time. Hence, whatever happens in EU-India relations, will largely happen in the economic sphere and not in the "political, diplomatic or military spheres" (Aiyer 2010).

Civil Society Elites

Alok Mukhopadhyay stated that the first EU-India summit was held in 2000 at Lisbon and there have been more than 10 summits since then. The trajectory and status of the relationship is contingent upon which country holds the EU Presidency and how much importance it accords to India. He stated that for instance, under "Slovenian Presidency or Lithuanian Presidency", we cannot expect EU-India relations to be the centre-piece of discussions (Mukhopadhyay 2010). Henri Tiphagne stated that the progress of EU-India relations is very slow owing to the fact that India is not in a hurry to speed up things and wants to unravel itself on the world stage at a slow pace (Tiphagne 2010). Karuna Raina stated that EU-India relationship has been pretty much stagnant for the past decade as the relationship has neither been showing considerable improvement nor has it worsened. She goes on to say that the EU was simply not visible on the scene in Copenhagen because the EU did not feel comfortable with the BRICs countries on one side, and was sidelined by the United States on the other. Therefore, India and the EU could not have considered taking their relationship one step ahead because of very visible differences and reluctance to compromise. The disappointing outcome of the talks at Copenhagen is attributed to the fact that the participating countries who found themselves on either side had agreed to disagree (Raina 2010). Mallika Joseph was of the view that EU-India relations have improved exponentially because EU provides alternative technologies to India that have proved to be extremely beneficial. She goes on to point out that there are no serious ideological differences between India and the EU as both espouse the same values and are ardent supporters of freedom and democracy. Hence, we seem to have a non-problematic feel-good relationship with the EU. But she points out that India is more interested in US as they provide Indians more opportunities in the economic sphere than in EU. Nevertheless, the relationship "has gone up quite a bit in the last 10-15 years". She added that although the condemnation of the nuclear test conducted by India in 1998 by the United States as well as the EU and the sanctions that followed were a bit of a setback, the sanctions did not hurt India at all and mending of fences started soon after (Joseph 2010). Jesim Pais stated that relations of India with the EU are improving because its relations with all other powers with the exception of China are progressing. He also reasons that there is no deep strategic conflict with the EU which makes it a smooth-sailing relationship. Moreover, the EU has recognised that India is a rising power and therefore the former has been tailoring its policies accordingly (Jesim 2010). Pratap Bhanu Mehta voiced similar views when he stated that the EU and India do not have "any deep, serious strategic conflicts" and economic cooperation between two powers "necessitates a degree of engagement which has a certain momentum" which is leading to a constant improvement in the EU-India relationship (Mehta 2010). Ranjana Kumari was of the view that India and the EU shall have "a very active friendly relationship" in the near future because of the involvement of mutual interests. She elaborated by saying that both India and the EU want to see the establishment of peace in the Middle East. Both do not want China to become "an uncontrollable giant". India and the EU do not want the US to assume the role of a hegemon and consequently have no say on important questions of international economy and politics. Besides, both powers believe in the doctrine of democracy and rule of law and aspire "to engage in good governance and bring more peace in the world" (Kumari 2010). Ruchira Gupta stated that EU-India relations are constantly improving. She said EU is understood in India "as a cultural and tourist destination". It is known for fashion and style and brands such as Versace and Prada. Some of the "best car designs and clothes designs" reach India from the EU. India also has "defence relationships" with EU member-countries "in terms of purchase of arms and technology". She advocates maximum number of exchange programmes of all kinds between EU and India that shall increase their visibility in each other's region (Gupta 2010). Sujit Dutta stated that there are very interesting elements that bind India to Europe. He stated that India and the EU went through a similar process of trying to unite its constituent elements into one bloc. He stated that there is huge scope for India and the EU to work together in order to construct a new world order in the 21st century that shall be stable and based on the ideals of democracy and liberalism. He exhorted that that this new world order should aim at helping the poorer constituencies in the world within Africa and parts of Asia. India and the EU should take steps to encourage collaboration in science and technology especially in the area of climate change. They should also engage with the question of adoption of ways and means to make welfare state functional in the EU and India (Dutta 2010). Wilson John stated that the EU-India relationship is largely stable and is improving incrementally. He stated that India has better relations with some of the EU member-states compared to others. Therefore, when India negotiates with the EU as a bloc, a complexity regarding motives and compulsions emerges. Then, the solidarity and cooperation give way to competition especially in the fields of energy security and economy (John 2010).

Perception of the Media Elites on Coverage of EU News Stories

All media elites stated that they report EU news stories as and when they happen. There is no advanced planning or targets laid down for a certain degree of coverage of EU news. Most of the time foreign wires supply EU news items to the Indian press because there are very few correspondents of Indian newspapers stationed in Brussels and European capitals. Sometimes the Indian media agencies are approached by the office of European Union Delegation to India when a major event is supposed to happen. The Delegation also provides press reporters with documents providing a background and information about the event. The reporters publish these stories as per their relevance and interest to the Indian reader.

All media elites stated that there is no special allocation of budget for coverage of the EU. They stated that this trend of special allocation of resources for a region has not caught on in the Indian media. Most of the media organisations including the largest and profit-making ones do not prefer to be directly involved in the process of news-gathering as it is a costly exercise. They prefer instead to rely on foreign news wires, stringers or at the most on a single correspondent who is more often than not stationed in London and is responsible for sending reports on news and events happening in all member-states of the EU. It is reasonably expected that news that he sends are analysed from the British perspective and thus what is reported about the EU in the Indian media is largely biased and fairly inadequate.

All the media elites stated that they do not hire more staff or experts to cover EU issues. Most of them stated that issues related to the EU are covered by the economic affairs correspondent or foreign affairs correspondent. Therefore, the need to hire extra staff does not arise. It was stated that the reporters themselves consult experts and include their bites when they write news articles. However, some did say that reporters might be sent on an assignment to cover an EU-related news story. Most of the time the coverage is issue-specific. Some lamented the fact that the

Indian media has not reached the stage where experts are hired for coverage of a specific geographical area. It was also admitted by some that although a decent coverage of economic issues involving the EU takes place, political issues find very seldom coverage.

All the media elites stated that they would welcome the proactive stance taken by the EU in disseminating news about itself. However, they clarified at the same time that they would not be able to accommodate all the news and information provided by the EU as their choice is limited by certain compulsions. One of the considerations for inclusion of a news item on the EU would be that it should be of interest to the Indian reader. The relevance of the news piece in terms of furthering India's interest is also taken into account. Besides, there is limited news space available in the newspaper and therefore the editors cannot publish everything available and have to prioritise.

The media elites had a varied range of opinions so far as predicting the tilt in the balance of reporting in future was concerned. Some stated that the developed world including United States, China and the EU would be the focus of reportage as before. A majority of the elites stated that the balance of reporting shall shift towards East Asia. China received a special mention by many of the elites. It was stated by some that China is likely to receive far greater attention in Indian foreign policy and it will not be long before Indian media agencies will have a sizeable number of reporters stationed in China. It was stated by many that the EU is widely recognised as a stable and key economic partner. But the coverage of the EU is unlikely to increase in future because media believes in reporting news of a sensational and controversial nature. Some of the elites were apprehensive about the euro crisis that might adversely affect EU-India relations in future. Others stated that it is possible that coverage of the EU might increase in the Indian media if the "Indian interest and the interest of the readers" is catered to in a remarkable fashion.

All media elites, with the exception of one, agreed that it is difficult sell a EU story. They were of the view that EU is too good an actor in international politics and hardly does or says anything controversial which is the main reason for less coverage. The other elites believed that there has to be an India-angle in the story in order to sustain the interest of the readers. A EU story, solely based on the EU, will not find many takers, as the readers are interested in news which impacts them directly or indirectly. Many of the elites stated that the Indian reader is more concerned about Pakistan, China, USA and themes like terrorism rather than areas such as Japan and the EU. Therefore, aEU story has to compete with stories emanating from more popular regions and also with unsubstantial but sensational news.

Organisation of Coverage of the EU and European Issues

Ajay Setia, Input Head of ETV stated that he constantly received emails from the "EU Asia Programme and EU's headquarters in Belgium at least twice or thrice a week" which helps him to organise the coverage of EU (Setia 2010). Amiti Sen, who writes for the *The Economic Times,* stated that there is no planned organisation of the EU issues as such and no target is imposed which compels the newspaper to mandatorily come out with two or three stories every week. She stated that as and when developments happen, they cover it in their newspaper. For instance, when there are any "big meetings" happening, revolving around EU-India relations that shall be attended by the Prime Minister and senior leaders in India or if they shall be visiting EU, they find coverage in *The Economic Times*. She stated that:' we also tend to cover news involving disputes over a product or commodity between EU and India.' Amiti Sen summed up by saying that her newspaper covers issues as and when they happen (Sen 2010). Anil Patni, DGM, Energy Security, Communication and External Affairs, Former Press Advisor to the European Commission, former Assistant Editor at British High Commission and former Sub-editor at *The*

Times of India, threw light on the subject by stating that coverage of EU and European issues in the Indian press is organised as part of the "overall international coverage of foreign news". The coverage is found to be much more "broad-based and extensive" in English language newspapers when compared to Hindi or regional language newspapers. There is not much coverage of the EU in Indian newspapers on a day to day basis. However, if there is news from the EU which involves or impacts India and its people staying either in India or in the EU, it is definitely reported in the Indian press. It can therefore safely be said that the India media is "open and receptive" to news coming from the EU and European capitals as long as it involves Indian interest. He stated that if there is an "India element" in the news piece on the EU, it definitely finds coverage. But a news item solely based on European affairs such as internal politics, European institutions and European policy, is not likely to be reported in the Indian newspapers (Patni 2010). Lalita Panicker, Senior Associate Editor at *Hindustan Times* Media Limited, stated that EU issues are covered by foreign news wires such as AP, AFP and Reuters. She said that coverage of an issue entirely depends on its newsworthiness. For instance, the nuclear issue which has become very important in France was reported (Panicker 2010). Manoj Joshi, Deputy Editor, *Mail Today*, stated that they do not undertake any special coverage for EU or for any other country. He stated that if "something of interest" is found to be happening, only then do they pay attention to it. He stated that since their newspaper is only two years old, they do not have any correspondent stationed abroad (Joshi 2010). Kumar Rakesh, Group Vice-President and Senior Editor, NE TV Group, stated that he does not find EU-India relations being pursued with adequate vigour. He stated that the print media coverage of EU issues is much better than that of the electronic media. He stated that there happens to be a communication gap and systemic problems that are preventing adequate coverage of the EU (Rakesh 2010). Ranjit Kumar, Special Correspondent at the

Nav Bharat Times News Bureau, stated that whenever a high-ranking European official or any European leader visits India, the press reporters of his newspaper make it a point to attend the press briefing organised by the European Union or the Ministry of External Affairs. He stated that the reporters also receive "press handouts, press releases and background documents from the European Union Delegation in New Delhi". He stated that the event is written about and reported "depending upon the importance of the event" (Kumar 2010). Shantanu Guha Ray, Business Editor of *Tehelka*, stated that business newspapers popularly known as pink papers carry the maximum number of news items on the EU. He was of the view that EU news is primarily highlighted during the World Economic Forum when "a plethora of economy-related news keeps coming up". Although Indian newspapers routinely carry EU news stories, "the bulk of this reporting is based out of news agency write ups because not many Indian publications have reporters there". He believed that no advance planning is required to do day to day reporting. He stated that when stories break particularly about agriculture, policy changes, economy and the WTO, the Indian newspapers routinely cover these and so do the magazines (Guha Ray 2010). Ms. Soma Das, Principal Correspondent of *The Financial Express,* stated that media organisations "are less geographic and more sectoral, and a clear-cut organised geographical coverage including that of the EU has not taken a concrete shape yet" (Das 2010). Mr. T.K. Arun, Economic Editor of *The Economic Times,* stated the news on foreign countries comes basically from wire and news agencies unless there is a major event for which their own correspondent is sent to cover the same. He added that the "European Union representative office in Delhi" gets in touch when they have a dignitary from the Commission or an important European representative coming to India and then "the newspaper might choose to take an article from them or carry a story" (Arun 2010).

Special Preparations Made in Advance for Coverage of EU News

Ajay Setia stated that there is no need for special preparations for reporting on EU because whenever a press conference is organised by the EU Delegation in Delhi, they provide the press reporters with background material and hence there is no additional requirement for research. He added that if he chooses to write on a specific subject, then he does research on that topic (Setia 2010). Amiti Sen stated that *The Economic Times* has a reporting team and reporters are allocated different beats. She further clarifies that if a reporter's beat is trade, he has to cover all trade-related issues, including the occurrences and developments that take place in the context of EU-India relations for which he doesn't need any special preparation. However, if an important meeting is about to take place, the reporter might prefer to find out in advance the agenda of the meeting, the dignitaries who shall participate and the developments so far on the issue. She says that a reporter may prefer to know all this in advance but no extraordinary measures are taken for coverage of the EU or any other region as such (Sen 2010). Anil Patni was of the view that the question of making special preparations for coverage of the EU "is an overall issue with the media". He stated that journalists are "in a perpetual hurry, jumping from one story to another and they find no time to specialise on anything". The editors prefer not to get into technicalities of any subject and leave the task of conducting research to journals and academicians. Newspapers tend to focus on the need of the day and minimum of analysis which he considers as a very wrong trend. He believes that if they "would research their subjects, their writing would be far more accurate, analysis would be deeper and their introspection would be far more revealing". But presently, the news pieces are merely a description of events, personalities and issues devoid of analysis and prediction (Patni 2010). Lalita Panicker stated that there are reporters who understand EU and have studied EU especially among the senior staff and editorial board. Therefore, no special preparations are made. However, she pointed out that much more research is done on the US, as well as India's neighbourhood, when compared to the EU (Panicker 2010). Manoj Joshi stated that unless there is an important event involving the EU, or an international conference in which India is also a participant, no special preparations are made for coverage. Besides, foreign news reported in the Indian newspapers is mainly about Pakistan, US and China, and the EU is not accorded "a very high priority" (Joshi 2010). Kumar Rakesh pointed out that efforts are not made frequently enough to approach the media and brief them about relevant events happening in the EU. He said that: 'we do have access to EU websites and we come to know about a couple of seminars every year. But beyond that, there is nothing much done by the EU to enthuse and inform the Indian media so that they are motivated to write about the EU.' (Rakesh 2010). Ranjit Kumar stated that special preparations are contingent upon the nature of the event. He explained further that if they are supposed to cover an annual summit level meeting, they try to find adequate background information about the ongoing programmes of cooperation in the economic and political fields as well as the viewpoint of EU and Indian leaders on international issues (Kumar 2010). Shantanu Guha Ray stated that "for a big feature for a magazine, certain things could be planned". But as far as newspapers are concerned, they cover news breaking over the day and they keep sending stories and doing updates. For instance, if the members of WTO are about to meet, it is expected that a whole range of contentious issues shall erupt between the EU and India which will be reported in the Indian newspapers. If the event is happening outside India, the organisation shall plan in advance the strength of the staff that shall travel to cover the event and the number of people they shall be meeting and interviewing. However, news of the "normal, routine and general nature" about the EU gets reported as and when it happens and no special preparations are required for coverage (Guha Ray 2010). Soma Das was of the belief that responsible media organisations at the national level do a lot of research on a EU story that has direct relevance to India. It is also made sure that the EU perspective is clearly spelt out irrespective of whether the news piece is pro-EU or anti-EU (Das 2010). T.K. Arun surmised that journalists do some minimal bit of research for writing any article. They talk to people who know about the subject and who make themselves available and give time to journalists. He stated that this in fact is the essential process through which people get familiarity with the subject on which they write (Arun 2010).

Allocation of a Special Budget for EU Coverage

Ajay Setia stated that no special budget is allocated and foreign affairs correspondents cover EU as "a routine beat" (Setia 2010). Amiti Sen and T.K. Arun agreed and stated that they do not "have any special allocations" for EU coverage. However, if there is a big meeting and the newspaper is satisfied that the reporter should be covering the event, then "they can spend some money". She reiterated that generally there is no "special budget for coverage" of the EU (Sen 2010). Anil Patni stated that Indian newspapers do not allocate "any special budget for any kind of news, not even foreign news let alone EU news". The reason attributed for this trend is that "news gathering" is widely known to be a "costly exercise". Keeping this in mind, the news outlets generally station a single person in London who is entrusted with the task of covering news emanating from all the member-states of the EU. He states that Indian newspapers should at least have their correspondents stationed in the "key capitals of the EU such as Paris, Rome, Berlin and in Spain and Portugal". But this is not the current trend. The journalist working from London collects news from secondary sources and redirects them to India as the sheer size of the region makes it impossible for him to do first-hand reporting. Moreover, most of the news that comes from other parts of the EU, including Brussels, is reported from a British perspective, which the journalist stationed in London picks up and sends to India. Hence EU news coverage in the Indian media is not based on objective and unbiased reporting. This has had a deleterious effect on the minds of the readers because most the news reported in the Indian media is through the Britain-based journalist. Besides, if a big event is required to be covered, the Indian media outlets rely on international wires such as Reuters, AP and AFP. He believes that the Indian media's decision not to have a permanent correspondent in Brussels is not a wise decision as adequate coverage of EU news becomes impossible. He further goes on to say that such "deficiency is then reflected" in the coverage and it has a long-term effect on the reader in India as he does not get a fair opportunity to read about the EU. Moreover, the space in the newspaper is limited and is already hijacked by news from "Pakistan, Sri Lanka, Bangladesh, Bhutan and America and China". Therefore, the Indian world view does not seem to encompass the European continent in totality. He concludes by stating that "news coming from UK, about the British royalty or cricket or about Indians living in London" finds space in the newspapers but "news about continental Europe is blanked out, which is the crux of the problem" (Patni 2010). Lalita Panicker stated that their newspaper does have a correspondent stationed in Beijing and in Washington. But they also rely on stringers who supply them with information and news stories. She said that they tend to deploy these resources for countries that have "a more crucial bearing on Indian foreign policy (Panicker 2010). Manoj Joshi categorically denied that their newspaper had a special budget for EU coverage (Joshi 2010). Kumar Rakesh stated that although there is no special budget set aside for EU coverage, their news channel decides upon assigning a reporter and cameraman to go to European meetings in India and covering the event contingent upon the fact that India will be immensely benefitted by the project or seminar (Rakesh 2010). Ranjit Kumar stated that there is no provision for a special budget for the EU and the correspondents who cover international affairs also cover events related to the EU (Kumar 2010). Shantanu Guha Ray stated that all news outlets hire the services of various news wire agencies that are paid on a monthly basis. He explains that the stories from EU would be supplied to the outlets along with other stories from across the world. He went on to say that sending reporters to the EU from India involves "a big budget" as the reporters would "need to fly, need to stay and the cover the complete thing". On being asked if a special budget is drawn for coverage of other parts of the world, he replied that Indian newspapers rarely follow this practice except for the United States, Pakistan and places like London. He stated that very few newspapers or magazines would allot a separate budget for covering "a whole zone like the European Union". He emphasised that "it does not happen that way" in India (Guha Ray 2010). Soma Das stated that since the coverage is not organised on those lines, no special budget is especially allocated for the EU as well as other major powers including the US. She stated that the "EU or any geographic region does not get any special privilege" when the broad organisation is taken into account. She pointed out however that a rethinking on the issue is taking place as the "globe is shrinking and we cannot be detached from coverage of such nature" (Das 2010).

Assigning More Staff and Hiring of Experts to Cover Specific EU Issues

Ajay Setia stated that journalists dealing with economic affairs and those dealing with foreign affairs generally cover the EU. Hence, his organisation does not feel the "need for planning a special assignment or hiring special staff" (Setia 2010). Amiti Sen stated that her organisation has a "big reporting team". She stated that reporters in general are expected to be well-informed and whatever they do not know, they are "supposed to find out and incorporate it in the news stories". For instance, trade related stories often have "outside voices". She stated that reporters are "expected to talk to people, take their opinion and talk to EU experts" and therefore they do not hire any experts (Sen 2010). Anil Patni stated that he wishes that "Indian media reaches there but it is far away from that stage" (Patni 2010). Lalita Panicker stated that her news outlet tries to include stories or articles based on and revolving around

EU meetings, but they do not go out of their way to have more staff strength for the purpose of EU coverage (Panicker 2010). Manoj Joshi acknowledged that they are not a very big organisation and therefore they do not have "excess of staff that they could assign for the purpose of EU coverage". He stated that they have a "diplomatic correspondent who would do most of the coverage on EU" (Joshi 2010). Ranjit Kumar stated that "no such arrangements are made" in his newspaper. He stated that he covers international affairs and if he considers an issue good enough for reporting, he covers the event and writes about it in his newspaper (Kumar 2010). Shantanu Guha Ray stated that in his magazine, "EU issues are routinely done and primarily by people who are based out of London, people who are economists and people who write opinion pieces". He said that the coverage of the EU is mainly done by people who are based abroad. He stated that however, they do not do this "on a regular basis but as and when things happen like WTO and Davos, correspondents are asked to go there and cover the event" (Guha Ray 2010). Soma Das stated that if there are "summits or WTO meets happening in the EU, their special staff is assigned the duty to cover the event and the duration of such a task can be 15 days or more. She emphasised upon the point that such tasks are issue-specific. She stated that when the issue involves the EU aspects, their "organisation hires experts to cover those issues" (Das 2010). T.K. Arun stated that no preparation of the sort is made. They have beat-wise correspondents. He stated that the foreign trade correspondent largely covers EU issues on trade and investment. However, he also admitted that at the political level, they do not have much coverage on the EU (Arun 2010).

News Disseminated by a Proactive EU

Ajay Setia was of the view that if the EU is proactive in disseminating news about itself and "it serves their organisation's purpose which means India's purpose", they would be interested (Setia 2010). Amiti Sen stated that the EU has an office and press team in Delhi and "they keep sending out releases". She explained that if any information or briefing is relevant for the country or the readers, her organisation would be interested in such stories (Sen 2010). Anil Patni stated that if any news about the EU is relevant for the readers, it would get the space that it deserves. However, he explained that it is a daily battle for the numerous news pieces to get into the news page which has a limited number of columns. Therefore, the news will generally be included on the basis of its own merit. If the "EU is more proactive and systematic in pushing out that news", then the chances of the EU news finding space in the newspaper will be enhanced considerably. The editor already has news items from a number of news sources. Therefore, the EU has to make sure that it is in the race so that "it makes its presence felt in the competition to get published and increases its prospects of finding space in the newspaper" (Patni 2010). Lalita Panicker stated that they have a system in place which they call "Project Syndicate" through which "they get articles from wherever they choose". She said that "news is news" and therefore they would be interested in any information disseminated from the EU side (Panicker 2010). Manoj Joshi stated that it is not that they do not receive EU news. He stated that they subscribe to news agencies like Reuters and therefore, EU news keeps coming. But, "at the end of the day", he states that the news should meet their criteria and hence they have to prioritise because news can be provided to the readers in a limited number of pages only (Joshi 2010). Kumar Rakesh stated that although the EU website gives information about the latest developments, professional journalists are always on the lookout for exclusive news. He said that the current arrangement that the EU has in place does not serve this purpose for the Indian media (Rakesh 2010). Ranjit Kumar stated that "any flow of reports or background information or news and press releases" from the EU would be welcome. Nevertheless, he pointed out that the coverage shall depend on its relevance to Indian interest and shall also depend on the availability of news space in the daily (Kumar

2010). Soma Das stated that if her organisation is able to get the "official EU perspective from time to time", that would prove to be "extremely important and a great help" (Das 2010). T.K. Arun stated that "any news that they give, we will not take". He said that it should be "relevant to India and our readers" (Arun 2010).

Shift in Balance of Foreign Reporting in Future

Ajay Setia was of the view that the United States would undoubtedly be given more coverage as far as diplomatic and foreign affairs are concerned while the EU would be given the topmost priority in economic affairs as "India has business interests in the EU and the EU has business interests in India" (Setia 2010). Amiti Sen stated that a look at the *Financial Times* or the *Wall Street Journal* for the past 10 years would reveal that EU and US have been "hogging the limelight for a long time solely because they represent the developed world". But she points out that coverage of the ASEAN region and that of Africa have also significantly increased. India is being written about on account of the fact that it has diversified its trade and political interests. She stated that the increase in coverage of these regions is not at the cost of other regions. She explained that the coverage of international issues as a whole has increased and therefore we witness an increase in the share of coverage of almost every region of the world (Sen 2010). Anil Patni stated that the balance of reporting shall shift towards "those countries where India has an interest. He stated that any of the "threads such as political, defence, strategic relationship, trade and commerce, academic and cultural exchanges and people to people movement that tie a country to India" shall be on the Indian media's "radar screen". He stated that if there is no "Indian interest" in a country which may be otherwise doing great things, the Indian media would not be interested in covering such a region. He believed that coverage would be more of countries where Indian students are studying in big numbers or where students are being increasingly attacked (Patni 2010). Lalita Panicker stated that we would be witnessing a far more "China focused and America focused" stance in the larger foreign policy picture which also includes consideration about "Pakistan, terror and domestic issues" apart from other regions. She categorically stated that she unfortunately does not see an increase in EU coverage in the near future. She reiterated that the coverage would be "America centric and China centric" (Panicker 2010). Manoj Joshi stated that the balance of reporting will shift eastwards towards China and South East Asia. He stated that the shift in balance of reporting towards the EU is "unlikely" because the EU is "a rich stable area" and "there is no riot or war happening there". He explained that newspapers by their very nature do not "do good news". He opined that the EU is nevertheless very important from the economic point of view but the "balance of power" is shifting towards the East (Joshi 2010). Kumar Rakesh stated that coverage of EU issues is likely to increase (Rakesh 2010). Ranjit Kumar stated that whenever the newspapers select different kind of news, it depends upon a number of factors such as national interest as well as interest of the readership (Kumar 2010). Shantanu Guha Ray stated that Indian media would definitely be spending more money on coverage of areas where Indian business and industry are expanding such as United States, China and EU. His emphasis though, was more on China and he stated that Indian newspapers will have to station their correspondents in China sooner than later so that "first-hand reporting can happen from there" (Guha Ray 2010). Soma Das stated that the balance of reporting in the future will depend on "wherefrom India's engagements unfold and business and investment increase". She said that coverage of the EU in future would depend upon the rate at which EU-India trade links shall grow and also upon the degree of importance of the EU as a market for Indian goods and services (Das 2010). T.K. Arun stated that there shall be a shift towards "East and other Asian countries". He stated that the EU is under strain as it has expanded too fast and perhaps too much. He further stated that coherence in economic policy which was considered to be a given, is being challenged by the Eurozone crisis and by countries like Greece, Spain and Portugal which in turn is putting pressure on the EU itself. He stated that coverage of the EU shall depend on the manner in which the euro crisis unfolds (Arun 2010).

Difficulties Encountered in Selling an EU Story

Ajay Setia stated that it is difficult to sell a EU story as news emanating from the bloc generally deals with economic issues. Newspapers normally give space to news items that are sensational, easily comprehensible and economic issues are generally left out in these criteria (Setia 2010). Amiti Sen stated that it is essential "to spot the point that is interesting" and the reader should be able to "relate to the story" which should have something to "identify with". The same applies to a EU story. For instance, the story about the confiscation of consignments of Indian drugs at European ports heading for South Africa was of interest to the pharmaceutical companies and Indian exporters and it highlighted issues revolving around TRIPS (Sen 2010). Anil Patni stated that a story about the EU becomes easy to sell if it can boast of "an Indian angle or if the news is extraordinary". He stated that a news story about a leader of member-state of the EU and his private life receives a lot of coverage. He opined that the European Union would not prefer that such a news article is published but it shall invariably appear on the front page of Indian newspapers. He said that it is extremely essential to understand "the nature of the beast" according to which "what is good, orderly, normal and planned is not news but whatever is wrong, abnormal, unplanned, accidental, sudden and unexpected is news". He elaborated upon the point and said that "the regular stuff" never gets reported but the sensational story "of a missile falling down or a sex scandal always finds news space". He stated he has been witnessing the same phenomenon for the past 20 years in the Indian media and things have only gone "from bad to worse" (Patni 2010). Lalita Panicker was of the view that to sell a EU story was far more difficult than selling a China or America story because the "EU is not very controversial which is good for EU but it does not make a lot of news". She said that their newspaper does have EU Commissioners as well as Chris Patten writing for them once in a while. But EU news coverage is more "individual specific" and there is far less coverage of "EU issues" as such (Panicker 2010). Manoj Joshi talked about the "readability factor" and stated that any region in order to get coverage needs to capture the interest of the readers. He stated that it is clearly evident that Indian readership is more interested in issues emanating from Pakistan, USA and China, while there are areas which are not that popular among the readers such as Japan and the EU (Joshi 2010). Kumar Rakesh hinted at the problems faced in communication and coordination with EU in India. He stated that "how you want to sell an EU story also depends upon the EU official", by which he meant that the EU should go a step ahead and ensure easy availability of authentic information about EU affairs (Rakesh 2010). Ranjit Kumar stated that the inclusion of a news story in the newspaper depends upon "concerns and interests of the Indian readers". He further explained that if an EU news story is solely about European countries and has no connection whatsoever with India and its people, it shall be extremely difficult to the sell the EU story in India because no one shall read it (Kumar 2010). Shantanu Guha Ray was of the view that EU always manages to find news space. He stated that if a Google search is done on the EU, plus India, countless links appear which are a reflection of the fact that "people do actually cover EU". He remarked that Indian newspapers cover EU very strongly and do loads of stories on EU themes (Guha Ray 2010). Soma Das stated that it is indeed difficult to sell a news story based entirely on EU but "the moment an Indian link is established" where Indians in general or Indian businessmen or any sector in India find mention, it becomes feasible to publish the story (Das 2010). T.K. Arun stated that the EU does not generate "a great deal of interest unless it is related to a corporate or economic development". He stated that the EU is a very nebulous entity unlike the US where one language is spoken and there are always a plethora of cultural activities taking place which includes pop music, films and celebrities that are keenly followed by Indians. He said that he cannot think of a major European band after Abba and Spice Girls that has had an impact on India. Therefore, the connection that India has with all things American, is conspicuous by its absence in the case of EU-India relations. (Arun 2010).

Importance of the EU to India in Relation to Other Prominent Regions

The United States and China are considered to be more important than the EU by most of the elites. Some consider Russia and Japan to be vying for importance with the EU. The political elites showed no inclination to compare one region with the other and most stated that all the regions were equally important.

Business Elites

The business elites consider the EU to be an extremely important region. The most important power that emerges is the United States after which the EU is considered to be extremely important. China and Japan also find frequent mention. The business elites consider engagement with the European Union to be an extremely rewarding experience although it does not occupy the top position in their rating of the most favourable regions for India. S.Harikumar remarked that

> ...again coming back to our own area, trade, I think EU is the biggest trading partner... EU is becoming a bigger market with accession of 27 member states... tomorrow it may be 30... so India itself is expanding ....wanting to increase its export business, import and all these things... I feel that India needs to have better relations with the EU. After this FTA agreement, I hope that it will improve even further. Number two is that even technology, if you take Germany... hi tech industry... particularly automobile and...they are key players as well

> as Spain and Germany. So, yes... India has to work in close coordination with these countries to improve our relations so... this is what I feel.

On being asked whether he considered EU-India relations to be more important than US-India relations, he replied that he considers US-India relations to be more salient than EU-India relations. Then, he was quizzed about the chances of EU overtaking the US to which he answered that

> ... not in the immediate future, maybe after 15 years provided EU remains as strong as it is because there are so many other issues to be solved so, that is the one reason I feel that Indo- US relations are more important than India-EU relations.

He was then asked about the relevance of EU to India in comparison to China and Russia. He commentated that

> ...of course, I still feel that India should have more...better relations with the EU, and it is a bigger market with more potential and we should have better relations with the EU ...we should take it seriously ...we should not be carried away by this China syndrome...rather we should have better relations with the West....because it would be helpful in the political scenario...security aspect also...in every sense we should have better relations (Harikumar 2010).

Political Elites

The political elites did not give a clear response. Almost all of them stated that all the partners of India are important or that the EU is important. A couple of them stated the US and Russia and our neighbourhood, especially China, were more important than EU. Japan also found mention. Prakash Javadekar stated that

> ...No, no... Asia, U.S, China... Asia, China also...Japan, Asia... that is not a correct comparison. EU is a confederation of different nationalities so the comparable thing is SAARC. Or now the Union built up by Latin America... being built up by Latin American countries but as I told you in the beginning, it is always very good that different nations come together for mutual advantage, that's a good sign...

He was asked whether EU-India relations are more important than EU-China relations to which he gave the following reply:

> No, no everything is important as far the relations of any country are concerned. We want to have good relations with all including EU, European countries individually and we want Europe to leave their insistence about agricultural subsidies and the treaty which they want to conclude in Doha.' (Javadekar 2010).

Civil Society Elites

Most of the civil society elites considered the United States and China to be much more important than the EU. Some of them talked about the immediate neighbourhood and South- East Asia to be very important:

> It is certainly not important to us as US and China, Japan and Russia, not yet. But although I think we have been making some attempts on our part especially on the economic front to help the relationship with EU... but I think we have not been able to really succeed in that... but either way... its say...it comes among the top three priorities of India (John 2010).

Issues in EU-India Current Relations that have the most Impact on India

The majority of the Indian elites consider EU to be an extremely important economic partner and consequently, consider economic issues to have the most impact upon EU-India current relations.

Business Elites

About fifty percent of the business elites consider trade to be the most important issue in India-EU current relations that has the most impact on India. The other issues mentioned by business elites are labour movement, environment, climate change, disaster management, tourism, non-proliferation and education. Sukh Nandan Singh stated that:

> I suppose there are...there are quite a few things going on like...and I think it is of course going on in the positive way because right now India is in talks with the EU for this free trade and bilateral agreements for the wages and all... and of course if everything goes well and if everything is in place as it is... like projected then of course, the relations are going to be further strengthened and all (Singh 2010a).

Political Elites

Five out of eight elites considered trade and economic issues to be most important. Immigration, WTO and the visa systems were issues relating to the economy that were cited. Climate change and diplomacy were other issues mentioned by the political elites. Prakash Javadekar was of the view that:

> ...I think there are three issues which need more active consideration on EU's part: A) Their stand in WTO and climate change- both these are very important for a just global order and in a just order, you will like that the polluter pays and at the WTO round, there has to be a real level playing field ....and EU must consider these concessions plus there is a problem of Europe with which India can help them out and that is about the young skilled manpower but for that they must change their

> stringent immigration rules because it is up to their benefit. Our boys will be demanded all over the world so EU will be at a loss in the end (Javadekar 2010).

Civil Society Elites

Eight of the ten civil society elites stated that economic issues are the most important issues impacting upon the current relations between EU and India. Other issues mentioned were energy, environment, disarmament, immigration, defence and military exchanges, education and technology. Sujit Dutta stated that:

> I think currently trade and industries...at this point of time, India is poised for rapid development and therefore trade, investment and technology questions play the most critical role in shaping the future of Europe-India relationship. We would like to see Europe invest in India... make productive investment, technology partnerships to grow... from there a huge and steady rising growth in India- EU trade which will benefit employment and growth in Europe and which will help employment and growth in India. We should never forget that India is a country emerging as the second largest market in Asia after China and Japan... so Japan and China... third largest but in the coming 20 years or so or 30 years, India could become the second largest or even the first. So given the nature of population based in India, there is a huge scope for rapid development, over the next 30, 40, 50 years... trade, investment and technology would be an engine of growth in India-EU relationship ...so economics will tie us together as the material connections are very important. We must see Europe as contributing to India's development, meaning for its policy circles... meaning for its intellectual circles... without that it will not be meaningful, so I think the economic energies are the most important (Dutta 2010).

Media Elites

Nine out of ten media elites believe that economic issues are the most important. Davos, WTO, Cancun and Doha summit were mentioned while discussing the economic aspect of the relations. The other issues mentioned were nuclear power, technology transfer, education and culture. Amiti Sen stated that:

> ...Well, right now, if you talk about trade, then we are negotiating this bilateral trade and investment agreement. It does have some problems now because they are trying to bring in extraneous issues like labour and environment... but if they manage to carry it through, then it will be a big....and because of the free trade agreement with such a big block... that is important and... maybe on the nuclear power front also because India is trying to woo some of the European countries to get supplies from them so... so in that area also EU is pretty important (Sen 2010).

Issues to be Kept in Mind in the Course of Developing Trade or Government Policy in Relation to the EU

An overwhelming majority of the elites consider trade and economic aspect as the most important issue that should be kept in mind for the future. This shows the immense degree of importance that the economic aspect of relations enjoy. It also hints at the neglect or lack of focus on the other aspects of relations.

Business Elites

At least six out of ten business elites consider trade to be the most important issue to be kept in mind in while developing trade or government policy in the future. This would include discussion about the FTA, keeping intact the interests of exporters, easing of visa restrictions and immigration. Saponti Baroowa was of the opinion that:

> …I think India, the Indian elite or the Indian government should, in my opinion... should try to increasingly see EU as one actor in terms of economics or in terms of development policy so… so till now I think most Indian elites have…would look more to the UK or Germany maybe for cooperation…so India's approach has been…is still I think a bit bilateral so... I think what India needs to do is to see the EU increasingly as a common voice, as a common platform so I think it would be beneficial for India if India begins to engage with Europe at the European level as one entity rather than focusing on its traditional bilateral ties which of course are important... but to try to tie down those bilateral ties in the framework of a larger European identity or of a larger European framework... so that will be more beneficial. I think both India and EU should maybe cooperate more in education... more on cultural exchanges and also at the same time keep up their...or step up their exchanges at the political level. Have more constructive engagements... till now, it is more about having a summit and then having a declaration at the end and I am not sure how far these are followed up in strong terms, they are taken seriously at the political level but at the same time it should encourage … more civil society exchanges, student exchanges, cultural exchanges which I think would contribute a lot (Baroowa 2010).

Political Elites

Seven out of the eight elites referred to trade as the most important issue. Other areas that were considered to be significant were exchanges in the areas of non-aligned policy, technology, nuclear arena, migration, new areas of development and diplomacy and no imbalance in dealing with each other. Mukut Mithi predicted that:

> …You know mostly that…we have been trading partners you know…for a long time and we should continue that and then also we should maintain a political relation and you know... the

> powerful countries like France and others ...that is now we are coming to an understanding for the exchange of technology in the nuclear area. So those are very important ...aspects for India so we should have a better bond of relationship (Mithi 2010).

Civil Society Elites

About eight out of the ten civil society elites stressed upon greater collaboration in trade and related spheres. Other areas of collaboration mentioned by the respondents included technology flow, labour movement, social development, EU standards, climate change, agriculture, employment and terrorism. They also suggested that it is important to keep in mind the manner in which EU views the Indian neighbourhood and also called for keeping in mind larger sections of society while formulating policy in future. Henry Tiphagne put forth his views by stating that:

> ...Well, I would say... while India and EU sit on trade-related discussions, what Europe, EU should not forget and India should remind itself not to forget because it conveniently forgets... is that what impact these trade arrangements are going to have on larger sections of the Indian population. All said and done, there was somebody saying that... this so called percentage of people who are above middle class etcetera., they forget that it is...it is about 7 percent of the population which reaches the university in this country and not everybody who crosses university is engaged in business in this country, the income tax paying population is something like 4 to 5 per cent in this country... so what are we talking about? Whom are we talking about? We are talking about a vast majority of the people who have nothing to do with your relations and I think ultimately if these relations have to be stable and have to continue, and have to be sustainable, then the interest of the majority of the population has to be determined (Tiphagne 2010).

Contact with Delegation of the EU to India

The majority of the business elites and political elites were either unaware of the Delegation or had no direct contact with it. The civil society elites on the other hand, were mostly aware of the Delegation and knew the exact nature of its activities. Most of them saw it in a positive light and expressed the desire of closely working with the Delegation.

Business Elites

Almost none of the business elites had come in direct contact with the Delegation of the European Union to India. However, they suggested various ways in which the Delegation could be of use to them and their organisation. The suggestions included that the Delegation could help them with relaxing the visa rules and other bureaucratic procedures, organise outreach programmes, workshops and informal discussions so that they could get more information on bilateral relations and policy-making and on the availability of opportunities for them. Saponti Baroowa stated that:

> I am not very sure how...I have not... to be very frank... we have not been exposed to...to too much of the outreach programmes of the EU delegation. I know it exists, I have been to a couple of seminars they have organised but I think there has to be a proactiveness on their part also to include corporate organisation like the one I represent. Of course, they engage in the academic community a lot...there are conferences... they are engaging the media.. but I think... what is needed is more engagement with the business community because now you see in economic terms... business is transnational, it is not only Indian businesses, we have different constituents, we have different stakeholders, European stakeholders, some other foreign stakeholders, Indian stakeholders... so its important for the EU Delegation positioned in India to maybe reach out more to business houses... to maybe ask them....so it is not that we are

> coming to them, if we come to the EU Delegation, it is maybe more to seek information on a particular issue, but it will be also good if they engage us more on proactive issues and organise some kind of workshop or informal discussions with us or try to explore what are the needs of the business community. From my organisation's point of view, we are basically an informational organisation, we deal with information, we analyse our risks on the basis of information that we have... so that way... I think it will be...we will always be...it will be useful for us if we have greater access to the European press so if there is some kind of documentation at the delegation or press clippings or press views through which they can give us greater access which we could use for our own analysis of events... that is at the more micro level...I think more outreach programmes are fine (Baroowa 2010).

Political Elites

About six of the eight political elites claimed that either they had no dealing with the Delegation or were not aware of it or that they had no direct relations with them or that it was of no use to them. Only one political elite referred to the Delegation as a positive and proactive team, but he also stated that the interaction is more at the governmental level and therefore politicians at large are not aware of its activities. Anil Madhav Dave stated that:

> ...I am afraid I can't say...afraid I can't answer because I was in the meeting where the EU parliamentary delegation was there... and the Indian parliamentary delegation as an Indian parliamentarian... I was there to discuss but I am afraid I don't have much of an idea of who they are and what they have (Dave 2010).

Civil Society Elites

Only one civil society elite was unaware of the Delegation of the European Union to India. A couple of elites were critical of the

EU and the Delegation owing to its cumbersome bureaucratic procedures. All others were well aware of the Delegation and its activities and made several suggestions such as to provide funds to NGOs, think tanks and research organisations, reach out more to the NGOs directly and not through the government, facilitate the meeting of scholars and traders from both sides and have discussions and work on projects concerning climate change, economy and trade. Jesim Pais was of the view that:

> One thing they do for sure is that they sponsor research…okay… issues that EU considers important in India so they make you study and you give them a report so they can come back …the EU office in India for sure has….by their standards... it is a very small budget but by our standards it is quite a big budget, you can do detailed study on many things so that's one thing with the EU office in India and something else which our institute or we have not been very successful is….beyond all these visits to these countries always helps in understanding things better and the EU office can have a major programme of exchange... scholars going this way and that way which is happening but very small... so that could be something that the EU office... for example, China has this institute which promotes… so Chinese scholars even if nobody else wants them, the institute in China sends them across to the world... you go, you visit, you see and you come back and in India's case we have small little programmes like that, it's not much. The EU office in India could do this, you can have traders going across... you can have scholars going across… some kind of exchange so we understand things better. The EU Delegation is actually not visible... you see because of our research interest, you go looking for them and then you find them, they are actually not visible, they are not visible...and but we have found them because of our needs …we are constantly looking for people for information, for data, that's how but by themselves...I don't think they are visible (Pais 2010).

Risks or Opportunities for India when New Countries Join EU

The responses seem to show a mixed bag of results. The business elites enumerated both risks and opportunities in abundance while the political elites were mostly unable to make up their minds and chose not to comment on this query. The majority of the civil society elites considered the phenomenon of new countries joining the EU to be positive in nature and hence considered it to be an opportunity.

Business Elites

Five out of the ten business elites see both risks and opportunities for India while four of the elites see only opportunities while one business elite only sees risks if new countries join the EU. The risks enumerated by the elites include the fact that increased availability of skilful and cheap labour will prove to be a threat for Indian businesses especially the IT industry. There will be increase in conflict on political issues and mistrust and it will be difficult to arrive at agreements which might be conducive for India on account of the increase in the number of member-countries of the EU. The elites were apprehensive that there might be an increase in the crime rate and insecurity as well as an increase in the frequency of terrorist acts and fundamentalism especially if Turkey joins the EU. The opportunities include the expansion and increase of market opportunities and the increment in volumes and competition as a result of free markets. There will be an increased opportunity to enter into strategic alliances with the new countries for India. The EU will emerge as a stronger and more stable player and will provide a better platform to engage with and a better system of regulations and controls will make it easier for India in turn to engage with the EU. The elites also believe that the euro will eventually be adopted by all these countries which will help it emerge as a strong and stable currency in the world. Akhil Alha stated that:

> ... risks and opportunities...lets talk about risks first because like some new members are about to join EU... Turkey is the first one in the list who is about to join EU so... the risk can be of this nature ...India enjoys a stronghold in many different things... like skilful and cheap labour...is one..I would say one forte of India and apart from this...the IT industry where Indian professionals... they are doing exceptionally well in all parts of the world especially US...so if a new member-country, starts providing labour, be it skilful or be it semi-skilled labour to other countries of European Union, then it will increase the challenges for India and it will be a competition for India so, that can be one risk. About opportunities I would say that... like...if the group or the pool of these countries is getting bigger and bigger ...so certainly India will have better opportunities to increase its trade and to increase strategic alliances with these countries...so that would be beneficial in creating more and proper opportunities and related things (Alha 2010).

Political Elites

Five out of the eight elites chose not to comment on whether new countries that join the EU will present a threat or opportunity to India. Two elites stated that this would present an opportunity as the market will expand and market shares will go up. One of the political elites stated that real integration of the member-states with the EU shall alone make a difference. Prakash Javadekar stated that:

> ... it is a good thing, as I told you, we look to the whole concept of EU as not that of a threat but that of an opportunity, if EU gets the bargaining power, we also get a unified market so our market share goes up (Javadekar 2010).

Civil Society Elites

Five out of the ten civil society elites see the joining of new states as part of EU as an opportunity. Three of the elites stated that it was a risk. One of the elites saw it both as a threat and as an opportunity while another elite chose not to comment. The risks pointed out by the civil society elites include the difficulties in negotiating and the fear that the interests of the larger sections of the people would be compromised. The loss of business for Indians in the EU region was also one of the risks pointed out. One of the apprehensions was that the addition of new member-states ought not to jeopardise relations with other countries such as Russia. It was also stated that EU will in all probability witness the diminishing of its ability to articulate its standpoint on issues. It was also pointed out that there is not much of a risk posed as the EU does not have a single foreign policy and a major loss of business may therefore not happen. The elites stated that generally there shall be no major risks and the opportunities for trade shall increase as a result of an increase in the number of member-states of the EU. Hence, Jesim Pais stated that:

> When the new countries join the EU, they come with some advantages, OK... for example Romania is an agricultural country, there is lots of agriculture, Bulgaria also...there is some agriculture....some of them have got energy, some country has gas...so to that extent they contribute to the EU so EU is happy. Romania has labour... cheap labour... Bulgaria has all these big new factories that are coming up... they came up in Hungary, Czech Republic and so on. Now to that extent EU imports less from countries like India...we have a Maruti Suzuki factory in Delhi, in India... we export... Suzuki has factories in China, not very big in Japan, India and in the EU. Now if they have a big factory in the EU then our chances of exporting to the EU are finished. The factory they have in Hungary is as big....actually bigger than the factory in India, Gurgaon which means they produce all the Suzuki cars, all the models and everything so we cannot export to the EU... it does not make sense because they are already producing the cars and this factory is in Hungary, it is one of the new countries which has come in... so to that extent

> our trade with them will go down because the new countries give them opportunity to trade internally so it is negative you can say… it is not so good for India. If we don't export too much meat or fish, but suppose we were exporting meat and fish and then another country joins which produces a lot of meat and fish, then our opportunities are gone. When these countries joined the EU, New Zealand which was exporting a lot of meat to the EU lost out. New Zealand is at the other end, you produce good meat alright but then transporting that meat to the EU doesn't make sense... why not buy it from neighbouring countries (Pais 2010).

Euro as an International Currency vis-à-vis the US Dollar

The majority of the elites in India consider the US dollar to be more important and the strongest currency of the world. However, elites in all the three categories acknowledge the importance of the euro towards ensuring world economic stability and its emergence as the only alternative global currency in the world.

Business Elites

Seven out of ten business elites consider the US dollar to be a more important and stronger currency vis-à-vis the euro. They however admit that the euro has tremendous potential which may be unleashed in future as it is still a recent currency. It was also credited to have survived the financial crisis quite well and that it was widely thought to be the only currency that can emerge as a substitute for the US dollar. Surjit Bhalla stated that:

> ...well and this is where I think is the biggest problem that the euro....the European Union comprises of many states that are at very different stages of development. For example the PIIGS countries are at a much lower per capita income level than Germany, France, Italy etcetera and I think this has a tendency to make some regions very uncompetitive particularly in the

> PIIGS regions... so therefore, you know, I would think that looking forward to the next two- three years, the euro is something like 135 now with a peak value of 160 and I think it will have a tendency to drift towards 118 and lower... so therefore I see the US dollar as strengthening gradually over time with respect to the euro (Bhalla 2010).

Political Elites

Six out of the eight elites stated that the US dollar is much stronger than the euro. One of the political elites considered both the currencies to be equally important while another considered the euro to still be in the phase of experimentation and therefore thought it to be too early to comment. Most of them however, stated that the EU had the potential to emerge as a threat to the US dollar provided it made some efforts, especially if it became more assertive in the political field. Vincent H. Pala was of the view that:

> ... euro is becoming stronger and stronger...when it started it was stable and it has become more stable now... so I think one day it may also... might be a threat to the US dollar (Pala 2010).

Civil Society Elites

About six out of ten elites considered the US dollar to be more important than the euro. Two of the elites considered the euro to be more important while another two refused to compare the two currencies and stated that it is important to have a currency like euro and that it is not fair to compare two currencies which have importance in their own right. It was stated by the elites that the US dollar is an international currency while the euro is still a political project. It has not been able to emerge as a strong currency due to internal squabbles and its weakness has become evident to the world as in the case of the Greek economic crisis. The euro is however, considered by the elites to be an extremely important currency and it continues to play and is slated to play an extremely important role in future as an alternate global currency which shall ensure world economic stability. Sujit Dutta commented upon the euro's feasibility and stated that:

> from an Indian perspective the growth of the euro is a very major development that reduces ....the dependency of the world on a single global currency, the dollar and therefore... try and avoid currency crisis or the kind of problems that the dollar has seen... devaluation or the dollar's instability might lead to the collapse of the world economy and therefore the emergence of euro as an alternative global currency is very, very important for the world, for the world economy, for world stability and for India. Normally we prefer the dollar but euro is an alternative currency that many travellers are now keeping but as you know, dollar still remains the principal, it relates to America's role...the first question that we address is which country is most important. Of course because of America's primacy in the world and both economically, politically, and militarily... the dollar continues to be the most important currency. Currently we still use the dollar as the most important currency but when we travel to Europe, of course...the Euro becomes the most vital one, makes it so easy... now you don't have to deal with so many separate currencies. Euro works, the common Schengen visa works... these are great achievements in Europe and has facilitated and rejuvenated the European ties... so the common visa and the common currency are great... hugely beneficial (Dutta 2010).

Information about EU

The internet and newspapers emerged as the most important sources of information about the EU.

Business Elites

About seven business elites stated that they get their information about the EU from newspapers. Four of the elites mentioned magazines in general while three elites mentioned *The Economist* in particular. Three of the elites stated that they got information about the EU from delegates and seniors who frequently travel to EU. The internet and television were mentioned as a source of information by three and two elites respectively:

> From newspapers, from TV channels, from our HRD departments who are there and from our seniors who keep on travelling abroad and if any good thing is happening over there... if anything that is impacting us or not impacting us, we conduct a meeting with all the senior staff and the people from there... and that meeting goes on for almost two to three hours..We have a boss, the director of the company tells us what is happening in the other countries and where we have to improve (Iqbal 2010).

Political Elites

Four each out of the eight political elites mentioned the internet and the newspaper as sources of EU information. One political elite each mentioned EU bulletins, seminar, Parliament Reference Library, magazines and journals as the sources of EU information. Mukut Mithi explained that:

> normally we browse the internet and through the newspapers and through journals and sometimes when we attend some kind of a seminar and through the process of the parliamentary debate, we come to know about our relationship with EU (Mithi 2010).

Civil Society Elites

Four of the elites specifically mentioned the EU website and another four mentioned the internet as a source of information about the EU. Three of the elites mentioned newspapers as a source. The other sources mentioned include think-tank linkages, seminars, conferences, books, journals, NATO delegation, regional offices in Europe and EU delegations. Ranjana Kumari mentioned that:

> they have a very smart, very nice newsletter which we receive regularly, we also look at their website very regularly because we are occasionally planning to apply for grants though we have not been successful in the past and we would like to do it more in future and also we have lots of....EU member nations are our partners, we exchange information with each other. Also there are seminars and conferences...we are visiting as an NGO....and also the EU off late made an effort of redrafting their policy in terms of development cooperation which we were very actively participating in, which happened in Delhi (Kumari 2010).

Specific Media to Access News about EU

Internet turns out to be the most important source of information followed by the newspapers across the three categories of elites.

Business Elites

Five out of ten business elites use the internet. Five business elites also access news about the EU by means of newspapers. The newspapers mentioned by the elites include *The Economic Times*, *The Times of India* (mentioned by two elites) and *The Financial Times*. A couple of elites mentioned that they chose to rely on the international media. Two elites mentioned that they relied on television to a very limited extent for accessing news about the EU. *The Economist* magazine was mentioned by three elites while magazines in general were mentioned by a couple of elites. Akhil Alha stated that:

> I think I would say internet is one big medium which provides me whatever information I need about the EU. Then I mean and

> I would say a small chunk is also obtained through newspapers also. I generally spend very little time on watching television (Alha 2010).

Political Elites

Five of the eight political elites stated that they accessed EU news by means of the internet. Four of them stated that they accessed EU news through newspapers while one political elite stated that he relied on his secretariat for EU news. Manishankar Aiyer stated that:

> I have no idea. You have to ask the media people themselves. But I understand that an enormous amount of information about the EU is now available on the web. Now when I used to deal with Europe, through a decade and a half from 1963 to 1976, there was a psychlo-styled pink bulletin written in extremely bad English which we would read in order to understand what was happening. But now the amount of information and its easy accessibility is much more than my day. But as I have not had any professional reason to deal with the nitty-gritty of Indo-European relations since 1976 when I left Brussels to go to Baghdad, I am hopelessly out of date (Aiyer 2010).

Civil Society Elites

Eight out of the ten elites stated that they access news about EU through the internet. Three elites mentioned that they accessed EU news through newspapers. A number of newspapers found mention by these elites. A couple of the civil society elites stated that they hardly made use of television to access EU news, though BBC proved to be useful in this respect. The civil society elites stated that they made use of all the material made available by EU institutions and research organisations on the internet. Jesim Pais stated that he accesses :

> the internet and for serious stuff, journal articles which give you some kind of comparison... EU and non-EU... and newspapers, there is *The Guardian* newspaper, there is a *Guardian Diplomatic*, and there is a *Le Monde Diplomatic*, they are both English, ...they have some collaboration,....so I regularly read from that and the *Wall Street Journal*, I am quite regular, *The Economist* also I am quite regular, though I find them not good but still just to have a sense of....*The Economist*, very often they get things wrong according to me but anyways so....and *The Hindu* in India is not so bad. *The Hindu* newspaper, its quite good especially when we are talking about international relations and so on .The Indian newspapers I read include the *Business Line*, *The Hindu*, regularly these two...*The Economic Times*.... *Financial Express*. I find them very superficial, not detailed enough because at some stage... all the superficial stuff... you know... we want details so *The Economic Times* doesn't have detail (Pais 2010).

Personal Contacts within Europe

Many elites have relatives who migrated to Europe, mostly to Britain. Some received education in Europe and therefore have many friends there. Additionally, a few of the elites sent their children to Europe for higher studies, mainly to Britain again. Moreover, plenty of elites always travel or have travelled to Europe. The civil society elites appear to have the least personal connection with Europe. Their connection to Europe is through meetings and seminars that they attend in Europe.

Business Elites

Six business elites claimed to have friends in Europe while seven had business contacts. One of the elites mentioned that he had family in Europe. The elites had associations with a whole range of countries. Sukh Nandan Singh stated that:

> Yes, I do definitely have personal contacts within Europe... No family contacts but ya ...my friends and business contacts... I have a lot... country you can say... if I have to name the country, it will be a long list, and basically I have travelled... throughout Europe. I have travelled to Italy, Greece, Spain, Portugal, Germany, France, Switzerland, Slovenia, Czech, Poland, Romania, Hungary, UK, Ireland and Belgium. So, these are all the countries I have travelled to so far within Europe (Singh 2010a).

Political Elites

Three of the eight elites stated that they had no personal contact whatsoever in Europe. Three elites stated that they had contacts on a professional level. Two elites revealed that they had friends in Europe while one of them claimed to have family in Europe. Manishankar Aiyer revealed that :

> Well, I have lots of personal contacts within Europe, inevitably most of them with the United Kingdom because I studied there and I have a lot of friends there... many of whom went into British politics and some into European politics and two of my closest friends at Cambridge, both of whom became Chancellors of the Exchequer are seriously divided amongst themselves on the European currency and the extent of European integration. Ken Clarke is a great advocate of Britain becoming a fully European country and Norman L'montis is keen on preserving the sovereignty of the United Kingdom from what he believes to be unnecessary and unfair and possibly dangerous encroachments by Europe into Britain's sovereign territory. So they are friends there. I lived for seven years in Belgium... so inevitably, I have a lot of friends in Belgium. I speak French fluently so that makes it comfortable going around France and in my days...Indians ...students only got Scandinavian girlfriends so I acquired one from Norway for myself...so I also feel you know... nostalgic

> about Scandinavia... my brother in-law worked for a German firm all his life. So one is...one is involved with Europe and I have friends there but I do think that at a political level, Europe is not giving India the attention we deserve (Aiyer 2010).

Civil Society Elites

About seven elites stated that they have professional contacts in Europe. Six elites stated that they have friends in Europe. Four of the civil society elites claimed to have family. One of the elites stated that he has no personal contacts with Europe whatsoever. The elites had contacts with a whole range of countries across Europe. Alok Mukhopadhyay stated that:

> ...yes I have, we have a lot of professional colleagues, we have friends, we have professional colleagues who are also you know working on South Asia and vice versa. We have friends in Belgium, UK, Poland, France and Germany. I have no family members there (Mukhopadhyay 2010).

Images of the European Union

The elites were asked about the images that come to their mind when they think about the term "European Union". The EU was referred to positively about 21 times while negative connotations were attached to the EU 11 times only. The phenomenon of European Integration was very fondly recounted by 21 elites. The image of the EU as an economic organisation was invoked by 11 elites. The euro found mention 7 times. The EU was recognised as a successful experiment by 5 elites. The cultural heritage of Europe was mentioned by 5 elites. The EU was described as a good experiment by 5 elites while another 5 applauded the great history of the bloc. The image of the EU as a political organisation, as a military power, as an educational hub, as a stable entity, the comfort of having a Schengen visa, good infrastructure and the EU flag were positive images that found mention a couple of times each.

Some of the other positive images included a good welfare system, friendship, cooperation, tourism, agriculture, transparency, technology, literature, centre of social democracy, liberal ideas, trading partner, possible new superpower, peace, progress, emissions and environmental standards, beautiful women, clean cities, beautiful place, gang of boys and extraordinary bureaucracy.

The negative connotations attached to the EU by the elites included that of being hard negotiators, economically strong but politically weak, lack of cultural engagement with India, voluminous documents, complexity and compromise in the EU, weak family ties, risky to travel, political questions like Turkey, challenge of gender justice, not very understanding of the compulsions of the other parts of the world, arrogant about prosperity, stability and human rights.

Importance of the EU to India at Present and in the Future

Increase in optimism was witnessed among all categories of elites about EU-India relations from the present to the future (see Figure 4.1). The business elites were most optimistic about EU-India relations both in the present and the future as most of them expressed the sentiment of exploring opportunities for increasing EU-India trade manifold. The media elites showed the least amount of optimism regarding the relations. This rating is a reflection of the trend of less than adequate coverage of the EU in the Indian media.

Figure 4.1: Importance of EU to India at present and in the future

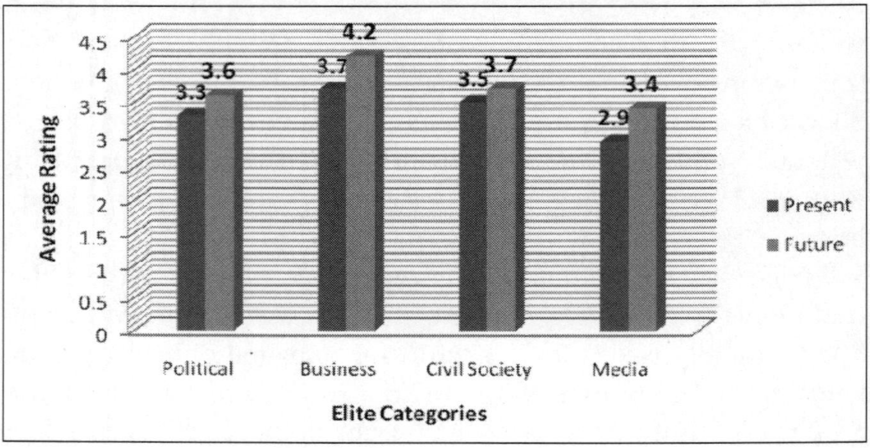

Conclusions

Elites enjoy a privileged status in society as they are largely regarded as the highest, best or excellent. Elitism refers to the belief in the rule of the elite. Classical elitism believed in the theory of circulation of elites and oligarchy and hence considered elite rule to be inevitable and unchangeable. Modern elitism tries to expose the damage elite rule does to democracy and that the belief in the indispensability of the elites is not true. Power elite are described as those elite who take key decisions which have major consequences. They are known to call the shots in the political, economic, military and social spheres and consequently enjoy power, wealth and celebrity status.

Two broad strands of conceptual understanding of the elite have emerged. The moral approach states that the rule of the single elite is justified on the basis of moral superiority while the functional approach believes that different types of elite share power, responsibilities and rewards and they are vital for the social functioning of a particular class or group. It is argued that the first approach leads to mysticism while the second approach encourages tautology. However, such conceptual moorings have been extremely useful for understanding modern industrial society which has witnessed a boom in the number and variety of elites on account of occupational and economic expansion of the society. The elites have thus been entrusted with the task of becoming a guardian of values and manager of goals.

The liberal-democratic perspective encourages participation of the common man in the process of foreign policy making unlike the realists who believe this should be an elite exercise. The critical approach agrees that the making of foreign policy is largely an elite exercise but it urges for a change in status quo unlike the realists who believe that the dominance of elites in the process is morally justifiable and should not therefore be subjected to any kind of change.

The pluralist model believes in the decentralisation and distribution of power among all sections of the society while the elite model holds the view that power is wielded by an influential few and the public is systematically ousted from all the power circles. The confabulation among elites takes place on key issues after which they also appear in the media and express their viewpoint on all kinds of affairs of the state. The Indian public watches these debates and internalises the opinion of the elites who always take stands which are amenable for perpetuation of their self-interest. The elites play a very clever game as they always urge for reform but not complete change as that would mean their ouster from power. Therefore, they are extremely interested in preservation of the status quo and this helps in checking reckless and uncontrolled pursuit of interests which might destroy the society altogether.

The Indian elites were actively involved in deciding the foreign policy priorities of independent India. There were basically three kinds of elites at the time that had considerable say in the governing of the country. The Congress Party was the political elite while the civil servants and officers of the armed forces were the other elite categories respectively. The Congress party always took a pro-India stance, while the bureaucrats and military officers were inspired more by British imperialism and western economic and political institutional frameworks. However, the Congress party, led by India's first Prime Minister Jawaharlal Nehru, made sure that the other two categories of elites functioned under the overall guidance and supervision of the political elite.

India's policy- making elites have keenly involved themselves with matters of India's foreign policy. They are largely based in Delhi and are known to consist of about a hundred members that include prominent journalists, retired civil servants, formal admirals, generals and air marshals, academics and scientists and a few politicians and businessmen. The socialising agents for the elite include conferences, workshops and seminars. They are known to be in demand for the purpose of giving advice and consultation to the major political parties of India.

The Indian elites are extremely confident about the stature of their country and look upon themselves as a newly emerging political heavyweight in international politics. They look upon the EU as the Old Continent, which is largely economically stagnant and is falling flat on welfares, which has led to the initiation of the rapid process of disintegration of intellectual and moral traditions. The Indian elite do not possess an accurate and comprehensive understanding of the EU. The only reason for familiarity with the EU is the robust trade and economic relations, but not many have a clue about the Schengen and the like. However, a gradual shift towards greater awareness about the EU and increasing familiarity with various aspects other than the economic dimension of the relationship has also been witnessed.

A total of 38 face-to-face in-depth interviews, of an average duration of 45 minutes each, were conducted as part of this study. A number of well-known personalities (ten from business, eight from politics, ten from civil society and ten from media) were interviewed which led to a number of interesting findings.

The Indian elites looked forward to professional involvement with the EU at present and in the near future. The business elites were very familiar with EU member-states and had several ties with them but the EU hardly figured in the scheme of things. The political elites talked about occasional brushing of shoulders with EU delegations but none of them talked about a concrete engagement with the EU. The civil society elites were most well acquainted with the EU and its structure and mode of working and they cited a project or two by which they got exposure to the prevalent practices in the EU, especially in the social sector.

Some of the business elites agreed that EU is a great power as it had played a commendable role in various spheres of international politics, while others considered EU to be a passive power largely owing to internal dissensions. The political elites were dismissive of the notion that the EU is a great power because they believed that it was not fair in the exercise of normative power and also because it had not come of its own to become a decisive political and military power in international politics. The civil society elite expressed their willingness to call the EU a social and cultural power but not a great power mainly because the EU was in the throes of an economic crisis. The media elites accepted that the EU was an established economic power but they did not consider it to be a leader in the normative, social and military spheres. They stated that lack of internal cohesion made it difficult for the EU to be recognised as a leader in international politics. Thus, it was only the business elites who recognised the EU as a great power.

The business elites were of the view that since the EU is economically powerful, it can make use of this strength to emerge as a leader in international politics. Most of them acknowledged that it had the potential to emerge as a leader on account of its worthwhile contribution in many areas of international politics. However, the EU has still not emerged as a leader as it did not possess the required capability and power to assume the role of a leader in international politics. The political elites were not willing to call the EU a leader in international politics. They were of the view that being a formidable economic power was one thing but becoming a leader in international politics called for assuming far greater power and responsibilities. Most of the political elites clearly spelled out the fact that they looked upon US as a leader in international politics and the EU at present did not even come close for the assumption of such a role.

The civil society elites believed that the EU should increase its involvement in Asia and Africa, as well as in global affairs. Some stated that despite taking a proactive stand on various issues, the EU has not emerged as a leader in international politics because it was largely seen toeing the line of the Unites States on global issues. Moreover, it failed to talk in unison on many global issues. including the Iraq war. The media elites similarly, also pointed out that the EU was many times found speaking in different voices as during the Copenhagen climate negotiations. The EU also seemed unwilling to manage its military and security matters on its own and therefore it could not be considered to be a leader in international politics. Thus, we see that the Indian elites recognise that EU has the capability to act as a leader in international politics. However, they believed that the EU needed to assert itself in many areas and project a unified front in order to be recognised as a leader by the world at large.

The business elites considered the relationship to be extremely positive and talked about the strong economic foundations that provided strength and durability to the relationship. They called for further cooperation between the two sides especially in the economic sector apart from encouraging cultural exchanges, museum exhibitions, promotion of tourism, movement of people and labour migration. The political elite were of the view that EU-India relationship could be further enhanced by taking the economic dimension of the partnership one notch up. Cooperation in the field of trade, terrorism, climate change and grass roots democracy was sought to be expanded. Besides, the political elite urged the staff at the Indian embassy to play a more active role in strengthening relations with the EU. The civil society elites also looked upon EU-India relations as a positive relationship, as there were no strong reasons for acrimony between the two sides. Besides, strong economic links, similar values and global aspirations were cited as uniting factors. The civil society elites were of the view that India had smooth sailing relations with EU member-countries on a bilateral level but it faced hurdles and problems in dealing with the EU as a bloc which could be significantly reduced by means of a fruitful intervention of the EU Presidency. They also said that a more powerful role of the EU in global politics would bring the two sides together. Thus, the Indian elites across all categories were convinced that EU-India relations are a positive relationship and cooperation in all possible areas should be taken forward. The EU and India were asked to build up an even stronger relationship on the basis of the commonalities that the two entities share between them.

The media elites state that no advance planning and no targets for coverage are set for reporting EU stories. The Indian press relies on news wires for EU news as there are not many Indian correspondents stationed in the EU. The EU Delegation to India is also known to get in touch with the media and request for coverage of an upcoming event. However, not all EU news finds space in the Indian newspapers because the editors have to prioritise keeping in mind the marketability of the news item and the interest of the readers.

The media elites do not allocate a specific budget for EU news coverage as the practice of allocating a budget for a region is normally not practiced in India. News gathering is an expensive exercise and therefore the Indian press mainly relies on foreign correspondents for this purpose or stations not more than a single correspondent mostly in London to report news coming from EU. Such news generally has the Anglo-Saxon influence, which ultimately conditions the perceptions of the Indian readers when such articles are published in the Indian press.

The media elites admitted that there is substantial coverage of economic news but scant coverage of political news about the EU. It turns out that most the coverage is done by economic reporters followed by foreign correspondents. More staff or experts are therefore not hired for coverage of EU issues. Besides, the reporters get in touch with experts on specific issues and include their bytes in the news articles. There are some occasions however, when the newspaper sends its correspondents for EU news coverage especially when the coverage is issue-specific.

The media elites had varied views as far as predicting a shift in the balance of reporting was concerned. Some were of the view that there would be no change and the developed world would always capture the maximum attention. Some however predicted that the balance of reporting shall shift towards East Asia especially China. Not many were hopeful that coverage of EU news would witness a substantial increase, because, it generally did nothing that was sensational or controversial in nature and publishing news that is basically routine, bland and placid has its limitations and cannot be carried on endlessly. However, a change may be noticed in case the EU serves Indian interests substantially and consistently over a period of time.

The media elites consider an EU story difficult to sell in India compared to articles from more popular regions such as Pakistan, China, USA and Japan, as news emanating from the EU fails to capture the imagination of the readers because EU is still considered to be a strange and distant land. EU does nothing which is an aberration in international politics. The EU fails to stand out for things good and bad in global affairs and therefore the Indian press does not seem to choose EU news stories over that of other regions.

US and China were considered to be the most important regions for India while others considered Russia and Japan to be more important to India than the EU. The political elites decided to refrain from calling one region more important than the other. The majority of the Indian elites considered the economic aspect of the relations to be most vital both at present and in the future. They stated that trade links and economic relations are the most important factors that should be kept in mind when India formulates policies in relation to the EU. This shows the immense respect and trust shown to the economic element of relations. However, this also amounts to ignoring other spheres and aspects of the relationship. The majority of business and political elites had no knowledge whatsoever about the Delegation and its activities. The majority of civil society elites were very familiar with the working of the Delegation and expressed keenness on working with the Delegation in future.

The business elites considered the accession of new countries to the EU as a challenge as well as an opportunity. The political elites skirted the issue and did not give clear-cut answers to this question. The civil society elites on the other hand considered accession of countries to the EU to be an opportunity.

The majority of the elites considered the US dollar to be the strongest currency in the world and much stronger than the euro. Most of them preferred to carry the US dollar over the euro while travelling. The Eurozone crisis had inflicted considerable damage to the confidence in the euro. However, none of them stated that it was a completely worthless experiment. Many of them acknowledged the advantage of having euro as a currency for ensuring economic stability and for breaking the monopoly of the US by emerging as an alternative global currency of the world.

The Internet, followed by newspapers, was the most important source of information for the elites about the EU. When asked to rate the importance of EU to India, the Indian elite across all categories expressed optimism that the relevance of EU to India would become even greater in future. The business elites were most confident and enthusiastic about the relations while the media elites were the most pessimistic about the partnership which is reflected in less than adequate coverage of the EU in the Indian press.

The elites were asked to mention the three images that came to their mind while thinking about the euro. The elites recalled more positive images than negative images. Some of the positive images mentioned by the elites included that of an economic bloc, the euro, a political organisation, a military power, an educational hub, a stable entity, good infrastructure, Schengen visa and the EU flag. The negative connotations attached to the EU included those of being hard negotiators, economically strong but politically weak, voluminous documents, weak family ties, challenge of gender justice, not very understanding of the compulsions of the other parts of the world, arrogant about prosperity, stability and human rights.

The study of perceptions of the Indian elites about the EU has provided useful insights about the EU-India relationship. We saw uniformity of opinion on salient issues regarding the relationship while stark differences persisted over others. The elites were largely forward-looking about the relationship but many of their responses were marked by pessimism, biasness, stereotypes and prejudices. A number of constructive suggestions were put forth by the elites for furthering the ties while they also pointed out the roadblocks in the relationship. Thus, the study helped us to understand the big picture of EU-India relations as it brought to light new and persisting trends of the bilateral relationship.

5

Conclusions

An attempt has been made to examine the strengths and weaknesses of the relationship and the ways and means of bolstering the EU-India partnership further especially in the light of the inputs based on the investigations about the perceptions of the print media and the Indian elites about the EU. This chapter shall summarise the broad findings of the study.

The interaction between India and Europe dates back to even before the Christian era. The Europeans made a mark in India through trade relations which culminated in colonisation of the country by the British. European thought had left an indelible imprint on the thinking of the intellectual intelligentsia and popular leaders of the Indian freedom movement who fought against the British. Independent India was worried about declining trade sops and benefits as a result of Britain becoming a part of the EEC. Nevertheless, through various instruments such as the GSP, JDI and CCA India was able to safeguard its economic interests. The Cold War led to the widening of gaps in relations on account of India's adherence to the doctrine of non-alignment. A steady rise in trade was witnessed through the 1990s but it was highly distorted in favour of EU. However, attempts were made during this period to provide relief to India by removal of quantitative restrictions on significant number of goods imported from India to EU.

Liberalism has become much more popular than realism in present-day international politics. Complex inter-dependence provides a closer portrayal of reality than realism. However, it is considered to be an ideal type. Reality is largely considered to exist between the two extremes. Apart from this, the shift from bipolarity and unipolarity towards multipolarity is said to have taken place. These developments indicate the growing salience of EU and India as international powers and it is considered logical for the two sides to come together for increasing their external credibility and legitimacy and attaining a mutually advantageous position in the international scenario.

The stupendous economic rise of India, the transformation of its population from a liability to an asset and recognition as one of the largest untapped markets of the world, made the EU realise that it needs to cultivate good relations with India, which led to the signing of a series of agreements with India and numerous meetings at all levels. It was the 1994 Cooperation Agreement which showed the way to broaden the political dialogue and it continues to be accepted as the legal framework for cooperation till today. This ultimately led to more institutionalised dialogues in the shape of annual summits. At the very first EU-India summit in 2000 at Lisbon, both sides expressed the desire of taking the relationship to a higher level of Strategic Partnership, in the wake of India's enhanced and sustained growth and on account of integration and enlargement in the EU. Consequently, the EU-India Strategic Partnership was adopted at the fifth EU-India summit, while the sixth summit saw the adoption of the Joint Action Plan, which provided strength and support to the Strategic Partnership endorsed in 2004. The progress and implementation of the Joint Action Plan was reviewed at the eighth EU-India summit. The leaders expressed their satisfaction at the progress achieved in the conduct of EU-India relations.

The bare perusal of the negotiations and agreements concluded between EU and India clearly indicate that the Strategic Partnership is the mainstay of EU-India relations. However, a lot remains to be desired in order to make the relationship more realistic and meaningful. The bilateral trade and investment agreement, for which negotiations began eight years back, have still not been concluded. Indian policy makers are not very convinced about a crucial and strategic role of EU in Asia at present and in the near future, which obfuscates the need to go the extra mile and extend a hand for greater cooperation. EU hardly figures as a power to reckon with in Indian foreign policy matters. Bilateralism seems to be the way out for getting deals done in the EU as EU member-states seem to prefer to deal with

India on a one- to- one basis, rather than under the EU rainbow with 28 shades of opinion and many more conflicts of interest. Thus, the strengthening of relations of India with the relatively more powerful member-states of EU is inversely proportional to the lessening of political will and weakening of relations with EU. Thus, the existence of the strategic partnership has not been able to prevent the spread of complacency and a lackadaisical attitude which seems to have diffused the enthusiasm to engage with each other on both sides.

The economic relation between the two partners is the most dynamic aspect of EU-India relations. Huge leaps in trade figures were witnessed in the period between 1980 and 1991 and the momentum continued throughout the 1990s. This momentum went on the back foot for a brief period of time during 2009, because of the dark clouds of global economic recession, after which EU-India trade recorded a quick recovery. The pace of EU-India trade has slowed down in the recent past due to various factors such as moderate increase in surplus trade, slowing down of India's GDP growth and the Eurozone crisis. Although the balance of trade has always been in favour of EU, India's exports to the EU are by far the largest, compared to other countries, as India happens to be one of the largest beneficiaries of the GSP system. The Indian services sector occupies a huge share of the EU market. Both partners appreciate and realise each other's potential and consequently make huge investments. The EU is India's largest trading partner which makes this relationship extremely special for India. India is leaving no stone unturned to bridge this gap and gain more from the economic partnership by constantly pursuing its interests and presenting its case in bilateral meetings between the EU and India, as well as before WTO and other global economic organisations, for redressal of disputes. Robust economic growth bears testimony to the fact that both sides share an element of trust with each other.

The rise in the strength of the middle class, and, especially accelerated increase of the upper middle class group, has led the EU along, with the rest of the world, to include India in the wish-list of markets that they would like to invest in and capture. India was also recognised as the largest English-speaking market. Outsourcing of knowledge- based services, especially low-cost IT services from India, has been a great pull to include Indian companies in their scheme of things. The recognition of the Indian calibre has led many European companies to promptly set up off-shore research and development centres in India.

It is a settled fact that the economic aspect is the most vital element of EU-India relations. Most of the energy is therefore channelised in order to get this equation right. This has led to a dogged determination on both sides to conclude the EU-India FTA, as too much time has been spent in negotiations since 2007. This is on account of the fact that both sides do not see eye to eye on many issues which has exacerbated the chances of reaching a deal. Standoff continues in the areas of agriculture, dairy sector, automobiles, wines and spirits, investment, public procurement, retrospective taxation, tariff and non-tariff barriers and climate change. The EU-India FTA is widely expected to increase trade volumes, create jobs and increase market access for both sides.

The economic interaction between the two partners continues to provide the building blocks of the relationship. It also cements the relationship on account of constant progress and growth of trade volumes, foreign direct investment and market access. The defence sector has emerged as a key sector for cooperation. There has been a noticeable increase in defence deals being concluded between EU-member states and India which is creating unease in the political and defence establishment in the United States. Mutual investment in defence is likely to increase in the near future, which will also have implications upon the future role of the EU and India in global affairs. Cooperation in this field may eventually lead to EU-India joint missions and throw open opportunities for strategic alliances in other parts of the world. Both sides have been partners in numerous prestigious endeavours in the field of science and technologyThe EU and India do not hesitate in directing huge amounts of funds towards various scientific projects and recognise and acknowledge the expertise, skills and acumen of the scientists from both sides in research and innovation. It would not be wrong to state that the EU has lent a helping hand to India since the very beginning of the relationship. It has made sizeable contributions towards Operation Flood Programme and Sarva Siksha Abhiyan initiative. Recently, India has transformed itself from an aid-seeking country and donned the new avatar of becoming a donor country. EU-India development cooperation has not stopped but continues in the form of EU assistance to India in helping the latter achieve the MDGs.

Values of democracy, rule of law, civil liberties and respect for human rights have led to a very strong bonding between the two partners. Both share an intrinsic belief in the potential of soft power in international politics. Commonality of values endears the partners to each other for it helps in bestowing trust upon each other. Belief in common values subsequently enhances mutual understanding and leads to consensus on most issues of common concern. It is this compatibility shared by the two sides which has led to a positive and sustainable relationship that reaches new milestones every year.

Despite the positive ambience in which the relations are conducted, there remain quite a few irritants in the relationship, which have been swept under the carpet, only to emerge yet again. It is important to take the bull by its horns and deal with the problems and aim at a permanent resolution of disputes rather than try to bring about quick-fix solutions. The over-emphasis on trade relations and currently with the EU-India FTA hogging the limelight, the EU tends to be largely seen as a trading bloc which diminishes its overall stature in the Indian-subcontinent. It would be prudent for both sides to highlight the other dimensions of the relationship which are equally important and contribute to the growth and endurance of the relationship. Providing only selective support to the Strategic Partnership will not hold the relationship in good stead. Carving out a pound of flesh from the entire beast will not completely satiate the hunger. It is important to develop a holistic and goal-based approach towards the relationship and work on every aspect and dimension of the relationship at all levels.

Excessive bureaucratisation is a red herring which needs to be streamlined in order to attain time-bound positive results in all spheres of the relationship. It has also been pointed out that the visibility of the EU in the Indian subcontinent is minimal when compared to that of the US. The EU should make concerted efforts towards an image correction so that it is recognised as a significant, responsible and veritable actor in international relations. The EU should categorically communicate its stand on Pakistan and condemn state- sponsored terrorist activities. India will embrace the EU in a tighter hug, if the latter shows solidarity with the former in countering violence and militancy. Joining hands to contain China would be a step taken by both sides in the right direction. However, if the two sides fail to strike when the iron is hot, it might become a case of too little too late. It would be a clever move on the part of the EU to support India's candidature for a permanent seat at the UNSC since Germany is also in the same race. If EU and India support and succeed in this endeavour, it will be a mutually advantageous scenario which will further consolidate their partnership. SAARC should be utilised as a platform for increasing levels of cooperation and for enriching and enhancing understanding between the regions of Europe and South Asia which in turn will enable the EU and India to better appreciate the nuances of their partnership. Greater interaction and cultural exchanges would be one of the surest steps on the way forward, as they would help in removal of inhibitions and misunderstandings and bring about an overall improvement in relations between the two countries. A thoughtful approach towards migration would undoubtedly increase the presence of the people inside each other's territory, which would lead to healthy growth of the diaspora—which would assume the task of mediation during highs and lows of the relationship. The diaspora would also play a crucial role in influencing the decision-making process on internal as well as external issues. The EU needs to be more vigilant for grasping all possible opportunities for forging stronger bonds and becoming more visible in India. The EU should try to be as sensitive and pro-active as the US if not more, to come out in support of India especially on issues concerning India's neighbourhood.

Making sense of the concept of perception and the manner in which we perceive our surroundings forms the core of understanding the processes of foreign policy formulation and implementation. Perception largely refers to an idea, notion or belief that people have on the basis of how things seem. It can be described as the effect that something external has on man. Perception formation involves decisions regarding the focus of our attention, organising the selected stimuli for evaluation and evaluating and attaching meaning to the stimuli.

Much more attention seems to have been directed towards the study of perceptions by psychologists rather than by scholars of international relations. Although, psychologists have contributed towards highlighting the salience of the concept, their approach appears to be deficient in nature when examined from the point of view of the study of international relations. The emotional quotient has been given much more weightage compared to cognitive aspects. There is always a doubt as to whether the settings and manipulations applied in the laboratory experiments will be completely applicable to real world events. The structure of the international system is largely ignored in these experiments, which many believe would not provide adequate results. Besides, international relations scholars believe that behaviour could better be explained and understood by means of policy analysis and not by an overdose of psychological variables. Thus, we see a clear tussle for superiority between the emotional and cognitive approaches of studying perception. However, it has been realised that both the cognitive model and emotional and motivational model can lead to similar faults and mistakes of judgment and decision. Since a cognitive model is found to be parsimonious and easily testable, it enjoys greater popularity among scholars of international relations.

Nevertheless, a shift in thinking was witnessed in the 1990s when it was realised that emotions are an inseparable part of rationality and that psychology is extremely useful to explain accurate judgments. The sentiments of trust and credibility were largely considered to be based on emotion as much as on cognition.

Image is the sum of cognitive, affective and evaluative structures of the behavior unit which can be the individual or the state. Similarly, in the psychological schema, image is referred to as a collection of features that come together in a meaningful manner. The image that is activated determines the reaction of the people to an action carried out by a foreign country. Thus, image plays a key role in the interpretation of action. Political identity, historical memories and socially-shaped conceptions of the world order are considered to be the main components of cognitive maps of a society. Position, interaction and power-related variables influence the perceptions of an external other based on the study of international relations and analysis of the intricacies of foreign policy.

Attempts are not being made to accurately fathom what the EU stands for, as it is considered to be a unique entity which does not qualify as a nation-state nor can it be referred to as a purely regional or traditional international organisation. Besides, the EU does not possess distinct and definite characteristics as it is still in the process of evolution. It is in fact very open to large-scale overhaul as was made evident by the changes brought about recently through the Lisbon Treaty. Thus, attempts to define the powers and functions of the EU have led to different interpretations of the identity of the EU, which in turn have endowed it with different nomenclatures. Efforts to draw the external identity of the EU on the basis of internal factors lead to ignorance about the external impressions of the EU. Thus, the viewpoint of outsiders about the EU and its role especially in global affairs is not factored in.

Perceptions are known to shape the foreign policy outlook of countries. The EU's uniqueness makes it difficult for outsiders to fathom what it exactly stands for. Thus, the values that EU espouses are interpreted differently by outsiders, which is contingent upon the cognitive maps of their society and country. This creates ample room for contradiction between what the EU tries to do and communicate and how the external others understand and perceive the EU. Thus, the EU is understood to be a bloc often known for complexity, ineffectiveness and delay. The EU could not afford such contradictions and misperceptions, which led to the establishment of the European External Action Service and the creation of the post of the High Representative for Foreign Affairs and Security Policy. These can be regarded as correctional measures that the EU took in order to refurbish its external image and ensure dissemination of correct information about itself.

External images about the EU make for a fascinating study as it spills out interesting findings. It is in fact a critical element that should be taken into account for the sake of the EU's foreign policy. Such studies undoubtedly facilitate better comprehension about the EU's external identity and help it in making an internal assessment of its failures and accomplishments abroad. It also assists the EU in deciding upon the future course of action in foreign policy.

The perception of the Indian elite about the EU is predominantly influenced by the Anglo-Saxon media, which tends to transfer a biased and opinionated view, which is lapped up by the Indian media which almost completely relies on these news sources —which in turn conditions the perceptions of Indian readers. Apart from the colouring of opinions, the EU has, to a large extent, become etched in the minds of Indians as non-negotiable territory which they would not like to explore. Most Indians feel intimidated by the apparent complexity of the working of the EU, not to mention its size and huge diversity.

It has also been noticed that the Indian government seems to be more at ease in dealing with EU member-states on a bilateral basis. There is a great amount of clarity regarding policies of EU-member-states among decision-makers and bureaucrats in India. However, they are found to be at a loss with respect to EU policy on the very same issues. The enthusiasm and urge to engage with India is also found to be missing on the EU side. In fact, very small clusters in EU seem to be interested in taking the relations forward. Any push or momentum is generated only when the most powerful member-states who are the driving forces of the EU think it to be necessary. The underlying motive most of the time is pursuit of their national-interest within the wider context of EU.

A major factor which has impeded cordial relations between nations has been misperceptions about each other. Democracies have an inherent safeguard against the spread of misperceptions about neighbouring countries, as citizens are able to conjure up really accurate images based on authentic information which is not media-controlled. The people in democratic states are also able to prevent demagoguery and propaganda by keeping in check the duly elected rulers who are accountable to the people for all their words and deeds. However, it has also been observed that partially correct perceptions are not able to prevent countries from dominating others. This miscommunication with the other gives rise to insurgency and to a sense of self-delusion, obstinacy and antagonism. Europe perceived Asia as an instrument for increasing trade, establishing colonies and spreading religion. The spiritual and material values of the two regions were as different as chalk and cheese and therefore the resultant interaction led to disparate opinions and perceptions about each other.

It was formally decided only a year after the signing of the Maastricht Treaty that the EU should raise its profile in Asia. Initially, the focus was on drawing attention towards EU's economic strength. But it was soon realised that economic and political relations could be hampered in the absence of a regular dialogue and enhanced understanding about each other. Therefore, the EU undertook a number of activities to increase its visibility in India such as spreading information about its economic and development activities, an enhanced visitor's programme, strengthening higher education and training links, town twinning and cultural exchanges, building up on European expertise in India and Asia, building networks at the university, media and enterprise level, intensifying EU-India dialogue by involving the civil society, media and the academic community on both sides and strengthening and broadening the network of Delegations . It was noted that the massive size and diversity of India requires special efforts for strengthening the image of the EU in India for which the press and media were called upon to play a special role. India was also expected to increase its visibility within the EU, by charting out its own communication strategy. The EU and India were required to inform and enrich public opinion and update media images on both sides in the wake of the rapidly changing domestic and global scenario. Thus, we see that both sides, especially the EU, had grasped the fact that despite a healthy partnership, more needed to be done in order to get due acknowledgement for the growth of the relationship in all possible spheres of cooperation.

A clear-cut absence of the EU was seen in Prime Minister Narendra Modi's list of foreign policy priorities. He has not been seen to have engaged with the EU in the same capacity as other powers of the world such as BRICS, United States, India's neighbours, East Asia, Russia and Australia. United States and China are more easily recognised as key partners of India, although the EU is India's largest trading partner and a vital source of high technology and FDI. Moreover, it has not assumed an aggressive economic stance like China, which is eroding parts of the Indian manufacturing sector by under pricing its exports. The EU has also emerged as a key defence partner of India next to Russia. However, the emergence of a common strategic culture between the two sides has not evolved yet. Cultural affinities and commonalties of values have not given rise to strong political and strategic bonds. Although, SAARC has desired to emulate the EU model, cooperation has not moved ahead beyond a point because of internal dissensions within SAARC.

The EU member-states are much more keen to ink bilateral deals with India for furthering their interests and do not intend to get lost in the maze of EU institutions and policies. Besides, it is the EU member-states rather than EU who seem to take a firm stand on global issues which leads to a loss of credibility of the EU at the cost of a highly assertive and isolationist role played by the member-states. It is therefore imperative that EU makes efforts towards emerging as a focal point of relations with India.

Others point out that the two sides are in fact very dissimilar in terms of history, culture and demography. Besides, the absence of geographic contiguity distances them from each other even further. Internal politics in EU and India is largely messy and compulsions of staying in power dictate the foreign policy agenda, which adversely affects relations. The two sides are known to be extremely overcautious regarding global ambition which reduces their economic clout. It is an established fact that EU-India relations have developed well beyond the economic aspect of relations. Therefore, it is necessary that traditional means of diplomacy, like the holding of EU-India summits, is promoted.

Many Indian opinion makers have expressed the hope of seeing the EU play a greater role in global affairs on the lines of the United States. However, this does not seem to be materialising, on account of the distinction between the strategy and goals of both sides. The expectation of the EU, that India would side with it on every issue in the UN and other international fora, has proved to be far-fetched as India has made sure to factor in its national interest before giving its verdict on any issue. Besides, India has emerged as an ardent campaigner for reconfiguration of the entire world order that will be devoid of traditional European and American hegemony. However, it is still believed that the EU and India will cooperate, if bad turns to worse, to ward off and contain China.

The Indian perception about the EU as a security actor is not very positive. EU is largely seen to make use of its civilian and normative identity in order to blanket its weaknesses in military capabilities and the absence of a sturdy and effective security and defence policy. The EU's engagement in Asia is limited to its contribution of NATO- led ISAF in Afghanistan and the anti-piracy mission off the coast of Somalia. The EU has no voting rights in the UN General Assembly and it is not a member of the security and military regimes, of which India seeks to be a member. It is the EU member-states that enjoy the member-ship and therefore it is they, and not the EU, who call the shots. Besides, the EU is not even a member of the UNSC, which undermines its position, compared to that of France and UK who are permanent members of the body. The EU seems to have no role to play in furthering India's security interests. The EU-India pledge to collaborate in the area of global security interests therefore seems very less convincing.

However, there are reasons for not being entirely dejected about the scope of EU-India collaboration in security affairs. The EU has been an approachable partner for smooth technology transfers which will enable India to build an indigenous manufacturing base. Besides, the EU appears to be a better partner as it has no inhibitions and hesitation in primarily engaging with the public sector in defence manufacturing unlike the United States. France and India have a rapidly growing partnership in space technology. Afghanistan is a likely area where the EU and India should cooperate on security matters, as thousands of lives are lost in Europe due to drugs smuggled from Afghanistan. The Asia-Pacific and Gulf Region are other areas where EU and India could form a united front. Both EU and India appear to be hesitant powers that are being urged by the United States to get rid of their inhibitions and play a much larger role in security matters in their neighbourhood and beyond. Both sides have been exhorted to look upon security issues with renewed vigour and vitality.

There are many doubts regarding India's willingness to engage with the EU on security matters. India is constantly working towards increasing its stature in military matters. It should join hands with the EU which happens to be an equally cautious international actor. It will be a mutually advantageous bargain as in the case of the economic aspect of the relationship. Besides, the member-states are engaged with India and South Asia in a big measure, which means that the EU does not have to tread on uncharted territory. The EU also needs to assure India that it would not unnecessarily meddle with or interfere in its internal matters as a result of their collaboration.

The present day India is not happy with the assumption of the role of a normative power in international affairs by the EU, especially when those norms and values are sought to be imposed upon developing countries. Indians are not ready to accept and appreciate the civilising mission of the EU. Nor do they think that the EU's path to development should be blindly followed by developing countries. The emerging nations are in the process of constantly remoulding the international order, which would be inclusive in nature and free from the condescending attitude of the West, which considers itself to be a moral superpower on a civilising mission. The normative disconnect is known to exist between the EU and India on issues such as climate change as the EU expects India to follow the standards set and understood by EU as suitable and appropriate. But they tend to ignore the fact that India and other countries have other compulsions to deal with, as they have not reached the level of development which the developed countries enjoy. The normative mission of the EU is largely regarded as a smokescreen for safeguarding its economic interests at the cost of the interests of developing countries.

India is also averse to be lectured on the issue of human rights. India claims that there is no issue pertaining to human rights violation raised by an INGO or external actors, which has not been raised previously in India itself, including the issue of Kashmir and Gujarat riots of 2002. Besides, India does not agree with the EU approach to stall EU-India FTA on the issue of human rights, which it believes should be dealt with at other fora such as the ILO. India has constantly been criticised by the EU for the manner in which it has voted on international issues concerning Afghanistan, Iran and Sri Lanka among others. India is most unhappy and accuses the EU of double standards because human rights violations never stand in the way when the EU negotiates with China where it invests almost twenty times more compared to India.

Cultural relations and exchanges are considered to be of vital importance and many consider it to be an end in itself. But there seems to be a long road ahead in achieving a respectable degree of cultural understanding between EU and India. Both sides are hugely ignorant about each other's culture and diversity that exists. Their impressions are marked by ignorance and stereotypical prejudices. UK is the only place that most Indians know in Europe or at the most they are distinctly familiar with Western Europe. EU- sponsored academic cooperation activities are not very popular because they involve a lot of paper work and lack transparency. Besides, humanities and social sciences are not given much weightage, when compared to the sciences in scholarship programmes offered by the EU. It is felt that the digital revolution that has swept India should be utilised by the EU in communicating with the Indian people, especially the youth on cultural issues. India could learn from the EU how to guard against nepotism in public affairs and ensure stability of the government which should be given support on the basis of issues rather than on the basis of parochial concerns of caste, class, race and religion. Many Indians feel that Europeans do not encourage assimilation and blending of cultures. They do not extend a warm welcome to people coming from other countries. Many allege that multiculturalism has failed as an experiment in Europe.

There are also differences in making sense of strategic issues. For instance, the EU understands the term sovereignty in the context of post-modernism while India refers to the traditional view of state sovereignty which involves protecting strategic autonomy. Hence, although EU and India share common values, they tend to differ in their approaches and strategies. Thus, the EU should lend an ear to India in order to comprehend the Indian understanding and interpretation of ideas and concepts.

It is the economic aspect of EU-India relations that has stood the test of time and is the mainstay of the relationship. However, there have been numerous short-lived as well as persistent obstacles along the way. Excessive bureaucratisation, lack of transparency, procedural hurdles and imposition of tariff and non-tariff barriers are some problems that both sides have had to contend with. The EU seeks greater liberalisation of the Indian market. However, India does not oblige as it seeks to protect the domestic market and producers. EU-India FTA negotiations have reached a deadlock. The issues involved therein have been highly politicised, which has made matters worse. But the Indian government and the EU authorities believe that the EU-India

FTA will see the light of day sooner than later. Both sides have expressed willingness to accommodate the other's interests and prerogatives as far as possible. The EU has urged India to make efforts to provide a better investment climate while India has constantly been working to ward off the effects of the Eurozone crisis on its economy. We also see that although there are economic disputes between the two sides on numerous counts, an effort is always made for amicable resolution of disputes as seen in the case of confiscation of Indian drugs at European ports or the lifting of the ban on export of Alphonso mangoes to the EU.

The growth of India from a developing to an emerging power with the potential to become a great power has brought about significant change in the nature of development cooperation between the EU and India. India is now a donor country and no longer an aid recipient. It has distanced itself from the traditional donor countries of the West, including the EU, and has opted to work within multilateral frameworks having Southern representation and leadership. Thus, India has not accepted many of the EU's normative assumptions about international development. However, change seems to be in the offing as EU member- states are moving towards greater South- South cooperation approaches. Thus, the EU has preferred to invest in social sectors such as health and education, while India has opted for investing in infrastructure projects. One of the new areas recognised for boosting development cooperation is that of information and communication technology because Indians can offer their efficient services at cheap rates. Besides, India can help the EU in building and maintaining their infrastructure and services as most countries of the EU have greying populations who are unable to do the same. The EU had taken a decision to phase out development cooperation in India after 2013, although regional and thematic programmes are still in operation. The EU is known to have extended cooperation to India to achieve the MDGs.

The EU and India have an extensive range of instruments for cooperation in the field of energy and climate change. However, such interactions have not yielded results on the ground as meetings have been irregular and the work has been slow-paced, despite the setting up of working groups on clean coal, energy efficiency and renewable energy. Some of the small scale projects in India funded by the European Commission and the EU member-states have been successful but they have not been able to ignite the pace of cooperation desired in this crucial sector. It is strongly felt that bilateral problems on technology transfer need to be resolved. The EU has urged India to decouple population, economic growth and poverty alleviation from rise in emissions. India's development priorities in fact need to be understood by EU and it could help India in technological leapfrogging and doing business in the area of conventional and renewable energy. Thus, there happens to be substantial scope for cooperation with India in the field of energy.

The climate change debate has always pitted the two partners against each other. The EU sides with the developed world, which is urging the developing countries to sign a legally-binding agreement on emissions. India on the other hand, belongs to the bloc of developing countries and has been urging the EU and the developed world to take responsibility for the damage that they have inflicted upon the environment and provide funds to the less developed nations so that they can do their bit in saving the earth from global warming. EU has stated in its defence that it is willing to negotiate with India despite difference of opinion. The EU has also tried to assure India that it would not be compelled to reduce carbon emissions in absolute terms, keeping in mind that it has still not attained its development goals and energy security.

Newspapers reflect the thought of a nation. They have been the source of information about important events taking place in other countries and foreign policy issues. Specialised wire services have played a key role in spreading information in a rapid and comprehensive manner across the world. Newspapers in America, China and Russia throughout have been utilised as the mouthpiece of the state and they have also provided space for airing of views of opinion makers and the general populace. The Indian media is known as the fourth pillar of democracy and its liberty has been duly safeguarded by the Indian constitution. Online access to news is posing a stiff competition to popularity and circulation of newspapers across the world. However, the Indian print media has drawn a lot of attention in this context especially from the developed world because Indian newspapers have registered a constant and significant rise in sales unlike many countries. India is known to have the largest number of newspapers in the world.

The current study aims to understand perceptions of India about the EU through the lens of newspapers. A total of three newspapers with the largest circulation in each category were chosen for the study. The three categories adopted for the choice of newspapers were English, Hindi and Business newspapers for which *The Times of India*, Dainik *Jagran* and *The Economic Times* were shortlisted for analysis of news items for the study. A total of 944 news items on the EU were reported in the three newspapers in the time-period of one year (1 July 2009 to 30 June 2010).

The Economic Times, which was selected as the business newspaper, contributed 61.1 per cent of the total EU news items reported in the three newspapers, which indicates the relevance attached to the economic aspect of EU-India relations. The coverage of the EU in *The Times of India* reported a total of 36.3 per cent of the total news items. Only 2.5 per cent of total EU news items were reported in *Dainik Jagran* in the span of one year of monitoring of the three newspapers. The distribution of coverage of EU news items validates the widespread perception that the economic aspect of the relationship overrides all aspects. Thus, we see major coverage of the EU in the business newspaper.

This also means that it is a very selective audience consisting of those who belong to the business community, know the English language, have an avid interest in financial matters and do not mind paying more for reading the pink papers and who actually get to read the maximum number of articles on the EU. Thus, the majority of the readers never get a chance to go through the various news stories where the EU has been mentioned and talked about. *The Times of India* reveals a modest coverage of the EU, which again is read by those who know how to read English and opt for the paper. It is a common saying that India's heart lies in its villages. *Dainik Jagran,* which is a Hindi newspaper and far more popular than English dailies, covered 2.5 per cent of news items on the EU. *Dainik Jagran* in fact enjoys the status of being the most widely circulated newspaper of the world. Thus, the readership of *The Economic Times* and *The Times of India* pales in comparison to that of *Danik Jagran*. The fact that EU was hardly reported in *Dainik Jagran* would mean that millions of Indians who read *Dainik Jagran* in urban and rural areas hardly get any information about EU.

The spread of monthly distribution of EU news over a period of one year reveals some interesting patterns. News output is seen to be in modest numbers in the first five months (July-26, August-36, September-44, October-33, November-35) followed by a sudden rise in coverage (61) in the month of December 2009 on account of the global climate negotiations taking place at Copenhagen. January recorded volume of reportage corresponding to the months before December (47). However, the months that followed, bucked the trend with the month of February (90), March (80) and April (106) registering a significant increase in coverage because of the Eurozone crisis, increase in intensity of negotiations, controversies regarding EU-India FTA and trade and industry-related issues. The Eurozone crisis, and its likely fallout in the EU as well as its impact on India and the world at large, led to the highest volume of news coverage in the month of

May followed by the month of June which covered a total of 167 news items.

A look at the dataset reveals that 31.8 per cent of the total news items were acquired from international sources. A total of 53.6 per cent of the articles were procured from local sources while only 14.5 per cent of the total articles on the EU mentioned no information about the source. This means that a total of 85.4 per cent of the total news items duly mentioned the source of reporting, which is testimony to the fact that the Indian print media takes the job of reporting seriously and carries articles with their sources duly mentioned. The scope of speculation and manipulation is thus significantly reduced. A significant percentage of international sources of news items shows that the Indian print media relies mainly on news emanating from the EU to be procured from an international source. This increases the credibility of the news item. However, this also means that the Indian print media is not interested in expanding its operations by means of stationing a foreign correspondent of their own newspaper in Brussels or in key-capitals of EU member-states. A little more than half of the EU news items have local sources which go on to suggest that Indians primarily have an appetite for news with a local angle. The Indian outlook is essentially tied to India-centric news. News items with no source mentioned are very less in number which is an encouraging trend for there is no way that the authenticity of such news items can be verified. Besides, the length of such news pieces is not found to be very long as they are mainly used to fill up vacant spaces in the newspaper and therefore leave negligible impact on the minds of the readers. Reuters emerged as the leading international news wire and contributed 44.08 per cent of the total news items. The overbearing presence of Reuters amongst the international sources of news corroborates the fact that the Indian media is highly influenced by the Anglo-Saxon media, which prevents the complete and real picture pertaining to matters of EU from reaching the Indian readership. The Press Trust of India which is regarded as India's leading news agency, was the only significant local news wire utilised by the three newspapers. *The Economic Times* and *The Times of India* relied on their own bureaus to contribute most of the local news items while *Dainik Jagran* mainly utilised PTI as the local source of news. An overwhelming reliance on local sources by all the three newspapers suggests that newspapers tend to be inward-looking outlets that do not accord priority to international news and more importantly to international sources. The media in India is expected to address the immediate cause of concern of the common man which is local and at the most national in nature. Even if international news finds space in the newspaper, it is procured from a local source rather than an international source. The newspapers have taken small steps towards including news supplied from international sources and stationing foreign correspondents abroad, but it can be regarded as a very slow-paced endeavour towards ensuring adequate coverage of international news. More worrying is the fact that *Dainik Jagran* which caters to the largest readership of the world did not feel the need to include a single news item contributed from an international source, which amounts to depriving a very large number of Indians from the opportunity to learn, understand and assess the EU as an entity and its role in India.

The focus of domesticity reveals that news items originating from EU amounted to 26.1 per cent of the total news items analysed. This is not an encouraging finding as it shows that Indian print media is hardly bothered about what is going on in the EU. The Indian press does not seem to be particularly interested in following important events taking place in EU. The distance between EU and India thus increases unfamiliarity with the ways of EU owing to the communication gap. It is not only the economic and political sphere of EU news that the Indian audience are being deprived of, they are also not being briefed about important developments in the field of culture and science and technology in the EU, which inevitably will render the EU as an alien continent for Indians for a significant period of time. Warmth in relations can increase only when there is ample and free flow of information about each other's economies and societies. No effort seems to be made for comparing India with EU or assessing the success or failures of EU policies for its people and the scope of emulating the EU. Such exercises do not take place, not because of the lack of will among the various stakeholders but on account of information deficit in India about all that is happening in EU. Journalists make no effort to unpack the complex entity called the EU so that the Indian readership could familiarise itself with what the EU is all about.

News items where the EU is mentioned in the course of covering news about a third country other than the EU and India comprised 21.92 per cent of the total news covered. This means a shift in focus from EU-India relations to the happenings in another country which is a clear diversion from what the agenda should be in order to enhance EU-India relations. The news story primarily is about the third country and not the EU and India. Both partners would not have a prominent role to play in most stories. Besides, no bilateral involvement of the partners is portrayed in these stories. Therefore, the Indian readers do not get to learn much from stories with a third country- focus.

News articles with a local focus contributed 51.9 per cent of the total news items which means that the articles that talked about EU and originated from India, form the major portion of news items of the dataset. Therefore, the local angle of EU news seems to get the topmost priority for reportage. This is welcome as concern about local news has led to the publishing of most number of articles on the EU. It also seems to hit the bull's eye as most people are interested in what is happening locally and this focus leads the way towards including the involvement of EU in India as part of the coverage in the news pieces. However, there is a downside to this development. Most of the news items reported lack a spark, and are mainly a record of events that took place. Critical analysis, assessment, review, projection and prediction are conspicuous by their absence in the news items. This hints at the lack of willingness on the part of journalists to bring the EU-India story to life, explore the inside story and give a background of the events taking place. Thus, inadequate coverage fails to enlighten and educate the readers about EU-India relations. Besides, the international dimension of such stories which would help situate EU-India relations in a global context is also completely ignored. Therefore, the Indian readers cannot entirely be blamed for not knowing much about EU-India relations.

The data analysis reveals that only one-fifth of the news items had a positive tone (19.38 per cent). It thus becomes evident that the Indian print media does not seem to make a conscious effort to portray the relationship with an underlying positive tone despite the fact that EU-India relations cannot be considered to be an acrimonious relationship from any angle. A total of 45.97 per cent of the total news items had a negative tone which can largely be ascribed to the Eurozone crisis and its fallout. News items with a negative tone led the tally in the case of *The Economic Times* (49.5 per cent) and *The Times of India* (41.1 per cent) while in the case of *Dainik Jagran,* the negative (29.1 per cent) and positive news (33.3 per cent) items were separated by a very narrow margin. The over-bearing presence of negative news involving the EU will not contribute towards enhancing the image of EU in the public eye. A sizeable number of news items were reported to have a neutral tone (34.63 per cent) which reflects the news to be presented in a recorded matter-of-fact manner that renders these articles extremely unattractive and leaves a bland taste in the mouth. It is also very difficult to recall the content of such of articles at a later date for the average reader.

EU institutions found place in a mere 14.5 per cent of the total number of news articles analysed. The EC found mention in only 7 per cent of the total number of articles followed by the ECB which was mentioned in 4.5 per cent of the news items in the entire dataset. A few institutions, such as the Council of the European Union, the Court of Justice of the European Union and the Court of Auditors, were not sighted in a single news article. Given the fact that the EU institutions hardly find any mention in the Indian press, it should not come as a surprise if the Indian reader fails to even recall the names of the EU institutions —and therefore the question of understanding the working of the EU institutions under the present state of affairs seems a far cry. The Indian reader is therefore not exposed to the mere existence of some of the EU institutions. This calls for a serious re-think of the EU communication strategy, as a complete blackout of EU institutions in the media implies that most Indians would have no clue about their structure, working, powers and functions. The queries regarding which EU institution does India negotiate with and for what and at which level remain unanswered. They would therefore be in no position to understand the linkages between India and EU institutions, thanks to the negligible coverage of EU institutions in the Indian print media.

The situation is no better when it comes to the visibility of EU officials. The most popular official happens to be Catherine Ashton. But the question is how popular? She appears only in 1.8 per cent of the total number of articles in the dataset followed by Jean Claude Trichet (1.27 per cent) and Jose Manuel Borroso (1.16 per cent). The percentage of visibility of all EU officials in the dataset is 6.46 per cent only. There is no EU official on the international political landscape who enjoys popularity among Indians. Some of the leaders of EU member-states do enjoy a fair amount of popularity in India, but not because of their policies and political acumen but because of their personal lives. Thus, the EU exists in India very much without a face and without a strong voice that does not augur well for EU.

The EU is portrayed to be playing a minor role in 34.21 per cent of the total number of news items. Such news pieces mention the EU only in passing and do not provide much scope to get an insight into the personality of the EU. Such articles reveal very little about the EU. These news pieces are more concerned about the bigger picture where the EU is a small insignificant piece of the jigsaw puzzle. This means that even dispensing with the role of the EU would not affect comprehending or running the story. However, such articles give an indication of the various areas in which the EU plays an active role. It also hints at the EU's allies and enemies in international politics. The portrayal of the EU in a minor role also helps in outlining the basic orientation of the EU towards themes and issues.

The EU played the role of a main actor in almost one-fifth of the total number of articles (19.7 per cent). Thus, there remains a lot to be desired as far as increasing the visibility of the EU is concerned. Efforts need to be made to push for publishing of more articles wherein the EU can be identified as the main actor. Only then, familiarising the Indian readership with the EU and all it does can become a possibility.

The dataset revealed that the EU is largely recognised as an economic actor with 70.4 per cent of the news coverage dedicated to this category. The recognition of the EU in the area of politics paled in comparison with only 11.8 per cent of news items while coverage of EU in environment (8.26 per cent) and social affairs (9.85 per cent) respectively was not so significant. Although the economic dimension is considered to be the strength of EU-India relations, the study reveals that the Indian press reported the EU to be playing a predominantly secondary role in the majority of news items (49.17 per cent). As far as political affairs are concerned, the EU is reported to be playing a main role in an abysmal share of the total news items. A meager 12.3 per cent of news items that portray the EU as a major player in political affairs cannot be expected to cast a magic spell on the readers. This clearly shows that the Indian print media has refrained from showing the EU cast in the main role in the theatre of international politics. It comes as no surprise then that the Indian readers do not consider the EU to be a decisive actor in global political affairs. The EU has donned the role of secondary actor in social affairs (48.71 per cent). This is mainly on account of the fact that news in this segment dealing with issues such as immigration, crime, health, education and research mainly had a third country focus. Thus, the Indian print media does consider the EU to be making a notable contribution in social affairs. The EU was projected as a minor actor in the environmental sphere (56.98 per cent) owing to the fact that it played a very subdued role in the recent climate change negotiations. Besides, the climate change negotiations had involved the participation of almost all the countries of the world that joined different blocs depending upon their strategies and priorities on the issue of climate change and the EU was largely seen to be one among them and simply a face in the crowd.

There were some recurrent themes found in the course of the study. The development angle found coverage in the context of India and the EU being urged to do more by way of helping the Tamils in Sri Lanka to get education, scholarships and job opportunities. The EU institutions and member-states pledged more than €400 million for emergencies and long-term development assistance to Haiti which had been struck by a massive earthquake leading to the loss of 200,000 lives. It was alleged that the EU had offered economic assistance to the developing countries in order to win their support for a legally binding agreement to cut carbon emissions. The implications of the IMF-EU aid package for Greece were also discussed in detail.

Glimpses of normative power EU could also be seen in the dataset. The EU raised its voice against the seizure of a Turkish ship by Israel-bound for blockaded Gaza. The EU adopted a strong stance in demanding the ouster of the Nepalese Prime Minister Madhav Kumar Nepal and the formation of a new inclusive all-party government. The ETA, which has been banned by the EU and the US as a terrorist organisation, was in also in the news, as it declared itself to be the leader of the armed struggle being waged for the independence of the Basque region. The diplomats of the EU and the US gathered outside a Beijing court to register their protest against the sentence of imprisonment of eleven years handed down to a Chinese writer and dissident for allegedly inciting subversion of state power through his writings. The visit of the EU Delegation to Kandhamal in Southern Orissa, sixteen months after violent communal clashes erupted in the district, was also reported. The EU along with the US put pressure on Iran to stop proliferation of nuclear weapons by including Iranian individuals and firms to a blacklist after the UN imposed a fresh set of sanctions. The EU was in charge of monitoring the Rafah Crossing after it was opened, as a result of a disengagement deal signed between the Israelis and Palestinians. The EU was exhorted not to encourage, in any manner whatsoever, the nefarious activities of Pakistan. The EU also made it clear to Sri Lanka that in order to continue drawing benefits from the Generalised System of Preferences extended by EU, it will have to repeal some of the sections of its emergency rules and adopt a human rights action plan.

The theme of integration was interspersed in the study. It was opined that the euro has been an incomplete currency from the start as the Maastricht Treaty of the EU established a monetary union without a political union. It was believed that the EU could get rid of its troubles by making efforts towards strengthening the euro by revising its structural framework. It was reported that the member-states of the EU stood up for the euro in solidarity, and helped debt-ridden member-states and did not leave them in the lurch. This is turn led to reinstating of confidence in the financial markets about the resurgence of the euro. The adoption of a proactive policy towards Russia for its inclusion as a member-state of the EU was opined. Member-states were reported to increasingly favour the creation of a European army which would make the EU a strong bloc to reckon with. The popularity of the Turkish language was discussed in the context of the possibility of accession of Turkey into the European Union. The Maastricht Discipline was recalled which allowed the EU member-states to become part of the Eurozone only if their fiscal deficit was well under 3 per cent and the economy was largely stable. It was pointed out that member-states of the EU have overcome challenges throughout history and have inextricably interlinked economies which have ensured their development and economic prosperity. The economic integration of the EU has largely been considered to be a source of inspiration for many trading blocs across the world including the ASEAN. Although a lot has been said and written about Britain's semi-detachment from the EU, a high degree of interdependence is said to exist between them.

The term 'elite' refers to the minority in society who is the highest, best or excellent and wields power, wealth and privilege. Elites enjoy a higher position in society. Elitism refers to belief in the system of rule by the elite. Classical elitism talked about the rule of elites as inevitable and unchangeable and hence, the phenomena of circulation of elites and oligarchy have been observed throughout history. Every human enterprise was believed to have given rise to its own elite. Modern elitism made an attempt to explain as well as challenge the concept of elites by highlighting the adverse impact their rule had on democracies and dispelling the notion of inevitability of their rule. Power elite were described as those who had power to take important decisions which had major consequences. They are known to rule big corporations, run the machinery of the state, direct the military establishment and occupy strategic command posts of the social structure, and the power, wealth and celebrity status that they enjoy are derived from these sources.

Two broad viewpoints about the question of elites have emerged. The moral approach believes that there is single elite which is socially decisive and their existence is justified on the basis of moral superiority, while the functional approach believes that there are different types of elites who share power, responsibilities and rewards and their relevance is attached to the social function of a class or group. However, both approaches seem to lose sense of purpose and direction, which leads the moral approach to be lost in mysticism while the second approach leads to tautology. Nevertheless, the concept of elite has been extremely useful in understanding the modern industrial society that has witnessed a proliferation of elites on account of increase in occupational and economic differentiations that have emerged as a guardian of values and manager of targets.

The liberal-democratic perspective advocates public participation in the process of foreign policy making unlike the realists, who do not support the involvement of the common man in the process. The critical approach agrees with the realists that the public are not largely involved in the process of foreign policy formulation. But they show disagreement with the viewpoint of the realists that elite domination of foreign policy is acceptable.

The pluralist model talks about devolution and distribution of power across all segments of the society while the elite model states that power is wielded by a small number of influential groups which include foreign policy officials, think tanks and representatives of large business interests, while the public is systematically ousted from this process. The discussions and debates among the elite circles eventually lead to organisation of debates in the media and the initiation of the process of public opinion formation. The Indian public is exposed to these debates and they tend to internalise and condition their views on the basis of what they see and hear. Needless to say, the analysis is always suited to the perpetuation of elite interest.

Nevertheless, it is also true that it is the self-interest of the elite that helps in binding the social, economic and political system together. The factor that keeps a check on the reckless and selfish pursuit of interests by the elite is the realisation that the system might disintegrate and collapse if such activities are not put on the leash. The contribution of the elite towards changing policies is of an "incremental" rather than a "revolutionary" nature. It is driven by the motive to protect their interests. Hence, existing policies are reformed but they are never replaced as the latter would be detrimental to the dominance of the elite (Wittkopf et. al. 2003: 291).

The Indian elites have been closely linked with the process of foreign policy making of independent India. The elite then comprised of the Congress party, which was the ruling political elite, while the bureaucrats belonging to the Indian civil service and the military were the other groups of elites that existed then. The elite had disagreements on many questions of foreign policy. The Congress party had an Indian outlook while the civil servants and officers belonging to the armed forces had been recruited, trained and worked under the British authorities for a long time and therefore their loyalties rested largely with British imperialism and with western economic and political frameworks. They were in charge of internal administration, defence and diplomacy after independence. However, India's first Prime Minister Jawaharlal Nehru made sure that that these two groups served India under the overall guidance and supervision of the political elite.

India's policy-making elites have concerned themselves with the issue of India's rightful place in the global order and its relations with the rest of the world. The country's strategic elite are largely known to be based in Delhi and they are known to consist of about a hundred members that include prominent journalists, retired civil servants, formal admirals, generals and air marshals, academics and scientists and a few politicians and businessmen. They are socialised through organisation of workshops and seminars. They are acknowledged as advisers on major issues of foreign policy to the key political parties of India.

It was stated that the Indian elites have a strong realisation about the economic growth of their country. However, the Indian state has been unable to reap optimum benefits as a result of the emergence of the country as a global economic power (Malone 2011). It has been stated that countries like India which do not possess the "material capabilities" to make a change in international politics are not very appreciative of the "concept of power in foreign policy making". Consequently, the word 'power' became associated with a pejorative connotation and the Indian political and strategic elite became sceptical about power politics. This has led to a progressive loss in India's ability to assert itself in international affairs (Pant 2011: 19).

The Indian elites are extremely confident of further increase in the recently acquired power and economic credentials of India. As far as perceptions of the Indian elite about the EU are concerned, they do not hesitate in terming the EU as a region that has stagnated economically and has accepted the outcome with a defeatist attitude. They are of the view that Europe is longer a power to reckon with and its intellectual and moral traditions have been uprooted. It has a very weak welfare state which is on the edge of disintegration.

The Indian elites, like the common man have a vague understanding of the EU and it is largely familiar to them solely on account of the economic aspect of the relations while other aspects of the EU like the Schengen is not understood by most Indians. However, a slow-paced trend of gradual increase in awareness about EU and shift of attention from the EU member-states to the EU have also been witnessed.

A total of 38 Indian elites belonging to the areas of politics, media, civil society and business were interviewed. A number of well-known personalities (ten from business, eight from politics, ten from civil society and ten from media) were interviewed as part of this study during the period (2 February -10 May 2010). The interviews were open-ended and each elite was asked a minimum of eighteen questions revolving around the issue of EU-India relations. The data collection technique involved face-to-face in-depth and semi-structured interviews of 45 minutes duration each and the content was recorded and transcribed for ready reference. All the interviews were conducted in Delhi, the country's capital. Content analysis of the data thus collected, was done for the purpose of understanding Indian perceptions about the EU and for analysis, comparison and identification of new trends in EU-India relations if any.

The Indian business elites were very well acquainted with EU member-states and had regular interaction and exchanges with them. They were very much aware of the economic affairs of the EU. However, the outlook to do business in Europe keeping in mind the EU's existence was conspicuous by its absence. They were very positive about doing business in Europe but the EU seemed to hardly matter in their scheme of things. The political elites talked about having occasional meetings with EU delegations but none of them were very particular about interaction within the EU structural framework. However, they were most magnanimous in recognising the EU as an extremely important partner of India and expressed the hope of more engagements with the EU in future. The civil society elites were very comfortable in answering questions about the EU compared to the business and political elites. They had a fair knowledge about the EU institutional framework and were pointedly able to explain the exact nature of their association with EU. They were able to make the distinction succinctly between the EU and its member states in the course of talking about their collaboration with the EU. Thus, we see that stakeholders across all categories looked forward to professional involvement with the EU at present and in the near future.

The majority of the business elites expressed their agreement that EU is a great power as it leads from the front in global markets, international diplomacy, military equipment, social diplomacy, agenda-setting and norm-setting. However, some considered the EU to be a passive power. Some were of the opinion that differences among EU member-states undermined the power of the EU. None of the political elites were ready to concede the title of a great power to the EU for a plethora of reasons. Some stated that the lecturing of EU on norms and values did not go well with the rest of the world. Besides, the EU never spoke in a single voice. Decolonisation had robbed Europe of its riches and this had affected its economic growth. Most of the political elites were dismissive of the notion that the EU is a decisive political and military power in international politics. However, they did express hope that it was most likely to become a great power in future. The civil society elites were most reluctant to accept the idea that the EU is a great power. Some relented to accept the EU as an economic power while others did not agree to the idea and pointed out that the EU is in the throes of an economic crisis. Besides, bilateral relationships ruled the roost and were preferred over collaborating with the EU as a single trading bloc. The civil society elites were of the view that the EU played a commendable role in social affairs and enjoyed the distinction of being a cultural power. The media elites were majorly convinced about the EU's economic prowess. But they did not consider the EU to be in the same league in the normative, social and military spheres. Most of them expressed the view that the EU was not a cohesive structure, which made it difficult for the rest of the world to appreciate better the perspective and role of the EU in world affairs. Thus, we see that apart from business elites, stakeholders from the other three categories were not willing to acknowledge that EU was a great power.

The business elites stressed upon the point that since the EU is an established economic power, it could utilise this strength to emerge as a leader in international politics. Quite a few elites acknowledged that the EU has the potential to emerge as a leader in international politics. The EU's political role in Afghanistan, its mending of relations with Iran and Iraq, its role in WTO, the acknowledgement of the EU as a worthy partner by the rest of the world and its effort to bring about democratisation were some actions of EU that were mentioned and found appreciation. However, the business elites did not go to the point of recognising the EU as an established leader in international politics as many believed that it does not possess the power to bend, change or determine the rules of the game in international politics. Many of the business elites also mentioned too many voices being heard from the EU which affected its status in international politics. Political elites seemed to be more forthright in stating that they did not look upon the EU as a leader in international politics. They stated that having robust economic relations with EU which has economic might, is indeed desirable but that does not translate into the EU becoming an established leader in international politics. Most of the political elites however, did not hesitate in declaring the United States as the dominant power of the international system and stated that the EU under the present circumstances does not come even close to assuming this status.

Some of the civil society elites believed that the EU plays a prominent role in international politics. They were of the view that the EU should increase its engagement in Asia and Africa and play a vital role in addressing global issues such as terrorism. The EU was exhorted to engage itself especially in these regions so that the civil society elites could partake a share of the largesse directed by the EU towards bringing about development in these regions. However, not all civil society elites considered the EU to be as eligible and agile and stated that the EU simply toed the line of the US and was unable to speak and take a unified stand on sensitive global issues such as the Iraq war. The EU's

China policy also drew a lot of flak from the civil society elites. The media elites similarly talked about the EU's global economic clout but stated that the EU has not emerged as a leader in international politics as it has not exhibited the will and ability to handle security and military issues on its own. The failure of the EU to project a unified standpoint on the Iraq war as well as the Copenhagen climate negotiations was also pointed out. They also suggested that the EU member-states should utilise their status and power in international organisations in order to sway the agenda in the EU's favour. Thus, we see a similar sentiment being expressed across all categories of elites that the EU is indeed an established global economic power and that it has the potential to emerge as a leader in international politics. However, it still has a long way to go and has to learn to speak in a single voice. It was suggested that the EU should be more pro-active in development cooperation and in military and security matters.

The business elites had an extremely positive outlook about EU-India relations and stated that it indeed has a lot of potential. They talked about the growing relevance of India to the EU and the mutually beneficial role played by the partners in each other's markets and in the world at large. The business elites advocated the enhancement of EU-India relations in the fields of finance, business and industry, cultural exchanges, museum exhibitions, promotion of tourism, movement of people and labour migration.

The political elites were of the view that EU-India relationship is a positive and stable relationship which can be further accelerated by increasing the level of economic engagement between the two sides. Cooperation in the field of trade, terrorism, climate change and grass roots democracy was sought to be enhanced. It was also suggested that the staff at the Indian embassy who deal with the EU affairs need to be briefed that they should work in order to bring vibrancy and dynamism in every aspect of EU-India relations. The civil society elites were of the view that EU-India relations can qualify as a cordial relationship on account of the absence of strategic conflicts and ideological differences between the two partners. A strong economic partnership has ensured the growth of EU-India relations. Besides, both partners have similar global aspirations, espouse the same values and believe in democracy, rule of law and good governance. Some civil society elites were of the opinion that irritants in the relationship tend to occur when India deals with the EU as a single bloc and not on a one to one basis with the EU member-countries and therefore, the EU Presidency has a vital role to play to ensure the smooth conduct of EU-India relations. It was stated that India would come closer to the EU if the latter would play a more visible and definite role in global affairs. Thus, we see that elites across all categories believe that EU-India relationship is going in the right direction and it is being spurred on by the robust trade links apart from other commonalities between the two partners. The elites also called for greater engagement of the two partners in a variety of areas and urged the EU to play a more assertive role in international affairs.

All the media elites stated that they carry stories about the EU as and when they take place. Nothing is decided fairly in advance or targets laid down for coverage of the EU. The media elites stated that they prefer to rely on foreign wires for supplying the EU news as not many Indian correspondents are stationed in the EU who can send news to the Indian press. The EU Delegation to India is also known to get in touch with the Indian press with regard to coverage of events organised by them. The Delegation is also known to supply background material and information about the event to the press. However, the articles are published subject to their relevance and interest for Indian readers as well as their marketability.

All the media elites stated that they do not have a specific budget allocation for EU coverage. This practice is not in vogue in the Indian media. News gathering is a costly exercise and most media organisations do not prefer to indulge in it and waste resources. They tend to rely on international news wires, stringers and sometimes a sole correspondent stationed more often than not in London who is responsible for sending in news from all the EU member states. It comes as no surprise that the news sent by the correspondent shall be reflective of the British perspective as most often than not, Indian reporters and journalists are stationed in London, which in turn conditions Indian perceptions about the EU.

The media elites explained that they do not hire more staff or experts for coverage of EU as most issues related to the EU are adequately reported by the economic affairs or foreign affairs correspondent. Hence, the need to hire extra staff for the purpose is not felt. Besides, reporters themselves consult experts in the course of writing an article and include their bytes. It was mentioned however, that sometimes reporters are sent on an assignment to cover an the EU related news story especially when the coverage is issue-specific. Indian media has not reached the stage when experts tend to be hired for coverage of specific regions and areas. Some media elites were candid in stating that there is substantial coverage of economic issues but coverage of political issues of the EU is very scant.

The media elites welcomed any overtures on behalf of the EU for coverage in the Indian press. However, they clarified that this would not automatically lead to increase in coverage of EU news because the editors have a number of considerations that they have to keep in mind when they ultimately make the selection of news stories to be published in the newspaper. For instance, the news piece should appear to be interesting to the reader. The news piece is instantly chosen if it is vital to national interest. The fact that all news stories cannot be published leads the editors to prioritise.

The media elites did not possess a single line of thinking as far as predicting the shift towards a region in the balance of reporting was concerned. Some of the elites stated that there would be maintenance of status quo and the developed world would remain the focus of reportage. However, the majority of the elites stated that there is bound to be an increase in coverage of East Asia, especially China, where it was predicted that the presence of Indian correspondents would increase exponentially in the near future. Although the EU is recognised as a trustworthy and stable partner, the future is unlikely to see an increase in coverage as it is never reported to be doing anything sensational or controversial in nature, and regular mundane news cannot be expected to be chosen over other news items endlessly. However, others were more hopeful and stated that EU news might capture the spot light for a considerable period of time in case the EU is reported to do something remarkable for India and its citizens.

The media elites believed that it is difficult to sell an EU story as EU does not lend any spice to news coverage for it does nothing which is politically incorrect or controversial. The other media elites believed that the Indian interest needs to be embedded in a EU news article in order to increase its appeal to the readers. Some stated that India is far more concerned about Pakistan, China and the USA rather than Japan and the EU. Therefore, an EU story is made to compete with stories emanating from more popular regions and also with unsubstantial but sensational news.

When asked about the importance of the EU in relation to other prominent regions, the United States and China were proclaimed to be more important than the EU. Some regarded Russia and Japan to be to giving tough competition to the EU in emerging as a promising and prominent international partner of India. The political elites mostly engaged in equivocation and refrained from calling one region more important than the other.

The majority of the Indian elites exuded confidence about the economic aspect of the EU-India partnership and consequently economic issues are regarded to have the greatest impact upon the relationship. Similarly, when asked about what issues should be kept in mind when India is formulating trade or governmental policy relating to the EU, it was found that trade and economic issues are considered to be of utmost importance. This reflects the great degree of trust bestowed upon the economic aspect of the relations. But this also reflects ignorance of other sectors and spheres of the relationship.

The majority of the business and political elites had either no knowledge about the Delegation whatsoever or had no interaction and links with it. The civil society elites on the other hand, were very much aware of the Delegation and its activities and expressed the desire to work closely with the Delegation. The question regarding the possible risks that may emerge for India in case new countries join the EU showed difference of opinion on the issue. The business elites considered the accession of new countries to be both a challenge and an opportunity for India. The political elites offered ambiguous explanations and chose not to address the issue. Most of the civil society elites welcomed the new countries joining the EU and considered this to be an opportunity rather than a challenge. The majority of the elites stated that the US dollar is the strongest currency in the world and is much stronger than the euro. However, the stakeholders across all categories acknowledged the importance of euro as a currency for ensuring world economic stability and its emergence as the only alternative global currency in the world.

The Internet, followed by newspapers, was the most important source of information for the elites about the EU. When asked to rate the importance of the EU to India, the Indian elites across all categories expressed optimism that the relevance of the EU to India would become even greater in future. The business elites were most confident and enthusiastic about the relations while the media elites were the most pessimistic about the relations which is reflected in less than adequate coverage of the EU in the Indian press.

The elites were asked to recall three images that came to their mind when they think about the term 'EU'. The elites recalled more positive images (21 times) than negative images (11 times). The theme of European integration was very popular among the elites. The EU as an economic bloc, the euro and cultural heritage of Europe were some of the images recalled by the elites. The EU was also looked upon as a political organisation, a military power, an educational hub, a stable entity, having good infrastructure, Schengen visa and the EU flag were other positive images invoked by the elites. The negative connotations attached to EU by the elites included that of being hard negotiators, economically strong but politically weak, voluminous documents, weak family ties, challenge of gender justice, not very understanding of the compulsions of the other parts of the world, arrogant about prosperity, stability and human rights.

Thus, the following hypotheses were tested by making using of statistical and analytical tools.

- Complex interdependence and the consolidation of multi-polarity are leading to greater engagement between European Union and India.
- The economic and political dialogue has contributed towards visibility of the EU in the Indian print media.
- On specific issues, the coverage of EU-India relationship creates prejudices and stereotypes.

The first hypothesis is supported by the research undertaken as part of the study. Indeed, the engagement between the EU and India has increased manifold. However, the crescendo of the relationship has not been reached yet and there remains a lot of potential for further engagement in all spheres. The engagement between the two partners is primarily in the field of economic affairs although there is still scope for a tremendous increase in trade volumes. The evidence generated by the research verifies the second hypothesis. The economic and political dialogue continues to offer new vistas of cooperation which has intensified the frequency and levels of engagement between the EU and India which has culminated in providing visibility to the EU in the Indian print media. However, the volume and nature of coverage have been found to be less than adequate. The third hypothesis stands verified by the results of the study undertaken. It was found that coverage of EU-India relations creates prejudices and stereotypes owing to media practices, prioritisation of certain considerations and basic orientation of the media towards coverage of news in general. Therefore, it can be stated on the basis of the findings that the EU did not emerge as a very popular international actor and partner of India.

Thus, it is extremely necessary to infuse more life, vigour, dynamism and enthusiasm into the relationship. The media especially the print media should work towards unpacking the complex organisation of the EU. There is a necessity to begin explaining what the EU is and what is stands for from the very beginning so that people in huge numbers are able to make sense of it. It is necessary to pool in not only the well-known educational institutions in the key cities of India but also second tier state colleges and universities that should be encouraged to engage with the issues pertaining to EU-India relations. There is an urgent requirement to bring novelty into the teaching and learning processes about the EU. Hence, it is imperative that the same set of people are not given grants for research unless they bring something new to the table and do not dish out the same salad with a slightly different dressing. It is necessary to point out the relevance of EU in international politics to the common man and how it is directly relevant to him needs to be clearly spelled out. The best way of reaching out to the common man for the sake of spreading awareness about EU issues is through the medium of the print media. This is so because newspaper reading for the average Indian is as regular and normal an activity as praying or brushing ones teeth every day.

It is necessary to engage the Indian elite in various spheres and ensure correct dissemination of information so that all sorts of stereotypes, biases, prejudices, confusion and ambiguity regarding the relationship are dispelled and subsequent debates on EU-India issues are based on authentic and concrete information. This in turn, will lead to the spread of goodwill about the relationship among the Indian readers.

All attempts should be made to do away with breaks and jerks in the EU-India economic and political engagement. The EU-India summits should be held on a regular basis and a huge hiatus, such as the one that followed after the EU-India Summit of 2012, should be avoided altogether. High-profile visits, summitry and famous handshakes and speeches by prominent leaders on both sides should be encouraged. The administrations of both establishments need to focus on large-scale overhaul and refurbishing of media and communication strategies in order to enhance the visibility of the relationship. A sincere effort needs to be made in order to make available authentic and adequate information devoid of speculation and bias about EU-India relations to the Indian elite as well as the Indian press. This would ensure the percolation of a holistic and balanced portrayal of the EU and EU-India relations into the Indian consciousness.

List of Appendices

Parameters Employed for Analysis of Print Media

A total of 944 new articles from three newspapers namely, *The Economic Times, The Times of India and Dainik Jagran* were scanned for EU news items for a period of one year (1 July 2009 to 30 June 2010).

SL No.	Parameters
1.	Title of the article
2.	Name of the newspaper
3.	Date
4.	Placement
5.	Length
6.	Sources -International wire/ Local Wire/ Foreign Correspondent / Local Correspondent
7.	Focus of Domesticity- EU news/ Local news/ 3rd Country news
8.	Degree of Centrality – Main / Minor/ Secondary role of the EU
9.	Main theme of the Article
10.	Actors – EU/ Europe/ EU officials/ EU Institutions/ EU member-states and officials
11.	Others- NGOs/ INGOs/ Important international institutions and organisations
12.	Character of the News- Prominence/ Timeliness/ Proximity/ Conflict/ Controversy
13.	Local Actors (Indian) – Leaders/ Government Officials/ Prominent Persons/ Public and Private Institutions
14.	Evaluation of News – Positive/ Negative/ Neutral
15.	Listing Actions of EU in the News Article
16.	Framing, Sub-framing and Sub-sub framing of news items

List of Interviewees

A total of 38 elites were interviewed during the period (2 February -10 May 2010).

The designation of the interviewees mentioned refers to the position they held at the time when the interviews were conducted.

Business Elites

Alha, A. (2010). Business Elite. Associate Analyst. Dunnhumby. Gurgaon. Interviewed in Delhi. 2 May.

Bhalla, S.S. (2010). Business Elite. Chairman. Oxus Investments Private Limited. 19 April.

Baroowa, S. (2010). Business Elite. Manager, Global Information Centre. Travel Security Services. Interviewed in Delhi. 20 April.

Dang, S. (2010). Business Elite. Group Head. Corporate Communications. Avantha Group. Interviewed in Delhi. 18 March.

Desai, S. (2010). Business Elite. MD & CEO. Future Brands Limited. Interviewed in Delhi. 19 April.

Harikumar, S. (2010). Business Elite. Senior Manager. Forex. Oriental Bank of Commerce. A Government of India Undertaking, International Banking Division. Interviewed in Delhi. 2 May.

Iqbal, N. (2010). Business Elite. Senior Merchandiser. Radhnik Exports. Interviewed in Delhi. 1 May.

Shashidhar, G.V. (2010). Business Elite. National Sales Manager, Wipro Limited. Infotech Division. Interviewed in Delhi. 20 April.

Singh, M. (2010). Business Elite. Publisher. Seminar Magazine. Interviewed in Delhi. 20 April.

Singh, S.N. (2010a). Business Elite. Manager. API Marketing. Ranbaxy Laboratories. Limited. Interviewed in Delhi. 26 April.

Political Elites

Aiyer, M. (2010). Political Elite. Former Union Minister for Pertroleum and Natural Gas and Panchayati Raj. Interviewed in Delhi. 2 February.

Dave,A.M. (2010). Political Elite. Member of Parliament. Rajya Sabha. Bharatiya Janata Party. Interviewed in Delhi, 8 May.

Javadekar P. (2010). Political Elite. Member of Parliament. Rajya Sabha. National Spokesperson of Bharatiya Janata Pary. Inteviewed in Delhi. 10 May.

Meinya, T. (2010). Political Elite. Member of Paliament. Lok Sabha. Indian National Congress. Interviewed in Delhi. 2 February.

Mithi, M. (2010). Political Elite. Member of Parliament. Rajya Sabha. Former Chief Minister of Arunachal Pradesh and former Lieutenant Governor of Pondicherry. Interviewed in Delhi. 2 February.

Pala, V.H. (2010). Political Elite.Minister of State for Water Resources. Member of Parliament. Lok Sabha. Indian National Congress. Interviewed in Delhi. 2 February.

Rudy, R. P. (2010). Political Elite. Member of Parliament. Rajya Sabha. Bharatiya Janata Party. Interviewed in Delhi, 13 March.

Sangma, A. (2010). Political Elite. Union Minister. Union Minister of State for Rural Development. Member of Parliament. Lok Sabha. Nationalist Congress Party. Internviewed in Delhi, 2 February.

Civil Society Elites

Dutta, Sujit (2010). Civil Society Elite. Mahatma Gandhi Chair. Nelson Mandela Centre for Peace and Conflict Resolution. Jamia Millia Islamia. Interviewed in Delhi. 21 April.

Gupta, R. (2010). Civil Society Elite. President. Apne Aap Women Worldwide, an Initiative to end Sex-Trafficking. Interviewed in Delhi. 17 April.

Henri, T. (2010). Civil Society Elite. Executive Director. People's Watch. Member, National Core Group on NGOs. National Human Rights Commission of India. Interviewed in Delhi. 13 April.

John, W. (2010). Civil Society Elite. Observer Research Foundation. Interviewed in Delhi. 20 April.

Joseph, M. (2010). Civil Society Elite. Deputy Director. Institute of Peace and Conflict Studies. Interviewed in Delhi. 8 March.

Kumari, R. (2010). Civil Society Elite. Director. Centre for Social Research. Interviewed in Delhi. 4 March.

Mehta, P.B. (2010). Civil Society Elite. President. Centre for Policy Research. Interviewed in Delhi. 16 April.

Mukhopadhyay, A.R. (2010). Civil Society Elite. Associate Fellow. Institute for Defence and Study Analyses. Interviewed in Delhi. 26 April.

Pais, J. (2010). Civil Society Elite. Assistant Professor. Institute for Studies in Industrial Development. Interviewed in Delhi. 3 May.

Raina, K. (2010). Civil Society Elite. Climate Campaigner. Greenpeace India. Interviewed in Delhi. 24 April.

Media Elites

Arun, T.K. (2010). Media Elite. Economic Editor. The Economic Times. Interviewed in Delhi. 6 March .

Das,S.(2010). Media Elite. Principal Correspondent. The Financial Express. Interviewed in Delhi. 3 March.

Guha Roy,S. (2010). Media Elite. Editor- Business. Tehelka Weekly News Magazine. Interviewed in Delhi. 19 March.

Joshi, M. (2010). Media Elite. Deputy Editor. Mail Today. The India Today Group. Mail Today Newspapers Private Limited. Interviewed in Delhi. 13 March.

Kumar, R. (2010). Media Elite. Special Correspondent. Nav Bharat Times News Bureau. Interviewed in Delhi. 6 March.

Panicker, L. (2010). Media Elite. Senior Associate Editor. Hindustan Times Media Limited. Interviewed in Delhi. 20 March.

Patni, A. (2010). Media Elite. DGM, Energy Security. Communication and External Affairs. Former Press Advisor to the European Commission. Former Assistant Editor at British High Commission and Former Sub-editor at The Times of India. 26 February.

Rakesh, K. (2010). Media Elite. Group Vice-President and Senior Editor. NE TV Group. Interviewed in Delhi. 8 March.

Sen, A. (2010). Media Elite. Economic Times Bureau. Interviewed in Delhi. 6 March.

Setia, A. (2010). Media Elite. Input Head.ETV. Interviewed in Delhi. 13 March.

Open-ended Questionnaire for Business, Political and Civil Society Elites

1. Could you describe the nature of your professional involvement with the EU?

2. Do you see the EU as a great power?

3. Specifically about politics, do you see the EU as a leader in international politics?

4. How would you compare the importance of EU to India in relation to other prominent regions?

5. How would you describe the relationship between India and the European Union (EU)?

6. In your opinion, which issues in India-EU current relations have the most impact on India?

7. Looking at the future, what issues should be kept in mind when India is developing trade or government policy relating to the EU?

8. The EU has its Commission Delegation in Delhi. How could the activities of the Delegation be of use to you and your organization?

9. What kind of risks and/or opportunities do you see for India when new countries join the EU?

10. How do you see the Euro as an international currency vis-à-vis the US dollar?

11. Where do you get your information about the EU?

12. Which specific media do you use to access news about the EU?

13. Do you have personal contacts within Europe, friends, business, family, travel?

14. On a scale of 1 to 5, where 1 is not important at all and 5 is very important, how would you rate the importance of EU to India in the present?

15. On a scale of 1 to 5, where 1 is not important at all and 5 is very important, how would you rate the importance of EU to India in the future?

16. When thinking about the term 'the European Union', what three thoughts come to your mind?

Open-Ended Questionnaire for Media Elites

1. How is the coverage of the EU and European issues organised?
2. Are special preparations made in advance?
3. Is a special budget allocated?
4. Do you assign more staff and hire experts to cover specific EU issues should the need arise?
5. What is the officially formulated policy on covering foreign news?
6. Does the news organisation assume a reactive or a proactive initiating role?
7. If the EU is proactive in disseminating news about itself, would your outlet be interested in considering such news?
8. Where do you see the balance of foreign reporting shift in the future?
9. When reporting about the EU, what news values lead to the selection of news?
10. How difficult is it to sell a EU story?
11. Do you see the EU as a great power?
12. Specifically about politics, do you see the EU as a leader in international politics?

13. In your opinion, which issues in India-EU current relations have the most impact on India?
14. On a scale of 1 to 5, where 1 is not important at all and 5 is very important, how would you rate the importance of the EU to India in the present?
15. On a scale of 1 to 5, where 1 is not important at all and 5 is very important, how would you rate the importance of the EU to India in the future?
16. When thinking about the term 'the European Union', what three thoughts come to your mind?

References

Abhyankar, R. M. (2007). "India and the European Union: Non-associable to Strategic Partner", in Sinha A. and M. Mohta (eds.), *Indian Foreign Policy Challenges and Opportunities*, New Delhi: Academic Foundation.

Afionis S. and I. Bailey (2012). "Ever Closer Partnerships? European Union Relations with Rapidly Industrializing Countries on Climate Change", in Compston H. and I. Bailley (eds.), *Feeling the Heat: The Politics of Climate Policy in Rapidly Industrializing Countries*, New York: Palgrave Macmillan.

Aggarwal, R.K. (2010, 8 March). "Chatroom Focus on GM R&D", *The Economic Times*, New Delhi.

Aiyer, M. (2010). Political Elite. Former Union Minister for Petroleum and Natural Gas and Panchayati Raj. Interviewed in Delhi. 2 February.

Alha, A. (2010). Business Elite. Associate Analyst. Dunnhumby. Gurgaon. Interviewed in Delhi. 2 May.

Anam, M. (2010, 2 February). "From Vision to Action India Should Think Outside the Box on Ties with Bangladesh", *The Times of India*, New Delhi.

Arun, T.K. (2010). Media Elite. Economic Editor. The Economic Times. Interviewed in Delhi. 6 March.

Austermann, F. (2014). *European Union Delegations in EU Foreign Policy A Diplomatic Service of Different Speeds*, New York: Palgrave Macmillan.

Azhar S. and P. Ullatil (2010, 18 May). "Window to the World, Seeking Less Scrutiny, Hedge funds flock to Asia", *The Economic Times*, New Delhi.

Babaria, P.J. (2010, 9 March). "Edit Page Mail box My Times my Voice Abolish Child labour", *The Times of India*, New Delhi.

Bagchi, I. (2009, 17 July). "Climb Down on 2 C Clause Done as a Last Resort?", *The Times of India*, New Delhi.

Balla, S.S. (2010). Business Elite. Chairman. Oxus Investments Private Limited. 19 April.

Bandyopadhyay, J. (1970). *The Making of India's Foreign Policy: Determinants, Institutions, Processes and Personalities*, Mumbai: Allied Publishers Private Limited.

Bandyopadhyayay, J. (2003), *The Making of India's Foreign Policy*, New Delhi: Allied Publishers.

Bannerjee, R. (2009, 20 July). "Backs India's Tech Route to Raising Crop Yield", *The Times of India*, New Delhi.

Baroowa, S. (2006). "The Emerging Strategic Partnership between India and the EU: A Critical Appraisal", *European Law Journal*, 13 (6): 732-749.

Baroowa, S. (2010). Business Elite. Manager, Global Information Centre. Travel Security Services. Interviewed in Delhi. 20 April.

Barua, P. (2010, 30 May). "River Basics", *The Times of India*, New Delhi.

Basu, N. (2013, 17 June). "India Offers to Slash Import Duty on Wines, Spirits to 40%", *Business Standard*, 8 January 2015, URL: http://www.business-standard.com/article/economy-policy/india-offers-to-slash-import-duty-on-wines-spirits-to-40-113061700046_1.html.

Bava, U.S. (2013). "The Efficiency of the EU's External Actions and the EU-India Relationship" in M. Telo and F. Ponjaert (eds.), *The EU's Foreign Policy: What kind of Power and Diplomatic Action* ?, England and USA: Ashgate Publishing Company.

BBC News Asia (2014, 17 December). "Reviving Stalled Process: EU Urges Pakistan, India to Resume Peace Dialogue", 10 January 2015, URL: http://tribune.com.pk/story/801553/reviving-stalled-process-eu-urges-pakistan-india-to-resume-peace-dialogue/.

Bennhold, K. (2010, 8 March). "Breaking the Glass Ceiling Science for Men? Not by a Long Shot", *The Times of India*, New Delhi.

Bhasin, M. (2009). "The India-EU Partnership: Strategic Alliance or Political Convenience?", in A. Ghosh et al. (eds.), *India's Foreign Policy*, New Delhi: Dorling Kindersley (India) Pvt. Ltd.

Bhat, U.R. (2010, 14 June). "The End Game in Europe", *The Economic Times*, New Delhi.

Bhatia, J. (2014, June) "Indo-European Defence Relations A Win-win Situation", India Strategic, 9 January 2015, URL: http://www.indiastrategic.in/topstories3391_%20 Indo-European_Defence_ Relations.htm.

Biesheuvel, T. (2010, 2 April). "Steel Rates May Go Up 21%: Mittal", *The Economic Times*, New Delhi.

Biggadike, O.(2010, 23 June). "Dollar Peg Aussie Canadian Dollars Rise at Euro's Cost", *The Economic Times*, New Delhi.

Bilefsky, D. (2010, 1 March). "Changing Face in Poland: Skinhead Puts on Skullcap", *The Times of India*, New Delhi.

Bomassi L. (2013)."Europe and India: Not So Different After All", Carnegie Europe, 16 January 2015, URL:http://carnegieeurope.eu/publications/?fa=50738.

Brajesh, T. (2009, 11 July). "Disagreement Surfaces on Economic Recession", *Dainik Jagran*, New Delhi.

Britsch, F. (2014). "Indian Views of Europe's Role as a Security Actor Why the EU Needs to Change its Role as a Security Actor", Friedrich Ebert Stiftung, 17 January 2015, URL: http://library.fes.de/pdf-files/iez/10717.pdf.

Cambridge Dictionaries Online (2015). "English Definition of Perception", 24 January 2015, URL: http://dictionary.cambridge.org/dictionary/british/perception.

Cameron, Fraser et al. (2005). "EU-India Relations (Including EU-India Journalists' Conference Report, 30-31 May)", *EPC Issue Paper*, 35: 1-47.

Castel, S. (2009, 16 November). "No Takers for Foreign Policy Post at EU", *The Economic Times*, New Delhi.

Centre for Education and Communication (2011). "EU-India FTA Background Note, EU-India Free Trade Agreement: For Whom", 11 May 2011, URL: http://www.cec-india.org/index.php?option=com_content&view=article&id=167:eu-india-fta-background-note-&catid=46:trade-and-labour-rights-main.

Chaban N. and M. Holland (2013). "Assuming Superpower Status? Evolving Asian Perceptions of the EU", *L'Espace Politique*,19: 1-21.

Chaban, N. et al. (2006). "The European Union as Others See It", *European Foreign Affairs Review, Kluwer Law International*, 11: 245-262.

Charlie, A. (2014). "European Companies in India: Reigniting Economic Growth Foreign Direct Investment", European Business and Technology Centre Enhancing EU-India Collaboration in Clean Technologies, URL: http://ebtc.eu/images/ebtc-website-assets/publications/sector-publications/cross-sector/market-reports/140505_REP_ebtc-eicc-report_european-companies-in-india.pdf.

Chatterjee, Bipul (2010, 15 March). "Perspectives: Copenhagen Lessons for Doha", *The Economic Times*, New Delhi.

Chaudhari, P.P. (2012, 21 June). "4-word Principle in India's Big Green Victory at Rio", Hindustan Times, 17 January 2015, URL:http://www.hindustantimes.com/world-news/4-word-principle-india-s-big-green-victory-at-rio/article1-876692.aspx.

Chaudhuri, S. (2010, 13 April). "Thinking of the Future and Its Challenges", *The Economic Times*, New Delhi.

Chaudhuri, S. (2010, 18 June). "Economic Outlook and Opportunity", *The Economic Times*, New Delhi.

Clark, N. (2010, 9 April). "Forging Partnership British Airways and Iberia Sign Merger Deal", *The Times of India*, New Delhi.

CNBC TV18 (2012, 10 February) "SIAM Opposes India-EU FTA; Says it can Kill Auto Mfg Sector", Money Control. Com, 8 January 2015, URL: http://www.moneycontrol.com/news/business/siam-opposes-india-eu-fta-says-it-can-kill-auto-mfg-sector_665357.html.

Cnn.Com/Asia (2011). "Zakaria: 'Spiralling Chaos' Possible in Pakistan", 12 May 2011, URL:http://articles.cnn.com/2009-04-22/world/zakaria.pakistan_1_swat-valley-taliban-militants-pakistan?_s=PM:WORLD.

Commission of the European Communities (1994). "Communication from the Commission to the Council Towards a New Asia Strategy", COM (94) 314 final, 15 January 2015, URL:http://aei.pitt.edu/2949/1/2949.pdf.

Commission of the European Communities (1996). "Communication from the Commission EU-India Enhanced Partnership", COM (96) 275 final, 15 January 2015, URL:http://aei.pitt.edu/3974/1/3974.pdf.

Commission of the European Communities (2001). "Communication from the Commission Europe and Asia: A Strategic Framework for Enhanced Partnerships", COM (2001) 469 final, 15 January 2015, URL: http://ec.europa.eu/development/icenter/repository/strategy_asia_2001_en.pdf.

Community Research and Development Information Service (1997) "EU-India Cross Cultural Programme", 15 January 2015, URL:http://cordis.europa.eu/news/rcn/8955_en.html.

Cowan R. & D. Fogarty (2009, 8 December). "Nations of the World Attend Nature's Call", *The Economic Times*, New Delhi.

D'Cruz, E. (2010, 9 March). "Dutch League Home Disadvantage Foreign Talent Causes Dilemma", *The Times of India*, New Delhi.

Dainik Jagran (2009, 17 December). "The Hope of Arriving at a Concrete Conclusion is Increasingly Becoming Hazy", New Delhi.

Dainik Jagran (2009, 3 December). "The Challenge Posed by the Developed Countries Will Be Met by the Formation of a United Front", New Delhi.

Dainik Jagran (2010, 11 May). "Greece Shall Get a 10 billion Dollar Package", New Delhi.

Dainik Jagran (2010, 11 May). "Rupee Spikes to Year's Highest", New Delhi.

Dainik Jagran (2010, 11 May). "European Package Sends Markets in a Tizzy", New Delhi.

Dainik Jagran (2010, 20 May). "Chaos among Foreign Investors in the Wake of Eurozone Crisis", New Delhi.

Dainik Jagran (2010, 20 May). "EU will Tighten Screws on Hedge Funds", New Delhi.

Dainik Jagran (2010, 21 April). "Visa Duration of Stranded Passengers in India has been Extended", New Delhi.

Dainik Jagran (2010, 22 April) "The European Skies Brightened Up with Resumption of Flights", New Delhi.

Dainik Jagran (2010, 23 April) "The Indian Government has Taken a Tough Stand on Dumping", New Delhi.

Dainik Jagran (2010, 23 May). "European Countries Shall Strictly Observe Budgetary Rules", New Delhi.

Dainik Jagran, (2009, 3 December). "The Challenge Posed by the Developed Countries Will be met by the Formation of a United Front", New Delhi.

Dang, S. (2010). Group Head. Corporate Communications. Avantha Group. Interviewed in Delhi. 18 March.

Das, S. (2010, 15 June). "Euro-pain: With Friends Like These...Traders Refer to Euro as a Derisory Amalgam of the Greek Drachma and the Deutschmark", *The Economic Times*, New Delhi.

Das, S.(2010). Media Elite. Principal Correspondent. The Financial Express. Interviewed in Delhi. 3 March.

Dasgupta, S. (2009, 19 November). "Ramesh Dismisses Talk of US-China's Side Deal", *The Times of India*, New Delhi.

Dasgupta, S. (2010, 12 February). "China Court Upholds Jail for Top Dissident, Sparks Global Outcry", *The Times of India*, New Delhi.

Dasgupta, S. (2010, 24 June). "Progress Nuked Back to Pre-Hagen Days with China?", *The Times of India*, New Delhi.

Dave, A.M. (2010). Political Elite. Member of Parliament. Rajya Sabha. Bharatiya Janata Party. Interviewed in Delhi, 8 May.

Deen M. and T. R. Homan (2010, 7 June). "US, EU Divided on Growth Story", *The Economic Times*, New Delhi.

Delegation of the European to India (2010). "EU-India Summit Joint Statement Brussels, 10 December 2010", 28 December 2014, URL: http://www.consilium.europa.eu/uedocs/cms_data/docs/pressdata/EN/foraff/118404.pdf.

Delegation of the European Union to India (2000). "A Milestone in EU India Relations", 21August2011, URL:http://eeas.europa.eu/delegations/india/ documents/eu_india/021_eu_india_reso_1st_page1_en.pdf.

Delegation of the European Union to India (2000a)."Joint Declaration", 26 December 2014,URL:http://eeas.europa.eu/delegations/india/documents/eu_india/021_eu_india_reso_1st_page1_en.pdf.

Delegation of the European Union to India (2000b). "Agenda for Action", 26 December 2014, URL: http://eeas.europa.eu/delegations/india/documents/eu_ india/021_eu_india_reso_1st_page3_en.pdf.

Delegation of the European Union to India (2001). "Overview", 23 August 2011, URL:http://www.eeas.europa.eu/delegations/india/documents/eu_india/021_eu_india_reso_2nd_page1_en.pdf.

Delegation of the European Union to India (2003) "A Secure Europe in a Better World

European Security Strategy Brussels 12 December 2003", 26 December 2014, URL: http://www.consilium.europa.eu/uedocs/cmsUpload/78367.pdf.

Delegation of the European Union to India (2005). "President Barroso to attend EU-India Summit in New Delhi on 7 September", 26 August 2011, URL: http://eeas.europa.eu/delegations/india/documents/eu_india/021_eu_india_reso_6th_page3_en.pdf.

Delegation of the European Union to India (2005a). "Political Declaration on the India-EU Strategic Partnership", 26 August 2011, URL: http://www.eeas.europa.eu/delegations/india/documents/eu_india/021_eu_india_res_6th_summit2_en.pdf.

Delegation of the European Union to India (2005b), "The India-EU Strategic Partnership Joint Action Plan", 26 August 2011, URL: http://www.eeas.europa.eu/delegations/india/documents/eu_india/021_eu_india_res_6th_summit1_en.pdf.

Delegation of the European Union to India (2006). "Council of the European Union EU-India Summit Helsinki, 13 October 2006 Joint Statement", 26 December 2014, URL: http://eeas.europa.eu/delegations/india/documents/eu_india/021_eu_india_ res_7th_summit1_en.pdf.

Delegation of the European Union to India (2007). "India-EU Joint Statement, New Delhi, 30 November 2007", 27 August 2011, URL: http://www.eeas.europa.eu/delegations/india/documents/eu_india/021_eu_india_res_8th_summit1_en.pdf.

Delegation of the European Union to India (2007). "India-EU Summit New Delhi, 30 November 2007", 26 December 2014, URL: http://eeas.europa.eu/delegations/india/documents/eu_india/021_eu_india_res_8th_summit2_en.pdf.

Delegation of the European Union to India (2008, 29 September). "EU-India Summit, Marseille, Global partners for global Challenges: EU-India Joint Action Plan (JAP)", 11 May 2011, URL:http://eeas.europa.eu/delegations/india/documents/eu_india/updated_jap_en.pdf

Delegation of the European Union to India (2009). "EU-India Summit New Delhi 6 November 2009, Joint Statement", 28 August 2011, URL: http://www.consilium.europa.eu/uedocs/cms_Data/docs/pressdata/en/er/110993.pdf.

Delegation of the European Union to India (2010)"EU-India Update Newsletter of the Delegation of the European Union to India", 9(8). 14 January 2015, URL: http://eeas.europa.eu/delegations/india/documents/press_corner/newsletter/eu_india_update_2010_2_en.pdf.

Delegation of the European Union to India (2010, 10 December). "EU-India Summit Joint Statement, Brussels", 11 May 2011, URL:http://www.consilium.europa.eu/uedocs/cms_data/docs/pressdata/EN/foraff/118404.pdf.

Delegation of the European Union to India (2010a)."Remarks by Herman Van Rompuy President of the European Council following the EU-India Summit", 28 December 2014, URL: http://www.consilium.europa.eu/uedocs/cms_data/docs/ pressdata/en/ec/118402.pdf.

Delegation of the European Union to India (2011). "Science and Technology", 10 May 2011, URL: http://eeas.europa.eu/delegations/india/eu_india/science_and_technology/index_en.htm.

Delegation of the European Union to India (2012). "Council of the European Union India-European Summit Joint Statement", 10 January 2015, URL:http://eeas.europa.eu/delegations/india/documents/press_corner/20120210_indiaeu_joint_statement.pdf.

Delegation of the European Union to India (2012)."European Union Factsheet EU-India Summit New Delhi, 10 February 2012", 28 December 2014, URL: http://eeas.

europa.eu/delegations/india/documents/press_corner/20120207_eu_india_summit_factsheet_en.pdf.

Delegation of the European Union to India (2012)"Promoting EU-India Research and Innovation Collaboration Awareness Raising and Information Campaign in India,10-28 September 2012", European Business and Technology Centre, 14 January 2015, URL:http://eeas.europa.eu/delegations/india/documents/snt_update_26_oct_12/10_presentations/european_business_and_technology_centre.pdf.

Delegation of the European Union to India (2013). "The European Union and India Fifty Years of Partnership", 31 December 2014, URL: http://eeas.europa.eu/delegations/india/documents/publications/the_eu_and_india_fifty_years_of_partnership.pdf.

Delegation of the European Union to India (2014). "Research and Innovation", 9 January 2015, URL: http://eeas.europa.eu/delegations/india/eu_india/research_ innovation/index_en.htm.

Delegation of the European Union to India (2014a). "Development Cooperation", 9 January 2015, URL: http://eeas.europa.eu/delegations/india/eu_india/ development_cooperation/index_en.htm.

Delegation of the European Union to India (2014b). "European Union Press Release Europe Calling- European Higher Education Fair held in Bengaluru- Hosting 100 World-renowned European Universities", 10 January 2015, URL:http://eeas.europa.eu/delegations/india/documents/european_higher_education_fair_held_in_bengaluru.pdf.

Deora, M. (2010, 3 April). "Be Mobile Without Risk We Need to Find Ways of Making Use of Cell Phones Safer", *The Times of India*, New Delhi.

Desai, S. (2010). Business Elite. MD & CEO. Future Brands Limited. Interviewed in Delhi. 19 April.

Deshpande, R. (2010.11 April) "Lack of Container Security Poses Threat of N-Smuggling", *The Times of India*, New Delhi.

Dey, I. and R. Watts. (2010, 22 February). "EU Prepares £22bn Bailout for Greece", *The Times of India*, New Delhi.

Dhawan, H. (2009, 16 October). "India in Talks With EU Over Mobility of Workers", *The Times of India*, New Delhi.

Dhawan, H. (2010, 4 June). "Everyone's Wooing Indian Tourists", *The Times of India*, New Delhi.

Dixit, J. N. (2000). "India and Europe: Perceptions and Misperceptions", in R. K. Jain (eds.) *India and Europe in the New Millennium*, Delhi: Radiant Publishers.

Doran, D. (2009, 30 November)."EU Back Continuity in Govt Aid", *The Economic Times*, New Delhi

Duggal, A. (2010, 25 March). "Resolve Now to Have Women on Boards", *The Economic Times*, New Delhi.

Dutta, Sujit (2010). Civil Society Elite. Mahatma Gandhi Chair. Nelson Mandela Centre for Peace and Conflict Resolution. Jamia Millia Islamia. Interviewed in Delhi. 21 April.

Dutta, V. (2009, 14 August). "Ministry Points Finger at Pharma Biggies over Drug Seizures in Europe", *The Economic Times*, New Delhi.

Edgar E. and P. Sedgwick (2007). *Cultural Theory: Key Concepts*, Oxfordshire, USA and Canada: Routledge.

Embassy of India Belgium Luxembourg & the European Union (2014). "Political Dialogue",

29 December 2014, URL: http://www.indembassy.be/pages.php?id=55.

Erasmus Mundus Students and Alumni Association (2014). "EMAInd Unites All Indian Students and Alumni of Erasmus Mundus", 14 January 2014, URL: http://www.em-a.eu/en/about-ema/regional-chapters/indian-chapter.html.

ETSI World Class (2014). "Project SESEI- The Seconded European Standardization on Expert in India", URL: 14 January 2015, URL:http://www.etsi.org/about/our-global-role/sesei.

Euractiv.com (2012). "The Latest EU-India Summit Managed to Touch Upon the Political Dimension of The Partnership, Yet There are Still Several Issues which Remain to Be Resolved, Writes Gauri Khandekar", 14 January 2015, URL: http://fride.org/download/Euractiv_Indiasummit_GK.pdf.

Euractiv.com (2014, 27 May). "EU-India FTA: Crucial to a More Favourable Business Environment", 8 January 2015, URL: http://www.euractiv.com/ sections/global-europe/eu-india-fta-crucial-more-favourable- business-environment-302457.

Europa (2011). "Europe in 12 Lessons", 21 August, URL: http:// www.europa.eu/pol/ext/overview in.html.

Europa, Press Releases (2010, 21 June). "EU-India Relations: General Background Note", 10 May 2011, URL:http://europa.eu/rapid/pressReleasesAction.do?reference=MEMO/10/265&type=HTML.

Europa, Summaries of EU Legislation (2004). "Communication from the Commission to the Council, The European Parliament and the European Economic and Social Committee An EU-India Strategic Partnership", 26 December 2014, URL: http://eur-lex.europa.eu/legal-content/EN/TXT/PDF/?uri=CELEX:52004DC0430&rid=2.

European Commission (2010). "Main Economic Indicators, India", 10 May 2010, URL: http://trade.ec.europa.eu/doclib/docs/2006/september/tradoc_113390.pdf.

European Commission (2011). "The India-EU Strategic Partnership Joint Action Plan", 12 May 2011, URL:http://www.delind.ec.europa.eu/en/political_dialogue/ summits/sixth/joint_action_plan.pdf.

European Commission (2014), "Trade Countries and Regions India", 3 January 2014, URL:http://ec.europa.eu/trade/policy/countries-and-regions/countries/india/.

European Commission Press Release Database (2010b). "Jose Manuel Durao Barroso President of the European Commission Statement by President Barosso Following the EU-India Summit", 28 December 2014, URL: http://europa.eu/rapid/press-release_SPEECH-10-749_en.htm?locale=en.

Eurostat News Release (2009). "EU-India Summit An EU27 Surplus in Trade in Goods with India Of 2.1 Bn Euro In 2008 Surplus Of 1.5 Bn in Trade in Services", 29 December 2014, URL: http://ec.europa.eu/eurostat/documents/2995521/5073538/6-04112009-BP-EN.PDF/5f669e28-734b-4300-8ba0-87cfe8cdc1c2?version=1.0.

Eurostat newsrelease (2010). "EU-India Summit EU27 Trade in Goods with India Relatively Balanced in the First Nine Months of 2010 Surplus of 13 bn in Trade in Services in 2009", 29 December 2014, URL: http://ec.europa.eu/eurostat/documents/2995521/5041778/6-08122010-AP-EN.PDF/112e2536-fb7f-4ec6-beca-969f1748c8e0?version=1.0.

Eurostat newsrelease (2012). "EU-India Summit EU 27 Trade in Goods with India Increased by 20% in the First Ten Months of 2011", 29 December 2014, URL: http://ec.europa.eu/eurostat/documents/2995521/5152694/6-09022012-AP-EN.PDF/97fd2c7e-6c3e-4337-9926-3d721a6d10f7?version=1.0.

Eurostat Statistics in focus (2009). "EU 27 Trade Surplus with India at Record Level in 2007", 29 December 2014, URL: file:///C:/Users/user/Desktop/KS-SF-09-026-EN.PDF.pdf.

Evan M. and L. Coen (2030. "Elitism and Agri-environmental Policy in Ireland", in Maura Adshead and Michelle Millar (eds.), *Public Administration and Public Policy in Ireland: Theory and Methods*, London, New York and Canada: Routledge.

F.Business, PTI (2014, 28 September) "EU Keen to Resume FTA Negotiations with India at the Earliest", 7 January 2015, URL: http://www.firstpost.com/business/ economy/eu-keen-to-resume-fta-negotiations-with-india-at-the-earliest-1992411.html.

Fiormonti, L. and S. Lucarelli (2007), "The EU Viewed by the Others: Drawing Some Conclusions", Forum on the Problems of Peace and War and GARNET, 5 February 2010, URL: http://www.garnet-eu.org/fileadmin/documents/working_ papers/1707/10%20 India.pdf.

Ganapathy, N. (2010, 17 April). "Modi Free to Travel, EU tells MEA", *The Economic Times*, New Delhi.

Ganesh, S. (2010, 20 June). "Markets Volatile Over Eurozone Debt Concerns", *The Economic Times*, New Delhi.

Gaur, M. (2005), *Foreign Policy Annual*, New Delhi: Gyan Publishing House.

Ghosh, D. (2010, 15 March). "Textile Cos Hiring As Demand Firms Up", *The Economic Times*, New Delhi.

Ghosh, D. (2010, 9 February). "With Recession Beginning To Ebb in Key Overseas Markets, Factories Are Humming Once Again", *The Economic Times*, New Delhi.

Girard, D. (2013). "Commentary: The Strength of Perceptions in the Dialogue between Asia and Europe", *Baltic Journal of European Studies*, 3(3): 195-206.

Good Governance (2011). "Development, Security Economic Statistics", 10 May 2011, URL: http://www.nationmaster.com/graph/eco_gdp_gro_ann-economy-gdp-growthannual&date=1971.

Goswami, U. (2014, 18 September). "EU wants India to Show Flexibility on Climate Change Talks", *The Economic Times*, 22 January 2015, URL: http://articles.economictimes.indiatimes.com/2014-09-18/news/54068344_1_climate-change-green-climate-fund-lima-round.

Goswami, U.A. (2010, 1 May). "45 Nations Bonn-homie over Climate Talks", *The Economic Times*, New Delhi.

Goswami, U.A. (2010, 10 April). "European Union Trying to Regain Stature in Climate Discussions", *The Economic Times*, New Delhi.

Goswami, U.A. (2010, 20 April). "Reduce Trust-Deficit in Climate Talks: India", *The Economic Times*, New Delhi.

Goswami, U.A. (2010, 7 June). "Merely Recycling Already Committed Development Assistance As Climate Funds", *The Economic Times*, New Delhi.

Government of India (2010), "Registrar of Newspapers for India", 31 July, URL: https://rni.nic.in/.

Government of India, Ministry of Commerce and Industry, Department of Commerce Annual Report 2013-2014 (2014). "Commercial Relations, Trade Agreements and International Trade Organisations", 30 December 2014, URL: http://commerce.nic.in/publications/pdf/anualreport_chapter6-2012-13.pdf.

Grant, C. (2006). "India and the EU: Strategic Partners?", Centre for European Reform Bulletin, 14 May 2009, URL : http://www.cer.org.uk/articles/46_grant.html.

Gucht, K. D. (2010, 4 March). "Bowled Over by Trade", *The Economic Times*, New Delhi.

Guha Roy, S. (2010).Media Elite. Editor- Business. Tehelka Weekly News Magazine. Inteviewed in Delhi. 19 March.

Gupta K.R. and V. Shukla (2009). *Foreign Policy of India*, New Delhi: Atlantic Publisher and Distributors (P) Ltd.

Gupta, R. (2010). Civil Society Elite. President. Apne Aap Women Worldwide, an Initiative to end Sex-Trafficking. Interviewed in Delhi. 17 April.

Gupta, V. (2009, 31 October). "Copenhagen after Kyoto", *Dainik Jagran*, New Delhi.

Gurav, V. (2010, 23 June). "Street Wary Retail Investors Stay on Sidelines Despite Rebound", *The Economic Times*, New Delhi.

Haksar, P.N. (2014)."Perception and Reality in the Making of Foreign Policy", Mainstream Weekly, LIII (1), 25 January 2015, URL:http://www.mainstreamweekly.net/article56.html.

Hamilton, A. (2010, 28 March). "For the Record 'Oxford Cannot Be Franchised Like Hamburgers'", *The Times of India*, New Delhi.

Harikumar, S. (2010). Business Elite. Senior Manager. Forex. Oriental Bank of Commerce. A Government of India Undertaking, International Banking Division. Interviewed in Delhi. 2 May.

Harshe, R. (2007). "European Union and India: A Critical Perspective", *Economic and Political Weekly*, 42(16): 1419-1422.

Henri, T. (2010). Civil Society Elite. Executive Director. People's Watch. Member, National Core Group on NGOs. National Human Rights Commission of India. Interviewed in Delhi. 13 April.

Heywood, A. (2008). *Political Theory: An Introduction*, New York: Palgrave Macmillan.

Hole, J. (2009, 23 August). "Fed, ECB Eye Recovery; Too Soon to Hit Brakes", *The Economic Times*, New Delhi.

Holger, H. and A. Rinke (2010, 20 May). "Germany Goes to War Alone, Bans Naked Short Selling", *The Economic Times*, New Delhi.

Holslag, J. (2009)."Europe's Normative Disconnect with the Emerging Powers", Brussels Institute of Contemporary China Studies, Asia Paper, 5(4): 1-21, 17 January 2015, URL: http://www.vub.ac.be/biccs/site/assets/files/apapers/2010301% 20%20 Normative%20disconnect.pdf.

Hughes, Kirsty (2005), "Britain Raises EU Standard in India", [Online: web] Accessed 5 February 2010, URL: http://www.europeanvoice.com/article/imported/ britain-raises-eu-standard-in-india/52425.aspx.

India-European Union Forum of Parliamentarians FICCI (2013). "India-EU Bilateral Trade Relations", 4 January 2015, URL:http://www.ficci-ineupf.com/trade.html.

Indian Express.com (2010, 23 July). "Open Economy to FDI: EU to India", 8 May 2011, URL: http://www.indianexpress.com/news/open-economy-to-fdi-eu-to-india/650753/.

Indian Wine Academy (2011, 18 July). "Wine and Spirits Delay EU FTA with India", 8 January 2015, URL:http://www.indianwineacademy.com/item_5_460.aspx.

Indianetzone, History of India (2009), "European Colonies in India", 10 August, URL: http;//www.indianetzone.com/9/european_colonies_india.htm.

Institute for Security Studies (2011), "Indian and EU Approaches to Security", 12 May 2011, URL:http://www.iss.europa.eu/index.php?id=18&no_cache=1&L=1&tx_ttnews%5Btt_news%5D=1183&tx_ttnews%5BbackPid%5D=13&cHash=5a25bd6e5e

Iqbal, N. (2010). Business Elite. Senior Merchandiser. Radhnik Exports. Interviewed in Delhi. 1 May.

Isar, Y. R. (2015). "India – Culture in EU External Relations", Preparatory Action Culture in EU External Relations, 17 January 2015, URL:http://cultureinexternalrelations.eu/wp-content/uploads/2013/10/INDIA-%E2%80%93-CULTURE-IN-EU-EXTERNAL-RELATIONS.pdf.

Jaffrelot, Christophe (2009), *Emerging States: the Wellspring of a New World Order*, New York: Columbia University Press.

Jagannathan, P. (2010, 24 February). "Imported Sugar Allowed into Maya Land", *The Economic Times*, New Delhi.

Jain R.K. and S. Pandey (2012). "The Public Attitudes and Images of the European Union in India", *India Quarterly*, 68 (4): 331-343.

Jain, R. K. (2007). "The European Union and SAARC: The First Enlargement and After", *Asia Paific Journal of EU Studies*, 5 (2):177-192.

Jain, R. K. (2009). "The European Union and China", in Wiesssala G. et al. (eds.) *The European Union and China: Interests and Dilemmas*, Amsterdam and New York: Rodopi.

Jain, R. K. (2011). "India's Relations with the European Union", in D. Scott (ed.), *Handbook of India's International Relations*, United Kingdom: Routledge.

Jain, R.K (2014). "India and Europe: Towards a new narrative", in Cremer M. et al. (eds.). *The Dwarfing of Europe? A Dialogue between Brazil, India, China and Europe Volume* 2, Amsterdam: European Cultural Foundation.

Jain, R.K. (2001). "Indian Foreign Policy on the Threshold of the Twenty-first Century" in F. Snyder (eds.), *Regional and Global Integration of International Trade*, Oxford and Portland: Oregon: Hart Publishing.

Jain, R.K. (2004). "India and an Enlarging European Union", *Asia Pacific Journal of EU Studies*, 2 (2):109-120.

Jain, R.K. (2005). "India, the European Union and Asian Regionalism", *Asia Pacific Journal of EU Studies*, 3(1): 29-44.

Jain, R.K. (2008). "Teaching the EU in India", in Holland M. et al. (eds.). *The Future of European Studies in Asia,* Singapore: Asia-Europe Foundation.

Jain, Rajendra K. (2000). *India and Europe in the New Millennium*, Delhi: Radiant Publishers.

James, L.R. (2013). *American Foreign Policy and Political Ambition*, United States of America: Sage Publications.

Javadekar P. (2010). Political Elite. Member of Parliament. Rajya Sabha. National Spokesperson of Bharatiya Janata Pary. Inteviewed in Delhi. 10 May.

Jervis, R. (1976). *Perception and Misperception in International Politics*, United Kingdom: Princeton University Press.

John, S. (2010, 25 April). "Ideas Just Waiting to Take Flight", *The Times of India*, New Delhi.

John, S. (2010, 30 April). "Kohli wins EU inventor Award", *The Times of India*, New Delhi.

John, S. (2010, 5 April). "People Spotting Father of Mass Market GPS is an Indian", *The Times of India*, New Delhi.

John, W. (2010). Civil Society Elite. Observer Research Foundation. Interviewed in Delhi. 20 April.

Johnston, A. (2006), *New Directions in the Study of China's Foreign Policy*, Stanford California: Stanford University Press.

Jones G. and S. Desai (2010, 19 May). "Window to the World Britain Cornered as EU Leaders Crack Down on Hedge Funds", *The Economic Times*, New Delhi.

Jones, H. (2010, 16 February). "Accounting Standards Board Shores Up Defences. Global Body Sets Terms to Protect Itself from Political Pressure", *The Economic Times*, New Delhi.

Jones, M. (2009, 4 December). "ECB to Cut Emergency Measures", *The Economic Times*, New Delhi.

Joseph, M. (2010). Civil Society Elite. Deputy Director. Institute of Peace and Conflict Studies. Interviewed in Delhi. 8 March.

Joshi, M. (2010). Media Elite.Deputy Editor. Mail Today. The India Today Group. Mail Today Newspapers Private Limited. Interviewed in Delhi. 13 March.

Kamerling, S. (2014, 1 October). "Maritime Security Cooperation: The Next Port Of Call", Cingendael Netherlands Institute of International Relations, 17 January 2015, URL: http://www.clingendael.nl/publication/maritime-security-cooperation-next-port-call.

Kanter, J and A. Revkin (2009, 12 December). "EU Vows $3bn A Yr For Climate Change Fund", *The Times of India*, New Delhi.

Kanter, J. (2010, 13 February). "EU Rejects Deal With US on Sharing Bank Data", *The Economic Times*, New Delhi.

Kapila, S. (2009), "Afghanistan: India Has Legitimate Strategic Interests in its Stability", South Asia Analysis Group, 12 May 2011, URL: http://www.southasianalysis.org/%5Cpapers32%5Cpaper3149.html.

Kaushal, N. (2009, 15 September). "Don't fear the Inflation, Yet", *The Economic Times*, New Delhi.

Keller, S. (1991), *Beyond the Ruling Class Strategic Elites in a Ruling Society*, New York: Random House.

Khandekar, V.K. (2013), *The Indian Media Business 4th Edition*, Sage Response: New Delhi.

Khattar, S. (2010, 15 March). "Q&A 'Success Calls for the Need to Learn' The Computer Society of India (CSI) has Launched its Knowledge Management Portal," *The Economic Times*, New Delhi.

Koley A. and D. Ghosh (2009, 2 July). "Textile Sector May see Rise in Demand", *The Economic Times*, New Delhi.

Kondapalli, S. (2009, 20 December). "Hot and Sour Taste of Growing Relations", *The Economic Times*, New Delhi.

Kris, U. (2003, 17 August). "Following the Roman trail', *The Hindu*, New Delhi.

Krugman, P.(2010, 12 January). "Europe's Better Life", *The Times of India*, New Delhi.

Kumar, R. (2009). "India as a Foreign Policy Actor- Normative Redux", in F. Heisbourg and M. Emerson (eds.), *Readings in European Security Volume* 5, Brussels, London, Switzerland, Geneva: Centre for European Policy Studies, International Institute for Strategic Studies, Centre for the Democratic Control of Armed Forces, Geneva Centre of Security Policy.

Kumar, R. (2010). Media Elite. Special Correspondent. Nav Bharat Times News Bureau. Inteveiwed in Delhi. 6 March.

Kumari, R. (2010). Civil Society Elite. Director. Centre for Social Research. Interviewed in Delhi. 4 March.

Laswell, H.D. et al. (2010). "The Elite Concept", in Peter Bachrach (ed.) *Poltical Elites in a Democracy*, New York :Atherton Press.

Levy, J.S. (2013). "Psychology and Foreign Policy Decision-Making", in Huddy L. et al. (eds.). *The Oxford Handbook of Political Psychology, Second Edition*, Oxford: Oxford University Press.

Lisbonne-de-Vergeron, K. (2014). "Chinese and India Views of Europe and the Role of Culture in European External Affairs" in Cremer M. et al. (eds).*The Dwarfing of Europe ? A Dialogue between Brazil, India, China and Europe Volume* 2, Amsterdam: European Cultural Foundation.

Livemint (2009). "Top 10 Dailies Show Growth in Readership", 16 July, URL: http://www.livemint.com/2009/11/23224235/Top-10-dailies-show-growth-in.html.

Lohia, Y. (2010, 12 April). "Shackling the Net", *The Times of India*, New Delhi.

Lomborg, B. (2009, 3 September). "Beyond the Carbon Crusade", *The Economic Times*, New Delhi.

Lomborg, B. (2010,14 June)."Perspectives: Europe's Determination to Decline", *The Economic Times*, New Delhi.

Lucarelli S. and L. Fioramonti (2009). *External Perceptions of the European Union as a Global Actor*, Rutledge / GARNET Series: Europe in the World.

MacAskill A. and J. Menon (2009, 3 December). "Fattening Banks in EU Sow Seeds of Next Crisis", *The Economic Times*, New Delhi.

Macdonald, A. (2010, 4 June). "Israel Resists Global Probe into Gaza Ship Raid", *The Economic Times*, New Delhi.

Macedonia.org (2002). "Alexander the Great", 10 August 2011, URL: http://faq.macedonia.org/history/Alexander.the.great.html.

Mahambare V. (2010) "European Sovereign Debt Crisis What does it Mean for India?", CRISIL Ratings, Economy View, 23 January 2015, URL:http://www.crisil.com/Ratings/Commentary/CommentaryDocs/CRISIL-Ratings_european-sovereign-debt_jul10.pdf.

Mahbubani, K. (2014, 4 February). "To the New Order, Strategically", The Indian Express, 10 January 2015, URL: http://indianexpress.com/article/opinion/columns/to-the-new-order-strategically/.

Malik A. and E. Roche (2011, 29 April). "India Shortlists European Fighter Jets", *Mint, Leading the News*, New Delhi.

Malik, A. (2010, 5 April). "Soft Power, Hard Battles India's goodwill-hunt in Afghanistan Needs a Degree of Hard Power to Complement it", *The Times of India*, New Delhi.

Malone, David M. (2011). *Does the Elephant Dance? Contemporary Indian Foreign Policy*, New York: Oxford University Press.

Manoharan, N. (2010, 10 June). "Taking Ties Forward India-Sri Lanka Relations are at an All-Time High but have Potential to Grow Further", *The Times of India*, New Delhi.

Markey, Daniel (2009). "Developing India's Foreign Policy "Software"", *Asia Policy*, 8:73-96, 5 February 2010, URL: http://www,nbr.org/Publications/Asia_policy/ AP8/AP8_Markey_India.pdf.

Martinuzzi, E. (2010, 18 February). "Goldman, Greece didn't Reveal Swap", *The Economic Times*, New Delhi.

Mary, L. (2010, 9 May). "Dealing with a New America the World's Biggest Economy Is Coming out Wiser from the Global Meltdown and Changing the Rules of the Game. Are We Ready?", *The Economic Times*, New Delhi.

Mattoo, A. (2005), "India's International Relations: The Search for Stability, Space and Strength", in Alyssa Ayres and Philip Oldenburg (eds.) *India briefing: Takeoff At Last?* , United States of America: Asia Society.

Mawdsley, E. (2014,). "Development and the EU-India Strategic Parntership: Missing Incentives and Opportunities", European Strategic Partnership Observatory, Policy Brief 14, 15 January 2015, URL:http://fride.org/download/PB14_Development_and_the_India_EU_Strategic_Partnership.pdf.

McPhail, Thomas I., (2010), "The Roles of Global News Agencies", in Thomas L. McPhail (eds.) *Global Communication Theories, Stakeholders and Trends*, United Kingdom: Wiley-Blackwell.

Mehta, A.K. (2010, 5 March). "Guest Column Lanka Tamils in Power Vacuum", *The Economic Times*, New Delhi.

Mehta, P.B. (2010). Civil Society Elite. President. Centre for Policy Research. Interviewed in Delhi. 16 April.

Mehta, Sharamana G. (2009, 7 July). "A Few Stitches, but not Tailored for Growth", *The Economic Times*, New Delhi.

Meinya, T. (2010). Political Elite. Member of Paliament. Lok Sabha. Indian National Congress. Interviewed in Delhi. 2 February.

Mills, Wright C. (2000). *The Power Elite New Edition with a new Afterword by Alan Wolfe*, New York: Oxford University Press.

Ministry of External Affairs (2004). "EC Communication Titled 'An EU-India Strategic Partnership'- India's Response", 27 August 2004, URL: meaindia.nic.in. See. Baroowa, S. (2006). "The Emerging Strategic Partnership Between India and the EU: A Critical Appraisal", *European Law Journal*, 13 (6): 732-749.

Mishra, P. (2010, 5 January). "India Losing IT to emerging rivals Top Outsourcers like GE, Citibank Opting for Nearshore Vendors", *The Economic Times*, New Delhi.

Mithi, M. (2010). Political Elite. Member of Parliament. Rajya Sabha. Former Chief Minister of Arunachal Pradesh and former Lieutenant Governor of Pondicherry. Interviewed in Delhi. 2 February.

Mitra, P.(2009,12 December). "Grameen Bank Founder Muhammad Yunus Calls for a South Asian Union, on the EU model", *The Times of India*, New Delhi.

Mitta, M. (2009, 28 September). "Worldwide, 200m Face Caste Bias: UN", *The Times of India*, New Delhi.

Mohan, Ram T.T. (2010, 13 May). "Why the Greek Rescue Won't Work", *The Economic Times*, New Delhi.

Muenchow- Pohl, B. V. (2012). "India and Europe in a Multipolar World", Carnegie Papers, 23 December 2014, URL: http://caregieendowment.org/2012/05/10/india-and-europe-in-mulitpolar-world/hz8g#.

Muenchow- Pohl, B.V. (2012, 23 August). "EU relations with China and India Courting the Dragon, wooing the Elephant", Carnegie Endowment for International Peace, 16 January 2015, URL:http://carnegieendowment.org/2012/08/23/eu-relations-with-china-and-india-courting-dragon-wooing-elephant/dkt4#.

Mukherjee, W. and S. Ghosal (2010, 4 January). "Your Wait for an IT Job May Just Get over This Year", *The Economic Times*, New Delhi.

Mukhopadhyay, A.R. (2010). Civil Society Elite. Associate Fellow. Institute for Defence and Study Analyses. Interviewed in Delhi. 26 April.

Mulay P. and G. Pai (2010, 10 April). "Re's Rise Against Euro May Hit IT, Textiles Cos", *The Economic Times*, New Delhi.

Nair, P.K. K. (2013, 3 July). "EU Threat to Indian Farmers", The New Indian Express 8 January 2015, URL: http://www.newindianexpress.com/columns/EU-threat-to-India-farmers/2013/07/03/article 1664241.e.

Nair, S. (2010, 18 May). "Guest Column Equitable Sharing of Carbon Space", *The Economic Times*,New Delhi.

Narendranath, K.G. (2009, 28 July). "A Multi-Pronged Strategy to Kill Generic Drugs Industry", *The Economic Times*, New Delhi.

National Dairy Development Board (2011). "Operation Flood", 10 May 2011, URL: http://www.nddb.org/aboutnddb/operationflood.html.

Neuger, J. and G. Viscusi (2010, 24 May). "EU to Toughen Sanctions on High-Deficit Countries", *The Economic Times*, New Delhi.

Neuger, J.G. (2010, 15 May). "Euro Breakup Talk Spreads as Germany Loses its Proxy", *The Economic Times*, New Delhi.

NFG Asian Perceptions of the EU (2013, 26-27 September)."Europe's Role for Security in a Muti-polar World Views from India and China", Freie Universitat Berlin, 17 January, URL: https://www.asianperceptions.eu/system/files/private/ NFG_Delhi_Report_Asias_views_on_EUs_security_role.pdf.

NYTC (2014). The New York Times Company, "The New York Times News Service/Syndicate", 11 June, URL: https://www.nytsyn.com/.

Oliker, O. et al. (2009). *Russian Foreign Policy: Sources and Implications*, Pittsburgh: Rand Corporation.

Pais, J. (2010). Civil Society Elite. Assistant Professor. Institute for Studies in Industrial Development. Interviewed in Delhi. 3 May.

Pala, V.H. (2010). Political Elite. Minister of State for Water Resources. Member of Parliament. Lok Sabha. Indian National Congress. Interviewed in Delhi. 2 February.

Panicker, L. (2010). Media Elite.Senior Associate Editor. Hindustan Times Media Limited. Interviewed in Delhi. 20 March.

Pant, Harsh V. (2011). "Indian Strategic Culture: the Debate and its Consequences", in Scott D. (eds.) *Handbook of India's International Relations*, United Kindgom, USA and Canada: Routledge.

Pant, M. (2009, 11 September). "WTO Talks: Waiting for Godot", *The Economic Times*, New Delhi.

Parashar, S. (2009, 30 November). "French Move on Carbon Tax Protectionism: UK", *The Times of India*, New Delhi.

Patnaik, B. (2010, 14 May). "Against the Grain FTA? Nothing Free About It", *The Times of India*, New Delhi.

Patni, A. (2010). Media Elite. DGM, Energy Security. Communication and External Affairs.

Former Press Advisor to the European Commission. Former Assistant Editor at British High Commission and Former Sub-editor at *The Times of India*. 26 February.

Pattanaik, Smruti S. (2004). *Elite Perceptions in Foreign Policy: Role of Print Media in influencing India-Pakistan Relations, 1989-1999*, Colombo and New Delhi: Regional Centre for Strategic Studies and Manohar Publishers and Distributors.

Pfanner, E. (2010, 9 February). "An International Crackdown on Illegally Copied Music, Movies, Designer Bags", *The Times of India*, New Delhi.

Plumber, K. (2010, 11 May). "Asian Policy Tightening may Take a Break Now", *The Economic Times*, New Delhi.

Pradhan, N. (2009, 12 September). "The Rich Countries Try to Woo India", *Dainik Jagran*, New Delhi.

Pragmatic Euphony (2009), "Indian Troops in Afghanistan", 12 May 2011, URL:http://us.cnn.com/2009/WORLD/asiapcf/04/22/zakaria.pakistan/index.htmlcnn.com/asia.

Pramugdha, M. and P. Mishra (2010, 8 February). "New EU VAT Rule to Make Offshoring Costlier by 15%", *The Economic Times*, New Delhi.

PTI (2014), Press Trust of India, "About PTI", 11 June, URL: http://www.ptinews.com/aboutpti/aboutus.aspx.

PTI (2014, 28 April). "EU Bans Indian Alphonso mangoes, 4 vegetables from May 1", *The Hindu*, 10 January 2015, URL:http://www.thehindu.com/news/international/ world/eu-bans-indian-alphonso-mangoes-4-vegetables-from-may-1/article5956482. ece.

Public Service Europe (2011). "Trade Deal Boost to India's Drug Monopolies", 11 May 2011, URL: http://www.publicserviceeurope.com/article/90/trade-deal-boost-to-indias-drugs-monopolies.

Raina, K. (2010). Civil Society Elite. Climate Campaigner. Greenpeace.India. Interviewed in Delhi. 24 April.

Rakesh, K. (2010). Media Elite. Group Vice-President and Senior Editor. NE TV Group. Interviewed in Delhi. 8 March.

Ram, A. N. (2010, 26 April). "Indo-China Relations are Likely to Improve", *Dainik Jagran*, New Delhi.

Ranganathan M and U. M. Rodrigues, (2010), *Indian Media in a Globalised World*, Sage Publications India Pvt Ltd: New Delhi.

Ranganathan, C. (2010, 23 June). "EU to Take up Single Work Permit Soon", *The Economic Times*, New Delhi.

Ray, A. (2010, 1 May). "6 days to go, it's Advantage Cameron PM Brown Floored In Final TV Debate Too As Focus Shifts from Economy to Immigration", *The Times of India*, New Delhi.

Ray, A. (2010, 12 April). "Curbs on immigration Top Labour, Tory Priority Lists", *The Times of India*, New Delhi.

Ray, A. (2010, 13 May). "Coalition Course Will Cameron keep his India Promise?", *The Times of India*, New Delhi.

Ray, A. (2010, 3 June). "Short of docs, UK Looks to Hire Indians to Staff NHS", *The Times of India*, New Delhi.

Ray, A. (2010, 30 June). "Cameron will be Here in end-July", *The Times of India*, New Delhi.

Ray, T. (2010, 15 February). "Higher Education is a Great Equalizer'", *The Times of India*, New Delhi.

Ray, T. (2010, 17 May 2010). “CEIBS Opens New Campus”, *The Times of India*, New Delhi.

Ray, T. (2010, 21 June). “New World Order a Master’s in International Relations Can be Challenging and Timely”, *The Times of India*, New Delhi.

Ray.A. (2010,25 June). “Q&A‘India and the EU are both Committed to Universal Values’”, *The Times of India*, New Delhi.

Reserve Bank of India (2014). “Weekly Statistical Supplement Foreign Exchange Reserves”, 9 January 2015, URL: http://rbidocs.rbi.org.in/rdocs/Wss/PDFs/2T_ WSS020115F.pdf.

Reuters (2011, 28 April). “Eurofighter, Rafale in Indian Fighter Race”, 8 May 2011, URL: http://in.reuters.com/article/2011/04/28/idINIndia-56634420110428.

Robinson, P. (2012). “Media and US Foreign Policy”, in Michael Cox and Doug Stokes (eds.) *US Foreign Policy*, New York: Oxford University Press.

Roy, B. (2009, 10 December). “Nobel Laureate for S Asian Unity on EU lines”, *The Times of India*, New Delhi.

Rudy, R. P. (2010). Political Elite. Member of Parliament. Rajya Sabha. Bharatiya Janata Party. Interviewed in Delhi, 13 March.

Sachdeva, G. (2009). “India and the European Union: Time to De-Bureaucratize Strategic Partnership”, *Strategic Analysis*, 33(2): 202-207.

Sachdeva G. (2008). “India and the European Union: Broadening Strategic Partnership Beyond Economic Linkages”, *International Studies*, 45 (4): 341-367.

Sachdeva, G. (2014). “EU-China and EU-India: A Tale of Two Strategic Partnerships”, *Strategic Analysis*, 38 (4): 427-431.

Sahay, A. (2010, 1 June), “Open Letter to PM Economic Costs of Mental Illness”, *The Economic Times*, New Delhi.

Saltmarsh, M. (2010, 24 April). “Greece Calls for Activation of Rescue Plan”, *The Times of India*, New Delhi.

Samovar, Larry A. et al. (2009). *Intercultural Communication: A Reader*, Boston: Wadsworth Cengage Learning.

Sangma, A. (2010). Political Elite. Union Minister. Union Minister of State for Rural Development. Member of Parliament. Lok Sabha.Nationalist Congress Party. Internviewed in Delhi, 2 February.

Sapir, A. (2010, 22 March). “Perspectives Can Globalisation be Sustained?”, *The Economic Times*, New Delhi.

Sedlar, Jean W. (1980). “India and the Greek World; A Study in the Transmission of Culture”, New Jersey: Sadhus and Yogis of India, 10 August 2011, URL: http://www.adolphus.nl/xcrpts/xcsedlar.html.

Sen A. (2009, 21 September). “Group Meetings are Fine, But WTO Talks Must Be Multilateral: Developing Nations”, *The Economic Times*, New Delhi.

Sen, A. (2009, 15 September). “India Won’t Take EU Word on Drugs Seizures”, *The Economic Times*, New Delhi.

Sen, A. (2009, 16 November). “Will it be Sweet November for WTO?”, *The Economic Times*, New Delhi.

Sen, A. (2009, 23 November). “Drug Seizure: Govt to Drag EU to WTO”, *The Economic Times*, New Delhi.

Sen, A. (2009, 26 December). “India Gives EU Another Chance to Settle Drug Seizure Case”, *The Economic Times*, New Delhi.

Sen, A. (2009, 3 July). "Exports Unlikely to Revive This Year", *The Economic Times*, New Delhi.

Sen, A. (2009, 5 October). "India to Haul EU to WTO over Customs Norms", *The Economic Times*, New Delhi.

Sen, A. (2010). Media Elite. Economic Times Bureau. Interviewed in Delhi. 6 March.

Sen, A. (2010, 1 June). "India Gets Help in Piracy Fight Nations From East Asia, Latin America and Africa Support Indian Stand", *The Economic Times*, New Delhi.

Sen, A. (2010, 10 May). "Poultry Import Curbs to Remain for Now", *The Economic Times*, New Delhi.

Sen, A. (2010, 19 June). "US, EU Cite Safety Issue in Defence of Piracy Law", *The Economic Times*, New Delhi.

Sen, A. (2010, 22 March). "India Ready to Move WTO Against EU Customs laws", The Economic Times, New Delhi.

Sen, A. (2010, 26 October). "Govt Won't Force States to Slash Tax on Imported Spirits", *The Economic Times*, New Delhi.

Sen, A. (2010, 8 May). "India to Keep EU, Japan Out of Govt Procurement Country Also Keeps Issues Out of FTA Negotiations With Australia", *The Economic Times*, New Delhi.

Sen, A. and K. Singh (2010, 29 April). "India Won't Let EU Play Drug Inspector", *The Economic Times*, New Delhi.

Sen, A. (2009, 3 July). "Exports Unlikely To Revive This Year", *The Economic Times*, New Delhi.

Sen, A. (2010, 14 April). "India Girding Itself For US, EU Carbon Tax Plans To Take On West Once Trade Barriers Are Set Up", *The Economic Times*, New Delhi.

Sen, A. (2010, 26 April). "India Moves WTO on Ambiguity in CVD Math Benchmark Sought to Ensure Penal Duties Imposed by West are not Arbitrary and Excessive", *The Economic Times*, New Delhi.

Sen, S (2009, 24 August). "Rabidly Protectionist About British Jobs", *The Economic Times*, New Delhi.

Sen, S. (2009, 8 November). "Blood pressure Now Impacts Bottom-line", *The Economic Times*, New Delhi.

Sen, S. (2010, 10 April). "Letter from London Iceland to Wall St, Cash Turns to Ash", *The Economic Times*, New Delhi.

Sen, S. (2010, 11 May). "$1,000,000,000,000 Aid Plan to Restore Confidence in Euro", *The Economic Times*, New Delhi.

Sen, S. (2010, 26 April). "Letter from London Talent, Skills and Immigration", *The Economic Times*, New Delhi.

Sen, S. (2010, 29 March). "Letter from London Sovereign Republic of Debt", *The Economic Times*, New Delhi.

Sen, S. (2010, 7 June), "Letter from London It's not Brown Man's Burden", *The Economic Times*, New Delhi.

Sethi, N. (2009, 12 Ocober). "US Throws Spanner into Climate Talks", *The Times of India*, New Delhi.

Sethi, N. (2009, 12 September). "Now, Law to Tackle Emissions? It Could Give India Bargaining Chip at Global Forum", *The Times of India*, New Delhi.

Sethi, N. (2009, 12 September). "EU Unwilling to Give India Funds for Climate Change", *The Times of India*, New Delhi.

Sethi, N. (2009, 19 October). "'India Must Listen More, Talk Less at Negotiations'", *The Times of India*, New Delhi.

Sethi, N. (2010, 19 February). "Biased' UN Climate Panel Chief Resigns India Wants Environment Secretary to Succeed Him", *The Times of India*, New Delhi.

Sethi, N. (2010, 21 April). "Quick Fix BASIC to Look for Options Beyond Kyoto", *The Times of India*, New Delhi.

Sethi, N. (2009,30 September). "India-led Effort Makes US Bite Dust on Climate", *The Times of India*, New Delhi.

Setia, A. (2010). Media Elite. Input Head. Etv. Interviewed in Delhi. 13 March.

Sharma, D. (2009, 23 September). "The Black Shadow That Looms Large Over The Farmers", *Dainik Jagran*, New Delhi.

Sharma, M. (2010, 22 April). "Meaty Discussions, Anyone?", *The Times of India*, New Delhi.

Sharma, M.M. (2009, 3 November). "No Fair Play in Pharma Industry", *The Economic Times*, New Delhi.

Shashidhar, G.V. (2010). Business Elite. National Sales Manager, Wipro Limited. Infotech Division. Interviewed in Delhi. 20 April.

Shibata, T. (2010, 7 June)."Market May Find A New Level After 3 Months", *The Economic Times*, New Delhi.

Sibal K., (2014, 13 October). "India should Look to Europe for An Economic boost", Mail Online India New from Mail Today, 16 January 2015, URL: http://www.dailymail.co.uk/indiahome/indianews/article-2791626/india-look-europe-economic-boost.html.

Singh R.K. and P. Priya (2014, 17 June). "What's Holding Back the India-EU FTA?", *The Diplomat*, 8 January 2015, URL: http://thediplomat.com/2014/06/whats-holding-back-the-india-eu-fta/.

Singh, K. (2010, 13 March). "Elder Hikes Stake in Bulgarian Arm", *The Economic Times*, New Delhi.

Singh, M. (2010). Business Elite. Publisher. Seminar Magazine. Interviewed in Delhi. 20 April.

Singh, N. (2009, 13 December). "The Confusion in Copenhagen", *Dainik Jagran*, New Delhi.

Singh, S. (2010, 21 June). "Innovative Technology", *The Times of India*, New Delhi.

Singh, S.N. (2010a). Business Elite. Manager. API Marketing. Ranbaxy Laboratories. Limited. Interviewed in Delhi. 26 April.

Sinha, P. (2009, 4 September). "WTO deal: India for all-round talks, Proposes Simultaneous Negotiations on Services, Agriculture and Non-Agri Market Access", *The Times of India*, New Delhi.

Sisodia, N.S. and C.U. Bhaskar (2005). *Emerging IndiaSecurity and Foreign Policy Perspectives*: New Delhi: Promilla & CO., Publishers in Association with Bibliophile South Asia.

Sruthijith, K.K. (2010, 25 January). "Niall Ferguson author, The Ascent of Money West Unlikely to See Robust Recovery in 10", *The Economic Times*, New Delhi.

Stiglitz, J.E. (2010, 18 January). "Perspectives: Overcoming the Copenhagen Failure", *The Economic Times*, New Delhi.

Strupczewski J. and L. Papadimas (2010, 12 April). "Euro Zone Approves € 30-b Rescue Package for Greece", *The Economic Times*, New Delhi.

Subhan, Malcolm (2005, 28 May), "Is India Neglecting the European Union?", *The Financial Express*, Brussels, 6 February 2010, URL: http://www.financialexpress.com/news/is-india-neglecting-the-european-union/ 146470/.

Subrahmanyam, S. (2005). "Taking Stock of the Franks: South Asian Views of Europeans and Europe, 1500-1800", *Indian Economic and Social History Review*, 42(1): 69-100.

Subramaniam, G.G. (2010, 22 March). "ET Interactive Karri Kaitue 'India is a Springboard to Asia'", *The Economic Times*, New Delhi.

Subramanyam, K. (2009, 9 August). "The Dependence of Inter-State Relations Upon Common Interest, The Prospects of Better Bilateral Relations Between India And America", *The Economic Times*, New Delhi.

Subramanyam, K. (2010, 14 February). "The Complexity of Buying Weapons", *Dainik Jagran*, New Delhi.

Subramanyam, K. (2010, 28 February). "Manipulaton and Crookedness is What Sustains Pakistan: Pakistan is Bent Upon Spreading Negative Propaganda against India", *Dainik Jagran*, New Delhi.

Suri, N. (2010, 13 April). "Investors Should Bet on Evergreen SIPs", *The Economic Times*, New Delhi.

Tannock, C. (2006, 13 February). "The India Option", Project Syndicate, 17 January 2015, URL: https://www.project-syndicate.org/commentary/the-india-option.

Tejaswi, M.J. and S. John (2010, 28 May). "E-major: Desi IT Strikes Cautious Note", *The Times of India*, New Delhi.

Tharoor, S. (2012, 28 May). "Reconsider Relations with the European Union", Indiatodayin, 16 January 2015, URL:http://indiatoday.intoday.in/story/european-union-india-ties-india-eu-joint-action-plan/1/189252.html.

The Economic Times (2009, 1 August). "10 m Euro for Solar Power R&D", New Delhi.

The Economic Times (2009, 10 December), "EU to Decide on 2 billion Euro Aid for Poorer Countries Today", New Delhi.

The Economic Times (2009, 11 December). "BIC Coordination after Tuvalu Breaks G-77 +", New Delhi.

The Economic Times (2009, 13 August). "Rift in UNSC over US Draft on Suu Kyi", New Delhi.

The Economic Times (2009, 14 September). "Fight Looms Over State Aid to Magna-led Opel", New Delhi.

The Economic Times (2009, 16 November). "Eurozone Out of the Hole", New Delhi.

The Economic Times (2009, 19 August). "India to Work for Rainbow Coalition at WTO", New Delhi.

The Economic Times (2009, 2 December). "Eurozone Jobless Rate Stable at 9.8% Shows Eurostat data", New Delhi.

The Economic Times (2009, 2 November). "India May Come Under Pressure at Barcelona", New Delhi.

The Economic Times (2009, 2 October). "EU Roaming Rate Cap Valid: Court Advisor", New Delhi.

The Economic Times (2009, 2 September). "WTO Officials in Warm-up Exercise Today", New Delhi.

The Economic Times (2009, 23 August)."Tech Aspects very Important for Trade Talks", New Delhi.

The Economic Times (2009, 23 September). "BoE's King may get EU Watchdog Role to Win Over UK", New Delhi.

The Economic Times (2009, 24 September)."EU Blueprint To Overhaul Bank Policing", New Delhi.

The Economic Times (2009, 27 October). "ING to Split in Two, Launch Rights Issue", New Delhi.

The Economic Times (2009, 29 September)."EU to Set Volume for MP3 Players", New Delhi.

The Economic Times (2009, 3 July). "Eurozone Jobless Data Hits 10-Yr High in May", New Delhi.

The Economic Times (2009, 3 October). "EU Aims to Make Antitrust Class Action Lawsuits Easier", New Delhi.

The Economic Times (2009, 31 August). "Boosting Trade is the Only Game in Town", New Delhi.

The Economic Times (2009, 4 December). "Euro Zone GDP up on Inventories", New Delhi.

The Economic Times (2009, 4 September). "EU Probes Oracle Bid for Sun", New Delhi.

The Economic Times (2009, 5 November). "Barcelona Talks Resume as African Nations End Boycott", New Delhi.

The Economic Times (2009, 5 November). "India, EU to Sign Deal On Civil Nuclear Energy This Week", New Delhi.

The Economic Times (2009, 6 August). "Patten Eyes Top EU Job", New Delhi.

The Economic Times (2009, 6 November). "Extraneous Issues to Delay EU-India FTA", New Delhi.

The Economic Times (2009, 6 September). "EU will Take Steps to Resolve Drug Seizure Cases, says Ashton", New Delhi.

The Economic Times (2009, 7 December). "Labour Pangs Likely to Hold Up India-EU Free Trade Agreement", New Delhi.

The Economic Times (2009, 8 October). "EU Officials Raid Ranbaxy French Unit", New Delhi.

The Economic Times (2009, 8 October). "MS Sees to EU Tiff Ahead of Report on Browser Remedy", New Delhi.

The Economic Times (2009, 9 August). "EU Missed Evidence in Intel Antitrust Case", New Delhi.

The Economic Times (2010, 10 February). "In a Nutshell Bulk of Foreign Trade to be Free from Barriers Soon", New Delhi.

The Economic Times (2010, 10 March). "EU Warns US Against Protectionism in Pentagon Deal, Says Terms Favour Boeing", New Delhi.

The Economic Times (2010, 11 February). "Europe Prepares to Bail Out Greece", New Delhi.

The Economic Times (2010, 11 May). "Vedanta buys UK Co's Zinc Biz Beats Xstrata & China Metallurgical to Buy Anglo American Unit for $1.3 B", New Delhi.

The Economic Times (2010, 11 May). "$1,000,000,000,000 Aid Plan to Restore Confidence in Euro", New Delhi.

The Economic Times (2010, 11 May). "Awesome EU solidarity but Expect a Stronger Dollar", New Delhi.

The Economic Times (2010, 12 February). "Booster Dose Oil Above $74 on Greek Rescue Hopes", New Delhi.

The Economic Times (2010, 12 February). "EU Raises Demand for Non-Rain Forest Palm Oil", New Delhi.

The Economic Times (2010, 12 February). "European Leaders Reach Agreement on Aid to Rescue Greece", New Delhi.

The Economic Times (2010, 12 February). "Losing Shine Gold Retreats from Highs As Euro Wilts", New Delhi.

The Economic Times (2010, 13 February)."IMF Pledges Support to Greece to Rein in Deficit", New Delhi.

The Economic Times (2010, 13 June). "Mauritius is Ready to Try and Imprison High Sea Pirates", New Delhi.

The Economic Times (2010, 15 April). "Short Takes, India to contest Steel Subsidy Complaint in EC", New Delhi.

The Economic Times (2010, 16 March). "Race for Climate Top Job Hots Up", New Delhi.

The Economic Times (2010, 17 June). "Short Takes, Govt Allows 10,000 Tonne Sugar Export to EU", New Delhi.

The Economic Times (2010, 17 May)."For a Stronger Bond", New Delhi.

The Economic Times (2010, 18 April). "Volcanic Ash Suspends Flights for Third day", New Delhi.

The Economic Times (2010, 18 February). "India Seeks Observer Status at WTO Government Procurement Pact", New Delhi.

The Economic Times (2010, 19 February). "Better to Talk Than Not Will Help Saner Elements in Pakistan", New Delhi.

The Economic Times (2010, 19 March). "Greece May Seek IMF Help for Bailout", New Delhi.

The Economic Times (2010, 2 February). "Imports rise 27%, Confirm Economy Back on Track 22.4% Rise in Non-Oil Imports in Dec Reflects Manufacturing Growth", New Delhi.

The Economic Times (2010, 2 September). "WTO Officials in Warm-Up Exercise Today", New Delhi.

The Economic Times (2010, 21 June). "Currency Fluctuations May Hit Exports: Ficci", New Delhi.

The Economic Times (2010, 22 January). "Across the World, Oracle Wins EU Nod For Sun Buy", New Delhi.

The Economic Times (2010, 22 March). "Foreign Hands Immigrants, The Favoured Ones", New Delhi.

The Economic Times (2010, 22 March). "In a Nutshell", New Delhi.

The Economic Times (2010, 23 March). "Barroso Challenges Merkel on Greek Plan", New Delhi.

The Economic Times (2010, 24 April). "G-20 may Press Hard for Yuan Rise", New Delhi.

The Economic Times (2010, 25 June). "Lanka Denies Visas to UN Panel on Rights Abuse", New Delhi.

The Economic Times (2010, 26 March). "Gold Firm at $1,093.45/oz as Euro Steadies Againt $", New Delhi.

The Economic Times (2010, 27 January). "BASIC Idea: Collectively Provide Financial Aid to Vulnerable Nations", New Delhi.

The Economic Times (2010, 27 January). "Euro, Price Fall Help EU Wheat Exports", New Delhi.

The Economic Times (2010, 29 April). "High Tariffs Shielding Auto Cos: Khullar", New Delhi.

The Economic Times (2010, 4 June). "Economic Govt for Eurozone Gets a Fillip", New Delhi.

The Economic Times (2010, 4 May). "Glenmark Inks $325-M Deal With Sanofi", New Delhi.

The Economic Times (2010, 4 May). "Watchdogs at Work EU Assures FTA Won't Lead to Costlier Life-Saving Drugs", New Delhi.

The Economic Times (2010, 5 April). "India Hopes N-Summit Will Boost Security Cooperation", New Delhi.

The Economic Times (2010, 5 February). "Re Falls as Investors Shun Emerging-Market Assets", New Delhi.

The Economic Times (2010, 5 June). "EU to Overhaul GM Crop System Countries To Be Free to Choose Whether to Grow Or Ban Genetically Modified Crops", New Delhi.

The Economic Times (2010, 5 June). "Sensex Logs 2nd Weekly Gain as India Outperforms Peers", New Delhi.

The Economic Times (2010, 5 March). "In a Nutshell: New Issues Crop Up in India-EU Trade Pact", New Delhi.

The Economic Times (2010, 5 May). "Central Banks Across The Globe Flock Back to US Govt Bonds, Hike Exposure To $2,709 B In Wake Of Eurozone Crisis", New Delhi.

The Economic Times (2010, 7 June). "Experts' Take on Money Trends for the Week", New Delhi.

The Economic Times (2010, 8 April). "Top Gear Daimler, Renault-Nissan Ink Small Car, Engine Deal", New Delhi.

The Economic Times (2010, 8 February). "Collage of Cultures", New Delhi.

The Economic Times (2010, 9 June). "EU Talks Austerity Again to Keep House in Order Spanish Public Workers Stage Strike; Hungary, Bulgaria in Trouble Spot", New Delhi.

The Economic Times (2011, 28 April). "India Shortlists Dassault's Rafale, Eurofighter Typhoon for $12 bn Jet Deal", 8 May 2011, URL: http://articles.economictimes.indiatimes.com/2011-04-28/news/29482911_1_defence-ministry-jet-deal-dassault-s-rafale.

The Economic Times (2014, 21 November). "India wants to Energise Trade Ties with European Union", IANS, 18 January 2015, URL: http://economictimes.indiatimes.com/news/economy/foreign-trade/india-wants-to-energise-trade-ties-with-european-union/articleshow/45229122.cms.

The Economic Times Foreign Trade (2014, 14 December). "European Union Hopes to Seal Free Trade Pact with India Next Year", PTI, 8 January 2015, URL: http://articles.economictimes.indiatimes.com/2014-12-14/news/57034553_1_trade-policy-eu-ambassador-joao-cravinho-fta.

The Economic Times, (2010, 10 February). "US, EU Ignoring India on Af-Pak to Appease Islamabad: Expert", New Delhi.

The Economic Times, (2010, 13 May). "Sugar Futures Ban May Be Lifted Soon", New Delhi.

The Economic Times, (2010, 15 April). "Short Takes, India to Contest Steel Subsidy Complaint in EC", New Delhi.

The Economic Times, (2010, 19 May). "Bridging Divide Huge Potential if Both Nations Collaborate", New Delhi.

The Economic Times, (2010, 20 April). "Air Carriers Seek End to Blanket Ban on Flights Across Europe", New Delhi.

The Economic Times. (2009, 18 July). "EU to Take India's Liquor Tax Hangover Before WTO", New Delhi.

The Financial Express (2005, 6 July). "EU Favours UN Reform; No Position on Permanent Seats", 12 May 2011, URL: http://www.financeexpress.com/news/eu-favours-un-reform-no-position-on-permanent-seats/142592.

The Hindu (2014, 28 April). "EU Bans Indian Alphonso Mangoes, 4 Vegetables from May 1", PTI, 23 January 2015, URL:http://www.thehindu.com/news/international/ world/eu-bans-indian-alphonso-mangoes-4-vegetables-from-may-1/article5956482. ece.

The Indian Express Group Finance Buzz (2011, 7 May). "India's Forex Reserves Surge", 10 May, 2011, URL: http://expressbuzz.com/finance/indias-forex-reserves-surge/272321.html.

The Times of India (1959, 3 November). "Increasing Exports to West Europe: Arrangements Made by Trade mission."

The Times of India (2009, 1 July). "EU Scraps Ban on Ugly Fruits, Veggies", New Delhi.

The Times of India (2009, 10 December). "Greece May Be First Nation to Default in EU'", New Delhi.

The Times of India (2009, 13 November). "Intel to Pay $1.25 B For Patent Dispute", New Delhi.

The Times of India (2009, 16 December). "Unlimited 1-year Loans by ECB", New Delhi.

The Times of India (2009, 17 December). "EU Woos Emerging Nations", New Delhi.

The Times of India (2009, 18 August). "FTP to Expand Markets For Exporters", New Delhi.

The Times of India (2009, 18 December). "Giving Only to Take", New Delhi.

The Times of India (2009, 18 November). "Somali Pirates Hijack Chemical Tanker", New Delhi.

The Times of India (2009, 2 October). "Iran to Allow IAEA to Inspect N-plants", New Delhi.

The Times of India (2009, 21 November). "Belgian PM Chosen EU's First Prez after Blair Bid is Dropped", New Delhi.

The Times of India (2009, 21 October). "Somali Pirates Turn Eastward, Seize China Ship", New Delhi.

The Times of India (2009, 26 August). "25 Yrs on, UK blunder Lets Porn be Sold Legally to Kids", New Delhi.

The Times of India (2009, 26 December). "Auschwitz Sign Stolen To Fund Terror Attacks?", New Delhi.

The Times of India (2009, 27 October). "France for Talking Out Wine Dispute", New Delhi.

The Times of India (2009, 28 August). "In Europe, It's Lights Out for Bulbs", New Delhi.

The Times of India (2009, 29 July). "New Proposal on Lufthansa/AUA deal", New Delhi.

The Times of India (2009, 29 September). "Saving Ears: EU to Impose Volume Limits on MP3 players", New Delhi.

The Times of India (2009, 3 December). "Empty Swiss Bank Accounts to Protest Ban on Minarets", New Delhi.

The Times of India (2009, 4 November). "EU Set to Exit Recession This Yr", New Delhi.

The Times of India (2009, 6 August). "Scots Lay Claim to Chicken Tikka Masala, Indians Fume", New Delhi.

The Times of India (2009, 6 September). "EU Will Take Steps To Resolve Drug Seizure Cases, Says Ashton", New Delhi.

The Times of India (2009, 8 October). "Power Biggies Fined $98m", New Delhi.

The Times of India (2009, 9 December). "Jerusalem Should Be Joint Capital: EU", New Delhi.

The Times of India (2010, 1 March). "ETA Chief Arrested in France: Spain", New Delhi.

The Times of India (2010, 10 June). "Hamas Win In '06 Triggered Tighter Curbs on Gaza", New Delhi.

The Times of India (2010, 11 May). "EU-IMF Prepare $1tn Plan To Avert Greek Tragedy", New Delhi.

The Times of India (2010, 11 May). "World Digest", New Delhi.

The Times of India (2010, 12 May). "Greece and Us Eurozone's Problems Concern India But are Unlikely to Singe It", New Delhi.

The Times of India (2010, 12 May). "Greece Wants $26bn as First Tranche Aid", New Delhi.

The Times of India (2010, 13 February)."After EU, IMF Offers Support to Greece", New Delhi.

The Times of India (2010, 14 June) "Green drive: EU to Ban Sex Toys", New Delhi.

The Times of India (2010, 14 May). "New Partnership Cameron Will Head Coalition Government in the UK", New Delhi.

The Times of India (2010, 14 May). "New Partnership Cameron Will Head Coalition Government in the UK", New Delhi.

The Times of India (2010, 15 February). "EU Quality Study", New Delhi.

The Times of India (2010, 15 January). "Yellow Metal Slips on Firm Dollar", New Delhi.

The Times of India (2010, 15 June). "Inflation Hits 19-Mth High of 10.16%", New Delhi.

The Times of India (2010, 15 June). "Moody's Cuts Greece Rating to Junk", New Delhi.

The Times of India (2010, 16 April). "Russia Looks to Join WTO by 2010-end", New Delhi.

The Times of India (2010, 17 April). "EU Directive Could Stump Cricket: Report", New Delhi.

The Times of India (2010, 18 August). "FTP to Expand Markets for Exporters", New Delhi.

The Times of India (2010, 18 June). "US, EU Tighten Screws on Iran N-programme", New Delhi.

The Times of India (2010, 18 May). "ECB Buys €16.5bn Bonds", New Delhi.

The Times of India (2010, 19 April). "Valedictory Gathering", New Delhi.

The Times of India (2010, 19 January). "Haiti on Edge, US Sends Extra Troops Senegal Offers to Rehabilitate Survivors in 'Land of Ancestors'", New Delhi.

The Times of India (2010, 19 March). "World Digest: Rocket Kills One in Israel as EU Diplomat Visits Gaza", New Delhi.

The Times of India (2010, 19 May). "Cross Border Murthy Pushes for Dreams Unlimited". New Delhi.

The Times of India (2010, 2 June). "EU Banks Face €195bn Loan Loss", New Delhi.

The Times of India (2010, 2 June). "Feeling Edgy World Marts Dip on Weak EU Finances", New Delhi.

The Times of India (2010, 20 April). "Ash Shutdown Costs Airlines Over $1bn Germany, UK, France To Open Air Space For Limited Flights", New Delhi.

The Times of India (2010, 20 June). "Somali Pirate Who Saved Hostages Left in the Lurch", New Delhi.

The Times of India (2010, 21 April). "India Should Legalize Gambling", New Delhi.

The Times of India (2010, 21 April). "When is it Safe to Fly? Debate Is On", New Delhi.

The Times of India (2010, 21 March). "Open Space", New Delhi.

The Times of India (2010, 22 April). "Out in the Open? France Moves a Step Closer to Banning Veil", New Delhi.

The Times of India (2010, 22 April). "All Eyes on TV for 2nd Debate Today", New Delhi.

The Times of India (2010, 23 April). "Greece 2009 Deficit Turns Out Higher", New Delhi.

The Times of India (2010, 23 March). "Nepal Should Be Hindu State, Says Rajnath", New Delhi.

The Times of India (2010, 23 May). "World Digest", New Delhi.

The Times of India (2010, 24 June). "Collapse of Euro Can't be Ruled Out: Soros", New Delhi.

The Times of India (2010, 24 March). "Short Cuts: Use Cellphone Without Touching It", New Delhi.

The Times of India (2010, 24 May). "Speak, Memory Digital Strongbox to Prevent Data Loss", New Delhi.

The Times of India (2010, 25 June). "Lanka Denies Visas to UN Panel on Rights Abuse", New Delhi.

The Times of India (2010, 26 April) "After Ash Chaos, World Mulls How to Live With Volcanos", New Delhi.

The Times of India (2010, 26 April). "Turkish Language Courses at Jamia", New Delhi.

The Times of India (2010, 27 March). "Solving Financial Woes Eurozone Agrees on Greece Bailout", New Delhi.

The Times of India (2010, 28 May). "Expert Soliloquy", New Delhi.

The Times of India (2010, 29 April). "Greece Will Get Aid in Time: EU", New Delhi.

The Times of India (2010, 29 April). "Worried Markets Looking at Angela Merkel", New Delhi.

The Times of India (2010, 3 May). "In Brief Medal Glory", New Delhi.

The Times of India (2010, 30 January). "India Digest", New Delhi.

The Times of India (2010, 31 March). "No Ransom Demand From Somali Pirates Yet", New Delhi.

The Times of India (2010, 4 June). "Economic Govt for Eurozone Gets a Fillip", New Delhi.

The Times of India (2010, 4 June). "Tel Aviv Rejects International Probe into Raid", New Delhi.

The Times of India (2010, 5 April). "Headley Effect: Tighter Visa Norms Spell Misery for PIOs and Tourists", New Delhi.

The Times of India (2010, 5 January). "Put Your Feet Up, This Car is Self-Driven", New Delhi.

The Times of India (2010, 5 March). "'India, EU Should Conclude FTA by Oct'", New Delhi.

The Times of India (2010, 6 January). "Mr. Bean Replaces Spanish PM on Hacked EU Website", New Delhi.

The Times of India (2010, 7 February). "Force One? EU Looking to Create One Army for Bloc", New Delhi.

The Times of India (2010, 7 June). "Hamas Win in '06 Triggered Tighter Curbs on Gaza", New Delhi.

The Times of India (2010, 7 June). "Visual Analytics", New Delhi.

The Times of India (2010, 7 March). "World Digest Iceland Votes on Foreign Debts", New Delhi.

The Times of India (2010, 8 February). "Debt Crisis in Europe Exaggerated, Says Sachs", New Delhi.

The Times of India (2010, 8 January). "EU Divided Over Use of Body Scanners", New Delhi.

The Times of India (2010, 8 May). "This was an Unhistoric Election'", New Delhi.

The Times of India (2010, 9 June). "EU Leaders Committed to Euro's Survival'", New Delhi.

The Times of India (2010, 9 May). "Europe Races to Secure Bloc From Predators", New Delhi.

Thornet, L. (2011, 11 May), "Border-Free Area", *Oman Daily Observer*, Sultanate of Oman, URL: http://www.pressdisplay.com/pressdisplay/viewer.aspx.

Torney, D. (2013). "Outsiders' Perceptions and EU Influence in the World: The Case of Climate Change", *NFG Working Paper Series*, 4: 1-25.

Torney, D. (2014). "External Perceptions and EU Foreign Policy Effectiveness: The Case of Climate Change", *Journal of Common Market Studies*, 52 (6): 1358-1373.

Traidcraft (2008). "The EU-India FTA: Initial Observations from a Developmental Perspective", Fighting Poverty through Trade, 17 January 2015, URL:http://www.indianet.nl/pdf/EU-IndiaFTAInitialObservations.pdf.

Upadhyaya, P. (2009, 13 December). "The Worthless Tug-Of-War at Copenhagen", New Delhi.

Varadarajan, S. (2005), "The Truth Behind the Indo-U.S. Nuclear Deal", Centre for Global Research ,14 May 2009, URL: http://www.globalresearch.ca/index.php?context=va&aid=756.

Varma, S.(2010, 7 June)."Guest Column Defence Investments Under Attack", *The Economic Times*, New Delhi.

Venkataramanan, K. (2010, 28 June). "Excerpts 'Don't Care What the World Thinks, It's India's View That Matters to Me'", *The Times of India*, New Delhi.

Venkateswaran, S. (2010, 17 May). "Goa to Refurbish Brand Image", New Delhi.

Vishakantaiah, P. (2010, 4 February). "ICT can Contribute Towards Sustainable Development", *The Economic Times*, New Delhi.

Webster's Online Dictionary (2015). "Definition of Perception by Webster's Online Dictionary", 24 January 2015, URL: http://www.webster-dictionary.org/definition/perception.

Winand, P. et al. (2015).*The European Union and India: Rhetoric or Meaningful Partnership*, UK and USA: Edgar Elgar Publishing Limited.

Wittkopf E. et al. (2003). *American Foreign Policy: Pattern and Process*, Belmont: Wadsworth Thomson Publication.

World Trade Organisation (2010, 24 February). "Dispute Settlement: DS352 India-Measures Affecting the Importation and Sale of Wines and Spirits from the European Communities", 8 January 2015, URL: http://www.wto.org/english/tratop_e/dispu_e/cases_e/ds352_e.htm.

Wouters, J. et al. (2013). "Some Critical Issues in EU-India Free Trade Agreement Negotiations", Leuven Centre for Global Governance Studies, 4 January 2015, URL: https://ghum.kuleuven.be/ggs/publications/working_papers/new_series/wp101-110/wp102-wouters-goddeeris-natens.pdf.

Wulbers, S. A. (2008). "Identity Configurations in India-Europe Relations", in Wulbers, S.A. (eds.) *EU India Relations: A Critique*, New Delhi and France: Foundation in association with EuroIndia Centre.

Zeebiz (2013, 29 October). "EU-India FTA: Unless Everything Is Agreed Nothing Is Agreed, Says Panel", 7 January 2015, URL: http://zeenews.india.com/business/news/economy/eu-india-fta-unless-everything-is-agreed-nothing-is-agreed-says-panel_87858.html.

Zimmerman, W. (2002), *The Russian People and Foreign Policy: Russian Elites and Mass Perspectives (1993-2000)*, United States of America: Princeton University Press.

Index